DEATH IN BABYLON

DEATH IN BABYLON

Alexander the Great & Iberian Empire
in the Muslim Orient

Vincent Barletta

THE UNIVERSITY OF CHICAGO PRESS
Chicago and London

VINCENT BARLETTA is associate professor of Iberian studies at Stanford University. He is the author of *Covert Gestures: Crypto-Muslim Literature as Cultural Practice in Early Modern Spain* (2005), winner of the *La corónica* International Book Award of the Modern Language Association, and the translator of Francisco Núñez Muley's *A Memorandum for the President of Royal Audiencia . . . and Kingdom of Granada* (2007), the latter published by the University of Chicago Press.

Frontispiece: Anon., *Alexander the Great* ("Inopos"). Marble, 95 cm. high (MA855). Hellenistic Delos, Greece (ca. 100 BCE). Louvre, Paris, France. Photograph © Réunion des Musées Nationaux / Art Resource, New York. Photograph: Hervé Lewandowski.

The University of Chicago Press, Chicago 60637
The University of Chicago Press, Ltd., London
© 2010 by The University of Chicago
All rights reserved. Published 2010
Printed in the United States of America

19 18 17 16 15 14 13 12 11 10   1 2 3 4 5

ISBN-13: 978-0-226-03736-3 (cloth)
ISBN-10: 0-226-03736-3 (cloth)

The University of Chicago Press gratefully acknowledges the generous support of the Program for Cultural Cooperation between Spain's Ministry of Culture and United States Universities toward the publication of this book.

Library of Congress Cataloging-in-Publication Data

Barletta, Vincent.
  Death in Babylon : Alexander the Great & Iberian empire in the Muslim Orient / Vincent Barletta.
    p. cm.
  Includes bibliographical references and index.
  ISBN-13: 978-0-226-03736-3 (cloth : alk. paper)
  ISBN-10: 0-226-03736-3 (cloth : alk. paper)
    1. Alexander, the Great, 356–323 B.C.—In literature. 2. Spanish literature—To 1500—History and criticism. 3. Portuguese literature—To 1500—History and criticism. 4. Spain—History—711–1516. I. Title.
  PQ6060.B37 2010
  860.9'351—dc22

                                                              2009034994

♾ The paper used in this publication meets the minimum requirements of the American National Standard for Information Sciences—Permanence of Paper for Printed Library Materials, ANSI Z39.48-1992.

For Laura, my most significant Other

CONTENTS

vested contributors to that chorus. Green, certainly aware of the Macedonian ghosts that haunted his sanctuary, admits what he likely knew before he ever boarded the ship: there simply is no such thing as a "plain" Alexander.

The present book can be fairly characterized as the product of a kind of contrary project to that undertaken by Green. With no interest in teasing out the unbiased or "plain" Alexander (a historical chimera, in any case), I decided from the beginning to travel in the opposite direction and focus directly on that distracting chorus—as literary scholars are trained to do—revolving around Alexander in the Iberian Peninsula during the fifteenth and sixteenth centuries. This period witnessed the initiation of a long period of Iberian colonial expansion into Muslim Africa and Asia, and it also saw a significant redeployment of Alexandrian references and images. My principal interest in this project was in coming to a deeper, more nuanced understanding of the place of Alexander the Great in the broader project of empire in the Crown of Aragon, Castile, and Portugal from roughly 1450 (when Gomes Eanes de Zurara completed his history of the Portuguese conquest of Ceuta) to the end of the sixteenth century, and this meant sailing away from my own Astypalaia (as one might frame the American state of California, in spite of its status as a former Spanish colony) into the swirl of ideologies and imperial ghosts (Alexander among them) that continue to haunt the Iberian Peninsula. To the extent that I feel comfortable placing myself in relation to a scholar of Green's stature (and except for purely heuristic and rhetorical purposes I do not), we can perhaps be seen as passengers on ships that pass one another at sea, one bearing a historian toward relative solitude and the sober consideration of established facts, the other taking a literary scholar toward the rich chaos of human politics and the darker forces at work within he theorization of empire and Muslim-Christian confrontation.

As a purely practical consideration, I should also point out that when I ᵊak of "Iberian empire" or "Iberian imperial expansion" throughout this ᵓk I am referring to a geographical region whose three principal Christian ʳdoms (Granada was still a Muslim kingdom in the fifteenth century)— ʲle, the Crown of Aragon, and Portugal—engaged in various forms of ʲial expansion during the late medieval and early modern periods, and ʲifferent results. In using the term "Iberian," I do not mean to suggest ᵊrian empire" or "Iberia"—whether the ill-conceived "union of arms" ᵗp in the seventeenth century by Gaspar de Guzmán y Pimentel, the ᵘke of Olivares (1587–1645), or the later unionist fantasies of Fran-

coists and at least one Portuguese Nobel laureate—should have any real political or historical significance in the fifteenth and sixteenth centuries. And
I certainly do not mean to bother the Bastetani and Turdetani tribes that
gradually lost out to the Romans (the latter with Alexander on their collec-
tive mind) in the centuries just before the start of the Common Era. Within
this book "Iberian" is merely geographical shorthand, to be understood in
much the same way that we might interpret terms such as "the Balkans,"
"North Africa," or "the American west."

~

In tracing out the place of Alexander in the literature that revolves around
Iberian imperial expansion into Muslim Africa and Asia, I felt it necessary,
first and foremost, to describe the project in some depth. For this reason,
the first chapter maps out the broader argument of the book as a whole,
including a discussion of the Levinasian framework (though it remains far
from orthodox) that I adopt. I begin with an account of the deeper phenomenological concerns regarding death and mortality that consistently emerge
from the literature I survey, and I follow this discussion through to a brief
introductory account of how Alexander—or, more accurately, his ghost—
operates within this literature.

In chapter 2, I attempt to trace out the ways in which Alexander is presented and employed in Greek, Roman, late antique, and medieval texts from
the Iberian Peninsula and beyond. This necessarily brief survey is by no
means comprehensive; rather, it focuses on the main textual and ideological
currents that form the basis for the late medieval and early modern texts
under analysis in the rest of the book. Where possible, I point to secondary
works that readers might consult to get a deeper, more detailed sense of the
Alexander that emerges in the periods passed through in this chapter, and
the ways in which writers—both Iberian and otherwise—made use of the
Macedonian king within a range of literary and political projects. My goal in
this chapter is merely to give my reader an overview of the rich and varied
discursive tradition from which authors such as Gomes Eanes de Zurara,
Joanot Martorell, and Luís Vaz de Camões drew.

Chapter 3 focuses primarily on the beginning and end of Portuguese
expansion into Morocco, with shorter accounts of Castilian and Aragonese
excursions into the Maghreb. The primary texts upon which I focus are Zurara's *Crónica da tomada de Ceuta*, written in 1450, and epistolary accounts—

for example, from the Castilian king Felipe II's ambassador to Portugal's king Sebastião—of the arrival of Sebastião in Morocco in 1578 and his ill-fated death march to al-Qaṣr al-Kbīr to aid the deposed Moroccan monarch Muḥammad al-Mutawakkil, and the aftermath of that battle. Focusing on specific elements of these texts, especially the emergence of Alexandrian references and discourse within them, I attempt to tease out the ways in which the Portuguese imperial project in Morocco was shaped by very deeply felt anxieties about mortality and the relational status of the subject vis-à-vis the Other, and how the texts associated with this project—insofar as they make use of Alexander—work to theorize them.

In chapter 4 I turn my attention to Asia, and the ways in which selected Iberian authors—in the first instance the Portuguese humanist João de Barros—frame the formation of a Western empire in Asia against the backdrop of a troubled reckoning with mortality. Alexander is at the center of this project, at one level because his Macedonian empire in Asia intersects geographically at many points with that established by the Portuguese in places such as Gujarat and Hormuz, but also because of all that is implied by his fame and "greatness," including his seeming victory over mortality itself.

The final chapter of this book examines the ways in which minority Crypto-Muslims in sixteenth-century Aragon engaged and reshaped the narrative tradition of Alexander as it came to them from Arabic sources. Focusing on specific Aljamiado (pronounced *al-xam-yAH-ðo* and referring to Ibero-Romance texts copied out in Arabic script) manuscripts copied out in late sixteenth-century Aragon, I attempt to draw out the connections that Crypto-Muslim readers constructed between Alexander the Great, frameworks of time and (inter)action, and the daily practice of being Muslim (even if secretly) within a burgeoning Christian empire committed to regimenting the cultural practice of its New Christian subjects within the Iberian Peninsula and beyond.

The Iberian Peninsula, from which would spring in the fifteenth and sixteenth centuries vast empires that exceeded in scope (and perhaps in the degree of cruelty and mismanagement) even the immense and diverse dominions of Alexander, inherited the full range of Alexandrian material produced within the Mediterranean. From Latin and Romance historiography to Jewish philosophy and Islamic epic, copies of manuscript and early printed texts dealing with Alexander represent a significant amount of written material produced within medieval Iberia. And as had been the case in classical Rome and Ptolemaic Egypt, these texts frequently served overtly political and ideological ends. The purpose of the present volume is to focus on specific examples of this textual corpus and develop frameworks for understanding their implications for both the phenomenological ground for early European empire and what we have provisionally come to describe as early modernity.

ACKNOWLEDGMENTS

OVER THE THREE YEARS THAT PASSED AS I WROTE THIS BOOK, I incurred numerous debts of gratitude to various persons and institutions. My former colleagues at the Department of Spanish and Portuguese at the University of Colorado at Boulder, especially Julio Baena and John Slater, shaped the project in its early stages, and frequent conversations with my new colleagues in the Department of Iberian and Latin American Cultures at Stanford University sent it moving in new and unforeseen directions. Special thanks go to Joan Ramon Resina and Sepp Gumbrecht, who continuously inspire and challenge me with their work and words. Also central to the development of this book were the questions and suggestions of several of my fellow travelers in medieval and early modern studies, among them Josiah Blackmore, Michael Gerli, Roland Greene, George Greenia, Alberto Montaner, Francisco Roque de Oliveira, Jesús Rodríguez-Velasco, and François Soyer. I am also grateful to the Program for Cultural Cooperation between Spain's Ministry of Culture and United States Universities for its generous support. My sincere thanks go to the staff of the national libraries of Catalonia, Portugal, and Spain, the Biblioteca da Ajuda, and the Arquivo Nacional da Torre do Tombo in Lisbon for their kind and expert assistance. Special thanks go to Randolph Petilos, Lindsay Dawson, and the rest of the staff at the University of Chicago Press, and to Barbara Norton (*correctrix textorum nec plus ultra*), of Norton Editorial; their professionalism and open-mindedness made working with them a pleasure. Two anonymous readers worked to make the original manuscript of this book a much more solid piece of scholarship, and I am heartily grateful to them for their valuable input. The errors that remain are, as always, entirely my own.

CHAPTER 1

DEATH AND THE OTHER
An Introduction

Isti cum omnia concuterent, concutiebantur.

[As these men were shaking the world, they themselves were being shaken.]
SENECA, *Ad Lucilium Epistolae morales*

Aschenbach's half-distracted, half-inquisitive scrutiny of the
stranger may have been lacking in discretion, for he suddenly
perceived that the man was returning his stare.
THOMAS MANN, *Death in Venice*

AS IS PERHAPS EVIDENT FROM THE SECOND OF THE TWO EPI-
graphs printed above, the present book has emerged in large part through
a reading of Thomas Mann's *Death in Venice*. This may at first seem odd,
because Gustav von Aschenbach's voyage into desire, illness, and mortal
rest has, on the face of it, little to do with either the figure of Alexander
the Great or the expansion of Iberian empire into Muslim Africa and Asia
during the fifteenth and sixteenth centuries. The story of an aging German writer, a young Polish boy, and an epidemic of Indian cholera in early
twentieth-century Venice is of course compelling in its own way; but it does
not concern itself with the epic sweep of imperial war, colonization, and the
quest for immortality that shape, as Alexander does, theorizations of early
modern Iberian incursions into Africa and Asia, and the resistance that these
incursions meet in the process.

The question of resistance, however, is a complex one, and it is here that
my reading of Mann has shaped, somewhat idiosyncratically, the present
book. From a historical point of view, it is generally accepted that during
the long initial push of Iberian expansion into Africa and Asia, more or less
from the Portuguese conquest of Ceuta in 1415 to the Battle of the Three
Kings at al-Qaṣr al-Kbīr in 1578, the kingdoms of Aragon, Castile, and Portugal were consistently engaged in tense commerce and at times open conflict

with Muslim kingdoms that were in many cases their political, economic, and technological equals. The consequences that the fifteenth-century rise of the Ottoman Turks had for the imperial and commercial pretensions of the Crown of Aragon in the Eastern Mediterranean and North Africa are well known.[1] Castile's ongoing conflicts with Granadans, Turks, and Moroccans throughout the fifteenth and sixteenth centuries have inspired an immense body of literature, including much of Miguel de Cervantes's written work.[2] With respect to Portugal, the chronicles of exploration and colonial government are nearly filled with examples of violent setbacks and resistance on the part of African and Asian Muslims, and much modern scholarship in history and literature has likewise focused on the tense struggles that dominated Luso-Muslim relations within Africa and Asia.

Leaving aside for the moment an analysis of the ways in which Iberian authors theorized the deep angst produced by Muslim power in Africa and Asia (not to mention, in certain contexts, the power demonstrated by Muslims in the Iberian Peninsula itself), it is useful to develop a broader sense of the direct ways in which that power expressed itself. To this end, we may take a brief example from Fernão Mendes Pinto's *Peregrinação* (Travels), namely, the situation faced by Henrique Barbosa and his men in the area of the Arabian Peninsula bordering the Gulf of Aden and its relation to the Turkish attack on the Portuguese fortress at Diu in 1538:

> Daqui desta paragem nos partimos para Arquico, terra do Preste João, a levar uma carta que António da Silveira mandara a um tal Henrique Barbosa, feitor seu, que lá andava havia três anos, por mandado do governador Nuno da Cunha, o qual com quarenta homens que trazia consigo escapara do levantamento de Xael onde ficaram cativos D. Manuel de Meneses e mais cento e sessenta portugueses, e tomaram quatrocentos mil cruzados e seis naus portuguesas, que foram as que Solimão Baxá, vice-rei do Cairo, levou com os mantimentos e munições da sua armada quando no ano de mil quinhentos e trinta e oito veio pôr cerco à fortaleza de Diu, por lhas ter mandado ao Cairo o rei de Xael, com sessenta portugueses de presente, e dos mais fez esmola ao seu Mafamede, como cuido que dirão largamente as histórias que tratam do governo da Nuno da Cunha.[3]

[From this stop we left for Arkeeko, in the land of Prester John, to deliver a letter that António da Silveira had sent to his factor, a man named Henrique Barbosa, who had been there for three years by order of the governor Nuno da Cunha. Barbosa, and forty men that he brought with him, had escaped from the uprising at al-Shiḥr, where Dom Manuel de Meneses and 160 Portuguese had been taken captive. The insurgents took 400,000 *cruzados* and six Portuguese caravels. These same caravels were those later used by the viceroy of Cairo, Pasha Suleyman, to transport supplies and munitions for his fleet when in 1538 he laid siege to the fortress of Diu. Pasha Suleyman had received the ships in Cairo, along with sixty Portuguese captives, as a gift from the king of al-Shiḥr. The rest of the captives were given to Muḥammad [the Sharif of Mecca], as I believe the chronicles that deal with the government of Nuno da Cunha will speak of at some length.]

The image that Mendes Pinto presents, of stranded Portuguese sailors and captives sold into slavery, of Portuguese caravels converted into Turkish supply ships during the first of many sieges on the colonial fort on the southern tip of the Kathiawar Peninsula in Gujarat, and of a continued search in Abyssinia for a nonexistent Christian king who might aid the Portuguese in their fight against the Turks, is one of unpredicted reverses and very real dangers for the Portuguese. What comes through in Mendes Pinto's narrative, beyond the material losses involved in Portugal's efforts to secure overseas colonies in Muslim territory, is the ability of African and Asian Muslims to respond to such efforts.[4]

Taking into account the bigger canvas of Portuguese expansion into Asia, C. R. Boxer has argued in terms that support the more focused view provided by Mendes Pinto. In his authoritative and sweeping *The Portuguese Seaborne Empire, 1415–1825*, Boxer argues that

> when all is said, the Portuguese achievement in establishing a seaborne empire in Monsoon Asia was no less remarkable than that of the Spaniards in establishing their land-based empire in America. Perhaps even more so, when we consider that the population of Portugal in the sixteenth century probably never exceeded about a million and a quarter souls; that there was a perennial shortage of Portuguese shipping; that Goa was the only Portuguese port in Asia with adequate dockyard facilities; and that the Portuguese had many other commitments in Morocco and West Africa, to say nothing of their efforts to colonise the Brazilian coast from 1539 onwards. Moreover, the technological gap between the Portuguese and the majority of their Asian opponents was much less than that between the Spaniards and the Amerindians of the New World. Diogo do Couto (1543–1616) and other contemporary Portuguese chroniclers were fond of pointing out that

their compatriots in Asia had to contend with well-armed opponents who were as skilled in the use of firearms as themselves; whereas the Castilian *conquistadores* of Mexico and Peru had to overcome primitive warriors armed only with stone and wooden weapons.[5]

Moving back from Boxer's description of the Iberian empire during the sixteenth century to an account of the first stage of Portugal's imperial push into North Africa at the start of the previous century, we see that the issues described by Boxer were there from the very beginning. The taking of the city of Ceuta, somewhat fancifully described by Gomes Eanes de Zurara (c. 1410–1474) in his *Crónica da tomada de Ceuta* (Chronicle of the Conquest of Ceuta) as a kind of epic pretext for the ceremony of chivalric investiture that runs through and underlies it, was in no sense the foregone conclusion that Zurara describes it to have been.[6] Even Zurara admits that João I (1357–1433) and his advisers had little sense of the heavily fortified city's basic layout prior to their expedition, a fact that could have proven disastrous even as nonintervention treaties with the Castilians and the Naṣri Granadans somehow managed to hold.[7]

For the Crown of Aragon, the Christian loss of Constantinople in 1453 to the forces of Mehmed II (1432–1481), especially given the kingdom's commitments in southern Italy, made an impact that is difficult to calculate. The taking of Constantinople ruptured, or at least drastically reconfigured, important commercial sea lanes through the eastern Mediterranean, and it rendered the promise of a seaborne empire—an Aragonese dream since at least the reign of Jaume I (1208–1276)—a chimera. This reversal quickly found expression in Catalan literature, and prose works of the fifteenth century, such as Joanot Martorell's *Tirant lo Blanc* (Tirant the White) and the anonymous *Curial e Güelfa* (Curial and Guelfa), reflect this tendency.

Looking briefly at *Curial e Güelfa*, we see how the scene of Curial's shipwreck near Tripoli, a shipwreck that would lead to a long period of enslavement, presents the very real dangers associated with sea travel in the Mediterranean and the violent confrontations that often characterized relations between Aragonese Christians and Maghrebi Muslims in that region, especially in light of the ascendance of the Ottoman Turks:

Emperò les ones creixien, e la mar bramava molt espaventablemente e tempestejava aquella mesquina galera, la qual feia molta aigua i era en punt de perdre's; e així anà tot aquell jorn e la nit següent, fins al terç jorn, que ferí en terra davant Trípol de Barberia.

E com hagués poc temps que certes galeres e terides del rei d'Aragó haguessen donats grans dans en aquella ribera, e se n'havien aportades moltes ànimes e dues galeras armades de moros e cremades moltes altres fustes menors, estava tota aquella ribera ab les orelles alçades; per què los moros, qui veren la galera venguda a través, corregueren allà, e, veent que eren cristians, aquells pocs que en la galera trobaren vius foren mesos a espasa e tots tallats en peces.

E no escaparen sinó Curial e un gentil home català, qui havia nom Galceran de Mediona, home valent e de gran esforç; e aquests no foren escapats, sinó que pensàvan que éran morts, qui així com a morts en la cambra jaïen. Emperò, passada la furor als moros, trobaren que eren vius, e traguerenlos de la galera assats vituperosament, e, ab les mans lligades, foren venuts a poc preu, car no pensàven que poguessen escapar en manera del món, e foren comprats per un moro estranger, lo qual dins terra més de quaranta llegües los més. E aquell moro, despuis, los vené a un cavaller de Tunis molt ric e avar, jove emperò, lo qual dins pocs dies, carregats de cadenes e de ferros, a peu, tots nuus, ab poc menjar e menys beure, plens de desaire e de mala sort, a Tunis los menà.[8]

[The waves grew, however, and the sea roared fearsomely and tossed around that poor galley, which took on a good deal of water and was on the point of being lost; and in this way it spent all that day and the following night, until the third day, on which it struck land off Tripoli, in Barbary.

Shortly before some galleys and frigates belonging to the king of Aragon had done great damage on that shore and had taken off many souls and two armed galleys filled with Muslims and burned many other smaller foists, and so that entire shore was on a state of alert; so the Muslims, who saw the galley come ashore, ran to it straightaway. Seeing that the few men that they found still alive in the galley were Christians, they put them to the sword, hacking them to pieces.

The only ones who escaped were Curial and a Catalan gentleman named Galceran de Mediona, a brave and strong man; and these men escaped the sword only because they were thought to be already dead, for they lay in their cabin like corpses. Once the anger of the Muslims had abated, however, they discovered that the two men were alive, and they dragged them harshly from the galley. Then, with their hands bound, they were sold as slaves at a low price given that it was believed that there would be no way that they would survive for long. They were sold to a Muslim man from another region, who took them inland more than forty leagues. That Mus-

lim then sold them to a very rich and tightfisted young gentleman from
Tunis, who in a few days led them—in chains and irons, completely naked,
with little to eat and less to drink, and full of misery and misfortune—
to Tunis.]

Beyond the broader question of fortune, shipwreck, Curial's seven-year enslavement in Tunis and his eventual liberation and return to power (the description of his reading the *Aeneid* in Arabic with the daughter of his captor
and of her Dido-inflected suicide over the love she feels for Curial is especially powerful), the image this passage presents of Christian-Muslim relations in the Mediterranean—developed to an even greater degree in *Tirant lo
Blanc*—is one of violence, retribution, fear, and enslavement, but also of intimacy and extreme mutual vulnerability. For the Aragonese, Maghrebi Muslims are not merely infidels to be summarily conquered, but rather a dangerous and highly forceful Other just as capable of enslaving Christians and
stripping them of their power as they are of being enslaved themselves.[9]

For the Crown of Castile, Muslim military and cultural power had been,
by the beginning of the fifteenth century, a daily fact of life for seven centuries. Although the Crown of Aragon had moved south as far as Murcia
under Jaume I (Jaume was stopped by the Castilians), its attentions and resources had long been focused on the Mediterranean and its naval power.
The Portuguese, who had forged their kingdom in 1143 out of a war with the
Almoravids and a state of almost constant conflict with the Castilians and
Leonese, were by the start of the fifteenth century principally focused on
expansion into the Atlantic and beyond. The Castilians, on the other hand,
were largely concerned with acquiring the vast stretches of Muslim land to
the south of them then held by the Naṣri dynasty and with their capital in
the city of Granada.

Writing in the aftermath of the late sixteenth-century war in the Alpujarras between Granadan Muslims and the Crown of Castile (won decisively
by Castile after nearly three years of fighting), Luis del Mármol Carvajal offers a vivid description of the conditions under which Isabel I of Castile and
her husband, Ferran II of Aragon, came to the decision to do away with the
kingdom of Granada once and for all:

La última guerra que los príncipes cristianos tuvieron en España con los
reyes moros, fue la conquista que los Católicos Reyes don Hernando y doña

Isabel hicieron en el reino de Granada, de la cual hacemos mención en esta historia, por no dejar atrás cosas de las que faltando podrían desgustar al lector. Todas las otras que fueron antes della se hallarán escritas en nuestra general historia de África, en el segundo libro del primer volumen. Siendo pues rey de Granada un valeroso pagano del linaje de los Alahamares, llamado Abil Hascen, cerca de los años de Cristo 1480, y del imperio de los alárabes 892, en la ocasión de la guerra que los Reyes Católicos tenían con el rey de Portugal, juntó sus gentes, y hizo grandes daños en los lugares de la Andalucía y del reino de Murcia. Y como no pudiesen acudir a todas partes, hicieron treguas con él, durante las cuales, en el año de nuestra salud 1482, siendo el moro avisado por sus espías que los cristianos fronteros de Zara, confiados en la tregua, estaban descuidados, y que era buena coyuntura para ocupar aquella fortaleza, rompió la tregua, y juntando sus adalides y escuchas, secretamente les mandó que fuesen a escalarla una noche de grande escuridad. Sucediendo pues el efecto conforme a su deseo, entraron los adalides dentro, y ocupando la fortaleza juntamente con la villa, trataron al alcaide y captivaron cuantos cristianos hallaron con muy pequeña resistencia. Esta pérdida sintieron mucho los Reyes Católicos; y porque el daño no fuese mayor, acudieron luego hacia aquella parte, proveyendo en la seguridad de sus estados; y poniendo después sus invictos ánimos contra los de aquella nación, que tan molestos eran al pueblo cristiano, determinaron de no alzar mano de la guerra hasta acabarlos de conquistar, desterrando el nombre y seta de Mahoma de aquella tierra.[10]

[The last war that Christian princes had with Muslim kings in the Iberian Peninsula was the conquest that the Catholic Monarchs Don Hernando and Doña Isabel carried out in the kingdom of Granada, of which we make mention of in this history in order not to leave out things the absence of which might displease the reader. All of the other conquests that occurred before it will be found written in our general history of Africa, in the second book of the first volume. The king of Granada in the Christian year of 1480 (892 according to the calendar based on the empire of the Arabs) was a valorous pagan of the al-Ḥamar tribe, named Abū al-Ḥassan. Taking advantage of the war that the Catholic Monarchs were then waging against the king of Portugal, he brought together his forces and did great damage within Andalusia and the kingdom of Murcia. And as the Catholic Monarchs could not be in all places at once, they signed a truce with him. During the period of this truce, in the year of our salvation 1482, the Muslim being informed by his spies that the Christian borders at Zara (covered in the truce) had been left unattended and that these provided good access to the fortress there, he broke the truce and, bringing together his generals and sentinels, secretly ordered them to scale the fortress one very dark night. Everything went as planned, and the generals took hold of the fortress along with the city. They captured the mayor and all the Christians that they found with very little resistance. This loss weighed heavy on the Catholic Monarchs; and so that the damage might not spread, they went to that region to provide for the security of their estates. Then, pitting their unvanquished spirits against that nation, which had been so bothersome to the Christian people, they determined not to end the war until they had conquered them completely, driving the name and sect of Muhammad from that land.]

As Mármol Carvajal frames it, it is as a response to a significant loss of Castilian life and property at the hands of the Naṣrids that the war to take the kingdom of Granada begins in earnest. Mármol Carvajal's historical narrative is undoubtedly shaped by his desire to cast the 1568–71 war in the Alpujarras, and the expulsions from Granada that followed, as part of a long pattern of Christian responses to Muslim aggression. As the present book argues, however, it is precisely such ideologically charged accounts of historical events, as well the "possible" events of fiction and legend, that form the basis for narratives of Iberian reconquest and expansion into Muslim Africa and Asia.

As events in al-Qaṣr al-Kbīr, Constantinople, Gujarat, Hormuz, La Golette, Oran, Safi, and Tunis were to prove, the Muslim kingdoms—and at least three Asian empires—against which the principal kingdoms of the Iberian Peninsula wished to assert their influence during the fifteenth and sixteenth centuries (although the expansionist heyday of the Crown of Aragon was arguably the early fourteenth century, a period nostalgically dramatized within narrative texts of the late fifteenth century) were quite capable of pushing back when provoked. Even within the Iberian Peninsula itself, and decades after the fall in 1492 of the kingdom of Granada to the matrimonially (but not constitutionally) conjoined crowns of Aragon and Castile, we see evidence of concerted resistance to official plans for the cultural assimilation of Muslim converts to Christianity, commonly referred to as *moriscos* (Mármol Carvajal's account of the Alpujarras war is in fact a powerful ideological tool aimed at justifying this effort). Such resistance ranged from the extreme case of the two civil wars fought between Muslim converts in Granada and King Felipe II's army to the more subtle issue of the continued production and use of manuscript copies of traditional Islamic narratives in Aragon and Castile. Even actions on the part of colonized Muslims and new Christian converts in the Iberian Peninsula that appear to have been aimed at straightforward appeasement—such as conversion to Christianity itself—in fact tend to reveal complex networks of negotiation and resistance by which these people sought to redeploy the material and ideological resources of empire in creative and strategic ways. The historical image that emerges, put briefly, is of the Christian subject of Iberian empire looking outward toward Muslim Africa and Asia while the Muslim subject persistently, even belligerently, looks back.

The general point that I am trying to make by citing these examples is that throughout Africa and Asia, the spread of the Iberian empire was consistently checked and tempered by African and Asian Muslims who were all too willing (and able) to contest and negotiate the terms of their relation to the Aragonese, Castilians, and Portuguese. How this fundamental fact shapes and gives deeper significance to the symbolic tools deployed by Iberian writers—whether Christian or Muslim—to theorize the spread of empire into Muslim Africa and Asia makes up a good deal of what shapes the present book. But the deeper implications of this question only became apparent to me after I had revisited *Death in Venice*.

The passage from *Death in Venice* that has most gripped me and sent the present book lurching along into existence occurs at the very beginning, before Aschenbach ever leaves Munich. In the passage that interests me, Mann describes his protagonist's walk to the tram stop at the Northern Cemetery on Ungererstraße and his brief encounter there with a red-haired man (the first of three red-haired men that appear in the novella). It is this encounter at the tram stop, in the shadow of both the cemetery and a storm forming over Föhring (to the east), which both snaps Aschenbach out of a waking dream and foreshadows his own descent into illness and death, that sets the action of Mann's novel into motion:

> Whether the man had emerged from the chapel's inner sanctum through the bronze gate or mounted the steps unobtrusively from outside was uncertain. Aschenbach inclined towards the first hypothesis. The man—of medium height, thin, beardless, and strikingly snub-nosed—was the red-haired type and had its milky, freckled pigmentation. He was clearly not of Bavarian stock and, if nothing else, the broad, straight-brimmed bast hat covering his head lent him a distinctly foreign, exotic air. He did, however,

have the customary knapsack strapped to his shoulders, wore a yellowish belted suit of what appeared to be loden, and carried a gray waterproof over his left forearm, which he pressed to his side, and an iron-tipped walking stick in his right hand, and having thrust the stick diagonally into the ground, he had crossed his feet and braced one hip on its crook. Holding his head high and thus exposing a strong, bare Adam's apple on the thin neck rising out of his loose, open shirt, he gazed alert into the distance with colorless, red-lashed eyes, the two pronounced vertical furrows between them oddly suited to the short, turned-up nose. Thus—and perhaps his elevated and elevating position contributed to the impression—there was something of the overseer, something lordly, bold, even wild in his demeanor, for be it that he was grimacing, blinded by the setting sun, or that he had a permanent facial deformity, his lips seemed too short: they pulled all the way back, baring his long, white teeth to the gums.

Ashenbach's half-distracted, half-inquisitive scrutiny of the stranger may have been lacking in discretion, for he suddenly perceived that the man was returning his stare and was indeed so belligerently, so directly, so blatantly determined to challenge him publicly and force him to withdraw it that Aschenbach, embarrassed, turned away and set off along the fence, vaguely resolved to take no further notice of him. A minute later he had forgotten the man. It may have been the stranger's perambulatory appearance that acted upon his imagination or some other physical or psychological influence coming into play, but much to his surprise he grew aware of a strange expansion of his inner being, a kind of restive anxiety, a fervent youthful craving for faraway places, a feeling so vivid, so new or else so long outgrown and forgotten that he came to a standstill and—hands behind his back, eyes on the ground, rooted to the spot—examined the nature and purport of the feeling.[11]

Mann leaves it unclear what precisely has caused the "strange expansion" of Aschenbach's "inner being," combined with his "restive anxiety, a fervent youthful craving for faraway places," but there can be no doubt that it stems, at least generally, from his interaction with the red-haired man (the first of three red-haired men that appear in the novella). In this exchange, in which Aschenbach stares and the red-haired man stares back, something within the former shifts and he begins to feel the first pangs of wanderlust that will eventually lead him to his death, from an outbreak of Indian cholera, along the shore of the Adriatic—ironically enough, after having stared at (and stalked) the beautiful young Tadzio for several days.

According to my reading of this passage, it is first and foremost the assertive and irreducible Otherness of the red-haired man that so disturbs and alters Aschenbach. Throughout Aschenbach's stay in Venice, he observes, follows, desires, and generally admires the young Tadzio, converting the young boy into something akin to a Kantian object of aesthetic judgment and a Hellenic object of pederastic desire.[12] The young boy never possesses, however, anything resembling the subjectivity or alterity that characterizes the red-haired man. It is in fact only as Aschenbach is dying in his beach chair (while watching Tadzio play) that he imagines a potentially disrupting subjectivity for the young Polish boy—a beckoning toward the "promising immensity of it all."[13] But this too is part of Aschenbach's projected fantasy subjectivity for Tadzio, a projection onto the boy that merely reflects back to Aschenbach his own existential anxieties. Tadzio moves Aschenbach as beautiful objects and objects of desire can, but he does not confront him as a potent and menacing Other in the way that the red-haired man does. He does not stand as a potential threat or mystery. Seen from this perspective, it is an outbreak of Indian cholera and his desire to remain in Venice, near Tadzio, that eventually kills Aschenbach, but it is the stare of the red-haired man— an act of infinite, untheorizable, and unrepentant Otherness—that plants the first seeds of death in Aschenbach. The rest is merely a funeral march to the sea, a *katabasis* to the edge of his possibilities and where he is overtaken— struggling to get out of his chair—by the ultimate Other that is death itself.

In the case of early Iberian empire, it is the vigorous and insistent—even homicidal—Otherness of African and Asian Muslims that provokes (though does not ultimately cause) an analogous existential shiver running down the spine and through the limbs of the fifteenth- and sixteenth-century literature that seeks to theorize and narrate it. Like the red-haired man at the start of Mann's novel, this Otherness engages and resists, refusing to be rendered a mere object of judgment or desire, a point on a map. The profound and potentially mortal alterity of the would-be colonized in Africa and Asia, not to mention within the Iberian Peninsula itself, in fact operates as a powerful countercurrent to the masculine subjectivity of empire. It meets its gaze, it fires back, it insinuates itself, it interrupts. In many cases, as discussed in the following chapters, this "firing back" of the Muslim Other occurs in a very literal sense and is conceived self-consciously as an attempt to end the possibility of imperial expansion into Africa and Asia. There is, however, a deeper level at which such resistance, here implying not only open conflict but also an interactional engagement or a simple assertion of subjecthood (an assertion that imposes a limit to the objectifying powers of the subject), operates and signifies. In Zurara's 1450 account of the first push of Iberian expansion into North Africa, this shiver is prompted at different moments by a diseased feminine body, to be quickly discarded (at night and in secret), and by a monstrous black African hurling rocks at the heads of Portuguese invaders, threatening to deprive the invaders of their *tento* (good sense, reason, understanding) along with their lives. For Zurara, as we will see (chapter 3), both the suppurating flesh of João I's English queen and the black enormity of his Muslim Polyphemus stand in the way of imperial progress and threaten— even if for a moment—to derail and undo it, as if the Muslim Other or the generally (or specifically feminine) abject were some sort of pestilent and persistent threat to the steely logic of European empire. In all cases what is being theorized is a very real and present mortal threat, a "looking back" that shakes the imperial subject to its core.

The disruptive power of the (Muslim) Other's returned gaze, as well as the central role of the human body as an instrument and object of perception, emerges in stark relief throughout the Valencian author Joanot Martorell's (1413–1468) chivalric masterwork *Tirant lo Blanc*, written by 1460 and published in 1490. Most salient in this regard, as I have mentioned above in my brief account of *Curial e Güelfa*, is the long episode that recounts Tirant's shipwreck and his subsequent adventures in North Africa.

Near the middle of Martorell's text, the eponymous hero is tricked into believing that his beloved princess, Carmesina, is engaged in passionate foreplay with her father's black Muslim gardener, Lauseta. Spying on Carmesina, with the aid of mirrors, through a small window in a country cottage, Tirant sees Carmesina emerge topless and with her hair down from her bedroom and sit down on a garden bench next to Plaerdemavida, a lady-in-waiting disguised as Lauseta (she is wearing a black mask made for the occasion). The Viuda Reposada, another of Carmesina's attendants and the author of the deception, had earlier instructed Plaerdemavida to fondle Carmesina's breasts and thighs and kiss her to make her laugh and feel merry, which she does. The scene devastates Tirant, who is convinced that Plaerdemavida is Lauseta. He stays hidden for a time before leaving to track down the innocent Lauseta (the real one). Upon finding the surprised gardener, Tirant decapitates him before sinking into a long depression. He eventually resolves to sail away to battle in service of Carmesina's father, the emperor of Constantinople.

Tirant learns of Carmesina's innocence from Plaerdemavida when he is already aboard his ship and it is too late for him to change his plans. As a storm grows around him, he sails into the Mediterranean feeling miserable for his lack of faith in Carmesina. The storm continues to grow, and he is soon left shipwrecked in Tunis. It is here that the tables are turned on Tirant: although he had shortly before spied secretly upon Carmesina in the garden near the cottage, it is now his body that serves as an object of inspection by various sets of Muslim eyes.

As Tirant's men swim to shore from the wreckage, they are captured by a group of Muslims, who kill many of them with their swords. Tirant and a companion manage to reach the shore alive and sleep through the night in a cave situated next to a vineyard. A Muslim hunter chases a hare into the cave and finds the wounded knight sleeping there. Reporting back to his lord, the ambassador of the king of Tlemcen in Tunis, the hunter explains what he has found in the cave:

> "Senyor, jo no crec que natura pogués formar un cos mortal ab més perfecció, car pintor no poguera pintar un cos més bell del que jo he vist. Oh fortuna!, ¿per què l'has tant perjudicat? No sé si es defalt a la mia vista, car, a mon semblant, me par ésser més mort que viu, per la color que té descolorida, ab més bella cara, e lo llustre dels ulls que per que sien rubins acunçats. En l'univers mon no pens se trobàs un cos mortal ab tanta perfecció de membres. Jo l'he vist tal que crec que de dolor e mals està ben acompanyat."[14]

> ["Sir, I do not believe that nature could have formed a mortal body with more perfection, or that a painter could have painted a more beautiful body than the one that I have just seen. Oh, Fortune!, why have you treated it so harshly? I do not know if it is due to limits of my eyesight, but it seems to be more dead than alive; the beautiful face is pale, and the eyes shine like twin rubies. In the entire world I do not believe that you would find a mortal body so perfectly formed. I have seen it, and it seems to be accompanied by much pain and suffering."]

The hunter here speaks at length about Tirant's body as an object of aesthetic judgment ("I do not believe that . . . a painter could have painted a more beautiful body"); significantly, he never associates it with the self (or the soul) that resides within it. The hunter does not speak of Tirant, but of his body, which is to the hunter merely an animate object to be beheld, a *thing* that is perhaps more dead than alive. It is in this way that Tirant is immediately, in one stroke, stripped of his clothes, his consciousness, his subjectivity, and his agency upon his arrival in North Africa. He eventually manages to gain all of these back through his efforts and heroism; however, also hovering over him, like the storm that shipwrecked him in the first place, is death itself.

Later on in the episode, the king of Tlemcen's ambassador takes up this link between Tirant's body and the imminence of death as he describes his compassion for Tirant and reveals his belief that Tirant is a knight of great valor:

> "E ajuda'm altra raó per confirmar la mia creença, car com te viu nuu, sens camisa, mirant lo teu ben proporcionat cos semblant lo de Sebastià, qui fon assagetat, e lo teu fon vist ple de ferides, qui les te donà no tenia gran pietat de tu, ni crec com les rebist no dormies ni les tues mans no devien estar ocioses."[15]

> ["Another reason helps to confirm my belief, for I saw you naked, without a shirt, and I watched your well-proportioned body that so resembles that of Sebastian, which was shot through with arrows, while yours is visibly full of wounds. Whoever gave those wounds to you had little pity on you, nor do I believe that you received them while sleeping or with your hands resting at your sides."]

The ambassador compares Tirant's body to that of Saint Sebastian *after* his "first" martyrdom, and so simultaneously frames Tirant as a naked object of aesthetic judgment (and interpretation) while linking him to the theme of violent death. This is by no means the end of Tirant's adventure in North Africa (before he leaves he has converted thousands of Muslims to Christianity and won several major battles); however, it is a beginning that reveals a deep concern over the status of the Western subject (e.g., as a body to be perceived and mortal) in settings of imperial contact and imagination.

At the end of Martorell's novel Tirant does in fact die, much like Alexander the Great, from an illness that takes him by surprise. Tirant's death also precedes a one-hundred-year period of peace and prosperity in Constantinople, a political situation that contrasts starkly with political realties affecting the Crown of Aragon at the time that Martorell composed his novel. Given the steady decline of Catalan and Aragonese prestige (and rights) after the Compromise of Caspe (1412) put Fernando of Trastámara (1380–1416)—a Castilian noble—on the Aragonese throne, it is difficult to see Byzantium's rise as anything but the mirror image of Aragon's downward slide (a slide acutely felt by Martorell and his family). Montserrat Piera has made exactly this argument, maintaining that

> it is hard to believe that the ending of *Tirant lo Blanc* can be interpreted as a return to society's harmony and also as a textual closure, that is, as a happy ending. What this ending signifies is the impossibility of social and political harmony after the hero's disappearance and also the impossibility of textual closure. The story is not finished; it will finish when fiction catches up with history, when Constantinople, under the rule of one of Hipòlit's descendants, finally succumbs to the Turks. Or perhaps we should say instead that the story finished at the precise moment Tirant died and an acute sense of loss and despair started to infiltrate the Court of Constantinople and, undoubtedly, the contemporary reader.[16]

For Piera, *Tirant lo Blanc* functions as a kind of historico-chivalric fantasy, not unlike the broader Arthurian cycle from which it draws, that is inevitably eclipsed by the difficulties of the present. In a sense, the true enemy within Martorell's novel is not the Turks, but the future that brings them to power in Byzantium and the Maghreb. In this sense, Tirant's heroic achievements, as well as his status as a shining example of knightly comportment in the East, find themselves overshadowed by a future that inevitably, from the perspective of Martorell's reader, brings with it death and defeat.[17]

Loss and despair are not typically associated with the discourse of empire; however, it is just these sentiments, expanded to include the responses and punishments of Nature itself, that have served as the focus of a good deal of Josiah Blackmore's critical work on the "disruption" of Portuguese empire through its literature. Blackmore has logically opted for metaphors and critical foci that are more explicitly related to oceanic navigation (e.g., "shipwreck," "storm," "moorings") in his analyses of the *História trágico-marítima* (Tragic Story of the Sea), Zurara's chronicles, and the poetry of Luís de Camões (c. 1524–1580); however, insofar as he is concerned with bringing to the surface the ways in which the discourse of Iberian empire brings with it—even if unwittingly—a powerful undoing of itself and the empire it seeks to theorize, the present book can fairly be considered to be of a piece with Blackmore's critical project.[18]

As I have suggested, the larger argument about Iberian empire, and the role of Alexander the Great within narrative theorizations of that empire, which runs through the present book consists of a sustained focus on the connections between the forceful alterity of African and Asian Muslims (as well as other marginalized participants in the imperial project) and the deeper anxieties this agency provokes. In my analysis, the persistent ungraspability of the Other indexes (as a very literal "pointing to") the ultimate Otherness of death, a murdering presence that forms much like Mann's storm clouds over Föhring: near and yet always not-here-yet.

It is precisely the indexical link that exists between the murderous agency of death (as a kind of Other *nec plus ultra*) and the agentive alterity of African and Asian Muslims, as well as its more proximal echo in the perceived Otherness of marginalized groups within the Iberian Peninsula, within the context of Iberian imperial expansion that generates what I have chosen to describe as the deep existential or mortal shiver that runs through much of the literature of fifteenth- and sixteenth-century Iberian empire. Like the red-haired man at the tram stop on the Ungererstraße, the Other of Iberian empire responds to the gaze of the imperial self with a penetrating challenge that stirs up and threatens the imperial self's very existence. In simple terms, this challenge, which takes place within the realm of the social, indexes the primordial assault launched at the subject by death itself. It is for this reason that much of the discourse of early Iberian imperial expansion demonstrates such a preoccupation (if not obsession) with the limits of human mortality and an almost obsessive desire to overcome them. And it is here that Alexander the Great, the young Macedonian king and would-be demigod who took power over a good part of western Asia and North Africa, enters into the picture.

Alexander, Looking Back

In many cases, late medieval and early modern Iberian writers seeking both to theorize empire and to carve out a path by which mortality might be overcome call on (or, perhaps more accurately, conjure up) Alexander the Great. This may seem a natural maneuver in the case of the Portuguese, because their overseas Asian empire overlapped to some degree, at least in theory, with that carved out by Alexander nearly two millennia earlier. With respect to João de Barros (1496–1570), whose histories focus on the Portuguese colonization of sections of India, it is in fact this relation between Alexander and the Portuguese that takes center stage in various sections. His account, for example, of the conflicts between the Portuguese and the kingdom of Gujarat recalls Alexander's earlier battles with King Porus along the Jhelum (Hydaspes) River in modern-day Pakistan, and his assessment of the king of Persia at the time of the Portuguese conquest of Hormuz invokes the memory of Darius III. Even in Barros, however, the issue of territorial overlap is a minor one when compared to the long passages that he devotes to the issue of death and immortality—passages in which Alexander also figures prominently. The epic discourse of Luís de Camões (c. 1524–1580), which also focuses extensively on Portuguese overseas expansion into India, likewise makes good use of Alexander, but for the most part in the context of the ongoing fight between Portugal and the Sa'adi kings of Morocco. Camões in fact closes Os Lusíadas (The Lusiads) by calling upon the young (and demonstrably unbalanced) Portuguese king Sebastião I (1554–1578) to initiate a war in Morocco so that the monarch's fame, bolstered by Camões's poetic encomia, might exceed that of Alexander. Fifteenth- and sixteenth-century writers working in Castilian and Catalan likewise made good use of Alexander, although almost exclusively within the context of their imperial adventures (real or imagined) within the Maghreb. I have already mentioned Joanot Martorell's Tirant lo Blanc, which makes mention of Alexander on several occasions and invokes various elements of the Macedonian king's history (taken mostly from Pier Candido Decembrio's Italian translation of Quintus Curtius Rufus's history of Alexander) within the section of his novel that deals with Tirant's exile and spiritual conquest in North Africa. It bears repeating that even Tirant's eventual death by sudden illness, described as a novelistic element of realism or theorization of love suffering by so many modern critics, parallels in many ways Alexander's own feverish, and equally sudden, demise in Babylon.[19] From the other side of the imperial project, for Crypto-Muslim scribes and readers working in rural Aragon during the sixteenth century, the Qur'anic figure of Alexander (whom they equate with the enigmatic Qur'anic hero Dhū al-Qarnayn) offers an almost direct response to Christian hegemony and persecution as well as a means of questioning issues of death, divine judgment, and the afterlife.

That Alexander should have functioned as a kind of symbolic tool to help Iberian writers and readers to work through and confront the awful limitations imposed by the disruptive alterity of various forms of the

Other—and mortality itself—is in some sense paradoxical given the trajectory of Alexander's own life. A king at twenty, an Asian emperor at twenty-five, and a corpse by his thirty-third birthday, Alexander is anything but an image of longevity or stability. Alexander almost singlehandedly willed his empire into existence, but he fought in vain for the better part of a decade to give it a durable foundation. Particularly problematic is the fact that Alexander's empire essentially died with him, as though the two were existentially coextensive—like some radically symbiotic version of the imperial map described by Jorge Luis Borges in his short poem "Del rigor en la ciencia" (On Rigor in Science).[20] Alexander conquered but hardly governed, and in any case, his model of kingship was in almost all ways modeled on a Persian form of despotism that ran counter to the at least nominally republican political ideologies of Greek and Roman historians and philosophers. According to Quintius Curtius Rufus, a Roman historian of Alexander who flourished during the first century CE, Alexander was in fact fully aware, as his death approached him, that the reconsolidation and maintenance of his empire upon his death would at the very least entail an extremely violent struggle among his successors:

> Intuentibus lacrimae obortae praebuere speciem iam non regem, sed funus eius visentis exercitus. Maeror tamen circumstantium lectum eminebat: quos ut rex adspexit, "Invenietis," inquit, "cum excessero, dignum talibus viris regem?" Incredibile dictu audituque, in eodem habitu corporis, in quem se conposuerat, cum admissurus milites esset, durasse, donec a toto exercitu illud ultimum persalutatus est: dimissoque vulgo velut omni vitae debito liberatus fatigata membra reiecit. Propiusque adire iussis amicis— nam et vox deficere iam coeperat—detractum anulum digito Perdiccae tradidit adiectis mandatis, ut corpus suum ad Hammonem ferri iuberent. Quaerentibusque his, cui relinqueret regnum, respondit, *ei qui esset optimus*: ceterum providere iam se, ob id certamen magnos funebres ludos parari sibi. Rursus Perdicca interrogante, quando caelestes honores haberi sibi vellet, dixit, tum velle, cum ipsi felices essent. Suprema haec vox fuit regis et paulo post extinguitur.[21] (Italics my own)

> [Tears welled up as they looked at him, and they appeared not as an army visiting its king but one attending his funeral. The grief was especially intense among those at his bedside. Alexander looked at them and said: "After my death will you find a king who deserves such men?" Incredibly, he maintained the same posture which he had adopted before admitting the

men until he had received the last salute from the whole army. He then dismissed the rank and file and, as though released from all life's obligations, collapsed in exhaustion. He bade his friends draw near since, by now, even his voice had started to fail, and then took his ring from his finger and handed it to Perdiccas. He also gave instructions that they should have his body transported to Hammon. When they asked him to whom he bequeathed his kingdom, he answered, "*To the best man*," but added that he could already foresee great funeral games for himself provided by that issue. When Perdiccas further asked when he wished divine honors paid to him, he said he wanted them when they themselves were happy. These were Alexander's last words; he died moments later.][22]

The source for this passage is Diodorus Siculus (fl. c. 70 BCE), who writes at the start of the eighteenth book of his *Bibliotheka historika* (Library of History): "When he was quitting life in Babylon and at his last breath was asked by his friends to whom he was leaving the kingdom, he said, 'To the best man; for I foresee that a great combat of my friends will be my funeral games.'"[23] The Greek word that Diodorus employs here for "best man" is *aristos*, which Curtius Rufus translates as *optimus* and Justin (fl. c. 200 CE), in his epitome of Gnaeus Trogus (fl. c. 50 BCE), renders as *dignissimus*.[24] Late fifteenth- and early sixteenth-century Ibero-Romance manuscript translations of Quintus Curtius Rufus, mostly based on Decembrio's Italian edition, likewise render the term as some version of *optimus*.[25] Madrid, Biblioteca Nacional MS 8549, and Madrid, Biblioteca Nacional MS 10140, for example, both present the following phrase: "preguntando ellos a quien dexava el rreyno, respondió 'a quien será mejor'" (they asked him to whom he was leaving his kingdom, and he responded, "to whomever proves best").[26] The use of the future tense *será* suggests in a subtle way Alexander's awareness of the struggle to come: he is not leaving his kingdom to whoever is best in some essential or constant (let alone moral) way, but rather to the one who proves himself the strongest. This likely reflects, in Decembrio's scholarship, a familiarity with Diodorus's text that informs his Italian translation of Curtius Rufus's Latin reworking of the Greek original: earlier in Diodorus's text, he recounts the same episode, using instead of *aristos* the more ambiguous term *kratistos*, which can mean "strongest" as well as "best." These two terms likely were much the same to Alexander's mind, at least in this context, and it is almost certainly this sense that Decembrio was attempting to transmit and that was preserved in the Castilian versions of his work. The earlier episode in Diodorus reads:

They asked him to sacrifice to the gods on a grand scale and with all speed, but he was then called away by Medius, the Thessalian, one of his Friends, to take part in a *comus*. There he drank a good deal of unmixed wine in commemoration of the death of Heracles, and finally, filling a huge beaker, downed it at a gulp. Instantly he called out as if hit by a violent blow and was conducted by his friends, who led him back to his apartments. His attendants put him to bed and watched him closely, but the pain increased and the physicians were called for. Nobody was able to help him. When Alexander, in great discomfort and suffering acutely, had lost all hope of living, he took off his ring and handed it to Perdiccas. When his Friends asked him to whom he would leave the kingdom, he replied: "To the best/ strongest" [*tô kratístô*]. He added, and these were his last words, that all of his leading Friends would celebrate his funeral by engaging in great battles amongst themselves. This was how he died after a reign of twelve years and seven months. He accomplished greater deeds than any of the kings who had lived before him and also of those who were to come later, down to our time.[27]

Arrian (c. 95–175 CE) also uses the term *kratistos* in his brief mention of this episode at the end of his history of Alexander; however, he does not list Diodorus Siculus as his source, stating merely that "but others wrote/have recorded [that]. . . ." (*hoi dè kaì táde anégrapsan . . .*),[28] The shift between *aristos* and *kratistos* in the extant Greek histories of Alexander, reflected in Decembrio's highly influential humanistic work, fostered a strange sort of ambivalence regarding Alexander and his legacy that spilled over into the early modern period. We see an early Roman example of this ambivalence in Justin's commentary on Alexander's supposed decision to leave his kingdom to "the most worthy" (*dignissimus*):

Tanta illi magnitudo animi fuit ut, cum Herculem filium, cum fratrem Arridaeum, cum Roxanen uxorem praegnantem relinqueret, oblitus necessitudinum dignissimum nuncuparit heredem: prorsus quasi nefas esset uiro forti alium quam uirum fortem succedere, aut tanti regni opes aliis quam probatis relinqui. Hac uoce ueluti bellicum inter amicos cecinisset aut malum Discordiae misisset, ita omnes in aemulationem consurgunt et ambitione uulgi tacitum fauorem militum quaerunt.[29]

[Such was his nobleness of spirit, that though he left a son named Hercules, a brother called Aridaeus, and his wife Roxana with child, yet, forgetting his relations, he named only "the most worthy" as his successor; as though it were unlawful for any but a brave man to succeed a brave man, or for the power of so great an empire to be left to any but approved governors. But as if, by this reply, he had sounded the signal for battle among his friends, or had thrown the apple of discord among them, they all rose in emulation against each other, and tried to gain the favor of the army by secretly paying court to the common soldiers.]

As Justin makes clear in this passage, Alexander's personal greatness is not to be questioned (Arrian also concludes his history with great praise for Alexander and a qualification of his many criticisms). His despotic manner of ruling, however, is also the cause of great discord and war among his successors, even before he has gone. It is not for nothing that Quintus Curtius ends his history of Alexander not with Alexander's death, but with the civil war that breaks out afterward. Having based the survival of his empire (as well as that of the members of his immediate family) on his own strength/excellence, Alexander falls flat. His empire splinters into several warring pieces, and his former companions systematically imprison and murder the surviving members of his family, including his infant son and rightful heir by his wife, Roxana. Alexander cannot even control his own remains: men working for the new Egyptian king, Ptolemy Soter (one of Alexander's generals and a childhood friend), steal his body as it makes its way back to Pella and transfers it to Alexandria before it goes missing sometime after the Roman period. In these and a host of other ways, Alexander fails utterly to overcome death, even as he tenuously establishes his own divine status as a son of the god Amun and achieves a kind of immortality through fame. His empire dies with him.

Beyond the thorny issue of succession, more than one Roman historian has pointed out that Alexander formed his empire through unspeakable acts of violence and by actively accommodating himself to Asian political, religious, and courtly traditions. Alexander's turn to the Orient was a far cry from what Athenians (or would-be Athenians, such as Aristotle and his Roman heirs) considered good or honest government. Quintus Curtius, for example, whose republican inclinations have been well documented by Diana Spencer, in fact expends a good deal of energy criticizing the despotic (framed as oriental) inclinations of Alexander.[30] Much of Spencer's study of the Roman Alexander, in fact, deals with how the Macedonian king's despotism served Roman authors as a foundation upon which to build arguments against the decline of republican government in Rome. It is in fact no stretch to argue that due to these and other issues—Alexander's perceived "descent" into oriental mores and drunken paranoia (the two were correlates, at least from the Greek and Roman perspective) figure prominently—Greek and Latin accounts of Alexander tend to present the Macedonian king as much as a cautionary tale as a powerful (or great) figure to be emulated. It perhaps also comes as no surprise that in both this literature and that of early Iberian expansion into Muslim Africa and Asia, Alexander ends up taking the indexical relation between empire and death to new and even more disturbing depths.

Within the literature of early Iberian empire, Alexander has the paradoxical effect of heightening the deep sense of mortal anxiety that underlies the imperial project, even as authors call on him to mitigate and overcome this anxiety. Yanked up from his Babylonian deathbed, Alexander—or, perhaps more accurately, the ghost he has left behind—operates within the texts of early Iberian empire like so much gasoline thrown onto a fire. He brings with him the singular achievements of his Asian expedition and his seeming immortality (encoded in his greatness), but he also drags behind him an early and mysterious death, a perceived loss of (Western) self within the excesses of the Orient, and the impossibility of succession. To put it mildly, Greek and Roman authors, as well as those Iberian authors working in late antiquity and the medieval period, had a troubled and complex relationship with the figure of Alexander the Great. From Aristotle through Arrian and Seneca the Younger and on to Paulus Orosius and the poet of the thirteenth-century Castilian masterwork *Libro de Alexandre* (Book of Alexander), the writers of classical and late antiquity and the Iberian Middle Ages saw Alexander as an inherently ambivalent and dangerous figure, linked at once to death and the thin, elusive promise of immortality. It is Justin once again who presents this ambivalence in the most economical and subtle manner, in his commentary on the death of Alexander: "Qua nocte eum mater Olympias concepit, visa per quietem est cum ingenti serpente volutari, nec decepta somnio est, nam profecto maius humana mortalitate opus utero tulit" (On the night that his mother, Olympias, conceived him, she saw herself lying with an enormous serpent; nor was she deceived by the dream, for she certainly carried in her womb a work greater than human mortality).[31] As Justin puts it, Alexander's power over death—a current that also runs through the rich corpus of legendary material revolving around

Alexander—is at once the thing of dreams and visions and a demonstrable, empirical fact.

The authors of the early Iberian expansion into Asia and Africa (mostly, but not exclusively, chroniclers and poets), self-conscious heirs to both the classical and medieval tradition and the burden of "oriental" empire, likewise understood Alexander to be a dangerous weapon that always threatened to cut both ways. One gets the sense, however, that these writers were often willing enough to run the risks that accompanied any situation of their imperial project within an Alexandrian frame, or that they felt confident that they could somehow hang on to the desirable bits of Alexander while parsing out what was undesirable about his life and legacy. In other cases, such as Camões's epic discourse and the Crypto-Muslim legend of Alexander, the mortal ambivalence that underlies any reference to Alexander in the context of imperial conquest seems to have been precisely the point that authors wished to make, and that readers wished to take away. In any case, that the appearance of Alexander within the literature of Iberian empire in Asia and Africa ultimately serves to heighten the presence of mortal anxiety—the existential shiver that I have mentioned—rather than mitigate it is an aspect of this literature with which we must reckon. From the perspective of the modern researcher, it is precisely the heightening effect that Alexander, already by the fifteenth century a common trope for Western imperial expansion and loss in a loosely conceived East, has upon the deeper mortal relations of Iberian imperial expansion that allows us to see these relations in play. As Martin Heidegger might have put it had he considered these specific issues, we may justifiably argue that Alexander, like language itself, serves as the house of Being.

In mentioning Heidegger, I should say that my approach to the issues of death, language, and existence in the present book in fact draws very little from his work, at least in a direct way. As may already have become clear, in fact, my analytical treatment of these issues, and the texts in which they arise, instead springs from an interrelated network of specific ideas and approaches rooted at once in phenomenological philosophy, literary criticism, and classical studies. In this sense the present volume can be much more accurately understood as a work of creative synthesis—a weaving together of seemingly disparate threads—than as an example of systematic, original thought. I am not seeking to rewrite the history of Alexander the Great nor that of early Iberian imperial expansion; rather, I am merely attempting to show how these two histories intersect and shape theories of fundamental human care (once again, in a Heideggerian sense) within late medieval and early modern Iberian literature.

In philosophical terms, the present volume is most directly shaped, as I have stated above, by the work of Emmanuel Levinas. Because so much of what I argue over the course of the next four chapters stems from my readings of Levinas's work, it is useful to speak briefly of how I read it and how I understand it to be useful to my broader analysis of literature and empire. I will begin with Levinas's reworking of Heidegger's approach to death, which is, along with Mann's narrative exploration of the theme, a foundational concept for the present volume.

Levinas, Death, and the Other

For Levinas, death is "absolutely unknowable" owing both to its essential futurity and to its power to efface the subjectivity and efficacy of the very subject who, in dying, feels it near.[32] Death, as Levinas frames it, "escapes every present" not because we evade it or choose to sweep it under the rug, but because it is itself "ungraspable [and] marks the end of the subject's virility and heroism."[33] It is quite simply beyond us. Levinas develops this idea in a direct and sustained way within his early work, first published in 1947 as *Le temps et l'autre* (Time and the Other); however, it is in his best-known work, *Totalité et infini: Essai sur l'extériorité* (Totality and Infinity: An Essay on Exteriority), that we see its place within his broader philosophical program. *Totality and Infinity* was published in 1961 (only months after a sudden stroke marked the end, somewhere in Paris, of the "virility and heroism" of France's other leading phenomenologist, Maurice Merleau-Ponty), and it is in this book that we see perhaps the fullest expression of the link that Levinas would forge between death, time, and alterity:

> One does not know when death will come. What will come? With what does death threaten me? With nothingness or with recommencement? I do not know. In this impossibility of knowing the after my death resides the essence of the last moment. I can absolutely not apprehend the moment of death; it is "out of reach" as Montaigne would say. *Ultima latet*—contrary to all the instants of my life, which are spread out between my birth and my death, and which can be recalled or anticipated. My death comes from

an instant upon which I can in no way exercise my power. I do not run up against an obstacle which at least I touch in that collision, which, in surmounting or enduring it, I integrate into my life, suspending its alterity. Death is a menace that approaches me as a mystery; its secrecy determines it—it approaches without being able to be assumed, such that the time that separates me from my death dwindles and dwindles without end, involves a sort of last interval which my consciousness cannot traverse, and where a leap will somehow be produced from death to me. The last part of the route will be crossed without me; the time of death flows upstream; the I in its projection toward the future is overturned by a movement of imminence, pure menace, which comes to me from an absolute alterity.[34]

The mystery of death resides in its unchanging and irreconcilable futurity, in our inability to confront it in a given present. We approach this mystery, as if running to the end of a precipice (also the end of our *Grund*, as Heidegger phrases it in his later analysis of reason), but we cannot make the leap; in the end death leaps at us, finding us wholly passive and unable to respond. It is for this reason that Levinas describes death as the end of the subject's possibilities, as being "no longer able to be able." Working in the first person plural, Levinas expresses this idea as "nous ne pouvons plus pouvoir."[35]

In presenting this analysis of death as mystery and the end of the subject's possibilities, Levinas is reworking in significant ways the argument regarding being-toward-death and authenticity developed by Heidegger:

> Being toward death, in Heidegger's authentic existence, is a supreme lucidity and hence a supreme virility. It is *Dasein*'s assumption of the uttermost possibility of existence, which precisely makes possible all other possibilities, and consequently makes possible the very feat of grasping a possibility—that is, it makes possible activity and freedom. Death in Heidegger is an event of freedom, whereas for me the subject seems to reach the limit of the possible in suffering. It finds itself enchained, overwhelmed, and in some way passive. Death is in this sense the limit of idealism.[36]

While Heidegger speaks of authenticity and freedom, Levinas speaks of death in terms of passivity. For Levinas, death implies an end of the subject's mastery and the approach of something that overwhelms its powers. Within this framework, death comes near and places us in a relationship with something that bears alterity "not as a provisional determination we can assimilate through enjoyment, but as something whose very existence is made of alterity."[37] In his introduction to the English edition of Levinas's *Time and the Other*, Richard A. Cohen elaborates on this crucial point:

> Levinas, then, in *Time and the Other*, sees in death and mortality not the uttermost possibility of subjectivity, but a countermovement against subjectivity. And in this countermovement, rather than in the Heideggerian projection, he finds time. The future is not what comes from out of me in my being-toward-death, in the resoluteness of my futural projection, but what comes *at* me, ungraspable, outside my possibilities, not as the mastery of death but as the very *mystery* of the death which always comes to take me against my will, too soon.[38]

For Levinas, death is absolutely unknowable (not, he insists, merely unknown), because it comes at us from a future that never arrives—is never part of our present—until we are no longer.

According to Levinas, the absolute unknowability of death derives not from the "limited horizon of our understanding," but rather from the fact that it "does not lie within any horizon."[39] It is by its nature impossible to grasp, in much the same way that we cannot, in any given present, grasp the future yet to come. Beyond this ungraspability, death further presents us with a form of violence against which we are not even afforded the possibility of struggle:

> [Death] takes me without leaving me the chance that I have in a struggle, for in reciprocal struggle I contend with the invisible. Struggle must not be confounded with the collision of two forces whose issue one can foresee and calculate. Struggle is already, or again, *war*, where between the forces that confront one another gapes open the interval of transcendence across which death comes and strikes without being received. The Other, inseparable from the very event of transcendence, is situated in the region from which death, possibly murder, comes. The unwonted hour of its coming approaches as the hour of fate fixed by someone. Hostile and malevolent powers, more wily, more clever than I, absolutely other and only thereby hostile, retain its secret. Death, in its absurdity, maintains an interpersonal order, in which it tends to take on a signification—as in the primitive mentality where, according to Levy-Bruhl, it is never natural, but requires a magical explanation. The things that bring death to me, being graspable and subject to labor, obstacles rather than menaces, refer to a malevolence,

are the residue of a bad will which surprises and stalks. Death threatens me from beyond.[40]

The idea that the Other is "inseparable from the very event of transcendence" and is situated within the "interval of transcendence" that stretches out—as time, not as space—between, say, two warring forces (or two men facing one another at a streetcar stop), is a key element in Levinas's thought. It places our very existence, as processual beings who *feel* the menace of death *through* the things (such as hurled stones and cholera) that bring it to us, within the realm of the interpersonal, expressed as a kind of commerce or responsibility. It is from this point that Levinas pivots and begins to develop his argument for ethics, rather than ontology, as a first philosophy, and it is here that he initiates his most dramatic break from Heidegger:

> This unknown that frightens, the silence of the infinite spaces that terrify, comes from the other, and this alterity, precisely as absolute, strikes me in an evil design or in a judgment of justice. The solitude of death does not make the Other [*Autrui*] vanish, but remains in a consciousness of hostility, and consequently still renders possible appeal to the Other, to his friendship and his medication. The doctor is an a priori principle of human mortality. Death approaches in the fear of someone, and hopes in someone.[41]

It is, of course, this "fear of someone/hope in someone" that forms the basis of the framework of responsibility and servitude to the human Other that is most associated with Levinas's philosophy, the "interpersonal order whose signification [death] does not annihilate."[42] As Simon Critchley has pointed out, readers and critics have often misunderstood this point, which underlies the very title of Levinas's most important work (i.e., *Totality and Infinity*):

> For Levinas, all ontological relations to that which is other are relations of comprehension and form totalities. The claim is that if I conceive of the relation to the other in terms of understanding, correlation, symmetry, reciprocity, equality and even, as has once again become fashionable, recognition, the relation is totalized. When I totalize, I conceive of the relation to the other from some imagined point that would be outside of it and I turn myself into a theoretical spectator on the social world of which I am really part, and in which I am an agent. Viewed from outside, intersubjec-

tivity might appear to be a relation between equals, but from inside that relation, as it takes place at this very moment, you place an obligation on me that make you higher than me, more than my equal. It might be argued that much philosophy and social theory persistently totalizes relations with others. But for Levinas, there is no view from nowhere. Every view is from somewhere and the ethical relation is a description from the point of view of an agent in the social world and not a spectator upon it.[43]

The situated, interactional, and pluralistic character of all human being is, for Levinas, the fundamental basis for any account of being itself. It is for this reason that he contends that it is ethics, understood as a relation of infinite responsibility to the human Other (*Autrui*), not ontology, that should be considered first philosophy (*prima philosophia*). As both Critchley and Hilary Putnam have pointed out, Levinas here borrows the formal structure of René Descartes's (1596–1650) relation between the *res cogitans* and an infinite God, but in effect substitutes the human Other for that infinite God.[44] As Levinas himself puts it, presenting both the fundamental shortcomings of Western philosophy vis-à-vis the other and his point of departure: "Western philosophy coincides with the disclosure of the other where the other, in manifesting itself as a being, loses its alterity. From its infancy philosophy has been struck with a horror of the other that remains other—with an insurmountable allergy."[45]

Returning to the specific focus of the present book, we might argue that for fifteenth- and sixteenth-century Iberian authors seeking to work through the innumerable unknowns, risks, and hostilities associated with imperial expansion, it is Alexander the Great who most explicitly and intentionally serves as that "someone" in whom there is great hope of overcoming the menace of mortality. At this level, it is his very "greatness" that serves as a hedge against death and a kind of bridge to the immortality that lies beyond the inevitable lunge death makes at the subject. That these texts also express, however, a simultaneous and overriding fear of Alexander, as though he were some form of allergen or an Other whose presence somehow ensures and even speeds the leap that death will make at the subject's throat, brings a new and immediate significance to them as theorizations both of dominion and of being-in-the-world. What is at the center of this particular double function is the unknowable alterity of death itself and a primordial and inescapably ethical relation to the (Muslim) Other.

Keeping these ideas about Alexander and Iberian empire in mind, it is important to mention that what follows from Levinas's framing of death as radical alterity and his mention of the "interpersonal order" that emerges from that relation is a pluralistic conception of existence itself:

> Right away this means that existence is pluralist. Here the plural is not a multiplicity of existents; it appears in existing itself. A plurality insinuates itself into the very existing of the existent, which until this point was jealously assumed by the subject alone and manifest through suffering. In death the existing of the existent is alienated. To be sure, the other [*l'Autre*] that is announced does not possess this existing as the subject possesses it; its hold over my existing is mysterious. It is not unknown but unknowable, refractory to all light. But this precisely indicates that the other is in no way another myself, participating with me in a common existence. The relationship with the other is not an idyllic and harmonious relationship of communion, or a sympathy through which we put ourselves in the other's place; we recognize the other as resembling us, but exterior to us; the relationship with the Other is a relationship with a Mystery. The other's entire being is constituted by its exteriority, or rather its alterity, for exteriority is a property of space and leads the subject back to itself through light.[46]

This mystery, this other that comes at us from an unknowable (but certainly proximal) future to undo our mastery and alienate us from our very existence, is thus—perhaps paradoxically—an essential aspect of our existence. That we can never grasp it, because it resides in a future that is "absolutely surprising," conditions our possibilities within being that is not *toward* a death sharing a common existence with us (as an end we reach), but rather within being that is both shaped and alienated by a death (as Other) *coming at it* and rendering it wholly passive. As Levinas puts it: "The future is what is not grasped, what befalls us and lays hold of us. The other is the future. The very relationship with the other is the relationship with the future. It seems impossible to me to speak of time in a subject alone, or to speak of a purely personal duration."[47] Always lurking, in the mysterious half-light of the future, is that other which comes at us and forms our utmost possibilities even as we move inexorably toward it, never to know fully or grasp it, and never to face it in anything but a position of utter passivity. It is in this sense that Levinas concludes that "the fear for my being which is my relation with death is not the fear of nothingness, but the fear of violence—and thus it extends into fear of the Other, of the absolutely unforeseeable."[48] It is this fear that Alexander, long after his own death in Babylon, is called on—perhaps paradoxically—to alleviate.

The Great White Trope

It is perhaps unnecessary to state that Alexander has long served, at least from the period of Roman dominance, as a trope for empire. To speak of Alexander, to utter his name (with or without the *magnus* tag that later imperial leaders such as Pompey (106–48 BCE), Charlemagne (742–814), and Peter I of Russia (1672–1725) would take on), is to conjure up the self-conscious origins of Western empire itself. He is in many ways the urtext of Western empire, as well as the template on the basis of which a long list of European conquests in Africa and Asia (not to mention the Americas—it is almost beyond doubt that Hernán Cortés would have studied selections of Quintus Curtius Rufus's history of Alexander while a student at Salamanca) took place.

The present volume does not seek to dispute the fact that Alexander has served as an explicit signifier for a wide range of imperially inflected signifieds; however, it is not with this level of signification that I am principally interested. My main concern, rather, is with developing what we might consider a phenomenological or, more generally, a pragmatic or interactional understanding of Alexander as a symbolic tool by which late medieval and early modern authors, scribes, and readers from the three principal kingdoms of the Iberian Peninsula reckoned with empire. My argument, simply put, is that Alexander was both a trope for empire and a trigger for the theorization of deeper, more immediate accounts of human being at a pivotal moment in world history.

To gain an adequately contextualized understanding of that moment, and what we in the twenty-first century have inherited from it (even as I write this introduction, my own country's armed forces are seeking to control areas of Afghanistan and Iraq once held by Alexander), it will be necessary to move beyond traditional modes of literary analysis and investigate the ways in which human agents have made use of written texts to shape and theorize both our social world and those structures that underlie it. Insofar as the present volume has methodological value for the field at large, it is through the exploration of modes of inquiry that might attend to this project. It is also here that my interest in specific aspects of the philosophy of Levinas comes in.

The Ibero-Roman historian Paulus Orosius (fl. c. 410 CE) famously described Alexander as "ille gurges miserarium atque atrocissimus turbo totius Orientis" (that abyss of miseries and most horrible whirlwind of the entire Orient).⁴⁹ As Orosius's treatment of Alexander suggests, the Macedonian king was by the dawn of the medieval period at once the light of empire and its penumbra—a perfect storm of bottomless seas and violent winds that shakes the East and is shaken in return. As a historian, Orosius tends to be more adept at synthesis than invention, and we find early echoes of his treatment of Alexander in another Ibero-Roman writer, Seneca the Younger (4 BCE–65 CE), who deals critically with Alexander, Pompey, and Julius Caesar:

> Isti, cum omnia concuterent, concutiebantur turbinum more, qui rapta convolvunt, sed ipsi ante volvuntur, et ob hoc maiore impetu incurrunt, quia nullum illis sui regimen est. Ideoque, cum multis fuerunt malo, pestiferam illam vim, qua plerisque nocuerunt, ipsi quoque sentiunt. Non est, quod credas, quemquam fieri aliena infelicitate felicem.⁵⁰

> [As these men were shaking the world, they were themselves being shaken, like cyclones that spin together what they have seized, but which before this are spun up themselves and from this attack with greater force, because they have no control over themselves; therefore with all the suffering that they have brought upon others, they also feel in themselves that pestilence with which they have injured so many. It is not so, as you might believe, that one is made happy through the unhappiness of others.]

From Seneca (and later, from Orosius and then a flood of Renaissance writers) there emerges the idea that Alexander is swept up in his own violent "shaking of the world," that murder is, in essence, a two-way street. What emerges from this undercurrent of imperial discourse (so powerful in such Portuguese writers as Zurara, Camões, and Mendes Pinto) is a sunless, mysterious region from which emerges the horror of death as a violent overtaking of possibilities—as, for example, a fever that strikes one down suddenly, by surprise.

The storm image just mentioned takes us back (or forward) to the Eastern storm approaching Munich as Mann imagines Aschenbach standing at the streetcar stop, in the shadow of the Northern Cemetery. It takes us also into the fictional last days of Tirant lo Blanc, as he sails off to the Maghreb and, later, as his fever rises and his infected pleurae slowly begin to squeeze

his lungs shut. In the last instance, it takes us back to Alexander's own feverish death in the Iraqi desert, his breath shallow and his purported immortality brutally, decisively debunked for all to witness. This death, like the life
that it finally confronts, darkens the rise and development of empire in what
would come to be the Latin West. It presents itself as a framework to theorize
the perceived glories and all-too-real dangers of empire, the mortal angst
that underlies and shapes colonial expansion.

By the late fifteenth century, the darkness associated with Alexander and
empire all but eclipses the light (e.g., of reason and Christian faith) within
which Iberian colonizers, and the writers who attempt to theorize and narrate their efforts and fantasies, seek to frame the expansion of empire into
Muslim Africa and Asia. To read (or write) through an Alexandrian lens implies opening the imperial project up to a retheorization or recalibration that
seeks to account for the radical agency of the Other and that Other's indexical
relation to death (from a Levinasian perspective). For late medieval and early
modern Iberian writers and their readers, Alexander was a study in contradictions: he was both a towering Greek hero and an unchecked oriental despot; an enlightened student of Aristotle and a mean and unpredictable drunk
(and he drank often); an unmatched military genius and a lucky fool convinced of his own pagan divinity. He was, in a sense, both the mortal illness
that haunted empire (and does to this day) and a common response to it.

Alexander is at once the totalizing vision of Western empire (the brutal
spontaneity of one's immanent destiny) and the infinite Other (*Autrui*). He is
totality and infinity; and he is fundamental for understanding early modern
Iberian empire as it develops in the fifteenth and sixteenth centuries. He is
our specter, a tormented shade that rises up from below to imbue current
events with a thousand troubling contradictions. From a modern perspective, the meteoric course of Alexander's life, combined with the towering
place that the Macedonian king has occupied within the cultural and political history of Europe, Egypt, and Western Asia, has made the development
of adequately contextualized historical accounts of his brief existence a central priority. To understand Alexander, goes the argument, is to understand
much regarding the formation of the Mediterranean world, the still per-
vasive divisions between East and West, and the psychology of power and
imperial expansion.

CHAPTER 2

THE STINKING CORPSE

Alexander, the Greeks, and the Romans

THE LAST DAYS OF ALEXANDER THE GREAT WERE FOR THE MOST part a blur of drinking and bad omens. The rapid downward slide began in Ecbatana (modern-day Hamadan, Iran) during the fall of 324 BCE, as Alexander and his army, much depleted from a sixty-day death march across the Gedrosian Desert, were making their way back to Babylon from the Punjab. It was here that Hephaestion, Alexander's closest companion throughout his brief life, succeeded in drinking himself to death. Already suffering from a high fever and under his doctor's orders to stay away from alcohol, Hephaestion nonetheless managed to down roughly two liters of wine during a meal on the seventh day of his illness. This excessive consumption caused his fever to spike, and he died almost immediately afterward.

Alexander was attending an athletic event when Hephaestion took his turn for the worse, and although he hurried to be at his friend's side, Hephaestion was already dead when Alexander arrived. Plutarch (46–120 CE) describes Alexander's reaction to Hephaestion's death:

> Alexander was so beyond all reason [*oudeni logismô*] transported that, to express his sorrow, he immediately ordered the manes and tails of all his horses and mules to be cut, and threw down the battlements of the neighboring cities. The poor physician he crucified, and forbade playing on the flute or any other musical instrument in the camp a great while, till directions came from the oracle of Ammon, and enjoined him to honor Hephaestion, and sacrifice to him as a hero. Then seeking to alleviate his grief

in war, he set out, as it were, to a hunt and chase of men, for he fell upon the Cossaeans, and put the whole nation to the sword. This was called a sacrifice to Hephaestion's ghost.[1]

Arrian (fl. c. 130 CE) disputes some of the more striking examples of Alexander's grief mentioned by Plutarch and other authors. He is particularly opposed to the contention of his mentor, Epictetus (55–135 CE), that Alexander ordered the local shrine of Asclepius, the god of healing, to be destroyed. Arrian describes this act as: "barbaric [*barbarikòn*], and not at all characteristic of Alexander, but more suitable to Xerxes's presumption towards heaven and the fetters they say he let down into the Hellespont, in the belief he could punish it."[2] This reference to Xerxes I of Persia (519–465 BCE) and his "punishment" of the Hellespont, drawn from book seven of Herodotus's *Histories*, was by Arrian's time a popular example of what Greeks considered to be the unbridled tyranny and arrogance of Asian kings.[3] Perhaps tellingly, Arrian has nothing to say regarding the Cossaean genocide.[4]

Modern readers might question Arrian's implicit claim that the slaughter of the Cossaeans is somehow in keeping with the rational (*eúlogos*) comportment of a Hellenic king, while the destruction of a religious temple stands out as barbaric and far-fetched.[5] We may also wonder why Arrian goes to such lengths, here and elsewhere in his *Anabasis*, to hold Alexander up as a distinctly Hellenic monarch against the foil of various "barbarian" kings such as Xerxes, when Alexander himself seems to have gone to such great lengths during his life to emulate the Achaemenid kings of Persia, especially Cyrus the Great (c. 580–529 BCE).[6] Beyond these reflections and doubts, it is nonetheless clear that much of what is at stake in Arrian's treatment of Alexander's metaphorical descent into Persian mores and modes of kingship, along with his very literal and sudden descent toward death, serves as the deep symbolic background for late medieval and early modern Iberian treatments of Alexander and empire. Within the historical as well as the legendary tradition (in both its Christian and Islamic avatars), Alexander is at once a Greek champion and an Eastern despot, a former student of Aristotle and an immoderate adventurer, an immortal hero and the fragility of human existence personified. Throughout late antiquity and into the early modern period, in fact, Iberian writers consistently frame Alexander, perhaps more than any other major historical figure, as both the Western self *and* the Eastern Other—a conflicted and powerful soul that in the end could not but turn on itself as it did.

Given that my concern is to come to a contextualized understanding of the place that Alexander the Great has within the initial push of Iberian empire into Muslim Africa and Asia, it is useful to take to the time to sketch out the centuries-long backstory that shapes later Iberian accounts of the Macedonian king. Self-conscious heirs to the language, literature, history, and political theories of the Romans, Iberian writers of the fifteenth and sixteenth centuries had no need to conjure up Alexander ex nihilo, and it is for this reason important to develop some understanding of the general contours of the various Alexanders fashioned by writers in classical and late antiquity. This point is worth repeating: Iberian writers who sought to theorize and justify the imperial activities of Aragon, Castile, and Portugal during the fifteenth and sixteenth centuries were willing and conscious participants in a long textual tradition revolving around Alexander, and in many ways their framing of the Macedonian king—as well as the self-conscious crusade against Islam in which they participated—was but a heightened version of what had come before. In the end, as Alfred Heuss remarked at the middle of the twentieth century, Alexander has always served, even while he was alive, as a container that could be filled "with any wine" (it is not clear whether Heuss's reference to wine is meant to be ironic), and the literature of Iberian empire "fills" him in ways that consciously play off of the philosophical and ideological complexity inherited from classical sources.[7] And central to this project is, as I argue throughout the present volume, the interplay between Alexander, the radical agency of the Eastern Other, and the horrific alterity of death itself.

Arrian, Reason, and Return

To understand Arrian's selectively nationalistic framing of Alexander—one that fourth-century BCE Greeks certainly would not have accepted for their Macedonian (and thus foreign) king—it is necessary to come to at least a provisional understanding of what it meant to engage in the project of writing Greek history within the context of what Philostratus (c. 170–c. 247 CE) would later term the "Second Sophistic." Like Plutarch, Arrian wrote during what consisted of a Greek cultural revival that took place during the second century CE, in which Greek intellectuals sought to reaffirm Hellenic cultural prestige within the context of Roman imperial domination. Spencer has characterized the Second Sophistic as a "fusion of Greek cultural revival and Roman political ideology and vocabulary"—a fusion that incidentally did as much to pour Roman wine into Greek flasks as the reverse.[8] Seeking to contextualize the movement within the imperial politics of Rome, she goes on to argue that

> For a Greek living under the rule of Rome, Alexander could represent a great Greek savior, a disseminator of culture to the barbarians (overtly, the Persians, but also tying in notions of Greek cultural supremacy over Rome). He could stand for the cultural supremacy of Greece, and Greek military prowess, and his fame could demonstrate the lasting greatness of a Greek over Rome. This becomes particularly important after the Julio-Claudians and in the second century CE, when philhellenism regained respectability. It may seem obvious that "Roman Greeks" of this period might want to re-write past and present, each in terms of the other, and fuse present Roman power with Hellenistic origins.[9]

In other words, with Roman power established over Greece, Alexander could now be called on by Greeks working within the Roman Empire to serve as a uniquely Hellenic hero within two projects at once: in the first place, to commemorate their victory over the Persians; and in the second, to defend Greek interests in the political and cultural tensions between the Greeks and their Roman overlords. Within this movement, Alexander was, at least superficially, an almost natural fit: wherever the Romans went in Asia or Egypt, the Greeks could claim that "their Alexander," for better or worse, had been there first.

It is not my intention to enter into a detailed examination of cultural movements in Greece and Rome or the subtle contours of Arrian's Greek prose.[10] Having said this, I do wish to linger a bit over the way in which Arrian's refusal to accept Epictetus's narrative of Alexander's descent into "barbarian" (read: Persian) comportment relates directly to the question of Haephestion's death and the imminent death of Alexander himself, because it is precisely this connection between imperial expansion into a loosely defined East and the alterity of the oriental Other—which derives its power as an index of the radical otherness and agency of death—that so profoundly shapes the discourse of late medieval and early modern Iberian empire, especially insofar as this discourse makes use of Alexander. This analysis is in keeping with the more general argument that to examine Greco-Roman theorizations of Alexander and the issue of the Orient, alterity, and death is thus in a very real sense an analysis of the discursive and ideological substratum for the literature of Iberian imperial expansion—an analysis that ultimately goes beyond more traditional forms of *Quellenforschungen* and established narratives of national and Western literary history.

Returning to Arrian's critique of Epictetus, we can agree that given the proximity of Alexander's death at the time of his supposed destruction of the shrine of Asclepius (as compared to his earlier, basically unproblematic torching of the Persian palace/temple at Persepolis), any "descent" into barbarism would be a final and decisive one. In other words, a final slide into barbarism and irrationality (*oudenì logismô*, as Plutarch puts it before granting Alexander a kind of return to his senses at the very end of his life) on Alexander's part would preclude, from the point of view of history, any possibility of return or redemption. This is key for the rhetorical strategies of the Second Sophistic, given that for the Romans—whose myth of imperial right in the Orient hinged on the initial "ascent" of Aeneas, an Asian (Trojan) hero who arrived in Italy (by way of a painful and tragic betrayal in Carthage) with the explicit mission to found an empire. From the Roman perspective, the question of a Western endpoint—framed as a physical, spiritual, and mental return—is crucial, regardless of the time that one has spent in the East or one's origins. Put in simple terms, we might consider that although Aeneas or Scipio Africanus could be presented as great heroes by imperial Rome (and then Petrarch), the opposite was true for Mark Antony, who famously "lost himself" in drunkenness and the luxuries of Egypt and never returned to Rome. For Arrian as well as Plutarch (who compared Alexander to no less an imperial figure than Julius Caesar), the political imperative that informed their historiographic project was relatively straightforward: the life of Alexander needed to read more like that of a Scipio Africanus than that of Mark Antony, in spite of the fact that there were very few historical data upon which to hang such a narrative. In the end, the problem for Arrian, Plutarch, and other Greek authors (not to mention Pseudo-Callisthenes) was that Alexander *was* in so many ways similar to Mark Antony—a point that writers from Aristotle (*avant la lettre*) to Seneca the Younger had long been eager to point out.

Arrian's strategy for reclaiming Alexander for Greece revolves in part around his efforts to manufacture a final "return" for Alexander—in essence, to give him a Greek rather than a barbarian death. Students of Greek literature may recognize in these efforts a neat intersection with the concept of *nostos* (homecoming) that so thoroughly drives epic works such as Homer's *Odyssey*. Karen Bassi, taking as her point of departure Douglas Frame's work,[11] elaborates in greater detail the ways in which the concept of *nostos* functions in the *Odyssey*, also pointing out the ways in which it is linked to the related processes of death and resurrection:

> Classicists, following the work of folklorists, have long equated [the negative] inertia [that "postpones and threatens to cancel" Odysseus's journey] with a deathlike state and read the hero's return home as symbolic of transcendence and resurrection. This reading is compelling and may be readily applied to the *Odyssey*, where Odysseus, feared dead by his family, must go to the Underworld before he can reach Ithaca. In telling his account of this funereal journey to Alcinous and the Phaeacians (bks. 10–12), Odysseus describes how Circe instructed him to go to Hades and seek out the prophet Tiresias, who would tell him "the way to go, the length of [his] journey, and [his] nostos" (10.539–40). Tiresias prophesies the perils that Odysseus will encounter before achieving his "honey-sweet homecoming [*noston meliedea*]" (11.100). Upon their return from the Underworld, Circe calls Odysseus and his men "twice dead [*disthanees*]" (12.22) because, unlike the rest of mankind, they will suffer death a second time. That the map of homecoming in the *Odyssey* includes this interlude in the land of the dead seems to validate the notion of the hero's return as transcendent.[12]

This link between *nostos*, death, and resurrection was certainly not lost on either Arrian or later Iberian humanists such as João de Barros, Antonio Nebrija, and the humanists attached to the Neapolitan court of the Aragonese king Alfons V (1396–1458). Barros's intense focus on the question of Alexander and immortality in the prologue to his *Décadas da Ásia* (Decades of Asia) can, in fact, be read as an extensive gloss on this link, albeit recontextualized within an explicitly Christian interpretive framework.

It is also important to consider that the concept of *nostos* is linked etymologically to the term *nóos* (mind), from which the verb *néomai* (to return) also derives.[13] As Gregory Nagy has pointed out, much Greek literature and philosophy worked to explore the connections not only between *nóos* and the concept of return, but also between *nóos* and the possibility of life after death:

> And the word *nóos* conveys life after death, not only by virtue of its usage
> in Homeric diction: *nóos* is the quality that allows the *psukhê* to be cogni-
> tive even after death, as in the case of the seer Teiresias. . . . In other words,
> *nóos* is the quality that reintegrates the *psukhê* of the dead with *thumos* and
> *menos*, the physical manifestations of consciousness in the body, and in this
> sense *nóos* is the quality that can reintegrate *psukhê* and body.[14]

These related notions of reintegration, life after death, and return all come crashing together in the *Odyssey*, within which Odysseus returns from two journeys, as Bassi (following Frame) points out: a physical journey home to Greece from Asia Minor and a spiritual journey down to Hades and back again. Within the Homeric text, the link between Hades and the East is explicit, as is the existential significance of Odysseus's return.

Turning back to Arrian, we begin to see how the issue of Alexander's slide into madness and failure to return—even after death—to Macedonia could present deep problems for Greek historians laboring to present him as an iconic Hellenic hero (flaws and all) within the cultural and ideological framework of Roman political dominance. For Odysseus, the hidden enemy of his *nóos* and *nostos*, highlighted in episodes such as "The Lotus-Eaters," is *lêthê* (forgetfulness); for Alexander, however, there is something much darker and disruptive eating away at him, something quite likely linked to the Asian cult of Dionysus, as John Maxwell O'Brien has argued.[15] It is in fact here in this Dionysian darkness—linked at once to the Orient, alterity, and death without return—that I would situate the prominent and highly disruptive role of Bacchus (as the Latin West referred to Dionysus) in Luís de Camões's *Os Lusíadas* (The Lusiads). It is not by chance, after all, that Camões's epic masterpiece both begins and ends with an explicit reference to Alexander the Great—in the latter instance, in the context of a direct address to the deranged and soon-to-be-deceased young Portuguese king Sebastião I (1554–1578).

It is precisely at the intersection between *nóos* and *nostos* (whether to Ithaka or Lisbon, the latter a city that popular myth holds was founded by Odysseus, or Ulixes, as the Latin West knew him) that Blackmore's arguments regarding Iberian expansion into Africa and the role of humoral physiology are central. Focusing on the *General estoria* (General History), a late thirteenth-century world history commissioned by the Castilian king Alfonso X (1221–1284), Blackmore explains how this work links the heat of the African sun to the supposed natural inferiority of Africans themselves:

> Alfonso invokes medieval physiology and psychology to explain the inferior alterity of Ethiopians and in so doing makes "Africanness" an interior, physiological quality, an organic and therefore "natural" disposition that is created and conditioned by the sun's heat. Alfonso also addresses the "natural" intellectual inferiority of Africans in the *General estoria* in a discussion of Genesis and Noah's son Ham, the primogenitor of African peoples. For having scoffed at his father, Alfonso writes that "Cam [era] de menor entendimiento que los otros [hermanos]" 'Ham was not as astute as his brothers.'[16] The lesser intellectual capacity of Ham would justify the presumed "right" of Europeans to invade and conquer Africa.[17]

Within this geo-humoral framework, a "descent" into the Orient could also imply a descent into madness—the sort that inspires a Hellenic king to destroy a religious shrine or a Roman triumvir to take up arms against his homeland.

It is not clear that the elaborate humoral schema that Blackmore describes necessarily informs Arrian's framing of Alexander. It seems clear, however, that Arrian was well aware of the likelihood that his readers would see Alexander's seven-year refusal to effect a *nostos* from Asia after having defeated Darius III as a tragic error that in the end cost him his kingdom, his mind, and his life. That Arrian—and the more openly critical Plutarch similarly works to rehabilitate Alexander at the very end—goes to such lengths to frame Alexander as a rational (*eúlogos*) hero of Hellenic culture even during the last, almost wholly unhinged days of the king's life strongly suggests this. In this sense, it is beyond ironic that even Alexander's dead body failed to make it back to Greece or Macedonia; it was stolen on its western journey and diverted to Memphis and then Alexandria, where it remained on display for at least five centuries before it was lost.

How, precisely, does Arrian try to salvage Alexander? As Arrian presents it, Alexander's response to Hephaestion's death stands as an extreme show of both grief and savagery. His response never ceases, however, to be inherently rational, although it is clear that he has flown into something like a rage. He is at no point either out of his wits or outside of himself, as Plutarch argues (before backpedaling). In this restricted sense, Alexander is not unlike Vasco Martins de Albergaria, discussed in the following chapter, who manages to kill a Muslim defender outside the city walls of Ceuta even after taking a boulder to the head. Within the logic of Zurara's *Crónica*, just as within Arrian's *Anabasis*, there is a significant threat to the Western colonizer, Portuguese in one case and Hellenic (if not properly Greek) in the other, who somehow remains in possession of his reason (*tento/logos*). Contact with the East, framed by Greeks, Romans, and Iberians as a descent or "going away" that requires the forceful retention of reason (and self) even in the most extreme of emotional circumstances if a "return" is to be achieved, is thus a threat not only to body, but also to mind and soul. In the case of Arrian's Alexander, any suggestion that he lost his reason during those difficult months between Hephaestion's death and his own must, in the end, be dealt with and neutralized.

The End That Comes to Alexander

However Arrian, or his readers, strives to present Alexander just after the death of Hephaestion, what he cannot change is the fact that Alexander passed away less than a year after his beloved companion, and from much the same cause: a high fever made worse by excessive drinking. The several months that separate these two deaths, during which Alexander established his court at Babylon and settled into the business of receiving official visits from foreign ambassadors and laying plans, it is supposed, for a military expedition into the Arabian Peninsula, were perhaps the worst of Alexander's life.[18] As Plutarch describes it, Alexander spent the short time between Hephaestion's death and his own in a downward spiral of paranoia and religious fanaticism:

> When once Alexander had given way to fears of supernatural influence, his mind grew so disturbed and so easily alarmed that, if the least unusual or extraordinary thing happened, he thought it a prodigy or a presage, and his court was thronged with diviners and priests whose business was to sacrifice and purify and foretell the future. So miserable a thing is incredulity and contempt of divine power on the one hand, and so miserable,

also, superstition on the other, which like water, where the level has been
lowered, flowing in and never stopping, fills the mind with slavish fears and
follies, as now in Alexander's case.[19]

All of this was worsened by frequent bouts of heavy drinking (images of
Jim Morrison in Paris come to mind) and a series of events that seemed to
reinforce the notion that the gods were planning his downfall. One day in
Babylon, for example, a donkey owned by the king somehow managed to
kick to death a fierce lion that Alexander kept in his menagerie. The king's
seers quickly worked to put a positive spin on this event, but it was hard to
deny, within the logic of omens, that the brutal slaying of a royal lion by
a lowly donkey could not bode well for Alexander. On another occasion,
while reviewing his troops, Alexander left his throne in order to get some re-
freshment. When he and his retinue returned, they found a Messenian man
named Dionysius seated on Alexander's throne and wearing the royal robe
and diadem. Those present saw this as a horrendous offense, and Alexander
immediately had the man tortured and interrogated to see if he was part of
some conspiracy. Dionysius denied being part of any plot to kill the king,
and his only explanation for what he had done was that "the idea had come
to him to do so."[20] Arrian claims that Alexander's seers were troubled by this
vague explanation and strongly recommended that the king have the man
executed, which he promptly did.[21] Some days afterward, Alexander himself
was dead, though not before achieving, as both Arrian and Plutarch present
it, a final return (*nostos*) to his Hellenic senses (*nóos*).

Alexander's death was not immediately suspected to be the result of an
act of regicide; however, six years later information surfaced that led many
to believe that Iollas, the royal cupbearer, had mixed in a strong poison with
the king's wine. Olympias, Alexander's mother, went so far as to have Iollas's
grave dug up and his ashes scattered to the wind, and Plutarch reports that
others even affirmed that "Aristotle [had] counseled Antipater [Iollas's fa-
ther] to do it, and that by his means the poison was brought."[22] Plutarch puts
little stock in these rumors, and Arrian directly dismisses them.[23] Quintus
Curtius Rufus (fl. c. 50 CE) hedges his bets on this issue, however, and likely
provides justification (Plutarch's pairing of Alexander with Julius Caesar in
his *Bioi parallêloi* (Parallel Lives) likely had a similar effect) for what came
to be the common belief that Alexander had in fact been murdered by those
closest to him:

Veneno necatum esse credidere plerique: filium Antipatri inter ministros, Iollam nomine, patris iussu dedisse. . . . Haec, utcumque sunt credita, eorum, quos rumor adsperserat, mox potentia extinxit. Regnum enim Macedoniae Antipater et Graeciam quoque invasit: suboles deinde excepit interfectis omnibus, quicumque Alexandrum etiam longinqua cognatione contigerant.[24]

[Many believed that his death was due to poison, administered to him by a son of Antipater called Iollas, one of Alexander's attendants. . . . Whatever credence such stories gained, they were soon scotched by the power of the people defamed by the gossip. For Antipater usurped the throne of Macedon and of Greece as well, and he was succeeded by his son, after the murder of all who were even distantly related to Alexander.][25]

Modern scholars generally do not believe that Alexander's death was the result of a conspiracy (divine or temporal), and they tend to explain his early end by means of much more banal diagnoses: a high fever exacerbated by the consumption of too much wine, general overexertion, and a poorly healed chest wound that he had received in India. Peter Green suggests that the underlying cause of the fever may have been pleuritis or perhaps malaria, but he also makes it clear that motives for killing Alexander, as well as people perhaps willing to do the job, were not hard to come by:

Whatever the truth concerning his last days, it is clear enough that at the time (a point not stressed as much as it should be) there were few men, and *a fortiori* fewer women, who lamented Alexander's passing. In Greece and Asia alike, during his lifetime and for several centuries after his death, he was regarded as a tyrannous aggressor, a foreign autocrat who had imposed his will by violence alone.[26]

Green goes on to cite the reaction of the influential Athenian orator Demades (c. 380–318 BCE), who had once been a supporter of Alexander and his father, Philip II of Macedon, when the news of Alexander's death finally reached Athens: "'Alexander dead?' he exclaimed. 'Impossible; the whole world would stink of his corpse.'"[27] In light of the fact that Alexander's generals (commonly referred to as the Diadochi, or Successors) began a long and violent process of chopping Alexander's empire (and each other) into pieces almost as soon as he was dead, it may be said that in some sense the "cadaveric stink" that Demades mentions did in fact quite nearly cover the entire Hellenic world for many years.

Dialoguing with the Dead

The image of Alexander that emerges from this brief account of his last year of life is a dramatic and complex one. A brilliant and lucky general in spite of his tyrannical tendencies as king, Alexander was brought down in his youth by sorrow and madness, and then finished off by what ultimately may have been the combination of too much alcohol and a parasitic infection (if Green's malaria theory is correct). This is certainly not the script that Alexander would have written for himself, and it creates real dilemmas for historians and philosophers of all periods who seek to find some sort of positive lesson for future generations encoded in Alexander's fate. As the cases of Arrian and Plutarch demonstrate, such difficulties did not stop Greek authors working within the Roman empire from trying to make some sort of sense of Alexander's life and death, and there is a broader tradition of classical authorship and narrative that emerges from at least the second century BCE seeking to foreground Alexander's status as a powerful trope for a range of deep-seated issues, such as the working out of notions of self and Other and the tense question of mortality, that emerge primarily from Alexander's extensive contact with the Orient.

The author of the Second Sophistic who perhaps most extensively develops the link between Alexander, Asian empire, death, and immortality is Lucian of Samosata. Born in what is today south-central Turkey (then part of Syria) during the first half of the second century CE, Lucian deals with Alexander in three short texts contained in his larger collection of satiric dialogues, referred to as the *Nekrikoi dialogoi* (Dialogues of the Dead). The first of these, a dialogue between Alexander, Hannibal, Minos, and Scipio Africanus (Dialogue 12), was a popular work in Europe as late as the fifteenth century, as evidenced by the many extant manuscript copies from that period in Castilian and Portuguese.[28] The dialogue begins with Alexander challenging Hannibal, claiming that he should take precedence over the Carthaginian. Hannibal stands his ground, and Minos, the mythical king of Crete, is brought in to judge between them. In his closing argument, Alexander states: "If men took me for a god, I cannot blame them; the vastness of my undertakings might excuse such a belief. But to conclude. I died a king: Hannibal, a fugitive at the court of the Bithynian Prusias—fitting end for villainy and cruelty."[29] Here Alexander claims innocence with regard to claims of divine parentage (earlier he states explicitly that Philip II of Macedon was his father), and he underscores his regal status at the time of his death. Just after Alexander's argument, Minos is ready to render his judgment; however, Scipio Africanus then steps in and settles the dispute: "Alexander is my superior, and I am Hannibal's, having defeated him and driven him to ignominious flight. What impudence is this, to contend with Alexander, to whom I, your conqueror, would not presume to compare myself!"[30] In keeping with the politicocultural goals of the Second Sophistic, Lucian presents Alexander as a Hellenic king to whom even the über-Roman general Scipio Africanus feels inferior.

In the next dialogue, between Alexander and Diogenes, Lucian ups the ante considerably, describing in great detail the paradoxes that revolve around Alexander's legend in Greece and elsewhere. The dialogue begins:

DIOG. Dear me, Alexander, you dead like the rest of us?

ALEX. As you see, sir; is there anything extraordinary in a mortal's dying?

DIOG. So Ammon lied when he said you were his son; you were Philip's after all.

ALEX. Apparently; if I had been Ammon's, I should not have died.[31]

Here Alexander admits his own mortal status, basing his admission on concrete evidence (i.e., that he is dead) that allows no other conclusion. Diogenes then goes on to address the legendary story of Alexander's birth through the union of his mother with the god Amun, who supposedly disguised himself as a giant serpent:

DIOG. Strange! there were tales of the same order about Olympias too. A serpent visited her, and was seen in her bed; we were given to understand that that was how you came into the world, and Philip made a mistake when he took you for his.

ALEX. Yes, I was told all that myself; however, I know now that my mother's and the Ammon stories were all moonshine.[32]

Here Alexander, forced in death to admit that the legendary account of his birth that would come to form the basis for the *Greek Alexander Romance* of Pseudo-Callisthenes (and the long literary tradition that would follow) is essentially a lie, appears to have accepted his own mortality. What is interesting, as in the earlier debate with Hannibal, is that Alexander claims not to be the source of these stories, but merely the recipient. In the passage that follows, however, Alexander reveals that his claims of innocence are likely dishonest, and Diogenes calls him out on them:

DIOG. Their lies were of some practical value to you, though; your divinity brought a good many people to their knees. But now, whom did you leave your great empire to?

ALEX. Diogenes, I cannot tell you. I had no time to leave any directions about it, beyond just giving Perdiccas my ring as I died. Why are you laughing?

DIOG. Oh, I was only thinking of the Greeks' behaviour; directly you succeeded, how they flattered you! their elected patron, *generalissimo* against the barbarian; one of the twelve Gods according to some; temples built and sacrifices offered to the Serpent's son! If I may ask, where did your Macedonians bury you?

ALEX. I have lain in Babylon a full month to-day; and Ptolemy of the Guards is pledged, as soon as he can get a moment's respite from present disturbances, to take and bury me in Egypt, there to be reckoned among the Gods.

DIOG. I have some reason to laugh, you see; still nursing vain hopes of developing into an Osiris or Anubis! Pray, your Godhead, put these expectations from you; none may re-ascend who has once sailed the lake and penetrated our entrance; Aeacus is watchful, and Cerberus an awkward customer.[33]

Alexander here reveals his hope to be "reckoned among the Gods," and Diogenes has some fun at his expense. As the dialogue closes, Diogenes reminds Alexander that the pleasures and honors of the living are impermanent (something, Diogenes maintains, that Aristotle should have made clearer to his royal pupil) and that the best course for Alexander now is to drink deeply from the waters of the Lethe and forget.

The notion of death and forgetting, as a foregoing of both *nostos* and *nóos*, is central to this dialogue, and it makes up a central current of various forms of the Alexander narrative throughout antiquity and the medieval period. In the Arabic narrative *Qiṣṣat Dhū al-Qarnayn* (Story of the Two-Horned One), a version of the Alexander story that for the most part blends aspects of the *Greek Alexander Romance* with the Qur'ān and other oral traditions, these waters of forgetting and death are in fact converted—through the powers of God—into waters of eternal life.

Within the thirteenth-century *Libro de Alexandre*, a long and erudite poem based for the most part on medieval Latin and French versions of the *Greek Alexander Romance*, the theme of death is likewise front and center for Alexander. The poem in fact ends with Alexander's death (by poisoning):

Fue el rey en tod' esto la palabra perdiendo,
La nariz aguzando, la lengua engordiendo;
Dixo a sus varones: "Ya lo ides veyendo,
Arrenunçio el mundo, a Dios vos acomiendo."

Acostó la cabeça sobre un façeruelo,
non serié omne vivo que non oviesse duelo;
mandó que lo echassen del lecho en el suelo,
ca avié ya travado del alma el anzuelo.

Non pudo el espíritu de la ora passar,
del mandado de Dios non pudo escapar,
desanparó la carne en que solié morar,
remaneçió el cuerpo qual podedes asmar.[34]

[In all of this the king was losing his voice
his nose sharpening and his tongue swelling;
He said to his men: "You now see it;
I renounce the world and I commend you to God."

He rested his head on a pillow,
there could be no man alive who would not be pained;
he ordered that they move him from his bed to the ground,
as he had already released his soul.

His spirit could not extend beyond its time,
from God's command it could not escape,

the flesh in which it had lived collapsed,
and only the body remained for you to see.]

Here the inescapability of death, presented as God's command, overrides the earthly powers of Alexander and takes him. All that he can do is accept its coming, and once it comes it leaves only his flesh, a lifeless object of judgment (encoded in the verb *asmar*).

Returning to the *Nekrikoi dialogoi*, we see that the last of these which deal with Alexander involves a conversation between Alexander and his father, Philip II of Macedon. Within this dialogue, which consists of only eleven exchanges (initiated and ended by Philip), the sting of mortality and the stark divide between the Hellenic West and the Orient take center stage. The passage begins with Philip confronting his son about the question of paternity and immortality:

> PHIL. You cannot deny that you are my son this time, Alexander; you
>   would not have died if you had been Ammon's.
> ALEX. I knew all the time that you, Philip, son of Amyntas, were my
>   father. I only accepted the statement of the oracle because I thought
>   it was good policy.
> PHIL. What, to suffer yourself to be fooled by lying priests?
> ALEX. No, but it had an awe-inspiring effect upon the barbarians. When
>   they thought they had a God to deal with, they gave up the struggle;
>   which made their conquest a simple matter.[35]

Philip does not accept Alexander's explanation. Going on the attack, he belittles his son's Asian accomplishments and accuses him of acting, at least for the most part, in a way not befitting a king:

> PHIL. And whom did you ever conquer that was worth conquering?
>   Your adversaries were ever timid creatures, with their bows and
>   their targets and their wicker shields. It was other work conquer-
>   ing the Greeks: Boeotians, Phocians, Athenians; Arcadian hoplites,
>   Thessalian cavalry, javelin-men from Elis, peltasts of Mantinea;
>   Thracians, Illyrians, Paeonians; to subdue these was something. But
>   for gold-laced womanish Medes and Persians and Chaldaeans,—
>   why, it had been done before: did you never hear of the expedition

of the Ten Thousand under Clearchus? and how the enemy would not even come to blows with them, but ran away before they were within bow-shot?

ALEX. Still, there were the Scythians, father, and the Indian elephants; they were no joke. And my conquests were not gained by dissension or treachery; I broke no oath, no promise, nor ever purchased victory at the expense of honour. As to the Greeks, most of them joined me without a struggle; and I dare say you have heard how I handled Thebes.

PHIL. I know all about that; I had it from Clitus, whom you ran through the body, in the middle of dinner, because he presumed to mention my achievements in the same breath with yours. They tell me too that you took to aping the manners of your conquered Medes; abandoned the Macedonian cloak in favour of the *candys*, assumed the upright tiara, and exacted oriental prostrations from Macedonian freemen! This is delicious. As to your brilliant matches, and your beloved Hephaestion, and your scholars in lions' cages,—the less said the better. I have only heard one thing to your credit: you respected the person of Darius's beautiful wife, and you provided for his mother and daughters; there you acted like a king.[36]

Lucian employs Philip, who admittedly has good reason to attack Alexander for denying him as his father in favor of Amun (although Philip had also attempted to disassociate himself from Alexander when he was alive), to deliver criticisms of Alexander's comportment during his Asian campaign that played well to Greek and Roman audiences during the second century CE. The image that emerges is of a Hellenic king converted into an oriental despot, and of a man who foolishly allowed himself to believe that he could overcome the radical alterity of death itself, folding it into his map of empire as though it were one more territory. Playing the chastising father, Philip calls Alexander out on his foibles and seeks to shame him for his presumptive actions. Caught on the defensive, Alexander then seeks to gain his father's favor:

ALEX. And have you nothing to say of my adventurous spirit, father, when I was the first to leap down within the ramparts of Oxydracae, and was covered with wounds?

PHIL. Not a word. Not that it is a bad thing, in my opinion, for a king to get wounded occasionally, and to face danger at the head of his troops: but this was the last thing that you were called upon to do. You were passing for a God; and your being wounded, and carried off the field on a litter, bleeding and groaning, could only excite the ridicule of the spectators: Ammon stood convicted of quackery, his oracle of falsehood, his priests of flattery. The son of Zeus in a swoon, requiring medical assistance! who could help laughing at the sight? And now that you have died, can you doubt that many a jest is being cracked on the subject of your divinity, as men contemplate the God's corpse laid out for burial, and already going the way of all flesh? Besides, your achievements lose half their credit from this very circumstance which you say was so useful in facilitating your conquests: nothing you did could come up to your divine reputation.[37]

Here Philip converts Alexander's bravery into foolishness and even calls into doubt the cult of Amun and the oracle at Siwa. The attack is direct, and what is most devastating is the way Philip (through Lucian) transforms Alexander from a conquering subject to a passive object: a stinking corpse laid out for burial. At this point Alexander reacts to his father's reproach and tries to defend himself and his fame. The result, however, is that Philip is able to ridicule him even further, calling on his son to recognize himself as one of the dead:

ALEX. The world thinks otherwise. I am ranked with Heracles and Dionysus; and, for that matter, I took Aornos, which was more than either of them could do.

PHIL. There spoke the son of Ammon. Heracles and Dionysus, indeed! You ought to be ashamed of yourself, Alexander; when will you learn to drop that bombast, and know yourself for the shade that you are?[38]

The argument that Alexander should "know himself" (gnôsê seautòn) for the "shade" (nekròs) that he is and quite literally "unlearn" (apomathêsê) his bombast is at once epic and philosophical: Alexander is being called upon by his dead father to make a nostos, to return from his Asian/Egyptian pretensions to immortality and accept his place in Hades as Philip's son. The phrase is held together syntactically by the *kaì* . . . *kaì* construction with which Philip makes his final charge: "kaì gnôsê seautòn, kaì sunês êdê nekròs ôn." Within this compact and highly satirical phrase, Lucian embeds a complex conceit that is central to any full account of the classical Alexander, namely that Western theories of knowledge, forgetting, death, immortality, and the Orient all collide within him to create the wreckage out of which European empire would emerge.

Alexander, Greece, and the Orient

Given that the focus of the present book is not merely Alexander, but the role of Alexander within narrative theorizations of late medieval and early modern Iberian imperial expansion into Muslim Africa and Asia, it makes sense to look briefly at the historical roots of Western notions of the Orient (however loosely framed) within antiquity. These notions rise to the surface in the work of Greek authors such as Lucian and Arrian writing on Alexander within the context of the Roman colonization of Greece, and in general, classical Greek and Roman texts dealing with the Orient are plentiful. Even the most cursory examination of this literature reveals what we may have expected: fifteenth- and sixteenth-century notions of imperial expansion into a loosely conceived "Orient," a region that held for Greeks and Romans, as well as their European heirs—what Edward W. Said has described as an inherently "vacillating" and "confusing" value within "the mind's geography"— hardly emerged from nothing.[39] Beyond this two-mindedness vis-à-vis the Orient, however, I am also concerned with the manner in which Alexander the Great, long after his death in Babylon, continued to function not only as a complex trope for, and exemplar of, Western empire in the Muslim "East," but also as a destabilizing force within the theorization of empire—a foreshadowing of its inevitable downfall, framed not as an end, but as a violent death.

In general terms, Alexander's prolonged contact with and demonstrated affinity for the Orient has consistently provoked within classical Greek and Roman authors and officials a conflicted sense of their relationship, and debt, to the East. From at least the end of the Second Punic War in 201 BCE, the Orient increasingly came to be for Rome a region, very much within "the mind's geography," that was at once the source of Rome's own myth of origin

(Aeneas was, after all a Trojan), the domain of the perennial enemy (Persia for the Greeks, and Carthage, whose mother city was Tyre, for the Romans), a land of utter enchantment and possible rebirth, and a region of horrifying yet strangely seductive despotism, cruelty, and amorality. All of this—the issues of Greco-Asian origins, of Asian and African enemies, of the notion of death, rebirth, and immortality, and of the horror of oriental seduction (as well as the seductive qualities of oriental horror)—runs continuously through popular images of Alexander, from antiquity through to the early modern period, when Rome's Iberian successors begin to build their own Eastern empires.

In emulating the Achaemenid kings of Persia, Alexander had chosen to turn his back, to a certain, measured degree, on much of what passed for political and cultural *doxa* in the Hellenic world. Most Greeks, and especially Athenians, considered Alexander, a Macedonian, something of an unsophisticated outsider, in spite of his paternal family's claim to be direct descendants of Heracles by way of Temenus of Argos (his mother's family, natives of Epirus, claimed to be direct descendants of Achilles). In Demosthenes' (384–322 BCE) *Third Philippic*, a formal diatribe against Alexander's father, for example, we see how Athenians could, on a bad day, frame the Macedonians as barbarians themselves:

> And further, you must surely realize that all the wrongs that the Hellenes suffered from the Spartans or ourselves they at least suffered at the hands of true-born sons of Hellas; and (one might conceive) it was as though a lawful son, born to a great estate, managed his affairs in some wrong or improper way;—his conduct would in itself deserve blame and denunciation, but at least it could not be said that he was not one of the family, or was not the heir to the property. But had it been a slave or a suppositious son that was thus ruining and spoiling an inheritance to which he had no title, why, good heavens! how infinitely more scandalous and reprehensible all would have declared it to be. And yet they show no such feeling in regard to Philip, although not only is he no Hellene, not only has he no kinship with Hellenes, but he is not even a barbarian from a country that one could acknowledge with credit;—he is a pestilent Macedonian, from whose country it used not to be possible to buy even a slave of any value.[40]

Although it is necessary to situate Demosthenes' claim that the Macedonians were not Hellenes in the context of his broader attack on Philip, we should not forget that Demosthenes was able to make this claim precisely because he knew that it would resonate with his Athenian audience. As for Alexander, who spoke fluent Greek (albeit as a second language and with a perceivable accent) and was undoubtedly a Hellene, his outsider status, coupled with his disturbing affinity for Persian and Egyptian culture and modes of kingship, made him a kind of lightning rod for Greece's significant concerns with respect to the Orient, especially Persia, during the fourth century and afterward.

Demosthenes' comments support the notion that for the Greeks, especially the Athenians, the known Orient was a region deeply linked to Otherness, racial impurity, and slavery.[41] From a concrete economic and political perspective, the East was at once the principal source of slaves (and there were many slaves in Greece) and the imagined home of a multitude of tyrannical regimes that had, in any case, converted their subjects into de facto servants. Spencer addresses this point in some length:

What kinds of intellectual preconception are revealed by our engagement with the East? For the Greek states, the East could be a land of wonder, wealth, and magic, and also a land of barbarians, of other peoples who spoke non-Greek languages, who were ruled over by kings, and whose culture could be antithetically opposed to that of the Hellenic world. This opposition is enacted on a grand scale in the story of Alexander, who drew together the warring Greek states under his leadership with the promise that this coalition would present a united front against the Persian enemy and avenge the Persian invasions of Greece. In Alexander we find a figure who could, temporarily at least, unite the Greek world under one banner, but in doing so he committed "Greece" to a monarchy; monarchy was always susceptible to accusations of despotism, of orientalism and excess. Conceptualizations of the geographical east in terms of a mythical "East," a land of mystery and marvel, of Dionysus, of Amazon warriors, of fabulous wealth and decadence, coexisted with a sense of the East as actively opposed to the cultural assumptions of Athens and the ideals of democratic government.[42]

The nexus of heroic (literally, in emulation of Heracles and Dionysus) Asian conquest and the despotism with which the mythological East was associated was a locus of conflict and rich hermeneutic possibility throughout the Hellenic world, even before Alexander died in Babylon.

Plato and Aristotle more or less express popular sentiment in fourth-century BCE Greece in their statements on this issue. In his *Menexenus*, for example, Plato offers a long passage on Athenian racial purity and Hellenic freedoms, framed in the context of a Socratic funeral oration touching on the events of the Greco-Persian wars:

> Now the [Persian] king fearing this city and wanting to stand aloof, when he saw the Lacedaemonians growing weary of the war at sea, asked of us, as the price of his alliance with us and the other allies, to give up the Hellenes in Asia, whom the Lacedaemonians had previously handed over to him, he thinking that we should refuse, and that then he might have a pretence for withdrawing from us. About the other allies he was mistaken, for the Corinthians and Argives and Boeotians, and the other states, were quite willing to let them go, and swore and covenanted, that, if he would pay them money, they would make over to him the Hellenes of the continent, and we alone refused to give them up and swear. Such was the natural nobility of this city, so sound and healthy was the spirit of freedom among us, and the instinctive dislike of the barbarian, because we are pure Hellenes, having no admixture of barbarism in us. For we are not like many others, descendants of Pelops or Cadmus or Aegyptus or Danaus, who are by nature barbarians, and yet pass for Hellenes, and dwell in the midst of us; but we are pure Hellenes, uncontaminated by any foreign element, and therefore the hatred of the foreigner has passed unadulterated into the life-blood of the city. And so, notwithstanding our noble sentiments, we were again isolated, because we were unwilling to be guilty of the base and unholy act of giving up Hellenes to barbarians. And we were in the same case as when we were subdued before; but, by the favour of Heaven, we managed better, for we ended the war without the loss of our ships or walls or colonies; the enemy was only too glad to be quit of us.[43]

Socrates' encomium to Athens revolves around a very subtle implementation of mythological genealogies. After asserting the purity of the Athenians, he states that "we are not like many others, descendants of Pelops or Cadmus or Aegyptus or Danaus, who are by nature barbarians, and yet pass for Hellenes, and dwell in the midst of us." This is a very specific attack against other Hellenic nations, such as the Thebans and Peloponnesians (and perhaps the Macedonians), who, according to Socrates, carry the stain of their barbarian origins. According to Greek mythology, Pelops was a native of Anatolia, but he came to be associated with the whole of the Peloponnese and especially

Olympus. Cadmus, a Phoenician prince, was the mythological founder of Thebes and maternal grandfather of Dionysus. Aegyptus and Danaus, twin brothers, were natives of North Africa. Aegyptus grew up to reign over the kingdom that bears his name, while Danaus came to be central to the foundation myth of Argos, in the Peloponnese. Not incidentally, Argos was also the mother city of the Argeads, the Macedonian dynastic line to which Alexander belonged.

Although Plato uses mythological genealogies to assert Athens's Hellenic purity in opposition to the oriental miscegenation that had produced, in other regions of Greece, nations willing to tolerate the transfer of Hellenes to Asia to serve as slaves for the Persians, Aristotle deals with issues of Eastern despotism in a more direct and systematic way. In a well-known passage from the *Politics* (7.1324b), for example, he speaks of despotic rule and those naturally suited to it:

> Yet most men appear to think that the art of despotic government is statesmanship, and what men affirm to be unjust and inexpedient in their own case they are not ashamed of practicing towards others; they demand just rule for themselves, but where other men are concerned they care nothing about it. Such behavior is irrational; unless the one party is, and the other is not, born to serve [*desposton*], in which case men have a right to command [*despozein*], not indeed all their fellows, but only those who are intended to be subjects [*alla tôn despostôn*]; just as we ought not to hunt mankind, whether for food or sacrifice, but only the animals which may be hunted for food or sacrifice, this is to say, such wild animals as are eatable.⁴⁴

The argument here is that imposing despotic rule over otherwise free people is an indefensible act, except in the case of those people who are naturally suited to despotic rule (*despostoi*). The reference to the non-Hellenic world that Aristotle leaves implicit in this passage of the *Politics* is made explicit in an earlier section (1.1252b): "alla ginetai hê koinônia autôn doulês kai doulou" ([the barbarians], both men and women, are but slaves). Aristotle then goes on to flesh out this idea (3.1285a):

> There is another sort of monarchy not uncommon among the barbarians, which nearly resembles tyranny. But this is both legal and hereditary. For barbarians, being more servile in character [*doulikôteroi*] than Hellenes, and Asiatics than Europeans, do not rebel against a despotic government.

Such royalties have the nature of tyrannies because the people are by nature slaves [*turannikai men oun dia to toiouton eisin*].[45]

Aristotle here describes a "legal and hereditary" form of despotism that has as its legitimating basis the naturally servile nature of its people. In a turn that Patricia Springborg has described as thinly veiled racism, however, Aristotle (himself a resident alien in Athens) links this quasi-tyrannical form of government with barbarians and, more specifically, with Asians.

The natural suitedness of Asians (and, to a lesser extent, European barbarians) to slavery and despotic rule lies, according to Aristotle, in the fact that as humans they are able to perceive reason, but as slaves(*douloi*) their souls lack a "deliberative faculty" (*bouleutikon*).[46] Aristotle goes on to describe women as having a *bouleutikon* that "lacks authority" and children as having a *bouleutikon* that is as yet immature.[47] According to Aristotle, the lack of deliberative faculty among slaves and, by extension, Asians also presents a risk of contagion for free Hellenes. The lack of *bouleutikon*, or at least the appearance of such a lack, seems, in Aristotle's thinking, to be at least to some extent transferable through social interaction and *praxis* (3.1277b): "ou gar eti sumbainei ginesthai ton men despotên ton de doulon" (certainly the good man and the statesman and the good citizen ought not to learn the crafts of inferiors except for their occasional use; if they habitually practice them, there will cease to be a distinction between master and slave).[48] This phrase, which gives the literal sense of an emergent "walking together" (*sumbainô*) of the master with the slave through the former's habitual carrying out of the activities of the latter, suggests the possibility of a convergence between the "natural" master and his "natural" slave. The question is what sort of link existed in the mind of Aristotle between the soul of the household slave (*douros*) and that of the Asian subject of tyranny (*despostos*). If the two are essentially the same, as Aristotle seems to propose through his initial equation, in section 1.1252b, of the barbarians with slaves (*douroi*), then any "walking together" with Asians, as was the case with Alexander even as Aristotle first composed the *Politics*, would lead to a state of confusion in which, from the Hellenic point of view, there would cease to be a distinction between the Macedonian king (who was, in any case, only marginally Greek) and those Asians that he sought to rule.

In general terms, these are the main currents that run through classical Greek notions of Alexander and the Orient. What they point to is a

THE STINKING CORPSE 57

tremendously conflicted sense of what Alexander, as a foreign/Hellenic king (and former student of the great Aristotle) who had successfully defeated the Persian enemy only to become all but Persian himself, was and had become through his rise to previously unknown heights of power. In the context of Alexander's prolonged expedition into the Hellenic "heart of darkness" (i.e., Persia and beyond)—a journey from which, even in death, he never returned—it can be said that Greek theories of genealogy, humanity, mythology, slavery, and praxis came together within the Macedonian king to form something resembling a fatal mixture of corrupting influences.

Alexander's Roman Ghosts

Roman authors do not tend explicitly to question the link drawn by Aristotle between the Orient and the concept of natural slavery (nor the racism that springs from it); however, they do reformulate it in complex and often contradictory ways. As Springborg has argued in her analysis of the oriental roots of Renaissance republicanism:

> if the East had for millennia been the repository of all images of luxury and decadence, as it continues to be today, this was not considered [by the second century BCE] such a bad thing. The excitement engendered by constantly expanding economic and social vistas captured the imagination of all those who followed the great Alexander, who led the march East. And it rekindled interest in his predecessors, Cyrus and the great marcher lords of Assyria and Babylonia, further back again.[49]

Within this surge of Roman economic expansion into Asia and Africa, still based in large part on the slave trade, Rome saw Alexander as its predecessor, much in the same way that the Portuguese and other Iberian kingdoms would look, roughly 1,500 years later (far back in the rear-view mirror, as it were), to the Macedonian king. The economic enthusiasm of the Romans did not erase, of course, the serious physical, moral, and political dangers that they continued to associate with the Orient, and it is the back-and-forth that exists between Roman (and later, Iberian) fascination and horror that constitutes, on a superficial level, the ambivalence to which I at times refer in the present book. In any case, it should be understood from the outset that Alexander—who was for Rome Greece's *hegêmôn* (though he ruled nonetheless as a king), the conqueror of Tyre and Persia, a self-declared god (as pharaoh of Egypt and, more problematically, as the son of Zeus-Amun), and a horribly cruel tyrant and drunkard—intersects with all of these images in powerful if not wholly manageable ways.

The confluence of Alexander's heroic and decadent attributes comes through vividly in the extant historical sources, all of them Roman, upon which all historians must inevitably base their understanding of Alexander and the events of his short (or all too long, if one is Athenian) life. As Heuss has argued, Alexander has always been, both in antiquity and ever since, a dynamic and protean figure of which different writers and regimes have made active use in order to support a wide range of arguments and ideologies. Even leaving aside the profoundly political legend of Alexander—falsely attributed to Callisthenes of Olynthos, Alexander's ill-fated court historian—that emerged from Alexandria during the third century CE and quickly spread throughout Western Asia and Europe (a text that posits, among other things, that Alexander's biological father was a deposed Egyptian king rather than Philip II of Macedon), we find from antiquity and into the modern period an expansive array of ideological, cultural, and political projects into whose service Alexander has been pressed through the seemingly simple act of having the events of his life put into writing.[50]

I have already discussed how Arrian more or less implicitly invokes a heroic Greek *nostos* for Alexander, in part through his dismissal of Epictetus's belief that Alexander had destroyed the temple of Asclepius at Ecbatana after Hephaestion's death. He is much more openly critical, however, in his treatment of Alexander's destruction of the Persian palace at Persepolis in 330 BCE, even offering a first-person criticism of what he sees as vengeful overzealousness on Alexander's part:

> He set the Persian palace on fire, though Parmenio urged him to preserve it, arguing, among other things, that it was not good to destroy what was now his own property, and that the Asians [*Asían ánthrôpoi*] would not so readily adhere to him, but would suppose that even he had not decided to retain the empire of Asia but only to conquer and pass on. Alexander said that he wished to punish the Persians for sacking Athens and burning the temples when they invaded Greece, and to exact retribution for all the other injuries they had done to the Greeks. I too do not think that Alexander showed good sense in this action nor that he could punish Persians of a long past age.[51]

Arrian here presents Alexander as a steadfastly Hellenic conqueror intent on exacting retribution for the harm done to Athens by earlier Persian invasions. Even when Arrian disagrees with Alexander's actions, in fact, he does so to accentuate the king's overarching desire (*pothos*) to avenge the Athenians.

Arrian's primary source for this episode is Ptolemy, who is notably silent, as is Arrian after him, about many of the details surrounding Alexander's destruction of Persepolis. Turning to Cleitarchus (as transmitted by extant sources), however, we find a very different version of the episode. According to Cleitarchus's history, which was possibly written as early as the end of the fourth century BCE and which enjoyed immense popularity in antiquity, the burning of Persepolis was "ordered by Alexander when he was under the influence of drink, and at the suggestion of Thais, the upmarket Athenian prostitute who just happened to be the current partner of Ptolemy."[52] Thais's Ptolemy is the same Macedonian general and Egyptian king who served as Arrian's principal source, and it is perhaps understandable that his description of the burning of Persepolis would leave out some of the key details, including the role that his mistress (with whom he would have three children) had played. Diodorus Siculus, a Sicilian Hellene whose expansive *Bibliotheka historika* (Library of History) represents the earliest (albeit incomplete) extant source for Alexander's life, presents the episode in the following way:

> While they were feasting and the drinking was far advanced, as they began to be drunken a madness took possession of the minds of the intoxicated guests. At this point one of the women present, Thais by name and Attic by origin, said that for Alexander it would be the finest of all his feats in Asia if he joined them in a triumphal procession, set fire to the palaces, and permitted women's hands in a minute to extinguish the famed accomplishments of the Persians. This was said to men who were still young and giddy with wine, and so, as would be expected, someone shouted out to form the comus and to light torches, and urged all to take vengeance for the destruction of the Greek temples. Others took up the cry and said that this was a deed worthy of Alexander alone. When the king had caught fire at their words, all leaped up from their couches and passed the word along to form a victory procession in honour of Dionysus. Promptly many torches were gathered. Female musicians were present at the banquet, so the king led them all out for the comus to the sound of voices and flutes and pipes, Thais the courtesan leading the whole performance. She was the first, after

the king, to hurl her blazing torch into the palace. As the others all did the same, immediately the entire palace area was consumed, so great was the conflagration. It was most remarkable that the impious act of Xerxes, king of the Persians, against the Acropolis at Athens should have been repaid in kind after many years by one woman, a citizen of the land which had suffered it, and in sport.[53]

Diodorus is quite open about the general drunkenness that facilitates the burning of the palace, as well as Thais's role in helping events along. It is also clear from this account, which may not be, we must remember, fully true, that Alexander had not originally intended to destroy the palace as he did. Interestingly, however, Diodorus converts the event into a Dionysian (and thus arguably Greek) celebration. In doing so, he appears to agree with the spirit if not the letter of Ptolemy's version of events by presenting the destruction of the palace at Persepolis as a ritually scripted act of revenge carried out first by Alexander and then an Athenian woman for damages inflicted upon Athens's Acropolis. In this sense, the destruction of the palace at Persepolis stands not as a drunken act of vandalism, but as an act of poetic justice on behalf of Athens, carried out under the divine protection and inspiration of Dionysus. Plutarch, the latest of our extant Greek sources, generally agrees with Diodorus Siculus, but he adds two important details: he claims that Macedonian soldiers gleefully participated in the act of vandalism because they saw it as a sign that their king "looked homeward, and had no design to reside among the barbarians"; and he argues that all sources are in agreement that Alexander "soon repented" of destroying the palace "and gave order to put out the fire."[54] Plutarch does not say more about Alexander's supposed repentance, and his reader is left to figure out whether Alexander was sorry because Parmenio's advice had finally sunk in or because he did not wish to give his Macedonian troops the wrong idea about his Asian ambitions. It is also possible that as he watched the palace—now his palace—burn, he finally came to realize fully that it was a much greater thing to be "king of Asia" than to be the avenging *hêgemôn* of a fractious and weak Greece.

As Arrian's, Diodorus Siculus's, and Plutarch's accounts of the episode at Persepolis show, a serious preoccupation with establishing Alexander's Hellenic bona fides for readers in Greece during the late republican and early imperial Roman period is an element that runs through the extant Greek historical sources. As I have argued above, it can be explained, in keeping with the loosely nationalistic goals of the Second Sophistic, as an attempt to claim Alexander—who as a Macedonian king had been seen during his lifetime as an unsophisticated and mostly unwelcome outsider by Attic Greeks—as a fundamentally Greek hero. That this ostensibly Greek hero set about fashioning himself into a Persian king almost immediately after defeating Darius III at Gaugamela (331 BCE) is something of an inconvenient fact for these historians, and there is abundant evidence, such as the ultimately ambiguous episode at Persepolis, to suggest that it was a matter of concern for Alexander's Macedonian troops and Greek subjects as well.

The response of non-Hellenic Roman authors to the dangerous tensions in force between the antidemocratic cultural mores of the mythical East and Alexander's (and thus Greece's) own descent into despotism was generally not to attempt to resolve them, but rather to make a concerted effort to use them as a footstool for Rome's own imperial ambitions.[55] In short, Alexander's downfall and death in Babylon became a powerful ideological tool with which Rome, especially after Octavian's victory in the civil war with Mark Antony, would labor to demonstrate its moral superiority to Greece and the Orient. We find strong evidence of this practice in a section of Seneca the Younger's epistle on drunkenness:

Alexandrum . . . tot itinera, tot proelia, tot hiemes per quas victa temporum locorumque difficultate transierat, tot flumina ex ignoto cadentia, tot maria tutum dimiserunt: intemperantia bibendi et ille Herculaneus ac fatalis scyphus condidit. . . . M. Antonium, magnum virum et ingeni nobilis, quae alia res perdidit et in externos mores ac vitia non Romana traiecit quam ebrietas nec minor vino Cleopatrae amor? Haec illum res hostem rei publicae, haec hostibus suis inparem reddidit; haec crudelem fecit, cum capita principum civitatis cenanti referrentur, cum inter apparatissimas epulas luxusque regales ora ac manus proscriptorum recognosceret, cum vino gravis sitiret tamen sanguinem.[56]

[Alexander . . . survived all the marches, all the battles, all the many winter campaigns (through which he made his way by overcoming the difficulties posed by time and place), the many rivers from unknown sources, and all the seas; it was intemperance in drinking combined with that Herculean and ultimately fatal wine goblet that sent him down to his tomb. . . . Mark Antony, a great man and one of noble genius: what was it that destroyed him and drove him into foreign habits and un-Roman vices if not drunkenness and, no less potent than wine, love of Cleopatra? It was this that made him an enemy of the state, this that rendered him no match for his enemies, this that made him cruel when, as he was dining, the heads of political leaders would be brought in, when during the most elaborate feasts and regal luxury he would identify the faces and hands of those whom he had condemned, when, heavy with wine, he still thirsted for blood.]

Seneca's linking of Mark Antony to Alexander serves to kill two very large birds with one rhetorical stone. It first reproduces the argument, advanced by Octavian both before and after his victory at the Battle of Actium, that Mark Antony had adopted Egyptian habits, had become so morally corrupt, had spurned Roman interests, and had so fallen under the power of Cleopatra that he had effectively ceased to be a Roman at all. By linking Mark Antony to Alexander, Seneca is also able to call upon an immense repertoire of ills associated with a Western hero's "descent" into the Orient and death. The pairing that Seneca makes between Alexander's "Herculean and ultimately fatal wine goblet" and Mark Antony's "love of Cleopatra" is significant, for he is able to make an oblique reference to what it was that Mark Antony so loved about Cleopatra by pairing (in what modern readers might recognize as a Freudian reference) the object of that love with the goblet from which Alexander enjoyed his last bout of drinking. The mediated pairing of Hercules with Cleopatra likewise mixes lines of genealogical descent with other, ideological ones: Alexander's family, the Argeadae, were considered to be direct descendants of Hercules, while Cleopatra herself was a descendant of Ptolemy I Soter, the Macedonian general in Alexander's army (mentioned above in connection with Thais) who established, largely on the basis of his close association with Alexander, a Hellenic dynasty in Egypt. By bringing them together, Seneca is able to situate Hercules and Cleopatra on a line of descent that passes, on a downward slope, through Alexander. Beyond this complex language game of family resemblances, Seneca is also able to situate Rome, with the Julio-Claudian Dynasty at its helm, above the fray: drunkenness, cruelty, sexual lust, despotism, and death are situated far from Rome, in a loosely defined and acutely dangerous Orient.[57]

Before the civil war with Mark Antony, as the story of the Trojan Aeneas came to become a foundational myth for Rome itself in the run-up to Octavian's seizure of power, the young emperor's propaganda machine was increasingly able to push the idea that while Alexander (as would be the case with Antony) had ultimately succumbed to Eastern influence and had never returned to the West, Aeneas had been able to go far enough west to "become Roman, . . . , defeat the 'joint' Greek and Roman enemy [i.e., the Carthaginians, whose "mother city" was Tyre], and . . . found Rome, a city and power that would outstrip Alexander's Egyptian city."[58] Far from seeking a univocal and coherent image of Alexander, imperial Rome sought to exploit the Macedonian king's conflicted status as a heroic Western king who had nonetheless "gone native" in the despotic East in order to declare its own moral preeminence and bask in the (Stoic) glory of its own return from that abyss. As Spencer argues, Alexander—as both Macedonian king and Asian emperor—was seen by the Romans as a much more conflicted and tragically flawed precursor to Virgil's Aeneas, and thus to the Romans themselves:

For a Roman in the first century BCE, the combination of Alexander's Greek identity with Rome's victory over the Greek world . . . makes Alexander a proto-Aeneas figure; Trojan Aeneas and "Macedonian" Alexander both, in their different ways, prefigure Roman expansion into the Mediterranean and Asia. For Rome, Alexander had *always* been there first. Evoking Alexander's intimate connexion with such a lowly state is part of a discourse of diminution of his achievements that we find in authors such as Lucan and Juvenal, and it is a discourse that carries a double-edged meaning. Macedon was a small state that came to dominate the Greek world, and as Livy's use of Pyrrhus as a quasi-Alexander suggests, Macedon could still signify "Greece," or even Alexander's "East" in a Roman worldview. For Rome, the ascendant Mediterranean power, the glories of Alexander's conquests and Macedonian supremacy were short-lived, and so by conjuring with Alexander "of Macedon," Romans were also, paradoxically, evoking an inbuilt discourse of the transitory nature of imperial greatness. This complexity of meanings surrounding Alexander's birthplace could diminish his glory in the light of Roman triumphs (the conqueror conquered), whilst also aggrandizing Roman achievement. The dialogue between both interpretations makes available a sense of the impermanence of empire and divine favour. In this discourse, as we shall see when looking at Livy, the role of Alexander's conquests is to be simultaneously impressive and puny in comparison with the might of the Roman war-machine. An alternative model that is also implicit in comparisons between Rome and Alexander suggests that if the empire conquered by Alexander stands as an interpretative model for Roman imperialism, it can offer a paradigm for the victory of a young, warlike nation over the decadence of an ageing civilization. In this cyclical scenario, the fall of the ageing, decadent, Hellenized East offers a warning against the dangers of over-expansion—Alexander's empire (like all empires?) became what it had conquered. This flexibility—an important feature for the development and enduring popularity of Alexander—meant that "Alexander" was at once available to those who wished to provide a critique of imperial policy or behaviour (e.g., the younger Seneca) and to those favourable to Roman achievements (e.g., Livy).[59]

These ideological projects were never completely successful (Rome had several of its own contradictions to deal with, especially as the Julio-Claudian Dynasty reached its end); however, they continued to exist and remained influential, largely through the continued influence of Roman histories of Alexander, for centuries.

For a concrete example of how Roman authors framed Alexander as a Greek hero drawn down into tyranny and madness by his prolonged contact with the Orient, we may turn to Livy (59 BCE–17 CE), who speaks of a hypothetical invasion of republican Rome by the Macedonian army in the ninth book of his *Ab urbe condita* (History of Rome):

Et loquimur de Alexandro nondum merso secundis rebus, quarum nemo intolerantior fuit. Qui si ex habitu novae fortunae novique, ut ita dicam, ingenii quod sibi victor induerat spectetur, Dareo magis similis quam Alexandro in Italiam venisset et exercitum Macedoniae oblitum degenerantemque iam in Persarum mores adduxisset. Referre in tanto rege piget superbam mutationem vestis et desideratas humi iacentium adulationes, etiam victis Macedonibus graves nedum victoribus, et foeda supplicia et inter vinum et epulas caedes amicorum et vanitatem ementiendae stirpis.[60]

[If he is to be judged from the tenor of his conduct in the new state of his fortune, and from the new disposition, as I may say, which he put on after his successes, he would have entered Italy more like Darius than Alexander; and would have brought thither an army that had forgotten Macedonia, and were degenerating into the manners of the Persians. It is painful, in speaking of so great a king, to recite his ostentatious change of dress; of requiring that people should address him with adulation, prostrating themselves on the ground, a practice insupportable to the Macedonians had they even been conquered and much more so when they were victorious; the shocking cruelty of his punishments; his murdering his friends in the midst of feasting and wine; with the folly of his fiction respecting his birth.]

Here Livy is using a popular image of Alexander that the early Christian historian Paulus Orosius (fl. c. 410 CE) would take up in turn, according to which the great king is converted into an orientalized degenerate through, one may imagine, the accumulation of almost unchecked power and, no less important, prolonged exposure to Persian mores.

Turning to the third-century CE *Epitome historiarum Philippicarum Trogi Pompeii* (Epitome of the Philippic History of Pompeius Trogus) composed by Marcus Junianus Justinus (more commonly known as Justin), a summary of Gnaeus Pompeius Trogus's (no longer extant) late first-century BCE history of the Macedonian empire, we find a description of the oriental decadence of Alexander that closely resembles the moral judgments of Livy:

Alexander habitum regum Persarum et diadema insolitum antea regibus Macedonicis, velut in leges eorum quos vicerat, transiret, adsumit. Quae ne invidiosius in se uno conspicerentur, amicos quoque suos longam vestem auratam purpureamque sumere iubet. Vt luxum quoque sicut cultum Persarum imitaretur, inter paelicum regiarum greges electae pulchritudinis nobilitatisque noctium vices dividit. His rebus ingentes epularum apparatus adicit, ne ieiuna et destructa luxuria videretur, conviviumque iuxta regiam magnificentiam ludis exornat, inmemor prorsus tantas opes amitti his moribus, non quaeri solere.[61]

[Alexander assumed the attire of the Persian monarchs, as well as the diadem, which was unknown to the kings of Macedonia, as if he gave himself up to the customs of those whom be had conquered. And lest such innovations should be viewed with dislike, if adopted by himself alone, he desired his friends also to wear the long robe of gold and purple. That he might imitate the luxury too, as well as the dress of the Persians, he spent his nights among troops of the king's concubines of eminent beauty and birth. To these extravagances he added vast magnificence in feasting; and lest his entertainments should seem jejune and parsimonious, he accompanied his banquets, according to the ostentation of the Eastern monarchs, with games; being utterly unmindful that power is accustomed to be lost, not gained, by such practices.]

As is the case with Livy's *History of Rome*, Justin's *Epitome* casts Alexander as a Western (or at least Hellenic) conqueror who lost his way owing to the pernicious influence of his own cult of personality and the luxurious enticements of Persia.

In a similar vein, the account that Quintus Curtius offers of Alexander's virtues and faults at the end of his *Historiae Alexandri Magni Macedonis* (History of Alexander the Great)—also known as the *De rebus gestis Alexandri Magni Macedonis*—speaks at length in the final book of his history of Alexander's affinity for Eastern culture, customs, and dress. Quintus Curtius, who uses Cleitarchus as his primary source, begins by listing Alexander's "natural qualities," which include bravery, loyalty, generosity, strength, and sexual moderation ("a sex-life limited to the fulfillment of natural desire; and indulgence only in pleasures which were socially sanctioned").[62] He then moves on to describe the king's weaknesses, all of which are attributable, as Quintus Curtius argues, to either fortune or youth:

> The following are attributable to fortune: putting himself on a par with the gods and assuming divine honors; giving credence to oracles which recommended such conduct and reacting with excessive anger to any who refused to worship him; assuming foreign dress and aping the customs of defeated races for whom he had had only contempt before his victory. But as far as his irascibility and fondness for drink were concerned, these had been quickened by youth and could as easily have been tempered by increasing age. However, it must be admitted that, much though he owed to his own virtues, he owed more to Fortune, which he alone in the entire world had under his control. How often she rescued him from death! How often did she shield him with unbroken good fortune when he had recklessly ridden into danger! She also decided that his life and his glory should have the same end. The fates waited for him to complete the subjection of the East and reach the Ocean, achieving everything of which a mortal was capable.[63]

A striking aspect of this passage is how Quintus Curtius frames the gifts of fortune as both a blessing and a curse for Alexander. Here fortune (even the good sort) seems to operate as a kind of Derridean *pharmakon* in that it could both save Alexander from death in battle and assist him in his conquests but also could cause him to slip into something resembling insanity.[64]

Among the weaknesses that Quintus Curtius attributes to fortune is Alexander's tendency to assume the dress and customs of the Asian and North African cultures he had defeated, even if before he had held them in contempt. This is, first and foremost, a veiled reference to Alexander's institution in 327 BCE of the Persian practice of *proskynesis*, or imposed obeisance to him. Paul Cartledge describes this practice:

> In Persia obeisance was a social gesture performed, in different ways and according to caste and class perhaps, by an inferior to a superior, and so by all Persians to the Great King. For the Greeks, however, it was a religious gesture, performed by mortal men in honor only of the immortal gods, and many Greeks crudely misinterpreted the meaning of the Persian gesture by illegitimate cultural transference. Callisthenes, Alexander's official historian and learned relative of Aristotle, led the opposition to Alexander's imposition of obeisance on Greeks and Macedonians. What he did not like, he claimed, was not the requirement to signify publicly obeisance to a supreme ruler but the implicit command to treat Alexander as if he were a living god.[65]

Callisthenes's opposition to Alexander cost him his life (although Alexander's role in his death and the manner in which he was killed differ from source to source), perhaps because his criticisms hit the mark. In all probability, Alexander's stated "fusion policy"—according to which Hellenic and Asian troops were mixed together to form combined forces, the former were compelled to take Asian wives, and the royal court took on a decidedly Persian character—served as political cover for the very controversial belief, instilled in Alexander after a visit to the desert oracle at Siwa (in modern-day Libya), that he was the son of the Greco-Egyptian god Amun. It is also likely, as Cartledge points out, that the reluctance of the Macedonians and Greeks to accept *proskynesis* in Alexander's court stemmed in reality from entrenched beliefs regarding the inferiority of the Persians and their political practices:

> As for the Macedonians who followed Callisthenes's lead, they would have been objecting to being required to perform a gesture that was perhaps suitable for the Persians as an inferior and defeated people, but utterly inappropriate for members of a master race like the Macedonians. The requirement was all the more unpalatable for them, because they saw the Macedonian king as a first among equals. In face-to-face contact between the king and his Macedonian courtiers a degree of social equality was the unspoken rule.

For three years, since 330, the Macedonians had had to put up with the existence of a parallel oriental court, with its lavish paraphernalia of cup-bearers, spear-bearers, eunuchs, concubines and so forth. What they were not prepared to put up with now was the forced amalgamation of the two courts by means of this imposed common gesture of obeisance. I suspect that what really outraged them was that they, the victors, were being compelled to make the major public concession by adopting a key custom of the generally despised "slavish" orientals.[66]

The Greek conviction that the Persians were inherently predisposed to slavery was, as I have mentioned, already a settled piece of Aristotle's political thought, and there is little reason to believe that even the Macedonian king's high-minded former tutor would have approved of the adoption of *proskynesis* at Alexander's court, which to him would have constituted just the sort of "walking together" (*sum-bainô*) between master and slave of which he warned his readers in the *Politics*. In a very direct sense, Alexander's adoption of *proskynesis*, which operated as a kind of power apparatus (*dispositif*) in his efforts to form a central jurisdiction with bases in Babylon and Susa rather than Athens and Pella, represented for Greeks and (although long after the fact and from a wholly different perspective) Romans the legitimation of the "slavish" practices of the Persians by a Hellenic king.[67] That the adoption of *proskynesis* and other Persian court customs signified for Alexander's Macedonian and Greek troops an undesirable inversion of cultural and political status, and an almost complete surrender of their rights as free men, is more than likely the real issue underlying Callisthenes's protests and what provokes Quintus Curtius to criticize him long after the fact for "aping the customs of defeated races for whom he had had only contempt before his victory." As Quintus Curtius sees it, in fact, the net effect of Alexander's incredible success in the East (achieved primarily through good fortune) was to convert the Macedonian king and Greek *hêgemôn* into a maddened oriental despot. In this he was following an already well-established tradition of Alexander scholarship—and Alexander-mediated politics—within imperial Rome.

Paulus Orosius and Alexander

In the early centuries of Christianity, the ambivalent and highly subjective Roman view of Alexander and the Orient continued to find its ways into the work of authors writing in Latin. Perhaps the best-known example of such authors would be Paulus Orosius (fl. c. 410 CE), whose *Historiarum adversus paganos libri septem* (Seven Books of History against the Pagans) is in many ways a continuation of the deeply ideological and openly political treatment of Alexander that characterized earlier Roman accounts of the Macedonian king. Orosius's *Historiae adversus paganos*, written under the indirect guidance and protection of Augustine of Hippo (354–430 CE), is commonly held to be the first universal history written by a Christian author.[68] More important for the present study, Orosius also holds the somewhat lesser distinction of being the first Iberian historian (he is thought to have been from Bracara, now modern-day Braga, in northern Portugal) to deal at any length with the complex figure of Alexander the Great.[69] The *Historiae adversus paganos* is a central component of Alexandrian literature in medieval Iberia, having served as a source text for a fair number of historiographical accounts of Alexander's short life; the *General estoria* (General History) of the Castilian king Alfonso X (1221–1284 CE) and the *Historia de regibus gothorum, vandalorum, et suevorum* (History of the Kings of the Goths, Vandals, and Suevi) of Isidore of Seville (560–636 CE) are examples of works that take whole sections directly from Orosius.[70] Beyond its utility as a source text for other works, the *Historiae adversus paganos* seems also to have been frequently recopied, glossed, and read throughout the Middle Ages, both within and beyond the Iberian Peninsula.[71]

Orosius's history of Alexander, which occupies chapters 16–20 of the third book of the *Historiae adversus paganos*, is not in any sense a sympathetic one. This is perhaps understandable given the work's openly polemical goal, namely to show, in the wake of the Visigothic sack of Christian Rome, that horrible calamaties were also common during the pagan era. For Orosius, Alexander is one of these calamaties, as he makes clear early on in the third book of *Historiae adversus paganos*, in which he describes Alexander as "ille gurges miserarium atque atrocissimus turbo totius Orientis" (that abyss of miseries and most horrible whirlwind of the entire Orient).[72]

Perhaps the most striking element of Orosius's sharp attack on Alexander—an attack that is as critical as it is deceptively complex—is that it seems to deny that Alexander was ever human at all. This is somewhat ironic, given that the fuller context of Orosius's presentation of Alexander is the latter's birth: "Quibus diebus etiam Alexander Magnus, vere ille gurges miserarium atque atrocissimus turbo totius Orientis, est natus" (It was at this same time

that Alexander the Great was born, that abyss of miseries and most horrible whirlwind of the entire Orient).[73] The other events that Orosius lists in
the context of Alexander's birth are all, perhaps predictably, unhappy ones.
He first mentions the arrival of Carthaginians in Rome to finalize the second navigation treaty between them and the Roman Republic. This treaty,
signed in 348 BCE, essentially mapped out zones of permissible navigation
within the Mediterranean between Rome and Carthage and put significant
restrictions on Roman territorial expansion. For Orosius, the presence of the
Carthaginians in Rome is associated with a "hailstorm of evils" along with
"continuous darkness," corresponding to omens, recorded in Livy's *History
of Rome*, that include an enormous hailstorm and a solar eclipse.[74] Orosius
then mentions the birth of Alexander before describing the forced deporta-
tion of Egyptian Jews to Hyrcania by the Persian king Artaxerxes III, who
had waged a bitter war on Egypt and the Levant that saw, among other hor-
rors, the total destruction of the wealthy city of Sidon. Orosius interrupts his
list of mid-fourth-century BCE calamities only to make comments regarding
the growing size of the Jewish community of Hyrcania and what he feels is
their imminent departure from the region: "quos ibi usque in hodiernum
diem amplissimis generis sui incrementis consistere atque exim quandoque
erupturos opinio est" (it is commonly held that [the Jews] have lived in that
region since th[e] time [of Artaxerxes III's war in Egypt] to the present day,
experiencing a great surge in population, and that one day they will abruptly
leave that place).[75]

As calamities go, the presence of Phoenicians in Rome to finalize a
navigation treaty that would limit Roman expansion seems to be a minor
concern. The demolition of Sidon and the forced relocation of thousands
of people from the Eastern Mediterranean to the southern coast of the Cas-
pian Sea are no doubt much larger issues; however, Orosius describes both
events in relatively dispassionate terms. With regard to Artaxerxes and the
Jewish exile, he says merely that "post transactum in Aegypto maximum
diuturnumque bellum plurimos Iudaeorum in transmigrationem egit atque
in Hyrcania ad Caspium mare habitare praecepit" (after a large and long war
in Egypt, [Artaxerxes] forced many Jews to emigrate, and he ordered that
they settle in Hyrcania).[76] The destruction of Sidon is described in a similarly matter-of-fact way. In all, although Orosius's comments regarding the
Carthaginians certainly have something of an Old Testament ring to them,
he saves his strongest language for Alexander.

Orosius begins his history of Alexander, at the start of chapter 16 of the third book of the *Historiae adversus paganos*, with Alexander's rise to the throne of Macedon in 336 BCE upon his father's assassination (Pausanias, one of Philip's bodyguards, stabbed him to death at the wedding of Alexander's sister). The rest of the history, which consists of only nineteen hundred words in all, includes the major events of the campaign against Darius III and Porus and then ends with Alexander's death in Babylon. The direct source of Orosius's history of Alexander is the *Epitome* of Justin; however, Orosius is in general much more inclined to subjective assessments than is Justin. We may take as an example Orosius's comments on Alexander's visit to the temple of Amun, after which Alexander began to proclaim himself the son of that god. Orosius introduces this episode in the following way: "Inde ad templum Iouis Hammonis pergit, ut mendacio ad tempus conposito ignominiam sibi patris incerti et infamiam adulterae matris aboleret" (From there, he continues on to the temple of Zeus-Amun in order to wipe out the ignominy, built up by a lie of circumstance, of his uncertain paternal filiation and the infamy of his mother's adultery).[77] Another striking example of Orosius's treatment of Alexander involves the death of the Macedonian king, which Orosius, following the rumors that had begun to circulate almost immediately after Alexander's death, attributes to poisoning: "Alexander vero apud Babylonam, cum adhuc sanguinem sitiens male castigata aviditate ministri insidiis venenum potasset, interiit" (Alexander died in Babylon when, still thirsty for blood, he had with ill-tempered zeal drunk the poison served to him through the treachery of a servant). As Orosius has it, Alexander is thirsty for blood but accepts wine instead, only to end up drinking poison.

As I have suggested above, Orosius presents Alexander not so much as a king or even as a man, but as a kind of natural disaster. Even in the context of Artaxerxes III's war in Egypt, Alexander stands out as a cataclysm sprung from the earth and sky itself: "gurges miserarium atque atrocissimus turbo." For Orosius, Alexander is no Julius Caesar, Hannibal, or Scipio Africanus (conquering figures to whom the Macedonian king was frequently compared in classical and medieval literature), but rather something more elemental and less human. For Orosius, Alexander is in essence a kind of mythological Charybdis or Eurus brought to life and set loose upon the world, and it is perhaps for this reason that Orosius calls attention to Alexander's birth several chapters before speaking of his conquests. Few

Iberian writers would echo Orosius's supernatural (or, perhaps more accurately, hypernatural) treatment of Alexander; however, many others, such as the author of the thirteenth-century Castilian poem *Libro de Alexandre* and the various Muslim scribes and storytellers throughout the Mediterranean who reshaped the legend of Alexander to harmonize with the Qur'an, would strive to rework the legendary and historical tradition that set the young emperor up as something more than mere flesh and blood. Both currents, in any case, serve simultaneously to participate in and subvert Alexander's own claims, consistently made throughout the last decade of his life, that he was the son of Amun and thus divine.

As Orosius puts it in his brief notice of Alexander's birth, the Macedonian king is also a figure irrevocably associated with and somehow framed by the East. Orosius inherits this Eastern framing from Roman historians such as Livy and Justin, although in the context of Rome's imminent collapse at the hands of the Goths and Byzantium's ascendance by the early fifth century, such a reference meant very specific things to Orosius's readers (Augustine of Hippo being the most immediate of these). Three centuries later it came to have very different meanings within the Iberian Peninsula in the wake of the Muslim conquests that eventually led to the establishment of an independent Muslim caliphate in Córdoba. From the time of the Muslim conquest to at least the beginnings of the fifteenth century, the Orient was in fact both a relatively distant geographical region and a local, quotidian reality for much of the Iberian Peninsula. Standing, as it were, at a streetcar stop on the Ungererstraße, the inhabitants of cities such as Lisbon, Toledo, and Valencia did not have to develop abstract theories of what it meant to come face to face with the disruptive alterity of an "Eastern" Other. Such intersubjective relations were in fact part of daily life, whether one was an Andalusian Muslim grappling with the demands of Moroccan (first Almoravid and then Almohad) overlords or a Valencian Christian looking to buy silk.

Alexander in Medieval Iberia

The role of Alexander within the medieval and early modern literature of the Iberian Peninsula is an issue that has received little systematic attention up to now. In his monumental and still unsurpassed study of medieval Alexandrian literature, George Cary, oddly enough, has very little to say about Iberian texts:[78] in the whole of his four-hundred-page volume, which considers "the conception of Alexander" within the works of moralists, theologians, mystics, moral philosophers, preachers, and "secular writers" in medieval Europe, he mentions the literature of medieval Iberia on only twenty-two occasions.[79] Of the passages that mention Spain and Portugal, seventeen are little more than brief comments or notes on the *Libro de Alexandre* and its relation to the *Alexandreis* of Walter of Châtillon (fl. c. 1175) and various vernacular texts, especially those first redacted in France. The remaining five instances in which Cary mentions medieval Iberia are similar in both scope and depth to an example from a brief caption below the image of a manuscript folio: "This page, from the Stockholm MS. of the French Prose Alexander, . . . was in Portuguese ownership in the fifteenth century and may well have been written and illustrated in southern Spain or Portugal."[80] There is no further discussion of the manuscript's provenance, and as far as I have been able to ascertain, this is the only mention of Portugal in Cary's study. On another occasion, and without further comment, he calls attention to the motif of Alexander's liberality in France, Italy, and Spain: "However rarely we find them, the fact that we find references of the *proverbial* type to Alexander's liberality in fifteenth- and sixteenth-century writers in France, Italy, and Spain shows that Alexander's proverbial reputation for liberality existed throughout the whole of the later Middle Ages."[81] Cary's discussion of Ibero-Arabic and Aljamiado versions of the Alexander Romance in fact occupies only one brief paragraph: "There must also be noticed two works produced in Spain but belonging to the Oriental Pseudo-Callisthenes tradition: the Arabic *Life of Alexander* edited and with a translation by Gómez and the Aljamiado *Alexander* discussed and edited by Nykl. These two Spanish Arabic works were neither influenced by, nor had any influence on, Western textual tradition."[82] Passing over Cary's conflation of Aljamiado with Arabic in the second sentence of this citation, we may agree that his decision merely to "notice" but not actually study these works leaves a significant gap in his ambitious study. Indeed, it is difficult to explain the scant attention that Cary pays to medieval Iberia in a work that purports to "summarize, not one but all the general and popular conceptions of Alexander the Great current in the Middle Ages."[83]

María Rosa Lida de Malkiel, for her part, has offered pointed criticism of Cary's broader arguments, rightly mentioning that many of the shortcomings that she finds in these are due precisely to the circumstances under which they were formulated: Cary died in 1953, at the age of twenty-four, with the manuscript of *The Medieval Alexander* still in very rough form (it was extensively edited by David J. A. Ross before being published by Cambridge University Press in 1956).[84] As Lida de Malkiel states in her review, there is little doubt that, given better circumstances, Cary would have corrected the faults in his volume.[85] D. S. Robertson, who oversaw the project in its early stages, agrees with Lida de Malkiel, explaining that, like all university dissertations, Cary's project was "done against time, with scant opportunity for polish or revision."[86]

Seeking to take on at least a portion of the emendational task herself, Lida de Malkiel, who unfortunately died—at the age of fifty-one—in the same year that her review of Cary's volume appeared in *Romance Philology*, published in the same journal a kind of catalog, with extensive footnotes, of medieval Castilian references to Alexander. This article remains the most comprehensive survey of Alexandrian literature in the Iberian Peninsula to date, in spite of its brevity.[87] Beginning with an account of thirteenth-century Castilian poetry and ending with a brief mention of *Celestina* and the two passages in that work which refer to Alexander, Lida de Malkiel offers her reader a dense and carefully researched list of primary sources and critical works that functions, together with Cary's volume, as a necessary first resource for any comprehensive account of Alexandrian literature in medieval Iberia.

I stress the fact that Cary's and Lida de Malkiel's studies are essentially first stops for scholars concerned with the medieval Iberian Alexander due to the frame of analysis that each author adopts. Cary, as I have already stated, is concerned with a remarkably broad corpus of European texts and so hardly mentions peninsular references to Alexander (his brief treatment of the *Libro de Alexandre* being a notable exception), while Lida de Malkiel focuses rather tightly on Castilian works from the Western Latin tradition and is, in any case, more concerned with providing detailed bibliographic references and source material than with engaging in the analysis of texts. The reader wishing to explore further the nature of Alexandrian literature within the Iberian Peninsula must thus piece together information from a very wide assortment of published and primary sources.

Most of the existing critical literature on Alexandrian texts in medieval Iberia focuses on the *Libro de Alexandre* and its influence on later prose and poetic works. Long a part of the Spanish literary canon, the *Libro de Alexandre* is a legendary account of Alexander's life based largely on Walter of Châtillon's late twelfth-century Latin epic, the *Alexandreis* and Alexander of Paris' immense *Li romans d'Alixandre* (Romance of Alexander). The Castilian poem consists of roughly 2,500 fourteen-syllable, monorhymed quatrains—the Castilian version of the French alexandrine also referred to as *cuaderna vía*—and is extant in two full manuscript copies (Paris, Bibliothèque Nationale ms. Esp. 488 and Madrid, Biblioteca Nacional ms. Vitrina 5–10) as well as various fragments that date from the thirteenth through the fifteenth centuries. Scholars such as Ian Michael, Francisco Rico, and Raymond Willis carried out important critical work on the *Libro de Alexandre* during the last decades of the last century, and a host of other scholars have more recently worked on issues that range from the text's unknown authorship and date of composition to its implied mode of interpretation.[88]

Beyond the extensive work that has been done on the *Libro de Alexandre*, the Iberian tradition of Alexandrian literature has been left relatively unstudied. I have already mentioned Cary's brief treatment of Alexandrian texts from medieval Iberia and Lida de Malkiel's thorough but Castile-centric catalog, and we can add to these a short list of other critical works.[89] More recently, Richard Stoneman, perhaps the world's leading scholar of the *Greek Alexander Romance*, has traced out a more detailed image of the Alexandrian currents that flow through the Iberian Peninsula during the medieval period.[90]

In an attempt to appreciate the gradual but decisive shift that took place regarding textual accounts of Alexander from the medieval to the early modern period (Gomes Eanes de Zurara, discussed in the following chapter, is very much a transitional figure in this respect, at least within the Iberian Peninsula), it is worth taking a brief look at the following passage from the *Libro de moralidades* (Book of Moralities), a late fourteenth- or early fifteenth-century Castilian compendium of ethical philosophy. In a section that deals with the question of what might be the greatest good in this world, the reader finds a short list of classical authors and other figures from the period together with their general stance on the issue:

Diversas sentençias fueron de los antiguos filosofos de qual era el mayor bien de aqueste mundo. Et dixeron algunos que riquesa, et fueron movidos por aquesto, et veían que riquezas eran preçiadas et que los omnes ricos eran honrrados. Et de aquellos fue Vergilio, que fiso libros en como pudiese omne aver riquesas, et César, que puso todo su entendimiento en las riquesas de aqueste mundo. Et otros dixeron que cavallería, ca por cavallería ama omne victoria de su enemigos et conquista de muchas tierras; et de aquellos fue Luchan, que fiso libros de cavallería et Alixandre, que por grant cavallería conquistó la mayor partida del mundo. Et ovo y de otros que dixeron que salud era conservamiento de vida, de los quales fue Galieno, que fiso libros como omne pudiese aver salut, et el emperador Costantinopol [sic] que por salut quería dar todo su inperio. Et ovo y de otros que dixeron que el mayor bien del mundo era amor, et por amor era omne alegre et plasentero, de lo quales fue Ovidio que fiso libros de amor, et Percas [sic], que por Elena fiso muchos honrrados fechos. Et otros dixeron que por buenas costunbres omne vil era ensalçado, de los quales fue Catón que fiso libros de buenas costunbres. Et otros dixeron que sevieza, ca por sevieza conoçia omne a Dios et a sus leyes et todas las criaturas de Dios. Et de aquestos fue Aristótiles que fiso libros de seuieza.⁹¹

[Diverse statements were made by the ancient philosophers regarding what might be the greatest good of this world. Some said riches, and were motivated by this, and saw that riches were highly valued and rich men much honored. Of these philosophers we may count Virgil, who wrote books on how one might become rich, and Caesar, who focused all of his thoughts and actions on the riches of this world. Others said that chivalry is the greatest good, as through chivalric pursuits a man learns to love victory over his enemies and the conquest of many lands. Of this group was Lucan, who wrote books of chivalry, and Alexander, who by great acts of chivalry conquered the larger part of the world. There were also those that claimed that good health equaled the preservation of one's life, among whom was Galen, who wrote books on how a man might have good health, and the emperor Constantine, who would have exchanged his entire empire for good health. There were also those who said that the greatest good of this world was love, and that through love a man becomes happy and pleasant. Among these was Ovid, who wrote books on love, and Paris, who did many honorable things for Helen. Still others said that through good habits a vile man could be praised. Among these was Cato, who wrote books on good habits. Others said that wisdom is the greatest good of this world, as through wisdom a man comes to know God and His laws and creatures. Among these was Aristotle, who wrote books on wisdom.]

As is perhaps apparent from the citation above, the *Libro de moralidades* is not a work of serious erudition; rather, it reflects what might be termed a middlebrow clerical concern with ethical philosophy and the natural world.

It makes extensive use of medieval philosophers such as William of Conches (ca. 1090–1154 CE) and Abū Hāmid Muḥammad ibn Muḥammad al-Tusī al-Ghazālī (1058–1111 CE), but frequently deals with them in a superficial manner. In the passage cited above, Virgil is presented as a kind of self-help get-rich author *avant la lettre*, the Roman emperor Constantine is confused with the city named for him (Constantinople), and Paris is presented as a gallant lover who performed many honorable tasks because of his love for Helen.

The popular, even folkloric images of classical authors and personages presented in the *Libro de moralidades* tell us a great deal about the limited direct access the compiler of the text had to historical and literary materials from antiquity. This lack of access does not stop him, however, from making use of these materials within the openly Christian ethical framework of his argument, and it is interesting to note that the treatment that Alexander receives (compared, for example, to Julius Caesar) is remarkably balanced: the Macedonian king is identified simply as a man who "conquistó la mayor partida del mundo" (conquered the larger part of the world) through force of arms. This, it must be admitted, is about as even-handed as appreciations of Alexander get.[92]

Nevertheless, it is important to keep in mind that Heuss's argument—that Alexander is a figure that from antiquity to present has consistently been embedded within strongly ideological interpretative frameworks—still holds in the case of the *Libro de moralidades*. That is, the compiler (and subsequent copyists and readers) makes use of Alexander, and other figures from antiquity, to develop a very specific argument regarding ethical comportment and Christian salvation. Linked explicitly to chivalry and world conquest, Alexander here enjoys something of the immortality for which he so energetically fought.

In tracing out the general contours of the rhizomatic system of narrative threads that stretch Alexander out from ancient Greece to the early modern Iberian Peninsula, we run into a host of problems. Foremost among these is the question of definition. By "Alexander" do we mean the man born in Pella, Macedonia to two human parents, the Egyptian and Greco-Libyan god, or the imperial phantasm? Is it even possible at this point to separate these elements of what Alexander has come to mean? These threads, which had their ideologically charged beginnings in Alexander's own focused attempts to control his story (although he paradoxically seems to have left almost completely to chance the running of his empire after his death), spread out across the period of Roman domination in the Mediterranean and emerged largely intact during the Middle Ages. While the medieval period—which stretched at least from the Visigothic sack of Rome in 410 CE to the sea voyages of Vasco da Gama—saw different works and genres of Alexandrian literature emerge, what did not change from the Roman period were the ways in which Alexander was called on to embody both the height of human excellence and the absolute nadir of human depravity. By turns a chivalric hero, student of Aristotle, pagan despot, and enemy/prophet of Islam, Alexander had a long, strange antique and medieval career. And it is out of this career that his newly-polished Renaissance self would emerge, as both a continuation of Roman and medieval traditions, and a sign that something new and ominous was taking shape as Iberian kingdoms went about the Mediterranean and the world fighting to take control of Muslim territory and lives.

CHAPTER 3

OBLIVION

Iberian Empire in the Maghreb

THE HISTORY OF IBERIAN EXPANSION INTO NORTH AFRICA DUR-
ing the late medieval and early modern period is a difficult narrative to tell,
largely because the goals, resources, and geographical foci of each of the
three principal Iberian kingdoms during this period were so different. The
Crown of Aragon, which had established footholds in the Balkans, Byzantium, and Italy, was primarily interested throughout the fourteenth and fifteenth centuries in developing a Mediterranean thessalocracy, and the various kingdoms of the Maghreb were of interest to the Catalano-Aragonese
Confederation to the extent that they threatened or could aid in this project.[1]
The Castilians, meanwhile, can be said to have arrived late to the game after
having taken control of the Canary Islands very early in the fifteenth century
(the taking of an abandoned Melilla in 1497 and of Oran in 1509 serving as
concrete evidence of renewed Castilian interest in the Maghreb, at least for
the purpose of protecting its southern coasts), but they nonetheless managed
to make a significant impact on Maghrebi dynastic politics and relations of
power throughout the sixteenth century. For the Portuguese, the prize was
always Morocco.[2]

The Portuguese empire in Morocco took shape in fits and starts over the
course of more than a century. Its fall, however, was dramatic. At both temporal poles of the Portuguese colonial adventure in the Maghreb—its establishment in 1415 with the conquest of Ceuta and its de facto end in 1578 with
the humiliating defeat and death of Sebastião I at al-Qaṣr al-Kbīr—we find

striking textual theorizations of issues central both to the workings of early modern empire and, in a more philosophical sense, to being-in-the-world.

The first of these issues is the powerful presence of death and oblivion that everywhere shapes the history of Portuguese expansion into Morocco. Looking, for example, at the most authoritative fifteenth-century account of the conquest of Ceuta, that of Gomes Eanes de Zurara (c. 1410–c. 1474), we see that the entire enterprise—from its early planning to its aftermath—has at its center a profound and explicit concern with the strict limitations imposed by, and the very real anxieties associated with, human mortality. Functioning within frameworks of praxis and meaning that are by dizzying turns chivalric, Christian, classical, and literary, Zurara's history of the capture of Ceuta by the Portuguese is at once an official history of dynastic power and a painstaking account of the deadly pestilence that lies just beneath the surface of that power.

The second issue that arises from narrative accounts of Portuguese colonialism in Morocco is a focused reconsideration, along what we might consider phenomenological rather than traditional Scholastic or Neoplatonic lines, of distinctions between subject and object (as well as those between mind and body). Central to this reconsideration are subtle narrative accounts of human bodies in settings of face-to-face interaction and the associated process of hypothesis building—regarding issues as basic as being, time, action, and experience as well as cultural frameworks of morality and power—achieved through a persistent and focused recounting of the microsocial details of bodies in contact and interaction.

If narrative accounts of the first and last moments of the Portuguese empire in Morocco can be characterized by their deliberate focus on human mortality and the phenomenological substratum of embodied interaction—especially between Iberian Christians and North African Muslims—then it is Alexander the Great that gives these accounts teeth and serves as their guiding historical and moral frame. While it may be an exaggeration to state that the Portuguese colonization of Morocco was theorized as an explicitly Alexandrian enterprise in the same sense that the colonization of Hormuz and parts of India were, it is also difficult to ignore the ways in which, for example, the Greco-Roman history of Alexander's conquest of Persia gives shape to Portuguese efforts to narrate the (partial, temporary, and all-too costly) conquest of a territory that was to them marked at once by "oriental" strangeness and vicinal familiarity.

Josiah Blackmore has recently argued that "the Portuguese model (or better, practice) of empire in Africa was not a simple exercise of dominance or subjugation but was regularly more negotiated, as practical and pragmatic as it was ideological."[3] Blackmore's argument here is that for the Portuguese, North African and Iberian Muslims could not stand as "undifferentiated figure[s] of otherness" given that they had represented, from the twelfth century through the fifteenth, a cultural and religious Other as well as "a closer, more intimate presence."[4] This ambivalent understanding, from the Luso-Christian perspective, of Maghrebi and Andalusian Muslims (collectively referred to, along with other Muslim groups, as *mouros*) brings with it not only complex and often fraught reconfigurations of the distinction between subject and object, but also considerations of death, as, according to Emmanuel Levinas, the ultimate Other.[5] Although according to the politico-theological logic of reconquest and empire, Otherness necessarily resided upon the foundation of a stable and firm distinction between subject and object, the pragmatic and proximal interaction of these two groups over the course of several centuries had made such distinctions difficult to sustain. Narrative inevitably reveals the web of cracks in these distinctions and brings to the surface the ambivalence and ambiguity that underlie even the most devoted of imperial narratives, such as Zurara's prose-epic account of the conquest of Ceuta.

These relations were no less vexed (and vexing) from the Muslim perspective, as evidenced by the case of the Sa'adi dynasty's supplantation of the Marīni-Waṭṭāsi dynasties in Morocco during the early sixteenth century. The ascendance of the Sa'adis marks a crucial moment in Maghrebi history and would eventually lead to what is often considered to be a kind of golden age for the highly diverse and often fractious Moroccan nation.[6] From the perspective of Iberian imperial history, the rise of the Sa'adis is significant in that it was based first and foremost on an impassioned call to *jihād* against the Portuguese. A small Arab dynasty with origins in the southeastern desert of Morocco, the Sa'adis rode this popular call to *jihād* all the way to Taroudant, Marrakech, and Agadir before finally conquering Fez in 1549. Domestic and international policy were deeply intertwined within sixteenth-century Morocco, and such policy even spilled over into conflicts within the broader Muslim *umma*, given that the unspoken, peripheral target of the Sa'adis' discourse of resistance and struggle was always the westward-expanding Ottoman Empire. In spite of their call to *jihād* against Christian intervention in

Morocco, the Sa'adis were also keen to rally the support of powerful local *shaykhs* and marabouts in an effort to fix the boundaries of the Turks' North African hegemony at the Atlas Mountains. These efforts of course had mixed results and employed means that differed depending on the political context. If Aḥmad al-Manṣūr (r. 1578–1603) had forcefully negotiated with Istanbul for meaningful Moroccan sovereignty, his brother and predecessor, 'Abd al-Malik (d. 1578), had come to power as a self-conscious Ottoman vassal who had even led a large body of Ottoman-Algerian troops into Fez.[7]

Beyond the subtle politics that characterized Sa'adi relations with the Turks and their Algerian clients, the Sa'adis were no less committed to the negotiation of treaties, agreements, and partnerships with Christian powers, including the Castilians and the Portuguese. This willingness to negotiate extended also to business matters, as an excerpt from a letter sent by 'Abd al-Malik to a group of English merchants demonstrates: "I will refuse the offars of all other chrysteans and bargayne with you, as the other kinge dyd and that for the valeew of the pelletts that you shall bringe in from tyme to tyme, you shall have leysens to bey and to transporte saltepetar, copper or anne commodetis whatsoavar I have within my reallme."[8] In engaging in such trade with the English, 'Abd al-Malik was acting with the blessing of the powerful religious councils that dominated Moroccan politics throughout the sixteenth century—their theory being that commerce with Protestants, who at least *seemed* less idolatrous than their Catholic counterparts, could serve the double benefit of providing funds for military spending (to fight Christians, of course) while undermining the economic position of the Catholic kingdoms of the Iberian Peninsula. This would all make perfect sense, of course, if 'Abd al-Malik and other Sa'adi kings were not also actively pursuing treaties and trade agreements with their sworn enemies, the Castilians and the Portuguese. Perhaps the real tragedy of al-Qaṣr al-Kbīr, in fact, is that the Portuguese king Sebastião had, in waging war with 'Abd al-Malik, turned away repeated efforts by the Sa'adi king to negotiate some sort of reasonable and mutually beneficial (not to mention Castile-brokered) arrangement to prevent the outbreak of hostilities. There were of course other, more open forms of collaboration as well. The example of Abū Zakariyyā Yaḥyá ibnu Muḥammad Tā'fūft, an early sixteenth-century Berber chieftain from the area around Safi, Morocco, is striking in this respect.[9]

As in many other colonial contexts, Portuguese administration of Safi and the broader Dukkālat 'Abdah region of Morocco relied to a great degree on a series of complex deals and contracts with local leaders. In fact, shortly after Portugal took control of Safi in 1508, Portuguese king Manuel I (1469–1521) issued a royal decree granting local power to Yaḥyá Tā'fūft. Yaḥyá had been, before his lucrative deal with Manuel I, openly opposed to Portugal's presence in Safi. According to letters currently held in the Torre do Tombo archive in Lisbon, Yaḥyá's cooperation cost the Portuguese Crown a yearly salary of roughly thirty ounces of gold in addition to his portion of the spoils taken in raids against local tribes. He was also allowed to equip and maintain, according to these letters, a private guard of one hundred mercenaries and to collect a significant income from bribes of local merchants and others seeking his protection.[10] Steady conflicts with Waṭāsīd forces from Fez and the growing power of the Sa'adi dynasty in the South eventually led to an untenable situation for the Portuguese in the Dukkālat 'Abdah region, and they were forced to abandon Safi in 1541. Yaḥyá himself was ambushed and murdered in 1518 while on his way to visit a friend whose brother had recently been killed.[11]

The image of Yaḥyá that emerges from one side of the historical record is not particularly flattering. Among the letters in the Torre do Tombo archive that deal with Yaḥyá is a scathing letter to Manuel I composed by a Rabbi Abraão from Safi. The letter begins:

Depues que este moro foy posto por alcayde, logo determino de fazer entender aos moros que ho mando era seu, e que nom avyão de conecer ao capytam se nom a ele, e logo se começo a chamar rey, e que lhe beijasem todos ha mão e ho pe, e estando o capytam diante lhe beijavam a ele a mão e nom ao capytam, e logo começo a dezir aos moros que ele hera o senhor, e que o capytam se avya de yr, e ele avya de ficar por senhor em Çafy.[12]

[After this Muslim was given the post of captain, he made it a point to inform the other Muslims that the command was his, and that they should recognize no other captain but him. Later he began to refer to himself as king and ordered that everyone was to kiss his hand and foot, and even in front of the [Portuguese] captain they kissed his hand and foot and not those of the [Portuguese] captain. Later he began to say to the Muslims that he was their lord, and that the [Portuguese] captain must leave, and that he must remain as lord of Safi.]

The sense that we gain from this letter, along with others written by Portuguese officials in Morocco, is that there was at the very least some real anxiety regarding the power that Yaḥyá exercised in the area. Whether he was abusing his authority or not is a matter that is now perhaps impossible to determine; however, what is clear is that Yaḥyá had many enemies apart from the king of Fez and the local tribes that he was expected to overpower. Among these were the Portuguese captain-major Nuno Fernandes de Ataíde and what the French historian Joseph Goulven has described as the entire Jewish community of Safi.[13]

The image of Yaḥyá that emerges from his own written correspondence to Manuel I and other royal officials is, as we might expect, quite different. For example, in a letter written just two years before his death, we find Yaḥyá asking for the support of the newly appointed Portuguese captain-major of Safi, Nuno Mascarenhas:

> Louvores ao seu Deus. Senhor D. Nuno, vosso servo Iáhia Tafufte vos faz a saber que desno dia que vim a esta terra, não vi nenhum prazer nem descanço com cristãos, nem menos com mouros. Os mouros dizem que sou cristão, e os cristãos dizem que sou mouro, e assim estou em balanças sem saber o que hei de fazer de mim, senão o que Deus quiser. . . . Deixei meus filhos e mulheres por servir elrei nosso senhor, e eu senhor corro e trabalho por fóra, e o capitão e Nuno Gato e o feitor e outros me destruem de dentro; e assim toto mouro que vem á cidade com proveito a comprar e vender não torna mais pera fóra, dizem logo que é enxovío, e toman-nos per força pera o capitão e pera os seus amigos, e tambem os mouros que vem á cidade com a lenha e palha, e agora lhes fazem treição, matam-nos e deitam-nos nas almotofías e nos poços até federem polas casas, e muitos mouros vendidos pera terras de cristãos, e isto claro e visto sem darem pena a quem por isto merecer.[14]

> [My Lord, Dom Nuno, your servant Yaḥyá Tā'fūft informs you that from the day that I arrived in this territory, I have seen no pleasure or rest either among Christians or Muslims. The Muslims say that I am a Christian, and the Christians say that I am a Muslim, and so I am caught in between not knowing what to do with myself except that which God wills. . . . I left my children and my wives to serve the king our lord, and while I, my Lord, run about and work outside our borders, the captain [Nuno Fernandes de Ataíde], [the royal auditor] Nuno Gato, the administrator, and others destroy me from within. Any Muslim who comes to the city with the idea of

buying or selling something is not allowed to leave, as they say later that he is from Shāwīya, and the captain and his friends take them by force. The Muslims that come to the city with wood and straw likewise are betrayed: they kill them and lay them out in graves and dump them in wells until the stench of the bodies reaches the houses; also, many Muslims are sold into slavery in Christian lands. This is done in the open without any of the guilty parties receiving punishment.]

As we see, this letter begins with an introduction that serves an explicitly ostensive and metadiscursive function. This brief introductory clause first addresses Mascarenhas directly, and then announces Yaḥyá's intention to inform him of something: "My Lord, Dom Nuno, your servant Yaḥyá Tāʿfūft informs you that. . . ." What is most interesting about this brief piece of text, however, is the way in which it serves to embed the very urgent and intimate first-person account that immediately follows it within the frame of an overtly formulaic, official, third-person narrative.

In essence, what starts as a more or less stock example of a letter to a royal administrator morphs almost immediately (in fact, just after the relative pronoun *que*) into something of a very different generic order indeed, a kind of confession and very personal (even if not necessarily sincere) call for help: ". . . your servant Yaḥyá Tāʿfūft informs you that from the day that I arrived in this territory, I have seen no pleasure or rest either among Christians or Muslims." The switch from third- to first-person narrative is as seamless as it is sudden, and it in many ways exemplifies the sort of generic, discursive, and even deictic hybridity that makes up Yaḥyá's letters. The change here is so abrupt (and linked to such a dramatic shift of tone and genre) that we are left to wonder what exactly Mascarenhas was supposed to make of this letter—and of the person who wrote it.

This last issue (i.e., who is speaking here?) takes center stage as Yaḥyá informs Mascarenhas of the particular predicament in which he finds himself as a *capitão de campo* in Safi: "The Muslims say that I am a Christian, and the Christians say that I am a Muslim, and so I am caught in between not knowing what to do with myself except that which God wills." Yaḥyá's letter presents a theory of identity and selfhood based squarely and explicitly on language use and interaction. Yaḥyá here presents his identity as one that is socially embedded and mediated by the words of others—he is, in a sense, the sum of what two powerful groups say he is, even if that sum is a seeming contradiction. In the end, it was his own countrymen who would kill him, either as part of the broader Sa'adi *jihād* or as part of a more localized conflict between different Berber groups in the Dukkālat 'Abdah region of Morocco. In any case, it is in such seemingly endless shades of gray that imperial politics within Morocco, from both the Iberian and the native Maghrebi perspective, took place.

Death, Chivalry, and Ceuta

In any discussion of the starting point of early modern Iberian empire, the Portuguese capture of the northern Moroccan city of Ceuta on August 22, 1415, rightly takes center stage. The conquest of Ceuta is not necessarily the first act of Iberian colonial expansion (the colonization of the Canary Islands and the conquest of the Guanche Berbers by the kingdom of Castile had begun thirteen years earlier); however, it does represent the beginning of a steady stream of expansion down the Atlantic coast of Africa by the Portuguese, a process that would culminate nearly a century later in the establishment of colonies as far away as the Persian Gulf, India, and the South China Sea. It would also lead, albeit nearly a century later, to the sea voyages of Christopher Columbus in search of both a western route to India and, less directly but more urgently, the Christian "liberation" of Jerusalem.

If the Portuguese conquest of Ceuta serves as something like the "shot heard 'round the world" for Iberian expansion—above all into Muslim Africa and Asia—this is largely due to the narrative efforts of Gomes Eanes de Zurara. Zurara was the kingdom of Portugal's official chronicler and curator of the Torre do Tombo royal archive in Lisbon throughout the last two decades of his life (posts that he had more or less inherited from Fernão Lopes (c. 1378–c. 1459), medieval Portugal's most famous historian). He was granted this double post by Afonso V (1432–1481) shortly after the redaction, in 1450, of the *Crónica da tomada de Ceuta* (Chronicle of the Conquest of Ceuta), in which Zurara recounts the heroic—if not divinely ordained—imperial exploits of Afonso's family.[15] Primarily concerned in his historical works with the epic undertakings of high-ranking nobles, Zurara is also widely known for his later *Chrónica do descobrimento e conquista da Guiné* (Chronicle of the Discovery and Conquest of Guinea, completed in 1453) and the *Crónica do Conde D. Pedro de Meneses* (Chronicle of the Count Dom Pedro de Meneses, completed in 1463), the latter of which, an account of the career and heroic death of one of Portugal's most successful colonial captains in Morocco, compelled Zurara to travel to al-Qaṣr al-Saghīr (on the northern coast of Morocco, approximately halfway between Tangier and Ceuta) to collect firsthand accounts of his subject, who had died only four years before Zurara began his biography.

In the first part of the present chapter, I will examine Zurara's earliest historical text, the *Crónica da tomada de Ceuta*. In specific terms, I will be focusing on two particular episodes within the book and what they reveal about the earliest moments of Portuguese expansion into Portugal. The first deals with the drawn-out death of Philippa of Lancaster (1360–1415), the wife of João I of Portugal (1357–1433) and mother to the three princes whose exploits in Ceuta made them national heroes (and knights). The second involves a brief and violent exchange between the Portuguese invader Vasco Martins de Albergaria and a Muslim soldier outside the fortress city of Ceuta.

Early on in Zurara's account of the death of Philippa of Lancaster, he makes use of what he believed to have been Aristotle's written comments to Alexander the Great, contained within the apocryphal *Secretum secretorum* (Secret of Secrets), regarding human mortality. The passage reads as follows:

> E Aristóteles que disto tomou mui especial cuidado, disse naquele livro que se chama "segredo dos segredos," que enviou a Alexandre acerca do fim de seus dias, que certamente, ele se maravilhava do homem, que comia pão de trigo e carne de dous dentes, poder naturalmente falecer. E, depois que os homens determinadamente conheceram que, por si mesmos não podiam durar, buscaram certas maneiras de semelhança, por que eles fossem aos presentes em certo conhecimento.[16]

> [Aristotle, who took great care in this matter, said in his book, entitled *Secret of Secrets*, which he sent to Alexander near the end of his days, that he was certainly amazed that even the man who lived on a healthy diet of wheat bread and small bits of meat could also quite naturally die. And once men established beyond a doubt that they could not endure on their own, they looked for certain ways to appear to endure, so that they might remain in the minds of the living.]

Zurara here implicitly frames the work of the historian as a kind of struggle against death, as a seeming immortality that keeps the dead in the minds of

the living. He then lists three ways in which (wealthy) people had traditionally sought to live on after their deaths, proclaiming as a climax the important role that the historian plays in the transmission of the virtuous deeds of
the dead to those still alive:

> Uns fizeram tão grandes sepulturas e assim maravilhosamente obradas,
> cuja vista fosse azo de os presentes perguntarem por seu possuidor. Out-
> ros fizeram ajuntamento de seus bens, havendo autoridade de el-Rei, por
> que o fizessem morgado para ficar ao filho maior, de guisa que todos os
> daquela linhagem descendessem, houvessem razão de se lembrarem sem-
> pre daquele que o primeiramente fizera. Outros se travalharam de fazer
> tão excelentes feitos de armas, cuja grandeza fosse azo de sua memória ser
> exemplo aos que depois viessem, por cuja razão honravam todos os autores
> de tais cousas, como diz Valério que fazia Cipião a Lucano e assim outros
> muitos aos seus autores.[17]

> [Some made large and marvelously fashioned tombs, the sight of which
> would cause the living to ask about their owners. Others gathered together
> their property, with the permission of the king, in order to leave it to their
> eldest son. The purpose of this was so that those who descended from that
> line might always have cause to remember the person who came first. Oth-
> ers worked to accomplish excellent feats of arms so that their greatness
> might be an example to those who came afterward; for this reason, these
> men honored the authors of historical texts, as Valerius said Scipio did with
> respect to Lucan and also many others with respect to those who wrote of
> their achievements.]

The connective leap that Zurara takes from the intentionality that underlies
the carrying out of great deeds to the honor that the people who perform
such deeds owe their historians effectively ties up his textual project into a
neat package. According to this logic, nobles (such as, for example, certain
members of the Avis dynasty) do heroic and virtuous things (such as conquer Ceuta) so that those things might be spoken of after they are gone and
so grant them a measure of immortality. The instrument by which this project succeeds or fails, as Zurara has it, is the historian, who should be honored
and amply remunerated when he or she gets the telling right.

The text from which Zurara cites at the beginning of this paragraph,
the *Secretum secretorum*, was believed during the late Middle Ages to have
been a letter written by Aristotle and sent to Alexander the Great after the

latter's conquest of Persia. In reality an encyclopedic work composed in Arabic during the tenth century (entitled *Kitāb sirr al-asrār* [Secret of Secrets]), the *Secretum secretorum* became, thanks to the combined translation efforts of Philip of Seville (fl. 1120) and then Philip of Tripoli (fl. 1220), one of the most popular Latin prose texts of the Middle Ages. Its popularity inspired many vernacular versions, and in the Iberian Peninsula it is worth noting the abridged Castilian version, entitled the *Poridat de las poridades* (Secret of Secrets), from which was derived the Catalan *Llibre de la saviesa* (Book of Wisdom) as well as other Castilian works of moral philosophy. It is not clear whether Zurara was working from the longer Latin text or the shorter Castilian one; however, the presence of a fourteenth-century copy of the latter in the Biblioteca Nacional in Lisbon (MS IL 46, ff. 1r–8v) suggests that he may have had, at the very least, direct access to a portion of the Castilian abridgement.[18]

Moving on from the *Secretum secretorum*, but not his defense of historians, Zurara speaks directly of a well-known episode in the history of Alexander himself:

E porém dizia Alexandre o grande rei de Macedónia, que ele seria bem contente de trocar a prosperidade que lhe os deuses tinham aparelhada, e afastar sua mão de toda a parte que lhe no Céu podiam dar, por haver um tão alto e tão sumo autor para seus feitos, como houvera Achiles em Homero, poeta.[19]

[In a similar way, Alexander, the great king of Macedonia, said that he would be happy to give up all the wealth that the gods had presented to him and to pull his hand away from any reward that Heaven might give him in exchange for having such a prestigious and talented author to write of his feats as that which Achilles had in the poet Homer.]

This is a scene of which late medieval and Renaissance writers made a great deal of use. As we will see in the next chapter, Camões himself closes his epic of empire, *Os Lusíadas* (The Lusiads), with a direct reference to this moment in the historical narrative of Alexander. As Arrian records the scene, Alexander arrived at the tomb of Achilles in Troy shortly after entering Asia Minor in 324 BCE. Placing a wreath on the tomb, "Alexander, so the story goes, blessed Achilles for having Homer to proclaim his fame to posterity."[20] The link that Zurara forges between Alexander, empire, and human mortality is not a casual one, and it speaks directly to the episode that he is about to relate, namely the death of Philippa of Lancaster as a pious and necessary (albeit dark and sobering) prelude to the establishment of Portuguese empire in Africa. In brief, it links the theme of human mortality to that of imperial expansion while making use of a moral framework composed in almost equal measure of chivalric, Christian, and classical components.

Shortly after his reference to Alexander's visit to Achilles' tomb, Zurara justifies his textual account of the death of the English queen of Portugal:

> E não somente filharam os antigos cuidado de escrever os feitos dos virtuosos homens, mas ainda das virtuosas mulheres, asim como se acha nas histórias da Brívia, da Rainha Ester e de Judic e assim nas obras de Tito Lívio de Lucrécia de Virginea e de outras semelhantes. E, se estes autores assim quiseram renembrar os feitos virtuosos, desta pequena culpa merecemos nós, ao diante, escrevendo o acontecimento e virtuoso fim desta Rainha, cujas grandes virtudes são dignas de grande memória.[21]

> [And not only did the ancients take care to write down the achievements of virtuous men, but also those of virtuous women, as is seen in the stories of the Bible: Queen Esther, and Judith; as well as in the works of Livy: Lucretia, Verginea, and others. And, if these authors saw fit to remember virtuous acts, we deserve very little blame for this ourselves, as we set down the virtuous end of this queen, whose great virtues are worthy of great memory.]

Zurara links Philippa to her "great virtues" (linking these in turn to biblical and Roman heroines) and spends the next seven chapters of his history of the conquest of Ceuta describing them, even as he narrates, with a remarkable sense of drama and pathos, the slow destruction of her flesh by the plague. Underlying and giving historical meaning to this slow process of dying, a gradual "end of virility" or loss of "mastery as a subject," as Emmanuel Levinas has put it, is the first act of the ritual of chivalric investiture by which the queen's sons become knights.[22]

In a very literal sense, we can read the entire *Crónica da tomada de Ceuta* as the account of an exceptionally elaborate knighting ceremony.[23] At the beginning of the text, João I has signed a peace treaty with Castile and Granada and is planning a large celebration in Lisbon, during which he plans to knight his sons, Duarte, Pedro, and Henrique. The three princes have other ideas, however, as they, in their own words, wish first *fazer de nossas honras* (meaning something like "to establish our honor") in some great undertaking. It is this desire on the part of the princes that leads them to seek out a new theater of action, as they make clear near the beginning of the text: "Ca pois as pazes de Castela são firmadas, e da parte da Grada não temos esperança certa, não há hi pelo presente, cousa nenhuma azada em que possamos receber estado de cavalaria, se novamente não for buscada" (Since the peace treaty with Castile has now been signed, and from Granada, we can have no certain hope, there is not at present any action in which we might receive the state of chivalry unless we go looking for it).[24] Shortly afterward, in a conversation with their father's trusted royal treasurer, João Afonso de Alenquer, they hit upon the idea of attacking Ceuta and in this way earning their new status as knights. What follows this initiative is a long process by which their ceremony of chivalric investiture becomes spread out over a period of several weeks and across two separate continents. What causes this prolongation of the ceremony, as well as the complexities with respect to bonds of vassalage that are introduced into it, is the gradual, untimely death of the princes' mother, Philippa of Lancaster.

The narrative of Philippa's final days begins, more or less, with her request to João I that he go against their sons' wishes and knight them before they leave Portugal for Africa so that she might witness the event. She also requests that the king make them knights with three swords that she plans to have made for the occasion:

"Senhor, eu vos peço, por mercê que se me Deus quiser dar dias de vida, que chegue até o tempo de vossa partida, que vós façais vossos filhos cavaleiros presente mim, ao tempo de vosso embarcamento con senhas espadas, que lhe eu darei e com a minha benção. Cá posto que seja dito, que as armas das mulheres enfraquecem os corações dos cavaleiros, bem creio que, segundo a geração de que eu venho, nunca serão enfraquecidos por as receberem de minha mão." Ao que el-Rei respondeu que lhe prazia muito.[25]

["My lord, I ask you, provided that God might give me sufficient life so as to see your day of departure, that I may be present when you knight your sons upon your embarkment, and that you do so with swords that I will give to you with my blessing. Although it has been said that the arms of women weaken the hearts of knights, I believe that, in light of my lineage, they will never be weakened by arms received from my hand." The king responded to this that it pleased him greatly.]

The queen's efforts here, as well as her explicit mention of her lineage ("a geração de que eu venho"), should be read as an attempt on her part to make sure that the natural bonds of vassalage formed through the investiture ceremony exist not only between the princes and the Portuguese House of Avis (embodied by their father), but also between them and the English House of Lancaster, to which she belongs. Given that João I had become king of Portugal due in large measure to the direct support of Philippa's father, John of Gaunt (1340–1399), and that Philippa's marriage to the Portuguese king was arranged in the first place to solidify the Anglo-Portuguese alliance, this move was as much an astute political maneuver (as João I likely had to admit) as it was a mother's sentimental wish. Upon receiving permission from her husband to do so, the queen orders the three swords to be made, one for each of her sons. Afterward, she engages in what reads like a sort of ceremonial vigil, spending the entire day in church and returning at night not to engage "em danças nem em outros nenhuns desenfadamentos deste mundo, somente em espiritual contemplação" (in dances or other pleasures of this world, but only in spiritual contemplation).²⁶

Some days later, João I and Philippa go to Sacavém to escape an outbreak of the plague that was then ravaging Lisbon. While there, Philippa busily hands out alms to the local monasteries and other people that she "knew to lead good lives."²⁷ Sacavém is not particularly far from Lisbon (its center is less than ten miles from Lisbon's palace square), however, and it was not long before cases of the plague began to show up there. João I pleaded with Philippa to go immediately with him to Odivelas so that they might distance themselves a bit from the outbreak, but Philippa insisted on staying in Sacavém to finish her charity work. It is here, while in the church, that she became infected with the plague, although she attributed her pain to some common illness mixed with fatigue. Shortly afterward, she left to join João I in Odivelas.

Once at the monastery at Odivelas, the full extent of the queen's illness became apparent. In a great deal of pain, she sent to Lisbon for the swords to give them to her sons. While she waited for the swords to arrive, she gave each of her sons a piece of wood from the cross upon which Jesus was crucified and begged them to carry the relics with them always, "cá não sabeis os dias, nem as horas dos perigos" (as one does not know the days nor the hours when danger will come).²⁸ The princes then ceremoniously kissed her hand, and she gave each of them her blessing.

Shortly after the scene with the pieces of the cross, the swords arrive from Lisbon. Each of the princes kneels down before Philippa in turn, and she gives them their swords along with her blessing, urging them to use the weapons when they are knighted and lamenting the fact that she will not live to see this occur. At this time, in spite of the pain that she is suffering, she also deals with certain administrative matters that are pending between her and the princes. After receiving the swords, as well as their mother's blessing and counsel, the princes each kiss her hand and rise with their respective swords.

What Zurara is describing in this touching scene of imminent death and filial love is the first act of a three-act knighting ritual. In the final two acts, the princes will use their mother's swords to kill Muslims in Ceuta and then, with the city captured, they will ceremoniously remove the swords, hand them to their father, and officially receive the order of chivalry from him. From a sociopolitical perspective, it is crucial to note also that the princes' bonds of vassalage are in this way divided between their (English) mother and father and predicated upon the forceful capture of a Moroccan city. Philippa herself emphasizes her role in the ceremony and the bond of vassalage (*dívido*) that her sons have to her and her dynastic line:

E como quer que seja cousa empachosa de os cavaleiros tomarem armas de mão de mulheres, eu vos rogo que vos não queirais ter acerca desta que vos eu dou, semelhante embargo. Cá, segundo a linhagem donde eu descendo e a vontade que tenho para acrescentamento de vossas honras, nunca entendo que vos por isso empecimento [*sic*] nem dano possa vir, antes creio que a minha benção e deles vos fará grande ajuda.[29]

[And although it may be a shameful thing that knights take their arms from the hands of women, I beg you to disregard this with respect to the swords that I wish to give you; because, according to the lineage from which I descend and the desire that I have for the growth of your honor, I do not consider that from this any impediment or harm may come to you; rather, I believe that my blessing, and that of my family, will be of much help to you.]

The full political and historical ramifications of this underscoring of the bonds that existed between the Avis princes and the Houses of Plantagenet and Lancaster in England (Philippa's father was, as I have mentioned above, no less a figure than John of Gaunt, and her nephew was Henry V (1387–

1422), at the time of her death the reigning king of England) are beyond the scope of the present study; however, it is important to point out the complex chivalric framework within which Zurara seeks to fit his history, because it corresponds directly to both the tale of African conquest and to that of human death (and desired immortality) that he wishes to tell.

This drama of investiture aside, the episode of the queen's passing is not so much about her death as her dying. During this long process, she does her utmost to forge, through the machinery of chivalric ceremony, natural bonds (*dívidos*) between her English family and her sons, the eldest of which will be the next king of Portugal.[30] She also speaks prophetically about her sons' departure for Ceuta (namely, that it would occur within the week) and foretells her own ascension into heaven before receiving a vision of the Virgin Mary. Shortly after this vision, her sons convince their father to leave Odivelas so that he might not become seriously ill through the sorrow caused him by watching Philippa die. Before leaving, he says goodbye to his wife for the last time. Zurara only partially describes this scene:

> Mais daquele triste espedimento que ele fez da rainha sua mulher, quando a foi ver antes que se partisse, não posso eu falar tanto como devia, porque a força das lágrimas me embargam a vista, que não posso escrever, considerando em cousa tão triste. Cá se me apresenta ante a imagem do entender, como o verdadeiro e leal amor é mais forte cousa daqueles daquelas que a natureza em este mundo juntou. Do qual Salomão disse, no *Cantar dos Cantares* que "era forte como a morte."[31]

> [I cannot speak as I should of the sad goodbye that [the king] gave the queen, his wife, when he went to see her before leaving Odivelas. Considering such a sad thing, the force of my tears clouds my vision such that I cannot write. And the idea appears before my mind that true and loyal love is the strongest of the things that nature has formed in this world. As Solomon said, in his Song of Songs, "it is as strong as death."]

After this scene, the three princes continue to attempt to cure the queen through a range of medicinal measures, but their resolve is broken when it becomes clear that she has decided that it is time for her to die. She receives communion and has her body anointed, at which time they discover that she has a carbuncle beneath her knee. This is taken as a clear sign that she will not live much longer, and the priests begin to administer her last rites, dur-

ing which she is lucid enough to correct them when they make errors in the
Latin prayers. After these prayers have finished, the queen dies, with a faint
and pious smile on her face.

Once their mother has died, the princes discuss what is to be done with
her body. They decide, because it is July and the weather is very hot, that
they must bury her that night, and with as much secrecy as can be managed:
"acordaram, porque o tempo era quente, cá era quando o sol estava em dois
graus do signo do Leão, que a soterrassem de noute, o mais secretamente
que se pudesse" (they agreed, because the weather was very hot, as it was
when the sun was two degrees within the sign of Leo, that they should bury
her that night and as secretly as possible).[32] The following morning, with the
body of the queen already enclosed in her sepulcher and the king far away,
the princes arrange for a funeral mass in their mother's honor.[33] Zurara then
ends the episode with a pronouncement regarding death, honor, and his telling of the queen's passing:

> Nos poderíamos aqui falar muitas razões acerca do grande dó que foi feito
> por esta senhora. As quais nos parece que se devem escusar, considerando
> como seu recontamento não traz honra às grandes virtudes daquela sen-
> hora, cujo falecimento escrevemos, porque todos certamente sabemos, que
> no dia, que entramos em esta presente vida, por lei determinada somos
> julgados à morte, ca nossa vida não é senão uma trasladação que fazemos
> do ventre ao sepulcro, segundo diz Job.[34]

> [We could speak at length here of the immense grief that was shown for this
> lady. I believe that we should not do so, given that its telling brings no honor
> to the great virtues of that lady whose death we have just recounted, because
> all of us know with certainty that on the day that we enter into this life that
> we are sentenced by a fixed law to die, as our life is nothing but a journey
> that we make from the womb to the crypt, as Job says.]

In this way, death seems to have the last word in Zurara's narrative. Zurara,
however, moves quickly from his Old Testament depression to find explicit
solace not in the Christian god of the queen he has just eulogized, at least not
in the first instance, but rather in classical literature and, just perhaps (this is
left implicit), the Christian "truths" that it foreshadows.

He first cites the poet Ovid (43 BCE–17 CE), whom he mistakenly cred-
its with Quintus Ennius's (239–169 BCE) famous Latin epitaph, "Nemo me

lacrimis decoret nec funera fletu faxit. cur? volito vivus per ora virum" (May no one honor me with tears nor weep at my funeral. Why? I fly, still alive, through the mouths of men).³⁵ The passage in Zurara reads: "E, portanto, dizia Ouvidio poeta: 'Não me honre nenhum com lágrimas, nem vá ao meu enterramento com choro, porque não deve, com razão, chorar a morte, que me leva à vida imortal" (And therefore the poet Ovid said: "May no one honor me with tears nor weep at my funeral, as it makes no sense to cry over the death that brings me to immortal life").³⁶ It is clear that for Ennius immortality is gained through the continued recitation of his poetry by the living; in this way, he allies himself with Alexander, who likewise saw in text-mediated fame (particularly that of Achilles) a means of besting the seeming totalitarianism of human mortality. Zurara's use of Ovid/Ennius, however, leaves it unclear what exactly he means by "immortal life." Is he referring to the Christian heaven and the immortality of the soul, or of the earthly fame to which he, as a historian, holds the keys? As if to add to the ambiguity, Zurara then moves on to a citation from book 8, chapter 7 of Xenophon's *Cyropaedia*:

> E Xenofonte conta que Ciro o maior, estando para morrer dizia: "Ó meus muito amados filhos, não queirais cuidar que, como me eu partir de vós, que me tornarei em nenhuma cousa, nem serei em algum lugar, porque, quando eu conversava convosco, certo é não podíeis ver a minha alma, mais entendíeis que morava em este corpo pelas cousas, que me vieis obrar. Pois aquela mesma alma crede que me ficará, para sempre, depois de minha morte, a qual então perfeitamente começará de viver. E, porém não me queirais chorar com dor."³⁷

> [Xenophon recounts that Cyrus the Great, as he was dying, said: "My beloved sons, you should not worry that as I take my leave of you that I will turn into nothing, or occupy no place, because when I was speaking to you it is certain that you could not see my soul, and so you thought that I resided in this body through the things that I did. Well, that same soul will remain with me forever after my death, and with my death it will begin to live in perfection. And therefore, you should not cry for me in pain."]

These sentiments, taken alone, are perfectly adaptable to Christian doctrine; however, it is worth questioning why Zurara has chosen Ovid/Ennius and the trope of fame first mentioned at the start of the episode in connection with Alexander, as well as a passage from the *Cyropaedia* (a book that greatly shaped Alexander's thoughts and actions in Asia), in a discussion of the eternal nature of the soul. I am not questioning here Zurara's commitment to Christian doctrine and belief (in the closing two paragraphs of the same chapter he engages in a discussion of Christian ethics that makes no reference to classical authors); rather, I am concerned with the ways in which he constructs discursive, and ultimately moral, authority through his simultaneous telling, within the *Chrónica da tomada de Ceuta*, of the death of Queen Philippa, the knighting of the three princes, and the opening shot of Portuguese empire. Mixing Christian doctrine with classical thought is certainly nothing new in the Iberian Peninsula by the mid-fifteenth century; however, Zurara's engagement in this practice, in particular his subtle, if not hesitant, indexing of Alexander—and the moral frameworks associated with Alexander's expedition into the East and bid for world empire—make new and more urgent use of these topoi. As Cyrus tells his sons not to weep for him, we are made to think also of Philippa, whose Christian life and death seem to order the same thing (she can also be read as an index—through her name—of Alexander's father, whose violent death in Pella facilitated Alexander's rise to power and assumption of the Asian campaign against Darius III). And of course there was historically very little weeping done for Philippa—João I ordered less than eight days of official mourning for her— because to do so would have put the Ceuta expedition in jeopardy. Hustled off to her tomb and mourned in a hurry, Philippa's Christian stoicism and piety comes to serve, within Zurara, as a justification for the material exigencies of empire and chivalry. But then there is also the matter of her body, of the carbuncle below her knee, the outward sign of disease and putrefaction that signals the inscription of death, framed as a loss of virility—an "end of being able to be able"—upon the project.[38] Like a pool of blood or ejaculated semen within a Kristevan framework of abjection, the body of the queen is cast off and hidden away, even as it is recognized, within Zurara's chronicle, as a part of the official whole.

The Portuguese conquest of Ceuta, framed as part of the knighting ceremony of the Avis princes, carries with it—is, in fact, supported by—the death of Queen Philippa. The gradual destruction of her body, as well as her hurried and secret burial, allows her to begin the knighting ritual for her sons that will end in a converted mosque in Ceuta and then move out of the way so that the armada may sail. As Zurara puts it, mixing classical and

Christian tropes, the pestilence that takes her body does not take her soul, even as the shadow of death that hangs over the Ceuta expedition does not block out the light of chivalric honor and crusading zeal. In the end, death joins the Moroccan defenders themselves as the "intimate Other" that must be confronted and outfought. This death, like the life that it finally confronts, casts a shadow over the rise and development of empire in what would come to be the Latin West. It confronts it as a framework to theorize the perceived glories and all too real dangers of empire, the high price of colonial expansion. Running through all of this is the image of Alexander, standing on an Asian plain, laying a wreath on the grave of Achilles and lamenting that he likewise will die, and without a Homer to tell his story. This combination of death and empire, as well as the will to theorize both through narrative, would shape Portuguese colonial efforts in Morocco right up to their bitter and inglorious end.

Before discussing the end of Portugal's Moroccan empire (which at its peak never amounted to more than a series of fortress cities along the country's Mediterranean and Atlantic coasts), it is useful to look at a particular scene within Zurara's account of the taking of Ceuta. Its utility lies not only in the way in which it suggests a scene from the history of Alexander's conquest of Asia, specifically his brutal campaign against the city of Gaza, but also in its adumbration of many of the complex relations that would always be in play throughout Portugal's—as well as Castile's and the Crown of Aragon's—continued presence in the Maghreb.

The episode is very brief, taking up barely a third of chapter 72. As the Portuguese advance force rushes toward the city gates of Ceuta, the Muslim defenders are forced to turn back. Among these defenders is "um mouro grande e crespo todo nu, que não trazia outras armas senão pedras. Mais aquelas que lançava da mão, não parecia que saía senão de algum trom ou colobreta tanto era forçosamente enviada" (a large and completely naked Muslim with curly hair, armed only with large rocks, who launches these [at the Portuguese] with tremendous force).[39] Zurara describes the last stand of this Muslim defender:

E, quando os mouros assim foram empuxados como já dissemos, aquele mouro virou o rostro contra os cristãos e dobrou o corpo e foi dar uma tão grande pedrada a Vasco Martins de Albergaria sobre o bacinete que lhe lançou a cara fora. Nem a vista daquele mouro não era pouco espantosa,

cá ele havia o corpo todo negro assim como um corvo e os dentes mui
grandes e alvos e os beiços mui grossos e revoltos. Mais a Vasco Martins não
esqueceu de lhe pagar seu trabalho, cá posto que aquela pedrada fosse mui
grande e em semelhante lugar, Vasco Martins não perdeu o tento, mas ainda
o mouro não havia vagar de se virar da outra parte, quando ele adiantou
seus pés e correu a lança pelas mãos, e passou-o com ela de parte a parte.
E, tanto que aquele mouro foi morto, logo todos os outros viraram costas e
acolheram-se à cidade, e os cristãos de volta com eles.⁴⁰

[And, when the Muslim force was thus pushed back as we have described,
he turned to face the Christians. Bending over, he picked up an enormous
stone and hurled it at Vasco Martins de Albergaria. The stone crashed
against Vasco Martins's helmet with such force that it knocked out his visor.
The very sight of that Muslim was frightening: his body was as black as a
crow, his teeth were large and white, and his lips were very fleshy and curled
back. Although the stone had struck Vasco Martins on the head with great
violence, he did not lose his senses, nor did he fail to pay his opponent back
for his efforts: scarcely had the Muslim turned back around when Vasco
Martins stepped forward and ran him through with his lance. As soon as
that Muslim was dead, all the others turned their backs to seek refuge in the
city, with the Christians chasing after them.]

As he does throughout the *Crónica da tomada de Ceuta*, Zurara explicitly
frames the violent efforts of Vasco Martins as those of a Christian fighting
against Muslims rather than those of a Portuguese soldier fighting against
Moroccans. Beyond this crusading religious framework, which continued to
have significant appeal and force within the Iberian Peninsula (as we will see
in the case of Sebastião I's fall at al-Qaṣr al-Kbīr in 1578), albeit to varying degrees, throughout the fifteenth and sixteenth centuries, Zurara goes to great
lengths to hold reason and the mental faculties of the Portuguese invader up
against the monstrous, corporeal, animal force of the Muslim.⁴¹

    Like the body of Philippa of Lancaster, this Muslim's body—which, al-
though free of carbuncles and disease, is marked by excessive features (most
notably its size and naked blackness)—must paradoxically be both thrown
away (*abjectum*) even as it is built upon in order for the imperial enterprise
to succeed. In one sense, Zurara presents this Muslim as monstrous and
animalistic, with curled-back lips and large white teeth—a kind of African
Polyphemus throwing boulders at ships and soldiers that are approaching
rather than attempting to escape. It is these monstrous, powerful, dark, and

primitive aspects of the Muslim that the rationally violent Portuguese must defeat and cast aside; but it is also this man, with all of his associated characteristics, who must also quite literally be run through—as with Vasco de Martins's lance—for the conquest and colonization of Ceuta to occur. His is the "heart of darkness" that, from Zurara's perspective, must be pierced, penetrated, and exposed to the cruel light of European reason, an act that serves as both the justification and the obligatory passage of European expansion into North Africa.

The Portuguese passage through the heart of darkness back to the (Western) light of day, a return trip that Alexander never made, operates in Zurara's text through a pointed contrast between the Muslim's body and the rational intellect of Vasco Martins: although the Muslim smashes the Portuguese soldier against the head with a rock, the latter keeps his senses (*não perdeu o tento*) and runs the former's body through with a lance. It is this maintenance of Western discretion in the face of African savagery, and a reasoned triumph over the disorienting force of Muslim Africa itself (a potential disorientation represented by the smashing of a large Moroccan stone against the head of a European invader), that serves as the base upon which Zurara attempts to build his account of imperial expansion and chivalric investiture in Ceuta. That he ends his narrative with the knighting of princes Duarte, Pedro, and Henrique within a Moroccan mosque that has been hastily converted into a Christian church seems to reinforce the importance of this successful passage through the "flesh" of Muslim North Africa to the broader narrative of empire. The question to which Zurara never attends, of course, is how and to what extent the Portuguese themselves are transformed—as was Joseph Conrad's Kurtz—by this passage.

Perhaps the most powerful intersection between Zurara's account of Vasco Martins's defeat of the black Muslim (and the subsequent conquest of Ceuta) and the classical histories of Alexander the Great is Zurara's participation in the Roman narrative of oriental penetration and return. Like Aeneas and Scipio Africanus, but unlike Mark Antony and Alexander himself, the Portuguese within Zurara's text pass through North Africa and return to Europe without being fundamentally changed themselves; to paraphrase Quintus Curtius, they assume control of the Moroccan fort city and return to Portugal without "externum habitum mutare corporis cultum, imitari devictarum gentium mores, quos ante victoriam sprevera[n]t" (assuming foreign dress and aping the customs of defeated races for whom [they] had only contempt before [their] victory).[42] The performance of the chivalric investiture ceremony, an extension of a Portuguese dynastic drama into a North African setting, seems to suggest that it is Africa itself that will be changed by their presence.

Vasco Martins's defeat of the black Muslim also provides a scene of Portuguese one-upmanship with respect to Alexander's feats in Asia. Citing Diodorus Siculus as his source, John Maxwell O'Brien writes that upon crossing the Hellespont, Alexander "took the helm of the royal flagship . . . , but as the coastline emerged he changed into a full suit of armor and was the first to leap from the ship and hurl his spear into the shore." Diodorus Siculus records the event: "[Alexander] personally sailed with sixty warships to the Troad. Upon arriving, he threw his spear from the ship and fixed it in the ground. He then leapt ashore, as the first of the Macedonians, declaring that he received Asia from the gods as a prize won at the point of a spear."[43] As O'Brien points out, Alexander was himself seeking to reenact and surpass a specific Homeric episode by means of his spear toss and leap onto shore, namely the fatal leap that the Greek captain Protesilaus took onto Trojan soil as the Achaeans landed in Asia at the start of the Trojan War.[44]

Turning back to Zurara's *Crónica*, it should be pointed out that Vasco Martins is by no means the first Portuguese invader to reach land; this distinction belongs to Rui Gonçalves (who would be rewarded with the command of Canha, a small city approximately fifty kilometers east of Lisbon), who wounded many Moroccans in his solitary fight to hold the beachhead and who managed to kill, with the assistance of a German mercenary, another "grande mouro que entre todos os outros mostrava maior fortaleza" (large Muslim who among all the others showed the greatest strength).[45]

Though not the first to hit the beach, Vasco Martins is nonetheless the first of the Portuguese to enter the city. And when he tosses his spear, an act Zurara describes in great detail, it does not merely stick into the sand as Alexander's does; it instead runs through the body of an African Muslim, piercing it and so piercing the darkness of Africa itself. In ideological terms, this small piece of the episode—a beach landing and a decisive spear throw—represents in just about every way the escalation (as well as the problematization) of a classical motif.

The other classical episode upon which Zurara seems to draw, or at least to obliquely refer, is Alexander's brutal defeat of the Arab city of Gaza, the final military hurdle before his entry into Egypt. The siege of Gaza lasted approximately two months and involved the destruction of high walls that circled the city. Quintus Curtius describes the early stages of the siege:

Ortoque sole, priusquam admoveret exercitum, opem deum exposcens sacrum patrio more faciebat. Forte praetervolans corvus glebam, quam unguibus ferebat, subito amisit: quae cum regis capiti incidisset, resoluta defluxit, ipsa autem avis in proxima turre consedit. Inlita erat turris bitumine ac sulphure, in qua alis haerentibus frustra se adlevare conatus a circumstantibus capitur. Digna res visa, de qua vates consuleret, ut erat non intactae a superstitione mentis. Ergo Aristander, cui maxima fides habebatur: urbis quidem excidium augurio illo portendi, ceterum periculum esse, ne rex vulnus acciperet. Itaque monuit, ne quid eo die inciperet. Ille, quamquam unam urbem sibi, quo minus securus Aegyptum intraret, obstare aegre ferebat, tamen paruit vati signumque receptui dedit.[46]

[The next day Alexander ordered the city walls to be encircled by his troops, and at sunrise, before moving up his army, he offered a traditional sacrifice, asking for the help of the gods. By chance, a crow which was flying past dropped a clod it was carrying in its claws. Hitting the king on the head, the clod disintegrated and the earth dropped in pieces from him. The crow meanwhile took up a position on the nearest siege-tower. The tower had been smeared with pitch and sulphur; the bird's wings stuck to this and after unsuccessfully attempting to fly off it was caught by some bystanders. The incident appeared to deserve consultation with a soothsayer (and Alexander was not untainted by superstition). Aristander, the prophet who commanded the greatest credibility, declared that while the omen did indeed predict that the city would be destroyed, there was also danger that Alexander would sustain injury, so his advice was that the king should take no initiative that day. Despite his annoyance that this city was all that stood in the way of secure entry into Egypt, Alexander nonetheless deferred to the prophet and signaled a retreat.][47]

Arrian's version of the episode agrees for the most part with that of Quintus Curtius, although for him the crow (*corvus*) was in fact a carnivorous bird (*sarkophâgos ornis*) and it was a stone (*líthos*) that he dropped from his claws rather than a clod or chunk of earth (*gleba*).[48]

Quintus Curtius's designation of the bird as a crow is significant for Zurara's account of the deadly episode between Vasco Martins and the black Muslim, in that Zurara explicitly describes the latter as being "negro assim

como um corvo" (black as a crow).⁴⁹ There are further parallels: both the
crow in Quintus Curtius's account and the crow-black *mouro* in Zurara's history hit European invaders (Alexander and Vasco Martins, respectively) on
the head with a piece of earth, whether a stone or a clod of dirt, and in both
cases the immediate course of the campaign stems from this action. In the
case of Alexander, it is decided to hold off the siege due to the king's superstition (*superstitio mentis*). In the case of Vasco Martins, the Portuguese siege of
Ceuta accelerates as a direct result of his ability to maintain his composure
(*tento*), push forward, and successfully run his lance through the body of the
black Muslim. In this way too, Zurara frames the conquest of Ceuta as an
upstaging of various classical—and specifically Alexandrian—motifs.

As we have seen in the first two chapters of the present book, superstition, hubris, and the adoption of oriental mores were but three of the many
tragic flaws from which Alexander suffered, at least from the perspective of
his Roman and medieval historians. In his official account of the conquest
of Ceuta, Zurara makes subtle use of these Alexandrian flaws to demonstrate the superiority of the Portuguese to their classical predecessors. In so
crafting this narrative of masculine, Christian conquest—a passage through
death to life and through darkness to light—he asks us to keep our attention
focused in front of us and not to look to the side, where lie at least two monstrous and excessive bodies upon which this conquest is necessarily built: the
diseased body of Philippa, quietly decomposing in its dark tomb, and that of
the giant black Muslim, its flesh picked away by seagulls and crabs, its bones
bleached white by the sun.

The Ghost of Alexander and the Embrace of Kings

On Tuesday, July 8, 1578, Sebastião I of Portugal, the twenty-four-year-old
king whom Luís de Camões (c. 1524–1580) had six years earlier somewhat
hyperbolically (and strategically) compared to Alexander the Great, arrived
at the northern Moroccan coast with a large expeditionary force.⁵⁰ Ordering
his armada to await orders at Cape Spartel, Sebastião sailed on to Tangier,
where he was met the next day by Abū ʿAbdallah Muḥammad II, commonly
referred to by the name al-Mutawakkil ʿalá Allāh (Trusting in God), a deposed Saʿadi king locked in a violent dynastic struggle with his uncle, Abū
Marwān ʿAbd al-Malik I.

Two years prior to Sebastião's arrival in Tangier, 'Abd al-Malik had defeated Muḥammad al-Mutawakkil with the direct assistance of Ottoman troops from Algeria and taken control of Sa'adi Morocco. The Turks saw 'Abd al-Malik's rise to power as a way of indirectly extending their influence into the region west of the Atlas Mountains, and his two-year reign was understood by all to be a period of de facto Moroccan vassalage to Istanbul. Nehemia Levitzion describes 'Abd al-Malik's assumption of power:

> In March 1576 'Abd al-Malik entered Fez, and the *khutba* [sermon] of the Friday prayer was said in the name of the Ottoman sultan Murād. Shortly afterwards 'Abd al-Malik gave rich presents of gold to the Turks on condition that they should leave Fez and return to Algiers. 'Abd al-Malik then began to build up an army of his own, composed of Andalusians, Turks, Berbers, and Arabs, which he organized, equipped, and trained according to the Ottoman model. Years of exile among the Turks had left their impact. The new sultan spoke Turkish and adopted Turkish costume and manners. But he could also speak Spanish and Italian, and shortly after he had been freed from the Ottoman troops he re-established contacts with Spain.[51]

As Levitzion's brief narrative suggests, 'Abd al-Malik was a complex figure who, like many other members of the Sa'adi dynasty, appears to have been prepared to play all sides of a conflict at once in order to derive maximum benefit for himself and his kingdom. Dahiru Yaḥyá seconds this belief, arguing that

> despite the fact that 'Abd al-Malik ascended to the Sa'adi throne through the intervention of a power that was regarded by a large section of the Moroccan establishment as well as by Iberian states as an enemy, it was unlikely that a person of his great experience in international diplomacy and political management would trudge for long in the cautious footsteps of al-Ghālib or show the lack of purpose that characterized the short reign of al-Mutawakkil. Prompt action was needed to tackle the complex tasks of reassuring the Moroccan establishment and the country's disturbed European neighbours that his undertakings to his [Ottoman] patrons would not compromise the sovereignty of his country and were not liable to cause a change in the traditional Hispano-Moroccan *entente*.[52]

Even 'Abd al-Malik's bond of vassalage to the Ottoman Turks was likely meant as a strategic and perhaps temporary one, at least if his decisions to assemble his own army and initiate direct bilateral talks with Felipe II are any indication.

'Abd al-Malik likely knew that he would find sympathetic ears in Madrid, because the ever impecunious Felipe II was all too eager to restore trade with Morocco and, in the wake of the very recent loss of Tunis and La Goulette (1574), to engage in a kind of rapprochement, even if through a perceived proxy, with the Ottoman Turks. Portugal, a relatively minor player in Morocco by 1576 (at that time the Portuguese held colonial outposts or *praças* only in Ceuta, Tangier, and Mazagão, and their North African adventure was rapidly winding down), was another story. Sebastião had been itching for a fight in Morocco almost all his brief life, and 'Abd al-Malik's alliance with the Ottoman Turks, coupled with Muḥammad al-Mutawakkil's request for military aid, must have seemed to him a golden opportunity to put his plans into action.

According to most modern historians, Sebastião's desire for armed conflict with Muslims seems to have been matched only by his lack of subtlety in diplomatic and military matters. Echoing the judgments of José Maria de Queiroz Velloso, Charles R. Boxer, and a host of other modern historians, Bailey W. Diffie and George D. Winius describe Sebastião as an "unbalanced" and "insolent" young man who "dreamed only of leading a holy Crusade against the Moors in North Africa" and nurtured delusions of "sitting on the sultan's throne in Byzantium."[53] Whether Sebastião was here invoking the image of Alexander the Great triumphantly seating himself on the throne of Darius III at Susa is unknown, but given his humanistic education and his professed enthusiasm for martial themes, it is plausible that his Jesuit tutors acquainted him, at the very least, with Plutarch's *Life of Alexander*.[54] It is also highly unlikely that Sebastião would have been unaware of the parallels that existed between him and Alexander: both were fatherless, headstrong, young kings (Sebastião would be twenty-four when he invaded Morocco, and Alexander was twenty-two when he crossed into Asia), and both were fully committed to waging war against an "Eastern" imperial enemy. Both also had little interest in sexual contact with women: Alexander, as his Roman historians (the ones to which Sebastião would have had access) describe him, was famously more interested in war than in sex with either men or women, and Sebastião, hampered by a chronic illness that affected his genitalia, was similarly averse to sex (and, more important for his kingdom, to marriage and the production of an heir), although accounts of his private liaisons with

men have survived.[55] Like Alexander, he would become the subject of numerous legends; however, beyond the boundaries of his small kingdom, he
does not seem to have been particularly missed immediately after his death.
Juan de Silva, Felipe II's ambassador to the Portuguese court, describes him
in openly unflattering terms to Gabriel de Zayas (1526–1593) after Sebastião's
brutal defeat at al-Qaṣr al-Kbīr: "Plujo a nuestro Sñor castigar aquel Rey
mancebo y orgulloso en la propria fama que su tio y quantos bien le querian
se lo avian adiviãdo, y no me falto a mi un pedaço de este espiritu, como
por mis ultimas cartas v. m. veria" (It pleased our Lord to punish that young
king who was so proud of his own fame; his uncle and those who loved him
well had predicted as much, and I lacked not an ounce of this spirit, as your
Mercy will have seen in my most recent letters).[56]

Andrew C. Hess, working from documents in Turkish archives, has
attempted to soften these judgments somewhat, arguing that there may
also have been perfectly rational strategic reasons for Sebastião to back
Muḥammad al-Mutawakkil against 'Abd al-Malik and the Ottoman Turks in
1578. Hess maintains that while the Portuguese were fighting a losing battle
with the Turks "in places as far off as Sumatra, [they] could hardly ignore
the new Turkish threat not only to their west African outposts but also to
their naval lines of communication in the Atlantic Ocean."[57] As Hess has it,
Sebastião saw 'Abd al-Malik's rise to power as the harbinger of a new Turkish
threat in the Atlantic. There may very well be something to this argument;
however, it does not undo what has become more or less the standard explanation for Sebastião's ill-fated military involvement in Moroccan dynastic
politics. As Hess himself admits, there is also "overwhelming evidence that
crusading attitudes influenced the subsequent Portuguese decision to invade
Morocco in the summer of 1578."[58]

Whatever Sebastião's ultimate motivations for invading Morocco in the
summer of 1578, the fact remains that his decision put Felipe II, as well as the
Ottoman emperor Murād III (1546–1595), in a very awkward position:

> While the king of Portugal elected to continue the war against Islam,
> Philip II adopted the opposite policy towards the Turk. Following the Otto-
> man victory at Tunis in 1574 and the state bankruptcy of 1575, Philip II
> made a dramatic new effort to resolve the manifold pressures bearing on
> his enormous empire. Sensing that the Turk had reached the limit of his

ability to expand in the west, the Habsburg ruler launched another secret attempt to secure a treaty with the Ottomans; at the same time a succession crisis broke out among the heirs to the Safavid state in Persia. As the imperial opponent of the Ottomans in the east lost political cohesion, the Portuguese king, in alliance with the deposed ruler of the Saadi dynasty, Muḥammad al-Mutawakkil, requested military aid from Spain in order to attack the Moroccan protégé of the Ottomans, ʿAbd al-Malik. Philip II then found himself in the difficult position of conducting secret negotiations with the enemy of the Faith while being petitioned to carry on his role as a defender of Christendom.[59]

In the end, Felipe hedged his bets. He agreed to supply his nephew with men and materials, but he took no active role himself in the Moroccan war against ʿAbd al-Malik. This maneuver allowed him to continue to pursue secret diplomacy with the Turks (as the English were also doing) while protecting, at least nominally, his much-prized status as *Hispaniarum et Indiarum Rex Catholicus*.

Aware of Felipe's diplomatic efforts with the Turks, Sebastião exerted a good deal of effort to make sure that no agreements would be reached that might harm Portugal's interests. There is even textual evidence, from as late as June 6, 1578, that Sebastião was attempting to join his Habsburg relative in a three-party treaty with Murād III. In a letter drafted by Jorge da Costa, a royal scribe, Sebastião states that he would happily enter into a treaty signed by Felipe II and the Turkish emperor, and that he trusts Felipe to set favorable terms: "Mandoume elRey noso Sōr que da sua parte Respondese ao Sōr embaxador que he contente de entrar nas tregoas que se tratão antre o Serenissimo Rey de Castella seu tyo e o Turco, polo tempo E com as condiçõis com que sua Magestade nellas entrar" (The King our Lord ordered me to respond to the [Castilian] ambassador on his behalf, saying that he is content to enter into the treaties signed by the Most Serene King of Castile, his uncle, and the Turk, for the time and under the conditions that His Majesty should agree to).[60] As a sign of the importance of events in Morocco, along with their interconnectedness with imperial politics throughout the Mediterranean and beyond, Murād III, upon learning in February 1578 of Portuguese plans to invade Morocco, first ordered his governor in Tlemcen to support ʿAbd al-Malik as much as possible and then sat back to await "the outcome of the impending frontier clash before settling with [Felipe] II's representatives."[61]

Sebastião's arrival in Tangier on July 9 was to signal the beginning of what was expected to be a short war between the allied forces of Portugal and Muḥammad al-Mutawakkil on one side, and the Ottoman-backed troops of ʿAbd al-Malik on the other. The war did in fact turn out to be a brief one—just not in quite the way that Sebastião (or the Turks) might have imagined. It is in fact doubtful that any of the war's participants could have predicted that Sebastião, Muḥammad al-Mutawakkil, and ʿAbd al-Malik would all end up dead by the end of its first major battle, and that ʿAbd al-Malik's brother Ahmad (later given the title of "al-Mansūr" [the Victorious])—who had no desire to maintain even nominal ties with the Ottoman Empire—would emerge from the chaos as the undisputed king of Saʿadi Morocco.

As the story goes, Sebastião decided on July 28 to march inland from Asilah (approximately fifty kilometers south of Tangier) to meet ʿAbd al-Malik's forces in a decisive battle. Sebastião had with him about 20,000 poorly trained troops and woefully inadequate supplies. De Silva indicates the state of affairs in a letter sent to Madrid from Asilah on July 17: "Partimos tan faltos de todo que despiden los soldados castellanos que vienen de Andaluçia por no tener armas que darles" (We leave so lacking in everything that they have dismissed the Castilian soldiers that have arrived from Andalusia because they have no weapons to give them).[62] Marching southeast from Asilah, Sebastião, Muḥammad al-Mutawakkil, and their disorganized forces quickly outpaced their supply lines, forcing soldiers in full armor to march through the Moroccan countryside in late July without water. Tired and disordered, they were met on August 4 near the town of al-Qaṣr al-Kbīr (roughly sixty kilometers from Asilah) by the seasoned forces of ʿAbd al-Malik, which numbered approximately forty thousand, and a battle took place. The aftermath of this battle is well-known: Muḥammad al-Mutawakkil was killed, ʿAbd al-Malik succumbed to an illness, Sebastião disappeared completely, and the better part of the Portuguese force was taken prisoner by ʿAbd al-Malik's army, now under the command of Aḥmad al-Mansūr. Sebastião had borrowed heavily to finance the doomed expedition, and whatever money was left in Portugal was largely spent on ransoming the captives, many of whom were high-ranking nobles.[63] Almost immediately after the battle at al-Qaṣr al-Kbīr, a dynastic struggle ensued in Portugal (Sebastião had no children or siblings), and when the dust had settled in 1580, Felipe II had made himself king of the entire Iberian Peninsula. Luís de Camões, who died that same year, summed things up in his own sharp way in a letter to the captain-general of Lamego, even as the cold of death began to creep up from his feet: "Enfim acabarei a vida e verão todos que fui tão afeiçoado à minha Pátria que não só me contentei de morrer nela, mas com ela" (In the end, I will finish my life and all will see that I was so fond of my country that I not only chose to die in it, but also along with it).[64] Even though Sebastião had all but finished off his own country, he had provided Morocco with a gift that continued to give for at least two decades: wealthy from the ransoms paid to free Portuguese captives of al-Qaṣr al-Kbīr, ʿAbd al-Malik's brother Aḥmad al-Manṣūr was able to consolidate his power and even lead successful military incursions as far south as Mali. All of these events, from the debacle at al-Qaṣr al-Kbīr to Felipe II's assumption of the Portuguese throne and the Saʿadi sack of Timbuktu, were set in motion less than a month after Sebastião's quayside meeting with Muḥammad al-Mutawakkil on July 9.

The significance of the meeting in Tangier between Sebastião and Muḥammad al-Mutawakkil stems not only from what it led to, but also from what it reveals about the relations in force between Iberian Christian and North African Muslim elites, even (or especially) when these two groups were working, at least temporarily, as allies within a broader imperial backdrop. Focusing on de Silva's brief narrative account of this encounter, we see both the complex political maneuvers that imbue it with meaning as an interaction among players upon an imperial stage and, at a deeper level, the chiasmic relations of perception and experience that it reveals. In a way analogous to earlier Greek and Latin judgments of Alexander the Great's perceived loss of self within the persona of a Persian king (a move that provoked a good deal of anxiety among his Macedonian troops as well as his Olynthian court historian), de Silva documents and denounces Sebastião's own partial transformation from Christian monarch to a piece of the Saʿadi puzzle, a process that began before the Portuguese king even touched African soil.

The first meeting between Sebastião and Muḥammad al-Mutawakkil in Tangier is recorded in a letter that de Silva sent to Madrid:

A los 9 por la mañana vino el Xarife a ver al Rey a su gallera, salio Su Mag. de la popa a recebirle e la escala, yo me halle presente y adverti quel Xarife no hizo al Rey reconocimiento alguno de ynferioridad. Abraçole enchandole el braço por el cuello con semblante de tanta arrogancia como si el fuera el que hazia el socorro, y no el que le pide.[65]

[On the morning of the ninth, the Sharīf came to see the king on his galley. His Majesty came out from the rear of the ship to receive him. I was present at this meeting, and I noticed that the Sharīf made no gesture of inferiority whatsoever to the king. He hugged him, wrapping his arm around his neck with such arrogance that you would think that he was giving assistance rather than requesting it.]

As de Silva reports back to Felipe II, he is shocked that the deposed Moroccan king does not pay what he considers to be proper deference to the Portuguese monarch. Given the circumstances of Sebastião's voyage to Morocco, de Silva perhaps reasonably assumed that Muḥammad al-Mutawakkil should kneel down before Sebastião in a gesture of gratitude and obeisance befitting the agreement that the two had reached earlier in Lisbon and the enormous risks that the Portuguese king was taking on behalf of his Moroccan ally, who for two years had been nothing but a former king with limited influence and resources. Seemingly oblivious to these conditions, Muḥammad al-Mutawakkil hugs the young king, wrapping his arm around his neck in a gesture that the Spanish ambassador interprets as a sign of arrogance and an inversion of preestablished relations of power. One has to imagine that Sebastião, who was from childhood characterized by a highly inflated sense of himself, was also likely shocked by the gesture.[66]

Muḥammad al-Mutawakkil's display of collegial affection for Sebastião was, in all likelihood, a calculated show before all those present, including the Spanish ambassador, that he was renegotiating the deal that he had struck with Sebastião in Lisbon, according to which the Portuguese would be granted the city of Asilah and an annual tribute from the Saʿadi monarch in exchange for their assistance. In not showing deference to the Portuguese king, Muḥammad al-Mutawakkil put this arrangement in doubt and strongly suggested that he had no plans of surrendering any of his territory or political autonomy to Sebastião, no matter what the outcome of the war might be. The hug that Muḥammad al-Mutawakkil gave Sebastião was an act of amity and, as de Silva stops just short of pointing out, a public show of defiance. The deposed Saʿadi king was well aware, after all, of the risks that came with Sebastião's assistance: even if they were to emerge victorious from their war with ʿAbd al-Malik, it would be extremely difficult, if not impossible, ever to get the Portuguese out of Morocco. It was because of the precarious nature of his situation in relation to the Portuguese—who represented a potentially killing cure if ever there was one—that Muḥammad al-Mutawakkil embraced Sebastião as an ally, rather than kneeling down before him as a vassal. That Sebastião allowed this is perhaps an early sign that he was operating well out of his political depth.

Beyond his show of resistance to renewed Portuguese colonial designs on Morocco, Muḥammad al-Mutawakkil's embrace of the (Christian) Portuguese king was also a message carefully crafted for a Muslim audience. Like other Sa'adi rulers before him, Muḥammad al-Mutawakkil was publicly committed not to enter into any bonds of vassalage with either European or Turkish powers, a tradition that had been openly broken by 'Abd al-Malik when he opened the doors of the Sa'adi kingdom, established in 1554 by Muḥammad al-Shaykh (d. 1557), to the Ottoman sultan. This commitment had spiritual as well as political foundations.

The Sa'adis were able to consolidate power and expand from their southern Moroccan base (they were natives of the Dra'a River Valley, southeast of Ouarzazate) for two principal reasons: their public, and very convincing, call for a *jihād* against the Christian (i.e., Iberian) invaders and their Muslim allies, and their claim that they were direct descendants of Muḥammad, the Prophet of Islam. Built on a foundation of military and political power, as well as spiritual prestige, the Sa'adi dynasty represented a threat not only to Iberian colonial expansion, but also to the authority of the Ottoman Turks.[67]

The Arabic title used by members of the Sa'adi dynasty, and consistently employed by de Silva in his letters to Felipe II, was *al-Sharīf*, a term that denotes nobility derived from a direct genealogical link to the prophet Muḥammad through his grandson Ḥassan ibn 'Alī ibn Abī Tālib, the son of Muḥammad's daughter Fāṭima and his son-in-law (and first cousin) 'Alī ibn Abī Tālib. It is a title that most importantly invokes the legitimate authority that the Sa'adīs had, throughout the second half of the sixteenth century, to assert their independence from the Ottoman Turks, even though the Ottoman sultans had held, since the defeat of the Mamluks in 1517, the title of caliph. If the Ottoman sultans were recognized as the political "successors" (the literal meaning of *caliph*) to the prophet of Islam, then the Sa'adis could counter that they were his genealogical descendants and thus had just as much, if not more, right to rule in Morocco.[68]

The genealogical authority of the Sa'adis, as well as their unifying call to *jihād*, does not mean that they ever enjoyed uncontested power in Morocco. Beyond their conflicts with the Ottomans and the Iberian kingdoms, they also had to deal with local *shaykhs* and marabouts who likewise had certain claims, albeit locally centered, to power and influence. Levitzion describes this situation his in his account of the political state of affairs as Muḥammad al-Mutawakkil's grandfather, Mohammed al-Shaykh (d. 1557), came to power:

> By assuming the caliphal title of *amīr al-mu'minīn* [Leader of the Faithful], the Sharif challenged the Ottoman sultan. He was apprehensive of the latter's ambition to incorporate the whole Maghrib into the Ottoman empire. He therefore negotiated secretly with the Spaniards and reached a common agreement about a common action against Algiers. Reasons of state came before religious considerations. The Sharifian dynasty, it should be recalled, had come to power on the wave of a jihad against the Christian invaders. Along with other marabouts, the Sharif agitated against the sultans of Fez because of their co-operation with the Christian invaders. By relinquishing the jihad and by acting in collusion with the Christians against another Muslim power, the Sharif exposed himself to the criticism of the marabouts, who had already been alienated by his taxation.[69]

The *jihādi* zeal of the Saʿadis had fallen at the first hurdle, and although they continued to keep up the appearance of religious enthusiasm and purity throughout the rest of the sixteenth century, the line that they walked was at times razor thin. To consolidate power and repel the Ottomans, for example, they willingly enlisted the help of Carlos V (1500–1558), and while they were famed for expelling the Portuguese from nearly all of their coastal *praças* during the first half of the sixteenth century, by the second half their deposed king was somewhat desperately asking the Portuguese for military assistance against the reigning Saʿadi king and the forces of the Ottoman caliphate.

It follows from this predicament that Muḥammad al-Mutawakkil's demonstration of parity with King Sebastião of Portugal served also as a sign to his own supporters that he had not sold out his family's fundamental principles (unlike his uncle ʿAbd al-Malik), and that any cooperation with the Christians was but a temporary collaboration meant to achieve the greater goal of preventing the Ottomans from converting Morocco into another piece of their world empire. Sebastião was an instrument to be used to regain power and establish Moroccan autonomy once and for all. From the Moroccan point of view, the Portuguese were an unattractive means to a greater end, and the trick was to benefit from their help without giving up too much ground in the process. Following this logic, any show of deference or vassalage to Sebastião on Muḥammad al-Mutawakkil's part would have been a step in the wrong direction.

What is most interesting to me, beyond the subtlety of Muḥammad al-Mutawakkil's message to the Turks, Ibero-Christian elites, and his own followers, is that Muḥammad al-Mutawakkil makes use of Sebastião's body as the medium for his message. In a figurative sense, Sebastião's body—pulled in toward the Muslim king by the latter's arm—can be seen as a manuscript folio upon which Muḥammad al-Mutawakkil writes his declaration of independence from the Portuguese even as he declares, in a different color of ink, his gratitude for the assistance they have extended to him.

The brief hug that Muḥammad al-Mutawakkil gives Sebastião (did the Portuguese king hug him back, or did he merely stand there, paralyzed by his ally's breach of royal and colonial protocol?) constitutes a key moment in the deeply ambivalent and fraught politics of empire carried out between the Moroccans and the Portuguese, not to mention the Castilians and the Turks, throughout the sixteenth century.[70] Sebastião had come to Tangier with a significant (if rented) military force in order to provide military assistance—whether bravely or foolishly—to Muḥammad al-Mutawakkil in exchange for control of the city of Asilah and other considerations. Like Alexander crossing the Hellespont, Sebastião arrives in Tangier intent upon establishing his dominion over a loosely conceived "Orient." Unlike Alexander, however, Sebastião begins his campaign with a symbolic but significant defeat: he has not even touched land before he is converted by Muḥammad al-Mutawakkil into an unwitting instrument of Saʿadi power, with respect both to ʿAbd al-Malik and the Turks and to the Iberian colonial powers. Like Gustav von Aschenbach in Thomas Mann's Munich cemetery, Sebastião and de Silva, who narrates the exchange for Felipe II, are looking at the deposed Moroccan king, and he is determinedly, even defiantly, looking back.

As Sebastião comes from the aft of his ship to meet Muḥammad al-Mutawakkil, the latter also moves toward him and locks him up in a brief but binding embrace that would have (and both must have realized this, although for Sebastião this realization would only come after the fact) global ramifications. This hug between kings is also the tense and dangerous clinch of two nations, one the colonizer and the other colonized. It successfully negates the asymmetrical power relations and feudal bonds that Sebastião is attempting to forge (as de Silva points out) even as it pulls both men together into a shared space.

I would argue that this brief embrace goes even further: that it serves to make manifest—to the horror of the Spanish ambassador—the basic relationality that obtains between the two monarchs. This relation, a dynamic, emergent, and pretheoretical arrangement according to which each of the kings sees the other and is seen in return (touches and is touched, etc.), enfolds both, along with those witnessing their exchange, into what Maurice Merleau-Ponty would describe as a single horizon of activity and perception, while leaving intact the profound and irreducible Otherness of each. Each king's body—the complex instrument by which each perceives the world and *is* in and of it (as *Dasein*)—is drawn to that of the other, and for a moment the entire discursive framework of colonial engagement, built as it is on an inviolable and totalizing separation between (e.g., Roman or Christian) subject and (e.g., Eastern or Muslim) object, threatens to come crashing down. At the heart of this momentary shiver that runs through meticulously crafted theories of empire and colonial rule, as well as correlative theses of Iberian crusading in the Maghrebi "Orient," is the manifestation of relations of intersubjectivity (or, more precisely, what precedes and provides the conditions for intersubjectivity within what William James termed "pure experience") that belie any stable distinction between subject and object.[71] The qualitative separation between the crusading Westerner and his "oriental" collaborator, established and maintained through various modes of Bourdieusian "misrecognition" (*méconaissance*), falls away to reveal, just for a single, pregnant moment, an intercorporeal mode of being that is embedded within the same horizon of activity and experience.[72] As Muḥammad al-Mutawakkil's arm wraps around Sebastião's shoulder and their bodies come into contact, the prism through which the Spanish ambassador and his companions strive to see relations of colonial mastery falls away, and the immanent world briefly but devastatingly imposes itself, as though a spell were broken. The ambassador's letter to Felipe II, an accusation of moral decadence on the part of the Saʿadi king, should be read as a desperate and direct attempt to repair this rift, to put the prism back in its place.

It is this "natural" intercorporeality that Muḥammad al-Mutawakkil reveals as he wraps his arms around Sebastião. Through this gesture, in which he and Sebastião are pressed together in a relation of touch, de Silva perceives that something fundamental has been altered in the relation between the two monarchs. As an official observer in attendance at their meeting ("I was present at this meeting, and I noticed . . ."), de Silva is similarly implicated in this coiling over of subjectivities, which, in a certain sense, have become interwoven and irreducible.

From a Levinasian perspective, the chiasm between the two monarchs that reveals itself does not go so far as to elide the agentive Otherness that each subject—each body—inherently possesses. It is for this reason that the efforts of Felipe II's ambassador to reestablish stark and stable distinctions between (European) subject and (African) object—a project that even a writer as deft as Zurara could not ultimately sustain—emerge as something resembling a life-and-death struggle: for the embrace that Muḥammad al-Mutawakkil gives to Sebastião is a powerful and disturbing index of the radically disruptive (and murderous) embrace of death itself. In other words, even as these two men's bodies come together and touch, unconcealing the shared field of perception that shapes their being, that touch points to something much darker and frightening. That something, presented as the gathering storm clouds over Föhring in Mann's novella and as the bubonic carbuncles that reveal themselves behind Philippa's knees in Zurara's chronicle, is the violent leap that death itself makes at us and our inevitable passivity before it.

The twofold revelation represented by the monarchs' embrace is, to say the very least, highly threatening to the logic of Iberian imperial expansion into Northern Africa. On one level, it effectively elides the stable distinction between European subject and African object that supports the ideologically charged notions of reason and right comportment that justify Iberian expansion into the Maghreb. On another, perhaps more profound level, however, it indexes the passivity of the self before the agentive alterity of death—a death that "always comes to take me against my will, too soon."[73] This is so even as the political statement encoded in Muḥammad al-Mutawakkil's embrace of his younger counterpart constitutes a threat to Iberian empire on another, more readily apparent level.

In a very literal sense, in allowing himself to be embraced by Muḥammad al-Mutawakkil, Sebastião has unconcealed his own passivity before death and foregrounded his own mortality. There before all to see, the king of Portugal is thus reduced to a simple human body with absolute limits to its possibilities. This is why, in his letter to Felipe II describing the meeting in Tangier, de Silva criticizes Sebastião even as he takes an explicit stab at Muḥammad al-Mutawakkil: according to de Silva, Sebastião has lost himself in the embrace of the other, has ceded identity, agency, and ultimately his kingdom in the momentary clutch of a deposed African king. Like Alexander, who was overtaken by death in a desert much farther to the east, Sebastião no sooner arrives in Africa than he publicly surrenders himself to the Otherness that indexes his own end. A Christian Alexander in sixteenth-century armor, he emerges from the stern of his ship already doomed never to return, Aeneas-like, to the West.

CHAPTER 4

IMMORTALITY

The Promise of Asia

Qua nocte eum mater Olympias concepit,
visa per quietem est cum ingenti serpente volutari, nec decepta
somnio est, nam profecto maius humana mortalitate opus utero tulit.

[The night that his mother, Olympias, conceived him,
she dreamed that she was entangled with an enormous serpent;
nor was she deceived by this dream, for she certainly bore in her
womb a work greater than human mortality.]

MARCUS JUNIANUS JUSTINUS, *Trogi Pompei:*
Historiarum philippicarum epitoma

Com imensos trabalhos de fome, de sede, de doenças e de perigos de
morte, com a furia e impeto dos ventos e passados 90 estes se vem na Índia em outros
despantosas e crueis batalhas com a mais feroz gente e mais sabedor na guerra e
abastada das munições parela, que outra nenhuma d'Ásia.

[They suffer incredible hunger, thirst, illness, and risk of
death owing to the fury and strength of the winds; and after having passed through
ninety of these, they find in India dreadful and cruel battles with the fiercest and
most well-armed and war-ready people in all of Asia.]

FERNÃO LOPES DE CASTANHEDA,
Historia do descobrimento e conqvista da India pelos Portvgveses

AS WITH GOMES EANES DE ZURARA'S ACCOUNT OF THE TAKING
of Ceuta, the Portuguese humanist João de Barros (1496–1570) frames the
process of writing the history of Portugal's African and Asian empire as an
effort to overcome human mortality and its unwanted consequences. Central
to this framing, developed most extensively within the first prologue to Barros's sprawling *Décadas da Ásia* (Decades of Asia), is an explicit and complex
reckoning with Alexander the Great—and in at least one instance, the text-
mediated activities of those who worked to conjure up his ghost. From the

very outset of his multivolume history, directly modeled on Livy's *Histories of Rome*, Barros works at a deep, philosophical level to theorize and defend the role of the historian within the broader workings of empire, even as he brings his considerable philosophical acumen to bear on the meaning of Portugal's path to (and through) empire in relation to being-in-the-world itself.

The principal focus of Barros's *Décadas* is, as the work's title suggests, Portugal's Asian empire, which stretched along the western Indian coast from Gujarat to Cochin, held large swaths of Sri Lanka, and extended eastward in a coastal and insular patchwork that reached as far as China and Timor. In spite of this stated focus, Barros spends a good deal of time discussing Portugal's clashes with (and in) Muslim territories in North Africa and the Persian Gulf from the foundation of the kingdom in the eleventh century to the mid-sixteenth century. The title of the first *Década* ("Dos feitos, que os Portuguezes fizeram no descubrimento, e a conquista dos mares, e terras do Oriente" [Of the feats of the Portuguese in the discovery and conquest of the seas and lands of the Orient]) more or less signals this focus, because the Portuguese conquest of the seas and lands of "the Orient" begins, as we saw in the previous chapter, with Ceuta.[1] Or does Barros suggest that it begins with the Portuguese victory at Ourique in 1139, at the very moment that the kingdom of Portugal came into existence? Beyond what the reader might infer about the opening frame of Barros's "Asian" history, we find in the title of the first chapter of the initial *Década* an explicit focus not only on North Africa, but on the Iberian Peninsula as well: "Como os mouros vieram tomar Espanha e, depois que Portugal foi intitulado em reino, os reis dele os lançaram além-mar, onde os foram conquistar, ali nas partes de África como nas de Ásia, e a causa do título desta escritura" (How the Muslims came to take Hispania and how, after Portugal became a kingdom, the Portuguese kings set out across the seas, where they conquered Muslim lands in Africa and Asia; and the reason behind the title of this text).[2] As Barros presents it, this first chapter of his first *Década* is meant to carry the relatively heavy load of describing the Muslim invasion of the Iberian Peninsula at the beginning of the eighth century, the formation of the kingdom of Portugal during the twelfth century, the first impulses of overseas expansion at the beginning of the fifteenth century, and the guiding principles of the volume as a whole. This is a lot of material to cover in a short chapter (it takes up scarcely fifteen pages in the octavo-sized 1778 edition, of which the twenty-four-volume 1973 reedition is a near facsimile), and all the more so given that Barros dedicates the entire first half of the chapter to a description of the spread of Islam from the Arabian Peninsula through the Maghreb and the internal conflicts that weakened the caliphate almost from its very inception.

What emerges in the brief first chapter of Barros's first *Década*, and throughout the four *Décadas* penned by Barros as a whole (after his death in 1570, Diogo do Couto [1542–1616], best known for the scathing critique of Portuguese colonial administration in India contained in his *O soldado prático* [The Practical Soldier], would pick up the project), is a general concern with developing a philosophy of Portuguese nationalism that revolves in large part around Portugal's long and thorny relation to Islam.³ In more specific terms, however, Barros makes use of the complex and often contradictory (Roman) frameworks for understanding oriental empire—frameworks that inevitably invoke Alexander and his Asian conquests—in order to bring to the surface deep anxieties regarding human mortality and the question of Otherness. On both counts, it is through Barros's development of the notion of an Islamic Orient—stretching from Morocco to India—as an Other at once hostile and seductive, distant and all too familiar, that we most vividly see the philosophical subcurrents that shape his work as a whole. In the end, Barros's account of relations between Muslims and Iberian Christians (most but not all of it conflictive) involves a subtle and fraught theorization of what it means to be alive in the face of looming death. According to this framework, the Muslim Orient and human mortality—both the most proximal of Others for the Portuguese, but Others nonetheless—are barriers to be overcome, worked around, and reckoned with. And it is Alexander who serves, perhaps more than any other figure, as a trope for this project, this matter of death and life.

Like his Roman predecessors, most notably Livy, Barros is very much aware that any invocation of Alexander within the context of a history of oriental empire can cut both ways. Nonetheless, Barros seems to accept the troubling fact that Alexander is both Rome's and Portugal's predecessor, the mark against which they must compare and understand themselves as they establish uneven dominion over Muslim lands in Africa and Asia. As Spencer has put it, referring to the relation between the imperial discourses of Rome and Alexander the Great: "For Rome, Alexander had *always* been there first."⁴ The Portuguese, as self-styled Christian (and, by the mid-sixteenth century, Counter-Reformation Catholic) heirs to the Romans—a mask that both the Castilians and the Aragonese would likewise put on in their dealings with the Muslim Orient—inevitably saw things in a very similar way. And like Roman authors such as Seneca and Quintus Curtius, Barros also understands that Alexander serves ultimately as a call to reckon with (or an index, as in a "pointing to" or a "presence effect," as Hans Ulrich Gumbrecht has defined this term)[5] deep-seated human concerns regarding death, the self, and immortality.

Barros begins his prologue, addressed to King João III of Portugal (1502–1557), by theorizing his activities as a historian in an openly Aristotelian vein. In specific terms, he speaks of the principle of reproduction as a means of achieving a kind of immortality within nature:

Todalas cousas, muito poderoso rey, e senhor nosso, tem tanto amor á conservação de seu proprio ser, que quanto lhe he possivel trabalham em seu modo por se fazerem perpétuas. As naturaes, em que sómente obra a Natureza, e não a industria humana, cada huma dellas em si mesma tem huma virtude generativa, que quando Divinamente são dispostas, ainda que periguem em sua corrupção, essa mesma Natureza as torna renovar em novo ser, com que ficam vivas, e conservadas em sua propria especie.[6]

[All things, very powerful king and our lord, are so committed to the pres-ervation of their being that they work as much as possible, and however they can, to give themselves perpetual life. Natural beings, upon which hu-mans have no influence, have in each of them a generative capacity; and when they are divinely disposed, although they are menaced by their own corruption, Nature itself renews them in the form of a new being, through which they remain alive and preserved in their own species.]

Barros takes this passage directly from the beginning of the book 2, chapter 4 of Aristotle's *De anima*:

The acts in which [the nutritive soul] manifests itself are reproduction and the use of food—reproduction, I say, because for any living thing that has reached its normal development and which is unmutilated, and whose mode of generation is not spontaneous, the most natural act is the produc-tion of another like itself, an animal producing an animal, a plant a plant, in order that, as far as its nature allows, it may partake in the eternal and divine.[7]

This notion of reproductive immortality, so much a part of the psychology of monarchy (according to which the sons and daughters of a monarch embody not only the immortality of the self but also that of the nation), is for Barros—and, we might imagine, the monarchical reader to whom he addresses his prologue, nothing short of axiomatic.[8]

For Barros (as with Aristotle), the distributive immortality achieved through reproduction runs up against a kind of brick wall in the case of human action. As Barros puts it, because human actions (*feitos*) lack any sort of regenerative power, but rather die with the individuals that perform them, it has been necessary for humans to develop a mediating means by which their actions might approach at the very least the sort of immortality achieved by natural beings through reproduction. Adopting a quasi-Scholastic approach to language and intellect (inspired in part by Ramon Llull (1232–1315), as we shall see below), Barros speaks of this mediating means as a kind of "divine artifice" (*divino artificio*):

> E as outras cousas, que não são obras da Natureza, mas feitos, e actos humanos, estas porque não tinham virtude animada de gerar outras semelhantes a si, e por a brevidade da vida do homem, acabavam com seu author: os mesmos homens por conservar seu nome em a memoria dellas, buscáram hum Divino artificio, que representasse em futuro o que elles obravam em presente. O qual artificio, pero que a invenção delle se dê a diversos Authores, mais parece per Deos inspirado, que inventado per algum humano entendimento.[9]

> [And other things, which are not the work of Nature, but rather human achievements and actions, these die with their author due to both their lack of any animate ability to generate something like themselves and the brevity of human life. These same humans, in order to conserve their name and memory, sought out some divine artifice that might represent in the future that which they did in the present. This artifice, although its development has been attributed to various authors, seems more likely to have been inspired by God than invented by some human intellect.]

According to Barros, the means—that is, the artifice or instrument—by which humans might collaboratively resolve this seemingly intractable conflict with human mortality and the process of forgetting that it entails, is language.

Adopting what resembles a kind of proto-Marxian definition of language (as a feature of actual life-processes (*wirklichen Lebensprozesses*), or at least of the desires and anxieties about death that condition those processes), Barros defines language in this passage as both an active, embodied process and an emergent morphosyntactic system:

> E que bem como lhe aprouve, que mediante o padar, lingua, dentes, e beiços, hum respiro de ar movido dos bofes, causado de huma potencia, a que os Latinos chamam *affatus*, se formasse em palavras significativas, pera que os ouvidos, seu natural objecto, representassem ao entendimento diversos significados, e conceptos segundo a disposição dellas.[10]

> [And it pleased Him that, through the palate, tongue, teeth, and lips, a burst of air moving from the lungs, caused by a power that the Latins referred to as *affatus*, should form meaningful words such that the ears, their natural object, should represent to the understanding various meanings and concepts, according to these words' arrangement.]

The "Latin" to whom Barros is referring here is the Mallorcan philosopher Ramon Llull, whose treatise on the *affatus*, or "sixth sense," entitled in Latin *Liber de affatu hoc est de sexto sensu* (Book on the *Affatus*, that is, On the Sixth Sense) and composed in 1294, was, like much of his work, actively studied in the Iberian Peninsula (and beyond) throughout the sixteenth century.[11] Llull's concept of the *affatus*, partially adapted by Barros in the first prologue to his *Décadas da Ásia* (each *década* has its own prologue, although none is as elaborate as the first), posits that verbal speech constitutes not just a human faculty, but also a sixth sense that is unique to humans and linked to the intellect and its modes of expression. Mark D. Johnston situates *affatus* within the broader development of Llull's thought:

> The *Libre de contemplació* [Book of Contemplation], the *Rethorica nova* [New Rhetoric], and the *Liber de praedicatione* [Book on Preaching] all offer psychological and epistemological explanations of eloquence that rely on the same basic strategy, namely, rectifying the exercise of language by making the exercise of language serve as closely as possible the moral finality of human existence. Around 1294, Llull attempted to seek this same rectification through a different tactic, the integration of language into human nature itself. The result is his extraordinary proposal to classify speech as a sixth sense, which he calls *affatus*.[12]

As John Dagenais has argued, Llull's characterization of speech as a sense that is nonetheless "nobler" than the other five senses ("because God can be named in speech but cannot be seen, smelled, tasted, or touched") is in essence a theorization of what Llull saw as the power or faculty that underlies the conversion of mental images into sensual phenomena:[13]

> Because of man's dual nature, he also had two ways of knowing: spiritual things could be known only through faith and illumination; the things of this world could be known through the senses, for these things are perceived through touching, tasting, seeing, and by hearing other people talk about them. Sense impressions moved from the outside world to the inside world, sensual things became images in the mind. In discovering *affatus*, Llull is merely broadening the definition of a sense. Through *affatus* mental images become sensual. Llull has only reversed the direction of flow of sense data; the endpoints remain the same. Indeed, Llull did not try to smooth over this difference: *affatus* ". . . es pus noble que *auditus*, car *auditus* es passiva potencia en la vou, en quant la pren, e *afatus* es potencia activa, en quant la forma" (101rb).[14]

The radical physicality that Llull associates with verbal communication stems from the unmistakably sensual character of the utterance: it is heard. Llull is aware, however, that the utterance does not originate in the ear, which only perceives it, nor in the tongue, which is present even in people who are unable to speak. According to Llull, it originates in a sixth sense that actively converts the images in our mind into perceptible phenomena—the utterances by which we express our thoughts, pronounce the name of God, and, importantly for Barros, speak of our past actions.

Barros accepts Llull's account of the physicality of verbal speech, but does not go so far as Llull in presenting speech as an innate, God-given sense, such as taste or touch. This does not mean, however, that Barros discounts the role that language use plays in the "moral finality of human existence"; rather, he seeks out a kind of compromise between the dictates of universalist reason and morality and the wholly contingent features of verbal interaction and human being-in-the-world. Barros's notion of language as both "divine" and an "artifice" designed to mitigate the undesired effects (in this world and the next) of human mortality essentially allows him to walk a thin line between the idea, on one hand, of verbal communication as a social, intersubjective tool and the Lullian concept, on the other, of its status as an innate human sense linked in some direct way to the divine and the "moral finality" of our existence.

Beyond his flirtation with the universal and the divine, Barros also posits, through the theory of language developed in the first prologue to the *Décadas da Ásia*, the full integration of socially embedded language use and grammar (the *disposição* of *palavras significativas*) within a system of practice. He repeats this theory, although in a much more matter-of-fact way, through the definition of grammar that he presents within his *Grammatica da língua portuguesa* (Grammar of the Portuguese Language), published in 1540: "*Grammatica* é vocabulo Graego; quer dizer, çiençia de leteras. E segundo a difinçám que lhe os Grammáticos deram, é hum módo çerto e iusto de falár, e escrever, colheito do uso, e autoridáde dos barões doutos" (*Grammar* is a Greek word that means the science of letters. According to the definition that the grammarians gave it, it is an exact and correct mode of speaking and writing, taken from the usage and authority of learned men).[15] In this introduction to his Portuguese grammar, Barros employs both the notion of "usage" and "authority" to embed grammar—and language itself—within the social sphere of action and interaction, speaking of it, as his medieval predecessors had done, as a "mode" of social praxis.

In describing grammar and speech as he does, Barros offers a theory of language that serves to bridge, albeit *avant la lettre*, the Saussurian distinction between *langue* and *parole*. For Barros, authoritative strategies of speech are what form the system of language (as grammar), while that system (the *disposição*, or arrangement, of letters and words) in turn functions as a resource for the achievement of meaning in the broader scheme of human participation within God's creation and neo-Scholastic understandings of the workings of the intellect. In this respect, Barros seems to have been willing to forge practical adaptations of the Erasmian and Scholastic currents that shaped his thought.[16] In the first prologue to his *Décadas da Ásia*, Barros adapts Llull's concept of *affatus* to his pragmatist-Christian linguistic scheme while developing a theory of the socially embedded workings of verbal speech as complemented and shaped by the *disposição* of words themselves, insofar as it is this arrangement that constrains and facilitates the construction of meaning between the ears (as a bridge between sound and thought) and the intellect.

Having presented language as a pragmatic and embodied system of signification linked to the divine order, Barros quickly points out the limitations of verbal communication for any attempt to overcome the durational and ontological challenges that language in general is called on to resolve. Speaking of verbal language use, he points out that "não tem mais vida, que o instante de sua pronunciação, e passa á semelhança do tempo, que não tem regreso" (it has no more life than the moment of its utterance, and it passes much like time itself and does not return).[17] Having established both the promise and the limitations of verbal language, Barros then moves on to the memorializing powers of written language.

The theory that written texts, especially historical texts, served principally as an aid to both ontogenetic and phylogenetic memory and practice was by no means a new one by the sixteenth century; it had been developed since the classical period and was reflected in the popular Latin maxim "Verba volant, littera scripta manet" (literally, "Spoken words fly (away), the written letter remains"). It is also evidenced by the very first line of Herodotus's *Histories*: "These are the researches of Herodotus of Halicarnassus, which he publishes, in the hope of thereby preserving from decay the remembrance of what men have done, and of preventing the great and wonderful actions of the Greeks and the Barbarians from losing their due meed of glory; and withal to put on record what were their grounds of feuds."[18] Although the notion of "publication" for Herodotus was obviously something quite different than, say, a twenty-first-century book deal with a university press (the exact phrase that Herodotus uses in the Greek text is *historiês apódexis*, which can be translated more literally as "a setting forth of the histories"), it is also clear that what he is referring to here is the production of a written text. By the sixteenth century, the notion that historical (and even literary) texts served as a kind of countermeasure to oblivion, and thus to definitive death—we may recall both Alexander's and Ennius's comments on verbal performance, text, and memory discussed in chapter 3—had become all but commonplace. Nonetheless, it is worth focusing a bit on what Barros does with this general notion, as he develops it in subtle and specific ways.[19]

As Barros puts it, written letters, because they are not animate, do not suffer the sort of corruption that affects natural beings and phenomena such as verbal language. As inanimate things, letters endure and, in addition, do not corrupt the elements from which they are composed. What complements this freedom from corruption and imbues written language with force and meaning, however, is the "living spirit" (*espírito de vida*) that resides within them:

> As letras, sendo huns caracteres mortos, e não animados, contém em si espirito de vida, pois a dam ácerca de nós a todalas cousas. Cá ellas são huns elementos, que lhe dam assistencia, e as fazem passar em futuro com sua multiplicação de annos em annos per modo mais excellente do que faz a Natureza; pois vemos, que esta Natureza pera gerar alguma cousa, corrompe, e altera os elementos de que he composta; e as letras, sendo elementos de que se compõe, e fórma a significação das cousas, não corrompem as mesmas cousas, nem o entendimento.[20]

[Written letters, being inanimate characters, yet contain within them the spirit of life, given that they speak to us of all things. They are elements that provide assistance to nature and make things last into the future, with the multiplication of the years, in the most excellent way that Nature can achieve; for we see that Nature, in order to generate something, corrupts and alters the elements from which it is composed; and written letters, being the elements from which the form and meaning of things are composed, corrupt neither these things nor human understanding.]

Moving on from the preservational properties of written language to its role within the social sphere of moral action and interaction, Barros goes on to argue that

> o fruto destes actos humanos he mui differente do fruto natural, que se produz da semente das cousas, por este natural fenecer no mesmo homem, pera cujo uso todas foram creadas; e o fruto das obras delles he eterno, pois procede do entendimento, e vontade, onde se fabricam, e aceptam todas, que, por serem partes espirituaes, as fazem eternas.[21]

[the fruit of human actions is very different from our natural fruits, which are made from semen through the innate mortality found within all humans (for whose use all things were created). The fruit of human actions is eternal, given that it proceeds from the understanding and the will, where all actions are produced and received and, given that the understanding and the will are components of the soul, they make these actions eternal.]

It is thus an approximation to divinity, expressed both as a form of immortality and permanence and as a means of moral perfection within the social sphere of action and interaction (with origins in the soul), that written language offers to human beings. A hybrid construct, both inanimate and animate, written language, especially historical writing, offers the possibility—through the use of cultural tools—of an unending and progressively perfect life.

In light of Barros's description of its moral, temporal, and ultimately ontological powers, it follows that for him historiography imposes itself upon human beings as something of an ethico-ontological imperative. Barros stresses the natural and just obligation (*natural, e justa obligação*) that all humans have to preserve, diligently and solicitously, our achievements so that these may serve in the future as ready examples of comportment for the common good:

> Fica daqui a cada hum de nós huma natural, e justa obrigação, que assi devemos ser diligentes, e solícitos em guardar em futuro nossas obras, pera com ellas aproveitarmos em bom exemplo, como promptos, e constantes na operação presente dellas pera commum, e temporal proveito de nossos naturaes.[22]

> [It follows from this that each one of us has a natural and just obligation diligently and solicitously to preserve our actions in the future, in order to profit from good examples; and we must now also actively and constantly engage in such preservation for the common and immediate benefit of our countrymen.]

In this brief statement, Barros economically links notions of futurity (and thus mortality) with writing, praxis, and the Portuguese nation in ways at which earlier historians, such as Fernão Lopes (c. 1378–c. 1459), Zurara, Ramon Muntaner (1270–1336), Alfonso X the Learned, and Jaume I of Aragon (1208–1276) had only been able to hint.

Having reached his ethical conclusions, based on the eternal spirit of human action and the ability of written texts to preserve, without corruption or decay, that spirit in a semblance of immortality, Barros goes on to lament the impoverished state of Portuguese historiography. Complaints about the poor state of Portuguese letters in general had become something of a topos of Portuguese humanism by the middle of the sixteenth century, and these complaints often revolve around the example of rulers from antiquity, such as Alexander and Julius Caesar, who engaged in serious learning, even with sword in hand. This focus on the learning of Greek and Roman leaders (as opposed to the limited command that Portugal's elites had of even the most basic humanistic ideas) is evidenced in part by the following passage from the tercets that Luís de Camões (c.

1524–1580) composed near the end of his life to Leonis Pereira on the subject of Pero de Magalhães Gandavo's *História da província Santa Cruz a que vulgarmēte chamamos Brasil* (History of the Province of Santa Cruz That We Commonly Refer to as Brazil), published in 1573–76.[23] Speaking as the Greek god Mercury, Camões writes: "Nunca Alexandro ou César, nas confusas / guerras deixaram o estudo em breve espaço; / nem armas das ciências são escusas" (Never did Alexander or Caesar, even in the confusion of war, set aside their studies for long; for not even arms are exempt from the sciences).[24] Camões's pronouncements on the matter in stanzas 95–98 of the fifth canto of *Os Lusíadas* are even more direct, and he once again makes mention of both Alexander's military prowess and his enthusiasm for learning, especially the verses of Homer:

Dâ a terra Lusitana Scipiões
Cesares, Alexandros, e da Augustos,
Mas não lhe dâ com tudo aquelles dões
Cuja falta os faz duros e robustos.
Octavio, entre as mayores opressões
Compunha versos doutos e venustos,
Não dirâ Fulvia certo que he mentira
Quando a deixava Antonio por Glafira.

Vay Cesar sojugando toda França
E as armas não lhe empedem a sciencia;
Mas, nũa mão a pena e noutra a lança
Igoalava de Cicero a eloquencia:
O que de Scipião se sabe e alcança
He nas comedias grande experiencia,
Lia Alexandro a Homero de maneira
Que sempre se lhe sabe aa cabeceira.

Enfim, não ouve forte capitão,
Que não fosse também douto e sciente,
Da Lácia, Grega, ou Bárbara nação,
Senão da Portuguesa tão somente;

Sem vergonha o não digo, que a rezão
Dalgum não ser por versos excelente,
He não se ver prezado o verso e rima,
Porque quem não sabe arte, não na estima.

Desamor de Portugal às boas letras.
Por isso, e não por falta de Natura,
Não há tambem Virgilios nem Homeros;
Nem averá, se este costume dura
Pios Eneas, nem Achiles feros;
Mas o pior de tudo he que a ventura
Tão asperos os fez, e tão Austeros,
Tão rudos, e de ingenho tão remisso,
Que a muitos lhe dá pouco, ou nada disso.²⁵

[Portugal has given to the world Scipios, Caesars, Alexanders, and Augustuses; but it has not provided those gifts of learning whose lack makes these men hard and rigid. Octavian composed erudite and graceful verses during the worst of times (as Fulvia found out after Antony left her for Glaphyra). Caesar conquered all of France, and the exercise of arms did not keep him from learning. Rather, with a pen in one hand and a spear in the other, he equaled Cicero in eloquence. It is known that Scipio [Africanus] reached great heights in his comedies. Alexander was so devoted to the reading of Homer that he slept with a copy of *The Iliad* under his pillow.

There has been no great commander, whether Roman, Greek, or barbarian, who was not also highly learned, except among the Portuguese. I cannot say without shame that the reason we have no excellent poets is that poetry is something that we do not care about; for who knows nothing of an art cannot cherish it.

It is because of Portugal's distaste for literature, and not any natural lack, that there are no Virgils or Homers among us; and if this custom endures, neither will there be any pious Aeneas or fierce Achilles. Worst of all is that circumstances have made the Portuguese so rough, austere, rude, and intellectually remiss that many of us have little or no genius whatsoever.]

While concerned primarily with the relative lack of skilled poets working in Portuguese during his lifetime, Camões is well aware of the link—also made by Barros—between the literary representation of past deeds (whether in poetry or prose) and the commission of future ones. As he puts it, if there are

no Virgils or Homers among the Portuguese to set forth the feats of the nation's heroes, then it follows, as a direct consequence, that there will soon be
no heroes about whom to sing. Seen from this perspective, literary and historical texts not only represent human activity and cultural practice, they also
entail it. As Barros and Camões present them, these texts, themselves specific
forms of cultural practice rooted in both the social and the eternal (through
the soul), possess the power to act in the world and thus constitute another
instance of human activity. It is in fact no exaggeration to argue that Barros's
entire historiographical project (and, a fortiori, his *Grammatica da língua
portuguesa*), as well as Camões's poetic efforts, has at its center a philosophy
of language that views written texts as pragmatic and mediational forms of
language use and socially embedded praxis rather than as exclusively two-
dimensional examples of mimesis to be received and interpreted.

Returning to the specific issue of Barros's critique of Portugal's lack of
interest in its own imperial history, we find him, in his prologue to the Portuguese King João III, directly denouncing the lack of historical works dealing
with Portugal and the achievements of the Portuguese since the taking of
Ceuta over a century earlier:

> E vendo eu que nesta diligencia de encommendar as cousas á custodia das
> letras, (conservadores de todalas obras,) a Nação Portuguez he tão des-
> cuidada de si, quão prompta, e diligente em os feitos, que lhe competem
> per milicia, e que mais se préza de fazer, que dizer; quiz nesta parte usar
> ante do officio de estangeiro, que da condição de natural: Despoendo-me
> a escrever o que elles fizeram no descubrimento, e conquista do Oriente,
> por se não perderem da memoria dos homens, que vierem depois de nós,
> tão gloriosos feitos, como vemos serem perdidos de vossos progenitores,
> maiores em louvor, do que lêmos em suas Chrónicas, (segundo mostram
> alguns fragmentos de particulares escrituras).[26]

> [And as I have seen that in this duty to entrust things to the care of writ-
> ten letters (preservers of all works), the Portuguese nation has so failed to
> care for itself—although it is so ready and diligent in its actions that it is
> famed for its military force—and lends itself to deeds rather than words,
> that I have decided through this undertaking to make use of the customs of
> the foreigner rather than those of my countrymen: setting myself down to
> write out that which was done in the discovery and conquest of the Orient,
> so that these glorious accomplishments are not erased from the memory of
> those who come after us, as has occurred in the case of your ancestors, who

deserve greater glory than what we read in their chronicles (according to what we see in fragments of particular texts).]

For Barros there is a disturbing lack of proportionality between the heroic feats of the Portuguese and the written account of these feats, and as we have just seen from Barros's discussion of mortality and history in his prologue, this gap has much more significance than simply what it might mean for Portuguese national pride. Given Barros's linking of historical writing to ethical comportment and a stake in the divine, it also intersects with deeper ontological concerns regarding death, both at the individual and at the national level (vertices that intersect in the person of João III and then in his successor, Sebastião I). According to the framework that Barros presents in the prologue to his first *Década*, to neglect to write down what the Portuguese have done in Africa and Asia is to sentence the entire nation to a kind of death, one that it does not, in Barros's very interested opinion, deserve.

Directly after his exposition of written language, history, and mortality, Barros speaks of Alexander the Great. In doing so, he shifts his argument a bit, comparing his own efforts as a historian with those of the chain of historians, especially those of late antiquity, who documented the exploits and conquests of Alexander:

E na aceptação deste trabalho, e perigo a que me dispuz, antes quero ser tido por tão ousado, como foi o derradeiro dos trinta, e tantos escritores, que escrevêram a passagem, e expedição, que Alexandre fez em Asia, o qual temeo pouco o que delle podiam dizer, tendo tantos ante si; que imitar o descuido de muitos, a quem este meu trabalho *per officio*, e profissão competia. Pois havendo cento e vinte annos, (porque de tantos trata esta escritura,) que vossas armas, e padrões de victorias tem tomado posse não sómente de toda a terra maritima de Africa, e Asia, mas ainda de outros maiores mundos, do que Alexandre lamentava, por não ter noticia delles, não houve alguem, que se antremettesse a ser primeiro neste meu trabalho, sómente Gomes Eanes de Zurara chronista mór destes reinos em as cousas do tempo do infante D. Henrique: (do qual nós confessamos tomar a maior parte dos seus fundamentos, por não roubar o seu a cujo he.)[27]

[In accepting this task and the danger in which it has placed me, I should like to be considered at least as daring as the last of the thirty-some-odd writers who documented the voyage and expedition that Alexander made into Asia. This man had little to fear with regard to what they might say of him, given that so many had come before him and the worst he could do was imitate the carelessness of many others. It is against him that this present work of mine—*per officio* and by my own assertion—must compete. For the past 120 years (and it is to this period of time that the present work is devoted), your arms and monuments [*padrões*] of victory have been taking hold not only of all the coastal land of Africa and Asia, but also of other, greater worlds over which Alexander would lament, having had no knowledge of them in his lifetime. During this time, there has been no one who might be placed before me in taking up this task, except Gomes Eanes de Zurara, the chief chronicler of Portugal during the time of Prince D. Henrique (and of whose arguments we must confess having made great use, so as not to steal what is rightfully his).]

An accomplished sixteenth-century scholar with good knowledge of Greek and Latin literature, Barros would have had access to various historical treatments of Alexander.[28] At the very least, he would have known Quintus Curtius's *De rebus gestis*, Plutarch's *Life of Alexander* (he in fact makes direct and extensive use of Plutarch's *Perì dusôpías/De vitioso pudore* (On False Modesty) in his *Diálogo da viciosa vergonha* (Dialogue on False Modesty), published in Lisbon in 1540), Arrian's *Anabasis*, and Paulus Orosius's treatment of Alexander in the *Historiarum adversus paganos libri septem*; and it is against these historical texts, and their authors, that he chooses to set his own history of Portuguese empire in Asia.[29]

It is also against the conquests of Alexander that Barros sets the achievements of the Avis dynasty of Portugal. Described by Barros as conquerors "of other, greater worlds over which Alexander would lament, having had no knowledge of them in his lifetime" (a reference to Eastern Asia and Brazil), the Portuguese had effectively outdone Alexander in both military and epistemological terms; their achievements far outstripped those of their Macedonian predecessor, and they were thus potentially better equipped to approach the sort of divinity that Alexander had actively sought during his life. This conceit is dramatically presented by Camões, who knew Barros's work, in the third stanza of the opening canto of *Os Lusíadas*:

As navegações grandes que fizerão:
Callese de Alexandro, e de Trajano
A fama das victorias que tiverão,

Que eu canto o peyto illustre Lusitano,
A quem Neptuno, e Marte obedeçerão.
Cesse tudo o que a Musa antiga canta,
Que outro valor mais alto se alevanta.

[Cease celebrating the great sea voyages of the wise Greek and Trojan; stop
speaking of the fame of Alexander's and Trajan's victories; for I sing of the
illustrious Lusitanian, obeyed by Neptune and Mars alike. Silence all that
the ancient muse sings, as another, higher value now emerges.][30]

Having claimed victory over Alexander (and Trajan, another Iberian who
had conquered wide swaths of Asia Minor), Camões makes reference to the
valor mais alto that emerges with the Portuguese. This "higher value" is, like
Barros's theory of language, a hybrid construct: it refers to the heroic exploits
of the Portuguese vis-à-vis the Greeks and Romans even as it announces the
uniquely Christian framework of (re)conquest within which the Portuguese
supposedly operate. As we will see later in the present chapter, Barros makes
extensive use of this notion within his own discussion of writing, death, empire, and immortality.

Before returning to Barros's first prologue and the place of Alexander
within it, it is worth considering Camões's mention of the Macedonian king
once again in stanzas 11 and 12 of the eighth canto, in a consideration of
Afonso Henriques (1109–1185), Portugal's first king:

"Este he o primeiro Afonso," disse o Gama,
"Que todo Portugal aos Mouros toma,
Por quem no Estigio lago jura a Fama,
De mais não celebrar nenhum de Roma:
Este he aquelle zeloso, a quem Deus ama,
Com cujo braço o Mouro imigo doma,
Pera quem de seu Reino abaxa os muros,
Nada deixando já pera os futuros.

"Se Cesar, se Alexandre Rei tiverão
Tam pequeno poder, tam pouca gente,
Contra tantos immigos, quantos erão
Os que desbaratava este excellente,
Nam creas que seus nomes se estenderão

Com glorias imortais tam largamente:
Mas deixa os feitos seus inexplicaveis,
Ve que os de seus vassalos sam notaveis."[31]

["This is the first Afonso," said [Paulo] da Gama, "who took all of Portugal from the Muslims, and for whom in the Stygian lake Fame swears never again to celebrate Rome. This is that zealous monarch, whom God loves, who defeats the enemy Muslim with his arm, and tears down the walls of the Muslim kingdom, leaving nothing for future generations.

"If Caesar, if King Alexander, had had so little power, so few people, against so many enemies (such as were lined up against this excellent king), do not believe that their names would stretch out so far in immortal glories; but leave for now his inexplicable feats and look now on those notable exploits of his vassals."]

For Camões, the military superiority of Afonso with respect to Julius Caesar and Alexander is not in doubt. Camões describes Afonso's victory over the Almoravids and consolidation of the Kingdom of Portugal out of the territory seized through force of arms as "inexplicable" (*inexplicaveis*) feats, largely due to the fact that Afonso was up against forces "much larger than his own" (*tam pequeno poder, tam pouca gente*)—a likely reference to the Battle of Ourique on July 25, 1139, but also to the kingdom of León, from which the Portuguese declared their independence after the victory at Ourique. By the sixteenth century, the victory at Ourique was widely considered to have been the result of divine intervention, which increased rather than diminished the status of Afonso Henriques as a crusading Christian king. As Camões presents them, the conquests of Caesar and Alexander are, on the other hand, something less than extraordinary: the result of the strength and discipline of their enormous armies (although it should be pointed out that Alexander was significantly outnumbered in all four of his major set-piece battles in Asia) and the superior strategies of the Greek and Roman generals themselves, these victories pale in the face of Afonso Henrique's divinely assisted and nation-forming exploits.

On the other side of things, however, the Portuguese, like the Romans, are also compelled to hold their exploits up to those of Alexander, because his Asian conquests represented something of an "elephant in the room" for any Western attempt at Eastern expansion well into the early modern period.[32] Portuguese ambivalence with respect to Alexander's Asian conquests mirrors a particularly Roman conceit according to which Alexander, as a Macedonian king, was seen as somehow puny in comparison to the Julio-Claudian emperors of Rome even as he was held up as the inevitable reference point for Eastern conquest and martial greatness. As Spencer argues (see chapter 1 of the present volume), there is an inherent two-mindedness to Roman accounts of Alexander: he is at once a solitary man from a peripheral, rustic, and small kingdom that Rome and its many skilled generals had easily conquered (although it also important to remember that it was in Macedonia that Marcus Junius Brutus and Gaius Cassius Longinus, and the last vestiges of the Roman Republic with them, were brought down by the forces of the Second Triumvirate), and he is a model of ambition and vital force to be emulated, as Julius Caesar actively did throughout his life. Barros, who is commonly referred to as the "Portuguese Livy," likewise saw Alexander through this seemingly conflictive Roman lens, made all the more complex by Christian eschatology and the Iberian Peninsula's long history of conflict and collaboration between Muslim and Christian powers.

Also important for Barros's account of Portugal's Asian empire is the idea that the Portuguese, like the Romans and unlike Alexander (as well as Mark Antony, whose adopted "orientalness" was used effectively by Octavian to present him as an enemy of Rome), had successfully returned from their overseas expeditions without having given themselves over to Eastern mores. As I have pointed out in chapter 1, the figure of Aeneas—a Trojan who made the reverse trip from Asia Minor to North Africa and on to Europe, where he would found Rome—is central to this idea, framed as ascent within imperial Rome. This Virgilian frame of crossing and return continues to be central for late medieval and early modern Christian Iberian accounts of penetration into Muslim territory in the Maghreb and Asia within the broader frame of religious crusade and rebirth. When, for example, the eponymous hero of the anonymous Catalan romance *Curial e Güelfa* (ca. 1460) spends part of his Tunisian captivity studying *The Aeneid* in Arabic with his Muslim captor's daughter, it is clear that there is much more at stake in this scene than a simple lesson in Western literature, especially when this young woman explicitly invokes Dido before jumping to her death. Within Portugal, other Renaissance authors besides Barros—most notably Camões, Couto, and Fernão Lopes de Castanheda—similarly framed Portugal as a nation whose heroes had managed to cross over into the Orient and return. In this way, they effectively surpassed Alexander, who had lost himself in the East, never to come back (although the fact remains that many figures associated with the voyages of discovery, including Vasco da Gama himself, eventually died in Africa and Asia).

Camões reinforces the issue of Portuguese return in the final canto of *Os Lusíadas* through his brief but dense description of the heroic return to Portugal of Vasco da Gama and his men from their first voyage to India:

Assi forão cortando o mar sereno,
Com vento sempre manso e nunca yrado,
Ate que ouverão vista do terreno
Em que nacerão, sempre desejado:
Entrarão pela foz do Tejo ameno,
E a sua pátria e Rey temido e amado
O premio e glória dão por que mandou
E com titolos novos se illustrou.[33]

[And so they went off to cut through the serene sea, with a wind that was always gentle and never angry, until they came within sight of the land in which they had been born, always desired by them. They entered the pleasant Tagus delta, and to their homeland and much feared and loved king they bestowed the riches and glory of their journey (because he had ordered it) and he took for himself new titles.]

This return, favored by nature ("foram cortando o mar sereno, / Com vento sempre manso e nunca irado"), is at once a reconnection with a European homeland to which Vasco da Gama and his men had never ceased wishing to return (as opposed to Alexander's early decision not to return to Macedonia) and a reinforcement of the preestablished, European feudal order: the one who most directly profits from their voyage is King Manuel I (1469–1521), the seignieurial lord who had commissioned the voyage in the first place.[34] Although Camões's perspective on the voyages of discovery and the functioning of Portugal's overseas empire is famously complex, he at the very least presents in this stanza (whatever his intention may have been) the notion of return, which was central to official Portuguese accounts of imperial expansion and which runs through both Zurara's and Barros's historical accounts of that empire.

We also see the theme of return developed through the figure of Monçaide, the Tunisian Muslim interpreter whom, according to Barros, Camões, and Damião de Góis (1502–1574), the Portuguese meet in Calicut and who returns (Aeneas-like) to Europe with Vasco da Gama in order to convert to Christianity.[35] A kind of personification of the imperial/crusading fantasy that informs at least one level of Camões's epic (not unlike Martorell's *Tirant lo Blanc*), Monçaide has his origins in an episode described in Álvaro Velho's *Roteiro da primeira viagem de Vasco da Gama* (Journal of the First Voyage of Vasco da Gama):

> E ao outro dia [Maio 21] isso mesmo vieram êstes barcos aos nossos navios, e o capitão-mor mandou um dos degredados a *Calecute*; e aqueles com que êle ia levaram-no aonde estavam dois mouros de *Tunes*, que sabiam falar castelhano e genovês. E a primeira salva que lhe deram foi esta, que se ao diante segue: "Ao diabo que te dou; quem te trouxe cá?" E preguntaram-lhe o que vinhamos buscar tão longe. E êle respondeu: "Vimos buscar cristãos e especiaria." Êles lhe disseram: "Porque não manda cá El-Rei de *Castela*, e El-Rei de *França* e a Senhoria de *Veneza*?" E êle lhe respondeu que: "El-Rei de *Portugal* não queria consentir que êles cá mandassem." E êles disseram que: "Fazia bem."[36]

> [The following day [May 21] these boats approached our ships, and the admiral ordered one of our convict crewmen to go to Calicut; and those that went with him brought him to where there were two Muslims from Tunis, who knew how to speak Castilian and Genoese. And the first shot that they fired at him was the following: "The devil take you! Who brought you here?" And they asked him what we had come looking for so far away. And he responded: "We've come looking for Christians and spices." And they said to him: "Why isn't the King of Castile, the King of France, or the Doge of Venice in charge of this expedition?" And he responded to them that: "The King of Portugal did not wish to consent that they be in charge here." And they said to him that: "He did the right thing."]

As Velho describes it, the Portuguese have essentially sailed halfway around the world only to find that Tunisian Muslims (Spanish-speaking ones at that) have already established themselves there as traders. Tellingly, Velho also characterizes the first contact that the Tunisian pair has with the Portuguese *degredado* (whom the eyewitness Gaspar Correia (c. 1495– c. 1561) lists as a Portuguese converso named João Nunez) as a "shot" or "opening salvo" fired at him: "a primeira salva que lhe deram foi esta" (the first shot that they fired at him was the following).[37] Like the red-haired man staring back at Gustav von Aschenbach at the Munich streetcar stop, the two anonymous Tunisians openly challenge the Portuguese at Calicut, who looks/fires/speaks right back at them even as they are looked/fired/spoken at. That Velho also describes the reaction of the Portuguese to the presence (and stance) of these Hispanophone Muslims as one of *espanto* (an equal mix of surprise, fear, and dread) adds to the sense that there is something truly disturbing—and triggered by contact with this Muslim Other—at work from the very first contact that the Portuguese have with their future colonies in India. It is essentially this feeling or mood, experienced as dread or anxiety, that the narrative figure of Monçaide (from the Arabic *musā'd*, "one who helps") is called on to mitigate in *Os Lusíadas*: rather than reckoning with a defiant (nameless, and plural) Muslim Other, Camões, following Barros and Góis, flattens out that Other into a single collaborator and future Christian convert whose very name indexes his supporting role in the imperial project. That Monçaide also accompanies the Portuguese back to Lisbon and converts to Christianity (a historical fact supported by mention of him, though not by name, in a letter from King Manuel of Portugal to Cardinal Jorge da Costa (1406–1508), sent after Vasco da Gama's return) situates his story, and that of Portuguese empire, squarely within a heroic, epic tradition that includes both Aeneas and Scipio Africanus.

For a more open critique of this notion of return, we may turn to Gil Vicente (1465–1537), who as early as 1509 had dramatized the enduring effect that Eastern exploration and expansion could have on those who participated in it. At the very end of his *Auto da Índia* (Act of India), Vicente presents the serially cuckolded husband of a Portuguese lady, recently back from a sea voyage to India. His wife, who over time had come to dread his homecoming, greets him: "Jesu, quão negro e tostado! Não vos quero, não vos quero" (Jesus, how black and tanned! I do not love you, I do not love you). This blackness that lingers upon the husband from his Asian journey is not, as Blackmore has argued, simply the effect of overexposure to the sun, but rather a symptom of contact with the melancholic humors associated with the Orient.[38] In essence, the husband has returned from the East, but he has brought the humoral ill effects of that region back to Portugal with him. The Virgilian return, at least as far as Vicente understood it, carried with it a lingering contagion, the seed of death (and social ruin) that was from the very outset associated with the Orient.

Barros takes a more subtle, philosophical tack than Vicente in the first chapters of his *Décadas da Ásia*; however, his framing of Portuguese expansion into the Orient as a response to Macedonian and Roman (and even mythological) incursions into the East serves to embed his account of Portugal's early imperial history within a ready-made narrative of heroism and Western dominance, but also of illness, loss, and death. This is Barros's debt to the classical tradition that he indexes, but it is also part of his more immediate debt to Zurara, who understood perhaps better than any fifteenth-century writer the long shadow of death that hung over Portugal's overseas colonial adventures within Muslim Africa. That Barros's central mission is to overcome Portugal's mortal limitations through an extended (if not Herculean) act of historical narration is what, in the end, most directly links him to Alexander, at least as he attempts to frame things.

As Barros has it, it is with respect to the entextualizing of their imperial feats that the Portuguese lagged far behind the Greeks and Romans, as well as some of their contemporaries. While Barros can cite at least thirty historians of Alexander's expedition into Asia (a rough estimate on his part, but not far from the mark), he acknowledges Zurara as his only predecessor, although it was years after Zurara's death in 1474 that the Asian empire even became a realistic possibility. And so Barros strikes out mostly on his own to document the workings of an empire that far exceeded, in terms of territory and distance between its many points, any imagined by Alexander. And for Barros, Portuguese exploration and colonial expansion in Asia takes on its true significance when compared to Alexander's earlier campaigns and accomplishments. Like Alexander, the Portuguese emerged from the periphery of Europe to take control of whole sections of Africa and Asia. Unlike Alexander, Barros argues, the men responsible for Portugal's expansion also put in place an administrative framework that allowed them to stay in power for an extended time. This is in part what is so difficult about Barros's task relative to that of Alexander's historians: he has a much greater period of time to cover and fewer previous studies to consult. Situating himself within the broader project of exploration and heroic achievement in the East, Barros in fact goes so far as to form a link between the navigational and military feats of the Portuguese and the challenge presented by trying to give a detailed account of them 120 years after the beginning of the process. According to Barros's logic, just as the Portuguese have eclipsed the achievements of the Macedonians, so he is taking on a greater and inherently riskier task than those historians (including such Latin authors as Quintus Curtius, Arrian, and Orosius, who could rest on the shoulders of those who had preceded them) who had documented Alexander's march to the Punjab and back as far as Babylon. That Barros also explicitly models his history of Portuguese empire on Livy's *History of Rome* and Zurara's chronicles relating the Portuguese conquest of Ceuta and Guinea lends even greater complexity to his account.[39] How does this framing play out within the *Décadas da Ásia* as a whole? This question is difficult to answer, given the history that surrounds the redaction and publication of this multivolume work. Barros wrote the first three *Décadas da Ásia* and published them in Lisbon in 1552, 1553 (both with Germão Galharde), and 1563 (this time with the printing press of João de Barreira). The fourth *Década*, also written by Barros, was not published until 1615 (Madrid: Aníbal Falorsi), over forty years after Barros's death. Near the end of the sixteenth century, Diogo do Couto (1542–1616), having no knowledge of the existence of Barros's as yet unpublished fourth *Década*, wrote his own version, which was published in Lisbon by Pedro Craesbeeck in 1602. It is for this reason that we currently possess two versions of the fourth *Década*, that of Barros, written before 1570 and published in 1615, and that of do Couto, written near 1600 and published in 1602. Do Couto managed to publish the fifth, sixth, and seventh *Décadas* between 1612 and his death in 1616 (all in Lisbon by Pedro Craesbeeck). His eighth *Década*, however, was not published until 1673 (once again in Lisbon, this time by João da Costa and Diogo Soares). The ninth, tenth, and eleventh *Décadas* of Diogo do Couto were never published; however, the first five books of the twelfth, also written by Couto, was published in Paris (publisher unknown) in 1645.

The popularity that the *Décadas* enjoyed during the early modern period, more outside of Portugal than within it, is evidenced in part through the two-volume Italian translation of the work published in Venice in 1562 by Vincenzo Valgrisio. Also noteworthy is a brief exchange in a short dramatic work by Vicente Suárez de Deza (fl. ca. 1657) entitled, "La casa de los genios y la dama general" (The House of the Geniuses and the Intelligent Lady) and published in 1663 as part of the *Parte primera de los donayres de Tersícore* (First Part of the Graces of Tersicore) in Madrid by Melchor Sánchez. In it, a woman listed as Dama 1 asks a Don Roque if Indian (i.e., South Asian) women are "as beautiful as the men are handsome." He responds by asking her if she has seen any Indian women before. Her response to this question makes direct mention of Barros's *Décadas* as well as Fernão Mendes Pinto's *Peregrinação* (Travels) and lends more weight to the hypothesis, advanced by Diogo Barbosa Machado (1682–1772) in his *Biblioteca lusitana* (Lusitanian Library), that Suárez de Deza himself was Portuguese: "Yo no, pero téngolo leído en las *Décadas* de Barros y en el Fernán Méndez Pi[n] to" (Not personally, but I've read as much in the *Decades* of Barros and in Fernán Méndez Pi[n]to).[40] The mention here of Barros and Mendes Pinto, two sixteenth-century Portuguese authors (albeit both widely known and translated throughout the Iberian Peninsula and the rest of Europe), is not casual; it speaks to the central place that Portuguese historical discourse had occupied by the seventeenth century in Western European notions of the peoples and cultures of Asia. As Barros had explicitly hoped in the prologue to his *Décadas*, the Portuguese had supplanted Alexander in both military and epistemological terms. That Suárez de Deza also links the sober and moralizing Barros with Mendes Pinto, the author of a highly entertaining, though largely exaggerated and picaresque, first-person account of travel from Lisbon to Japan and back near the end of the sixteenth century, speaks to the varied images of the Orient that had taken shape within the Iberian Peninsula—and more specifically within the court society of Madrid—by the middle of the seventeenth century.

Chapter 1 of Barros's first *Década* begins with a dense account of the expansion of Islam from the Arabian Peninsula into the once-Roman province of Hispania:

> Alevantado em terra de Arábia aquele grande antecristo Mafamede, quási nos anos de quinhentos noventa e três de nossa Redenção, assi lavrou a fúria de seu ferro e fogo de sua infernal seita, per meio de seus capitães e califas, que em espaço de cem anos, conquistaram em Ásia toda Arábia e parte da Síria e Pérsia, e em África todo Egipto aquém e além do Nilo.[41]

> [Brought up in the land of Arabia around the year 593 of our Redemption, that great Anti-Christ Muhammad exercised the fury of his steel and the fire of his infernal Sect through his Captains and Caliphs, and in the space of one hundred years, they conquered in Asia all of Arabia and part of Syria and Persia, and in Africa all of Egypt on both sides of the Nile.]

It may seem somewhat strange to modern readers that Barros begins his history of Portuguese empire in Asia with an account of the rise of Islam in the Arabian Peninsula, but this account is in fact an integral and necessary part of his broader argument. Conscious of his Roman and Greek predecessors and committed to placing the Portuguese at the zenith, because of their Christian faith and the global reach of their domain, of a progressively higher chain of Western empires, Barros frames Dār al-Islām as the Romans had framed Carthage and the Macedonians had framed Achaemenid Persia: as encroaching Eastern enemies not only to be defeated but to be decisively supplanted by a new, even more expansive Western empire. As a kind of night to Portugal's day, the broader Muslim *umma* serves within Barros's imperial vision as an oriental empire threatening the very order and safety of Western Christian society. Having established this ideological frame, Barros then goes to great lengths to present his history of Portuguese expansion into Asia as a response to the threat of Muslim aggression and a continuation of the Christian crusade against Islam that had begun in the Iberian Peninsula, and out of which the kingdom of Portugal had emerged in the twelfth century.

Before speaking of Luso-Christian advances, however, Barros must identify for his readers precisely whom it is that they are fighting and how their initial victories and eventual schisms fit into the larger Christian scheme of crime, punishment, and redemption. In a highly economical account of the Muslim invasion of the Iberian Peninsula in the early eighth century and the seventh-century split between Sunni and Shīʿa Muslims over the issue of the caliphate, Barros mixes history with Christian theology in a passage reminiscent of several sections of the universal history of Paulus Orosius:

Os quais a força de armas devastando e assolando as terras, se fizeram senhores da maior parte da Mauritânia Tingitânia, em que se compreendem os reinos de Fez e Marrocos, sem até este tempo a nossa Europa sentir a perseguição desta praga. Peró vindo o tempo té o qual Deus quis dissimular os pecados de Espanha, esperando sua penitência acerca das heresias de Arrio, Elvídio e Pelágio de que ela andou mui iscada (posto que já per santos concílios nela celebrados fossem desterradas), em lugar de penitência acrescentou outros mui graves e púbricos pecados, e que mais acabaram de encher a medida de sua condenação, que a força feita à Cava, filha do Conde Julião (ainda que esta foi a causa última e acidental, segundo querem alguns escritores).

Com as quais cousas provocada a justiça de Deus, usou de seu divino e antigo juízo, que sempre foi castigar púbricos e gerais pecados, com púbricos e notáveis pecadores, e permitir que um herege seja açoute de outro, vingando-se per esta maneira de seus imigos per outros maiores imigos. E como naquele tempo estes arábios eram os mais notáveis que ele tinha, infestando o império romano e perseguindo sua católica Igreja, primeiro que per eles castigasse Espanha os quis castigar na sua heresia, acendendo antre eles um fogo de compitência, sobre quem se assentaria na cadeira do pontificado de sua abominação com este título de califa, que naquele tempo era a maior dinidade da sua seita.[42]

[The force of their arms devastating and ruining the land, the Arabs made themselves lords of the greater part of Mauritania and Tingitania, in which are contained the kingdoms of Fez and Morocco, although at this time our Europe did not as yet feel the persecution of this plague. The moment arrived, however, when God decided no longer to overlook the sins of Hispania or to await its penitence for the heresies of Arius, Helvidius, and Pelagius that so contaminated the region (holy councils celebrated in the province had already ordered their exile). Instead of penitence there grew other very grave and general sins, and in the end the region sealed its condemnation when the Cava, the daughter of King Julian, was taken by force, although this was the final and accidental cause, according to some writers.

Having through these things provoked the justice of God, Hispania received his divine and ancient judgment, which has always been to punish the general and public sins of notable and public sinners, and permit that one heretic be the whip that lashes another, avenging himself in this way of his enemies through his greater enemies. And at that time these Arabs were the most notable enemies that he had, infesting the Roman Empire and persecuting his Catholic church. Although it was through the Arabs that God punished Hispania, he wished also to punish them for their heresy, and so he had even earlier ignited within them a conflictive fire that revolved around the question of who would occupy the pontifical seat of that abomination they call the caliph, which was at that time the greatest title in their sect.]

Barros cites as the direct source for his account of the schism over the succession of the caliph and the early spread of Islam a text called *Larigh*, "hum Sumario dos feitos, que fizeram os seus Calyfas na conquista daquellas partes do Oriente" (summary of the feats of the caliphs in the conquest of the Orient).[43] This *Larigh* is almost certainly a corruption of the Arabic and Persian term *tārīkh*, which means, in the most generic sense, "history." It is not known with complete certainty which Arabic or Persian text Barros is referring to here; however, it is known that he made extensive use of a Portuguese translation of the history of the kingdom of Hormuz (no longer extant) written in Persian and attributed to a Hormuzi king named Tūrān Shāh (though not Tūrān Shāh IV, who occupied the throne, much diminished by the Portuguese occupation, until his death in 1521). It was the original version of this text that the Portuguese converso Pedro Teixeira (fl. c. 1600) studied and translated during his stay in Hormuz from 1593 to 1597, and he seems not to have been aware of an earlier Portuguese version of the text when he composed his own translation, in Portuguese and then in Spanish, as part of his *Relaciones de Pedro Teixeira d'el origen descendencia y succession de los reyes de Persia, y de Harmuz, y de un viage hecho por el mismo autor dende la India Oriental hasta Italia por tierra* (Narrative of Pedro Teixeira on the Origin, Descent, and Succession of the Kings of Persia and Hormuz, and on a Land Voyage that the Author Took from East India to Italy), published in Antwerp in 1610. In book 2, chapter 2 of his second *Década*, Barros even mentions Tūrān Shāh's *Tārīkh* by name before presenting his own summary of the origins of the kingdom of Hormuz: "O princípio deste Reyno Ormuz, (segundo contam as *Chronicas dos Reys* delle, que nos foram interpretadas de Persico) foi per esta maneira. . . ." (The beginning of this kingdom of Hormuz [according to what is recounted by the *Chronicles of the Kings of Hormuz*, which was translated for us from Persian] came about in this manner . . .).[44] The period that Barros describes as the beginning of the kingdom of Hormuz is much later than the first century of Islam (he situates it at 1273 CE), so it is unlikely that Tūrān Shāh's *Tārīkh* is the text to which he is referring at the beginning of the first *Década*. A more likely source would be the Persian historian Abū Jaʿfar Muḥammad ibn Jarīr al-Tabarī's *Tārīkh al-rusul wa al-mulūk* (History of the Prophets and Kings), an Islamic history stretching from Creation to 915 CE. This expansive chronicle, completed not long before al-Tabarī's death in 923 CE, was a canonical work of history by the sixteenth century, and it is entirely possible that Barros commissioned a Portuguese translation of certain sections of it while writing his *Décadas*.[45]

Beyond Barros's use of Arabic and Persian sources for his history of Islamic expansion, what is most important for an adequate understanding of the ideologies that underlie his work as a whole is that he explains that expansion into the Iberian Peninsula as part of God's plan to root out Christian heresies in that region. Barros presents this notion very clearly: "it was through the Arabs that God punished Hispania."[46] As Barros has it, God is perfectly willing to use one group of heretics to punish another—"and [He] permit[s] that one heretic be the whip that lashes another"—a point that underscores the sense, common within learned circles during the Middle Ages and into the early modern period, that the origins of Islam were not those of a wholly other faith but rather a heretical splitting off from Christianity.[47] God's punishment for the Muslims, however, is to place within them "a conflictive fire" that causes dissent and schism within their community and ultimately provides an opening for Christian victory over them.

Having framed the expansion of Islam into the Iberian Peninsula during the early eighth century as part of a divine plan to root out Christian heresy and having likewise pointed out the internal flaw of schism—with respect to the Christians and one another—that will prevent the Muslims from remaining in power (a flaw graphically depicted by Dante in canto 28 of the *Inferno*), Barros is then free to describe the process of Christian reconquest out of which the kingdom of Portugal will emerge.[48] This notion of reconquest leads him almost immediately to forge a link between the Portuguese nobility and the concept of martyrdom:

> Donde podemos afirmar que esta casa da Coroa de Portugal está fundada sobre sangue de mártires, e que mártires a dilatam e estendem por todo o Universo, se este nome podem merecer aqueles que, militando pola fé, oferecem suas vidas a Deus em sacrefício, e dotam suas fazendas a sumptuosos templos que fundaram; como vemos que fez el-Rei Dom Afonso Hanriques, primeiro fundador desta Casa Real, e o Conde Dom Hanrique, seu padre, e toda a nobreza e fidalguia que os seguia nesta confissão e defensão da fé, da qual verdade são testemunho mui dotados e magníficos templos deste reino.[49]

> [From which we can affirm that this royal house of Portugal is founded on the blood of martyrs; and martyrs stretch and extend this house throughout the entire universe if they are worthy of this name who, fighting for the faith, offered their lives to God in sacrifice and then donated their estates to the construction of sumptuous temples, as was done by the king Afonso Henriques, the founder of this royal house, and the count Henrique, his father, and all of the higher and lesser nobility who followed them in this confession and defense of the faith. Proof of this is found in the very rich and magnificent temples of this kingdom.]

In what reads at once as a superficial celebration of Portuguese nationalism through the blood of its noble martyrs and a deeper account of the nation's efforts to render itself eternal (if not absolutely timeless), Barros frames Portugal's birth as a process rooted in death and martyrdom. What makes this framing especially complex is that for Barros this process of martyrdom, and the problem of human mortality for the discourse of empire that he is attempting to construct, is ongoing and without any foreseeable end. The violent struggle against Islam out of which the Portuguese nation was forged has, in effect, never ended but merely evolved into the battles and wars associated with Portugal's occupation of formerly Muslim lands in Africa and Asia: a perpetual "state of exception" that defines both Portuguese sovereignty and the rise of Portugal as a modern nation state.[50] Moving from the defensive, Portugal has taken the offensive, but the process—and the shadow of death that covers it—has not changed. Portugal's battle against Islam is, as Barros presents it, what Portugal is; it is a war that is ultimately waged against itself and the specter of death that waits for its heroes and historians alike, a continuous presence always lingering, but never fully present.

The dark stain of mortality that so discolors the imperial cloth that Barros attempts to weave is not, of course, unique to Barros. As I discussed in chapter 1, it likewise characterized nearly all Roman accounts of Alexander's conquests, and it gave shape to Roman theories of national origin and destiny. Barros makes explicit reference to this in his account of the earliest moments of Portuguese expansion overseas:

E assi estava limpa deles no tempo del-Rei Dom João o primeiro, que desejando ele derramar seu sangue na guerra dos infiéis, por haver a bênção de seus avós, esteve determinado de fazer guerra aos mouros do reino de Grada e por alguns inconvenientes de Castela, e assi por maior glória sua, passou além-mar em as partes de África, onde tomou aquela Metrópoli Ceita, cidade tam cruel competidora de Espanha, como Cartago foi de Itália.

Da qual cidade se logo intitulou por senhor, como quem tomava posse daquela parte de África e deixava porta aberta a seus filhos e netos pera irem mais avante. O que eles mui bem compriram, porque não somente tomaram cidades, vilas e lugares, nos principais portos e forças dos reinos de Fez e Marrocos, restituindo à Igreja Romana a jurdição que naquelas partes tinha perdida depois da perdição de Espanha, como obedientes filhos e primeiros capitães pola fé nestas partes de África, mas ainda foram despregar aquela divina e real bandeira da milícia de Cristo (que eles fundaram pera esta guerra dos infiéis) nas partes orientais da Ásia, em meio das infernais mesquitas da Arábia e Pérsia, e de todolos pagodes da gentilidade da Índia de aquém e de além do Gange, parte onde (segundo escritores gregos e latinos) excepto a ilustre Semirames, Baco e o grande Alexandre, ninguém ousou cometer.[51]

[And so Portugal was clean [*limpa*] of Arabs by the reign of King João I. This king, wishing to spill his blood in the war against the infidels, in order to have the blessing of his grandparents, was determined to make war against the Muslims of the kingdom of Granada and to address some of Castile's affronts; to his greater glory, he went over the sea to Africa, where he took Ceuta, a city that competed so cruelly with Hispania, as Carthage had done with Italy.

He later became lord of this city, and he took possession of that part of Africa and left the door open to his children and grandchildren to move even further forward. This they managed to do very well, because they not only took cities, villages, and territory in the principal ports and forts of the kingdoms of Fez and Morocco, restoring, as obedient sons and captains of the faith, the Roman Church's jurisdiction in these parts of Africa that it had lost after the conquest of Hispania, but they also unfurled that divine and royal banner of the army of Christ (which they founded for this war against the infidels) within East Asia, in the midst of the infernal mosques of Arabia and Persia, and among all the pagan pagodas of India on the near and far side of the Ganges, a place where (according to Greek and Latin writers) no one dared to enter, except the famous Queen Semiramis, Bacchus, and Alexander the Great.]

These two paragraphs contain a dense blend of many of the major concepts that shape Barros's history of empire. He begins by speaking of João I's desire to spill his own blood (*seu sangue*) in a war against Muslims, thus invoking the notion of martyrdom that lies at the center of his version of Portuguese nationalism. He then explicitly links the Iberian Peninsula to the Italian Peninsula and Ceuta to Carthage, in this way suggesting a similar link between (imperial) Portugal and (imperial) Rome. This linking of Portugal to Rome, through the 1415 conquest of Carthage's would-be Moroccan doppelgänger, effectively forges a connection between Renaissance Portugal and the complex ontological and epistemological frameworks, discussed in chapter 1, that directly linked Roman conquest in the Orient with their most notable (and notorious) predecessor, Alexander the Great. As if to drive home this association, Barros then goes on to mention Alexander by name, presenting him along with Bacchus and the legendary Ninevite Queen Semiramis, who, according to the second book of Diodorus Siculus's *Historical Library*, had likewise extended her dominion into India. Barros joins the Portuguese to this ancient trio, making the claim that the former had "unfurled that divine and royal banner of the army of Christ" on both sides of the Ganges River, a

place that only Bacchus, Semiramis, and Alexander—at least, if Greek and
Roman historians are to be trusted—had dared to venture.[52]
There is an almost Joycian density of reference to the preceding two
paragraphs. Barros brings together the Portuguese struggle against Islam, a
struggle out of which the kingdom had come to be and continued to grow,
with the Roman struggle against Carthage and then moves deftly to speak
of his nation's continued military efforts in the name of Christ within Persia,
Arabia, and India. It is in India that he links the campaigns of the Portuguese
to those of Alexander, and through the concept of overseas crusade—begun
in Ceuta—that he links the struggle against Islam to Alexander's military
conquests. Barros's contemporary, Fernão Lopes de Castanheda (c. 1500–
1559), whose *História do descubrimento e conquista da Índia* (History of the
Discovery and Conquest of India) came to eclipse, at least within Portugal,
the popularity of the *Décadas da Ásia*, frames the Portuguese conquest of
India in almost exactly the same way:

> Tito Livio, Historiador romano, muyto alta e sereníssima Raynha N.S., Pola
> história que escreveu da fundação de Roma e do mais que os Romãos fize-
> rão na conquista de seu Império, foy antreles tão celebrado, que por isso
> ho teverão em grande admiração nas províncias estranhas. Em tanto que
> muytos naturais delas, sendo Roma naquele tempo a mais notável cousa
> do mundo, mais hião a ela por ver a Tito Livio que a suas grandezas. E ho
> mesmo fizerão outros muytos historiadores de suas cousas, que por ven-
> tura não forão tão famosas, se aqueles que as escreverão as não souberão
> tão bem representar. Porque na sua eloquencia consiste muyto, serem elas
> grandes ou pequenas. O que sentindo bem aquele grande Alexandre, teve
> Aquiles por tão bem-aventurado em ter Homero por escritor de suas fa-
> çanna, (como testificam aqueles dous versos tão notorios que disse quando
> vio a imagem d'Aquiles) e desejou tanto que Homero fora em seu tempo
> pera escrever suas cousas, que, dizendo-lhe hûa vez um seu que lhe levava
> hûa grande nova, perguntou se era de Homero resucitado.[53]

> [Livy, the Roman historian, Most Noble and Serene Queen, was so cel-
> ebrated among the Romans—due to the history that he wrote of the
> foundation of Rome and of what the Romans did in the conquests that
> built their empire—that he was even held in great admiration in the for-
> eign provinces. This was so much the case that many of the residents of
> these provinces, Rome being the most notable thing in the world, more
> frequently went there to see Livy than any of Rome's great wonders. And

many other historians did the same for their nations, which would not have been that famous had those who wrote about them not known how to represent them well. Because much rides upon the eloquence of writers, whether one's accomplishments are big or small. Alexander the Great was well aware of this when he held Achilles to be so fortunate in having Homer to document his feats (as evidenced by the two well-known verses that he uttered when he saw the image of Achilles) and when he expressed his wish that Homer were alive then to write of his conquests. Alexander once even asked one of his men who brought him some great piece of news if he was Homer brought back to life.]

This passage from the prologue to the third volume of Castanheda's text touches on many of the same elements introduced by Barros, although it lacks the philosophical depth of the prologue to the *Décadas da Ásia*. Castanheda presents written history as a weapon against oblivion, enters into open competition with the Greeks and Romans (as well as Greek and Roman literati), and makes explicit mention of Alexander the Great, specifically the Macedonian king's lament that Homer was not alive to sing of his exploits.[54]

In invoking the connection between Homer and Alexander, Castanheda reproduces a commonplace that ran through various Iberian texts of the medieval and early modern period. The *Libro de Alexandre*, for example, makes a direct reference to Alexander's acknowledgment of the poetry that served to immortalize Achilles. Arriving at Troy, Alexander and his army arrive at the tomb of Achilles, which is adorned with "good verses" (*buenos viersos*). The *Libro de Alexandre* does not mention Homer by name, but it does speak to the skill of the poet: "qui lo versificó fue omne bien letrado, / ca puso grant razón en poco de dictado" (who wrote those verses was a learned man, as he put a good deal of meaning into very few lines).[55] The lines themselves read:

Achilles so, que yago so est mármol çerrado,
el que ovo a Éctor el troyano rancado;
matóme por la planta Paris el perjurado,
a furto, sin sospecha, yaziendo desarmado.

[I am Achilles who rests below this hard marble, he who defeated the Trojan Hector; the lying Paris killed me with a devious shot to the sole of my foot while I was lying unarmed.][56]

Alexander's reaction to this epitaph is an echo, by way of Walter of Châtillon, of the scene at Troy described by Arrian:

> Quando ovo el rey el pitafio catado,
> dezié que de dos viersos nunca fue tan pagado;
> tovo que fue Achiles omne aventurado
> que ovo de su gesta dictado tan honrado

> [When the king had read the epitaph, he said that never had he profited so much from two verses; he held Achilles to be a lucky man that his feats should be expressed with such admirable words.[57]

Turning back to the passage from Castanheda's *História* that I have just cited, we see how Castanheda deals directly with the scene of Alexander at Troy, using it to argue that the greatness or insignificance of one's accomplishments rests squarely on the eloquence of the historian or poet: "much rides upon the eloquence of writers, whether one's accomplishments are big or small. Alexander the Great was well aware of this when he held Achilles to be so fortunate in having Homer to document his feats."[58]

Turning our attention back to Barros, it should be pointed out that the *Décadas da Ásia* is not the only work in which he forms a conscious point of intersection between Islam, Portugal, Alexander, and the theme of empire. In his *Ropicapnefma* (Spiritual Merchandise), a work of moral philosophy published in 1532 (Lisbon: Germão Galharde), Barros speaks of the conflict between Muslims and Christians in terms of Alexander's supposed solution to the problem of the Gordian knot:

> Se [a] alma era imortal, se ha pena e gloria, quem tem a verdade do que se deve crer de Deos e de suas obras: Gentios, Judeus, Cristaos ou Mouros. E esta derradeira, a meu ver, tem piores nos pera desatar que os de Alexandre. Razão. Pera isso trago comigo a verda-le, que corta mais que a espada de Alexandre, pera rr.e não deter em desatar laços infernais, mas decepa-los em raiz.[59]

> [If the soul is immortal and experiences punishment and glory, who is right with respect to what should be believed about God and his works: Pagans, Jews, Christians, or Muslims? It is, as I see it, this last group that has greater knots to be untied than those of Alexander. For this reason I carry with

me the true law, which cuts more than the sword of Alexander, because it doesn't waste time untying infernal bonds, but severs them at their root.]

The reference here is to the legendary wagon of Midas that was held in the acropolis of Gordium (modern-day Yassihüyük, Turkey). The wagon's yoke was fastened to a pole by a knot that was supposedly impossible to untie, although a local legend also held that whoever succeeded in untying the knot would rule all of Asia. As both Justin and Quintus Curtius present the episode, Alexander was unable to untie the knot, so he cut through it with his sword.[60] Although Barros is explicit about the immortality of the soul and presenting Christian "law" as a sword to cut through the Gordian knot of Islam, he leaves implicit what such an act of cutting—a severing at the root—might bring about: the right, at least within the logic of the example, to rule all of Asia.

Moving forward within the first volume of Barros's *Décadas da Ásia*, we find another reference to Alexander in the context of a brief description of Portuguese colonial rule in the kingdom of Hormuz, a small but wealthy island off the southern coast of Iran.[61] Taken in 1515 by Afonso de Albuquerque (1453–1515), a figure at the center of many of Portugal's early military exploits in Asia, Hormuz quickly became the linchpin of Portuguese commercial activities through the Persian Gulf to India and Eastern Africa. In strategic terms, Portuguese control of Hormuz and its important trading port simultaneously served to block Arab trade in the Persian Gulf and provided a valuable staging area for Portuguese ships on the long sea journey to and from India. Hormuz remained an important part of Portugal's overseas empire until 1622, when a joint attack by British and Persian forces compelled the Portuguese to abandon the island for good. The account that Barros offers of Hormuz under Portuguese administration, embedded as it is within a multivolume work explicitly modeled on Livy's *History of Rome*, is of a piece with the former's broader apologetic of Portuguese empire. This does not diminish the work's continued importance, however, given that much of what we know about Hormuz during the sixteenth century stems directly from the *Décadas da Ásia*, as well as other works by Portuguese historians and travelers such as the *Relaciones* (Accounts) of Pedro Teixeira (1570–1640), and the *Livro de Duarte Barbosa* (Book of Duarte Barbosa), completed in 1518.[62]

In his second *Década*, Barros deals with the history of Hormuz and the manner in which the Portuguese came to take control of it.

Como este Reyno de Portugal per hum particular dom de Deos lhe he concedida esta prerogativa, ganhar os titulos de sua Coroa per conquista de infieis, e este he o seu verdadeiro patrimonio, principalmente dos Arabios, que, como no principio dissemos, discorrendo das partes Orientaes da sua patria Ababia, vieram ter a estas Occidentaes; parece, que com Deos permittia que elles fossem flagello, e castigo dos peccados de Hespanha, destrundo, e assolando a terra aos naturaes della, assi ordenou que, passados tantos seculos, a gente Portuguez a mais Occidental de Hespanha, e do proprio solar della, não sómente dentro na sua esteril Arabia per o mesmo modo a poder de ferro fossem executar esta natural prerogativa, destruindo-lhe suas Cidades, queimando suas casas, cativando-lhe mulheres, e filhos, e fazendo-se senhores de suas fazendas, e patria, mas ainda a gente Persia mui célebre em nome, nobre per antiguidade de Reyno, armas, e policia, pagasse esta offensa feita a Hespanha, por se converterem á secta destes barbaros Arabio, té os sobmettermos debaixo do jugo, e potencias de nossas Armas com as victorias que delles houvemos em a conquista do Reyno Ormuz, cujo estado se contém nestas duas partes, Arabia, Persia.[63]

[To the kingdom of Portugal is conceded the prerogative, as a gift from God and its true patrimony, of winning the titles of its Crown through the conquest of the infidels, especially the Arabs. As we said at the beginning, the Arabs spread out from their native Arabia in the East and conquered parts of the West as well. It seems that God permitted them to serve as a whip to punish the sins of Hispania, destroying and leveling the land of the natives of that region. After several centuries, God ordered that the Portuguese people—the westernmost of Hispania and natives of that region—should execute their natural prerogative over the Arabs by military means: destroying their cities, burning their houses, capturing their women and children, and making themselves lords of their properties and homeland. And this was not the case only in Arabia, but also in Persia, a land much renowned for the ancient nobility of its Kingdom, arms, and civilization. God ordered that Persia, because it had converted to the sect of these barbarous Arabs, should also pay for the offense committed against Hispania by submitting themselves to the yoke and power of our arms with the victories that we had over them in the conquest of the kingdom of Hormuz, whose state is contained within these two regions: Arabia and Persia.]

Here the overseas conquests of the Portuguese are grounded once again in the idea that it's all payback for the conquest of the Muslims, which was a "whip of God." Portugal's very coming-to-be is linked to this invasion, and so the seeds of its empire are contained in its very birth. Persia, which was not part of the invasion of the Iberian Peninsula, is here included in the war of expansion because of their conversion to Islam, an idea that is altered somewhat by the treaty into which the Hormuzi king and King Manuel I of Portugal enter through the efforts of Afonso de Albuquerque and the Hormuzi negotiator (the latter described as an "homen apessoado, e vistoso, tambem vinha como quem se queria mostrar gentil homem" (a stately and pleasant-looking man, who also came as one who wished to present himself as a gentleman)):[64]

Finalmente elle se resumio nisto, que podia dizer a ElRey, e ao seu Governador Cóge Atar que o enviára, que elle era vindo per mandado d'ElRey seu Senhor a notificar a ElRey de Ormuz, que se queria pacificamente navegar os mares da India, que lhe havia de pagar hum certo tributo em final de vassallagem, por quanto elle tinha guerra com os Mouros em as partes Occidentaes de seu estado: que esta herança herdára de seus avós, e que por haver sua benção, não sómente lhe fazia guerra nas partes de Africa, mas ainda na India, que tinha mandado descubrir. Porque como os Arabios per impeto de cubiça, leixando suas terras, se foram entendendo per armas té chegar a Hespanha, lançando os naturaes de suas proprias casas, assi os Reys de Portugal, que são Senhores de boa parte della, per lei de restituição os lançáram della, e das partes de Africa que tinham por frontaria; e ao presente ElRey D. Manuel que reinava, mandava a elle seu Capitão que lhe fizesse crua guerra em esta propria Arabia. Porém porque esta lei podia ter alguma excepção ácerca d'ElRey de Ormuz, por seu estado não ser todo na Arabia, elle seguramente podia navegar os mares da India, e em ElRey seu Senhor acharia amizade pera suas necessidades, pagando-lhe algum tributo, e que esta era a condição da paz, e a da guerra não lhe limitava.[65]

[Finally, it came down to this: that Albuquerque could tell the king and Cóge Atar, his governor whom he would send, that he had been sent by the order of the king his lord to notify the king of Hormuz that if he wished safely to navigate the waters near India, that he would have to pay certain tribute as a sign of vassalage. With respect to the fact that the king of Portugal was at war with the Muslims in regions to the west of Hormuz, this was a war that he had inherited from his grandparents and with their blessing. Not only did he wage war in Africa, but also in India, which he had ordered discovered. The Arabs, motivated by greed, had left their land and made their way westward through force of arms until arriving in Hispania, where they forced the natives from their homes. The kings of Portugal, who are lords of a good portion of Hispania, forced the Arabs out of the peninsula and the coastal portions of Africa by virtue of the law of restitution. The king who was then in power, Manuel, ordered his captain to wage open war in Arabia itself. There could be an exemption to this order in the case of the king of Hormuz, however, because his kingdom was not in Arabia. He could therefore safely sail the seas around India, and in the Portuguese king, his lord, he would find friendship with respect to his needs provided that he pay that king some tribute. These were the conditions for peace, and those for war were not limited by them.]

As Barros presents it, Manuel I has inherited the war with the Muslims to the west of Hormuz, which was begun by their "greedy" westward expansion. And as the Hormuzis were not part of the Arab groups who had carried out this expansion and against whom the Portuguese were committed to fight, they could be exempted from the war—Muslims or not—in exchange for some form of monetary tribute. Manuel I invokes the law of restitution (in short, the remedies assessed by reference to a gain made by a defendant rather than a loss suffered by a claimant) to justify his kingdom's conquests in the southern portion of the Iberian Peninsula and the African coast and essentially expands the scope of the remedies assessed for this invasion to the Arabian Peninsula and India itself. Like the Hellenic invasion of Asia launched in 334 BCE with Alexander at its head, the rise of the Portuguese empire against Islam is here presented as a righting of past wrongs, an act of just restitution.

Beyond the parallels just mentioned, perhaps the most interesting aspect of Barros's account of Portuguese colonial expansion into the Persian Gulf is the way in which he once again makes explicit and idiosyncratic use of classical images and figures directly related to the Asian conquests of Alexander the Great:

O reino de Ormuz, já per si, era maior em estado, riqueza e gente que estes três juntos, e o que o fazia ainda mais poderoso era a vezinhança da Pérsia, donde podia ser socorrido. E se o Rei da Pérsia, que naquele tempo reinava, chamado Xeque Ismael, tomara posse dele, como tinha tentado, quando Afonso de Albuquerque o tomou, como veremos, nossa contenda fora com outro príncipe maior em estado e potência que o grande Dário, sob reverência de quanto os gregos escreveram dela, por dar maior glória ao seu Alexandre.[66]

[The kingdom of Hormuz, by itself, was greater in status, wealth, and population than [Adem, al-Shihr, and Fartak] together, and what made it even more powerful was its proximity to Persia, from which it could receive aid. And if the King of Persia, who at that time was Shāh Ismaʻīl, were to take possession of it, which as we will see he had been trying to do at the time that Afonso de Albuquerque took it, our struggle would have been with a prince greater in status and strength than the great Darius, of whose power and wealth the Greeks wrote with much reverence in order to give greater glory to their Alexander.]

In this brief passage, Barros first fashions Afonso de Albuquerque and his men into a kind of "thin red line" that prevented Shāh Ismaʻīl I of Persia (1487–1524 CE) from taking control of Hormuz and thus gaining an even greater level of power, status, and wealth in the region. He then makes a subtle comparison between the Portuguese and Alexander the Great that is much more difficult to make sense of, at least from the perspective of his stated goal, expressed in the prologue to the first *Década*—namely, "a escrever o que elles fizeram no descubrimento, e conquista do Oriente, por se não perderem da memoria dos homens, que vierem depois de nós, tão gloriosos feitos" (to write out that which was done in the discovery and conquest of the Orient, so that these glorious accomplishments are not erased from the memory of those who come after us).[67]

Barros argues that if the Portuguese had not successfully taken Hormuz when they did, then they would have been forced to fight, by the middle of the sixteenth century, a Persian king more powerful and wealthy than Darius III (380–330 BCE), the Achaemenid emperor of Persia against whom Alexander fought three violent set-piece battles before securing power over Western Asia. Immediately after setting up this comparison, however, Barros indirectly undermines the place of the Portuguese within it, stating that Darius's power and prestige had, in any case, been described with so much awe by Hellenic historians mainly in order to make the victories of "their Alexander" (*o seu Alexandre*) appear all the more dramatic. This is a conceit that runs through the *Décadas da Ásia*, as Barros repeatedly argues, like Castanheda, that although the Portuguese had accomplished much more through military and navigational feats than any other nation before them, they nonetheless placed far behind others in their commitment to making these accomplishments known to the world through writing. In this particular case, Barros is rightly arguing that what we know of the feats of Alexander (and specifically the threat that was posed to Alexander by Darius III) is to some extent the result of the systematic exaggeration of these feats by politically savvy historians looking to boost the prestige of their nation. In bringing down Darius, however, Barros also implicitly brings down the Portuguese, given that he here suggests that Isma'il I and Tahmasp I (1524–1576), the Persian kings that the Portuguese had managed to prevent taking hold of Hormuz, would have been greater than Darius had they successfully taken hold of the island kingdom. That they did not leaves Barros's reader to infer that they had not reached the status and power of Darius, which, in any case, had been much exaggerated by Hellenic historians.

It is unlikely that Barros would be seeking in this passage to diminish the heroic impact of Portuguese exploits in the Persian Gulf; however, there is a subtle and telling ambivalence that runs through his comparison of Isma'il I and Tahmasp I to Darius III (and, by extension, that of the Portuguese to Alexander). On one hand, he explicitly links the conquering exploits of the Portuguese to those of Alexander, a rhetorical strategy also employed, though somewhat less subtly, by Castanheda and extensively developed by the Romans before them. On the other hand, however, Barros's unfavorable comparison of the sixteenth-century Safavid dynasty with their Achaemenid predecessors at the end of the fourth century BCE implicitly places the exploits of figures such as Afonso de Albuquerque at a level below that of even the chauvinistically exaggerated achievements of Alexander. In other words, if the taking of Hormuz by Albuquerque had prevented the king of Persia from achieving power and wealth on a par with Darius III, and the power and wealth of the Achaemenid emperor had been exaggerated by Greek authors seeking to aggrandize the achievements of Alexander, what precisely does Barros wish to say about the Portuguese and their struggles against the Persian Safavid dynasty throughout the sixteenth century?

Barros further complicates things, and still within an explicitly Alexandrian framework, in his description of the struggles of the Portuguese with the kingdom of Gujarat, which directly follows his passage on Hormuz:

"Mais adiante tínhamos el-Rei de Cambaia, com que tevemos per muito tempo guerra e ainda temos, ao qual nem Xerxes nam Dário nem Poro chegaram em poder, estado e riqueza, e animo militar" (Later we faced the king of Gujarat, with whom we engaged in war for a long time, and still do, than whom neither Xerxes, Darius, nor Porus ever achieved a level of power, status and wealth, and military zeal).[68] Barros frames the war to gain power over Gujarat (a war in which the ascendant Mughals were also participants) as an ongoing struggle with an unknown outcome, describing its king (who was Nasīr al-Dīn Maḥmūd Shāh III at the time that Barros was writing) in terms of the principal Asian enemies of the Greeks and Alexander: Xerxes I of Persia (519–465 BCE), whose invasion of Greece was the explicit justification for Alexander's expedition into Persia; Darius III; and Porus, the Pauravan king whom Alexander defeated in the Battle of Hydaspes in 326 BCE.

Once again participating in the rhetorical strategy by which the Portuguese are to be judged in terms of Alexander's achievements—above all with respect to their conquests throughout the Persian Gulf and Asia—Barros defends the inability of the Portuguese to take definitive control of the kingdom of Gujarat in decidedly Alexandrian terms by mentioning Xerxes I, Darius III, and Porus and then arguing that Nasīr al-Dīn Maḥmūd Shāh III was more powerful than all of these. This description serves the double purpose of employing classical standards to excuse the Portuguese for their failures while once again presenting the key political argument of Barros's history, namely, that although little had been written about the Asian exploits of the Portuguese, they met or exceeded—at least in scope and daring—those of the Greeks and Romans, about which so much had been written. What is front and center, once again, is the role of the historian in delivering the story of Portugal's imperial adventures against Islam from the oblivion that it faced in the middle of the fifteenth century.

Barros's theorization of empire, death, and history in relation to what we might term phenomenological considerations of being-in-the-world is a project that did not fail to have an impact on other Portuguese authors (and literary genres) during the sixteenth century. Perhaps the most complex and celebrated continuation of Barros's framing of Portuguese empire in Asia is that found in Camões's *Os Lusíadas*. Camões composed the majority of *Os Lusíadas* while serving the Portuguese Crown in India and China, and much of the poem was also written while he was marooned in Southeast Asia, waiting for passage back to Goa and then Lisbon. Given Camões's (mostly bitter) experiences with the Portuguese empire in Asia and Africa in the middle of the sixteenth century, his perspective on the imperial enterprise—like that of Couto, who also spent years serving in Goa—is an understandably complex and fraught one. When we add to this the fact that Camões only managed to publish his epic poem, much altered, upon his return to Lisbon and only six years before the death of his royal patron (and, as far as Camões knew, the end of Portugal's very independence) at al-Qaṣr al-Kbīr, the place of *Os Lusíadas* in the broader narrative of Portuguese empire, and the role of Alexander the Great within Camões's epic, becomes an even more complex and important theme for analysis. It is worth considering, at least, why Camões would both begin and end his epic with explicit references to Alexander, Islam, immortality, and the text-mediated practices of the poet. In very direct ways, the historiographical work of Barros—which served Camões as both a textual and an ideological source—does much to answer this question.[69]

CHAPTER 5

JUDGMENT

The Aljamiado Alexander

IBERIAN AUTHORS AND READERS BELONGING TO THE CHRISTIAN
majority were by no means the only ones who conjured up the ghost of Alexander during the late medieval and early modern period. Within the minority Muslim communities of Castile and Aragon, for example, a textual
tradition inherited from the East drew upon Alexander in ways that differed
sharply from the uses to which the Macedonian king was put by authors such
as Barros, Martorell, and Zurara. Unconcerned with Virgilian epic and Roman historiography, Ibero-Muslim and crypto-Muslim scribes, storytellers,
and readers nonetheless engaged actively in theorizing imperial expansion,
focusing at once on the hard-fought spread of Islam throughout the East
and West, matters of philosophy, the message of the Qur'ān, and the rise of
Christian hegemony in the Iberian Peninsula and beyond.

In spite of the obvious differences between the texts and discursive traditions that make up Ibero-Christian accounts of Alexander and those of their
Muslim counterparts throughout the fifteenth and sixteenth centuries, there
are also important parallels that warrant careful examination. A deep-seated
concern with death and the afterlife, as well as the role of language and the
Other in the development of theories of mortality, oblivion, and the self,
all emerge from Ibero-Muslim texts dealing with Alexander, features that
these texts share with contemporary Ibero-Christian accounts. As with the
works of Barros, Martorell, and Zurara (among others), late medieval Ibero-
Muslim texts that deal with Alexander fight to work through issues revolv-

ing around death and life, and it is Alexander—a trope for the bitter fruits of empire and a trigger for the theorization of deeper, phenomenological accounts of human being-in-the-world—that operates at the center of this philosophical and pragmatic enterprise.

In the present chapter I will be discussing key elements of the Ibero-Muslim tradition of Alexandrian literature as it manifested during the fifteenth and sixteenth centuries. My goal is not to present anything resembling a comprehensive catalog of Ibero-Muslim references to Alexander in literature from the period, but rather to engage in a more focused analysis of specific manuscript texts in Aljamiado that deal with Alexander the Great and reflect dominant currents of late medieval Ibero-Muslim literature concerned with the Macedonian king. The main text upon which I will be focusing, the *Rekontamiento del rey Ališandre* (Story of King Alexander), speaks of empire in a focused way, developing this theme within the frame of a persistent exploration of Islamic concerns regarding human mortality, knowledge, the afterlife, and the Day of Judgment. By their very existence and use an open contestation of the dominant narrative of expansion and crusade put forth by the Christian majority in sixteenth century Castile and Aragon (it was illegal even to possess them in Castile after 1502 and in Aragon after 1526), Aljamiado texts nonetheless put the ghost of Alexander to work on issues of life, death, and the Other in ways that parallel in significant ways the work of their Christian contemporaries.

For readers unfamiliar with the status of Muslim and crypto-Muslim minorities in the Iberian Peninsula during the fifteenth and sixteenth centuries, it is perhaps necessary to provide a brief historical overview. Such an overview is by no means intended to serve as a substitute for the important work of historians such as Ahmed Boucharb, Louis Cardaillac, Antonio Domínguez Ortiz, Isabel Drummond Braga, Mikel de Epalza, Mercedes García Arenal, L. P. Harvey, Rogério de Oliveira Ribas, and Bernard Vincent (not to mention earlier work by Henry Charles Lea and Pedro Longás Bartibás); however, it can provide a kind of abbreviated orientation to readers unaware of the historical context out of which the texts in question emerge, and which they in turn helped to shape.[1] My goal here is not to offer new information or perspectives on the history of Iberian Islam from the beginning of the fifteenth century (when the practice of translating Arabic texts into Aljamiado really began to pick up steam in Castile and Aragon) to the end of the sixteenth century (shortly before the final expulsion of these communities from the Iberian Peninsula), but rather to help my reader to understand a bit better the significance of the texts upon which I will be focusing.

Mudéjares *and (Then)* Moriscos

It is widely known that much of the Iberian Peninsula has been shaped by the presence of Muslim kingdoms and communities in that region from the beginning of the eighth century until the very end of the Middle Ages. Over the past two centuries much has been written about Andalusi society and learning, and the existence of extensive networks of cultural contact and exchange between Christians, Jews, and Muslims in medieval Aragon, Castile, and Portugal has long been something of a commonplace within disciplines as diverse as literary studies, history, philosophy, archaeology, and art history. Within literary studies, the subtle philosophical and poetic works of Muslim intellectuals such as Ibn Ḥazm, Ibn Rushd (better known in the Latin West as Averroes), and ibn Quzmān, as well as their many Jewish counterparts, have served, at least since the middle of the twentieth century, as important foci for research on the history of philosophy, science, and literature, as well as for modern theories of Iberian nationhood. The title of María Rosa Menocal's most popular work to date, *The Ornament of the World: How Muslims, Jews, and Christians Created a Culture of Tolerance in Medieval Spain* (published just months after the World Trade Center and Pentagon attacks), demonstrates the extent to which modern scholars and even nonspecialists have come to look to al-Andalus, and medieval Iberia more generally, as a kind of high point not only of sophisticated cultural production, but also of functional multiculturalism.

The mainstream sophistication of caliphal Córdoba, as well as the complex back-and-forth that existed between Christians, Jews, and Muslims within other medieval Iberian cities such as Valencia, Toledo, and Lisbon, was admittedly something quite different from the realities faced by the Muslim communities of late fifteenth- and sixteenth-century Aragon and Castile (the case of Portugal, discussed in greater detail near the end of the present chapter, is somewhat distinct, but it is nonetheless part of the larger Iberian equation). These later communities, though in some sense the trickle-down heirs of the cultural riches of Muslim Córdoba and Granada, in fact had little connection to the philosophical and courtly discourse of Andalusi elites from the tenth and eleventh centuries, or even to the urbane courtly lyric of the later Granadan courts of Yūsuf III (d. 1417) and Abū ʿabd-Allah Muḥammad XII (c. 1460–1533). Primarily concerned with the maintenance and practice of Islam in everyday settings that presented significant and growing challenges (exemplified in part by the translation of canonical religious texts, and even the Qur'ān itself, into Castilian), the Muslims of fifteenth-century Castile and Aragon—commonly referred to as *mudéjares*—found themselves compelled to dedicate a good deal of their intellectual energy to the translation of Arabic works into Aljamiado for wider distribution among readers and their listening public in much of Castile and Aragon who had lost, through linguistic assimilation, all but the most rudimentary proficiency in Arabic.[2] By the beginning of the fifteenth century this process had become so widespread that it provoked a kind of religious crisis among Islamic scholars such as Iça de Gebir (fl. c. 1462), who took the radical step of producing a Castilian translation of the *sunna* to aid in the religious instruction of Castile's still sizable Muslim communities.[3] Many of these translated works were treatises of (Maliki) Sunni Islamic jurisprudence, Qur'anic commentaries, treatises of practical science and philosophy, and popular narratives dealing with the prophets of Islam and other religious figures. It is within the last of these generic groups that we may situate the *Rekontamiento del rey Ališandre*.

After the fall of Granada to King Ferran II of Aragon and Queen Isabel I of Castile at the very end of 1491 (they would become known as the "Catholic Monarchs" after this victory), things began to change in dramatic ways for the Muslims of these two kingdoms. In the first place, the conquest of Granada brought about a large exodus of Muslim social and intellectual elites from the Iberian Peninsula. Many of these émigrés settled in Fez and Tunis, where they made significant cultural and political contributions that are still in evidence to this day.[4] Those who could not afford to emigrate stayed behind, with legal assurances from the Christian authorities (which were infamously not extended to Castilian and Aragonese Jews) that they would be allowed to continue practicing their religion as they had before. This arrangement, inherited from existing treaties of capitulation dating to the Middle Ages, was accompanied by a high degree of mischief and violence on the part of royal and local officials, whose support for these concessions (in the face of intense land speculation in the former kingdom of Granada) was lukewarm at best. In any case, it would not be in place for very long.

Five years after the surrender of Granada to the Catholic Monarchs,

King Manuel I of Portugal decided to push for a marriage between himself and Isabel (1470–1498), the daughter of King Ferran and Queen Isabel. As a condition of this royal union, the Portuguese monarch was compelled by his future in-laws to order the expulsion of all of his Muslim and Jewish subjects. The king acquiesced, and in late 1496 he signed the order of expulsion, according to which Portuguese Jews and Muslims would have ten months to convert to Christianity or leave the kingdom. This order affected Portuguese Jews severely, given that they did not have the option of simply crossing the border into Castile, because that kingdom had expelled its own Jewish subjects in 1492. As a result of the many difficulties associated with emigration and the strong incentives put in place by Manuel I for the Jews to stay in Portugal and convert to Christianity, many did so—a reality that became extremely dangerous for them with the formation of the Portuguese Inquisition in 1536. The Muslims of Portugal, on the other hand, had a much softer option: since there had been no previous order to expel Muslims from Castile, many simply left Portugal by crossing the border into that kingdom. Paradoxically, the Crown of Castile had pressured Portugal to expel thousands of its Muslim subjects only to allow these Muslims to enter into Castile.

The Portuguese Muslims who immigrated into Castile, as well as the Muslims native to the region, saw their fortunes change dramatically in 1502. On February 12 of that year, Queen Isabel ordered that they must convert to Christianity or face exile. The conversion order reads:

Acordamos demandar salir a todos los dichos moros e moras destos dichos nuestros reynos de Castilla e Leon e que jamas tornen ni buelvan a ellos alguno dellos, e sobre ello mandamos dar esta nuestra carta, por la qual mandamos a todos los moros de XIII años arriba y a todas las moras de hedad de XII años arriba que biven e moran y estan en los dichos nuestros reynos . . . salgan de todos los dichos nuestros reynos e señoríos e se vayan dellos con los bienes que consygo quisieren llevar, con tanto que no puedan llevar ni sacar ni saquen ellos ni otros por ellos fuera de los dichos nuestros reynos oro ni plata ni otra cosa alguna de las por nos vedadas e defendidas.[5]

[We agree to order the expulsion of all of the aforementioned Muslims (men and women) of our kingdoms of Castile and Leon, and that not a single one of them ever return. To this effect we order that this our letter be registered. We order that all Muslim men over the age of thirteen and all Muslim women over the age of twelve that reside in our kingdoms and

dominions leave these lands with whatever they might be able to carry with
them, with the understanding that they may not take nor export nor have
someone export on their behalf any gold or silver (or any other item that we
have likewise prohibited) from our aforementioned kingdoms.]

As is left more or less implicit by this portion of the order, Muslim girls
under the age of twelve and Muslim boys under the age of thirteen did not
have the option of leaving; they would be converted to Christianity by force
and, if necessary, separated from their parents. A very similar order would
go into effect within Aragon in 1526.[6] These Muslim converts to Christianity,
formally referred to as *cristianos nuevos de moros* (New Christians formerly
Muslims), came to be known more commonly as *moriscos*, a designation that
persistently cast them as *"from* the Muslims" in spite of their new status as
baptized Christians and subjects of the *catholicus* Habsburg crown.

Many of the Muslims who converted to Christianity and stayed in the
Iberian Peninsula after 1526 continued to practice Islam in secret, in spite
of the fact that such practice made their lives increasingly difficult and unpredictable. Now nominally Christians, they began to attract the attention
of the Inquisition and faced stiff penalties and in some cases death for instances of perceived backsliding. In a very real sense complements of the
external colonies that drew so much of the Crown of Aragon's, Castile's, and
Portugal's resources and attention, these internal communities of Crypto-
Muslims—which made up just over 4 percent of the total population of the
Iberian Peninsula by the sixteenth century—served persistently to under-
mine official narratives of empire building and expansion from a homoge-
neous and unified metropole.

For *morisco* communities with little or no knowledge of Arabic and perhaps even less contact with Muslims residing in other regions (Valencia was
in many ways the exception to this rule: there higher levels of Arabic fluency and relatively steady contact with Maghrebi Muslims was maintained
throughout the sixteenth century), the production and use of manuscript
texts in Aljamiado became a crucial tool in the widespread effort to maintain
the practice of Islam. These books were copied out in secret and in many
cases hidden in caves, under false floors, and in the walls of homes so that
they might not fall into the hands of the Inquisition and other royal and
church authorities. As I mentioned above, Aragonese and Castilian Crypto-
Muslims working in Aljamiado were able to build upon a textual system

that had been established at least a century before their forced conversion to Christianity; however, during the sixteenth century this practice necessarily took on a more complex and anxious character and, at least in Aragon, became more widespread as it was incorporated into broader processes of cultural practice and negotiation shaped by the Islamic principle of *taqiyya*, or sanctioned religious dissimulation.[7] Consuelo López-Morillas has asserted as much, arguing that the production and use of Aljamiado manuscripts accompanied what can be understood as a highly innovative period for Iberian Muslim language and culture:

> Rather than finding the Moriscos' language as debased as their economic and cultural state, I see it as a sign of their continuing vitality as a people. It was not only the New World chroniclers who had to stretch language to the bursting-point in order to encompass the new reality of their discoveries; their Spanish Muslim contemporaries were performing a parallel feat in accommodating the language to their own reality, which was Islam. Far from undergoing what López Baralt terms "este lento proceso de des-semiticización" [this slow process of desemitization],[8] Mudéjar and Morisco Spanish was in fact becoming actively re-Semiticized, and specifically Islamicized, the better to serve the needs of its speakers. The creative force required by this process calls for a mitigation of the image of the Morisco as a hapless victim of circumstance; it certainly testifies to a strong sense of cultural and religious identity.[9]

The "mitigation" that López-Morillas calls for requires, at least in part, that scholars of *morisco* language and culture adequately attend to the ways in which the use of Aljamiado texts—based at once on established and self-consciously conservative religious traditions and the dramatic innovations facilitated by the framework of *taqiyya*—mediate the processes by which linguistic and cultural innovation took place. Linguistically assimilated (although their speech remained marked from the perspective of the Christian majority) and for the most part belonging to a functionally illiterate class of agricultural workers and tradespeople, the *moriscos* of Castile and Aragon, whether as readers, scribes, or members of the listening public, had a very practical and immediate need for vernacular texts that dealt with Islamic themes as well as with other issues important to the cultural and even personal survival of members of these communities. It is within this context, as well as within the broader context of Iberian nation-state formation and expansion into North Africa and beyond, that the recopying and employ-ment of the *Rekontamiento del rey Ališandre* and other texts that make use of Alexander must be understood. And although these texts, as I have ar-gued, played a central role in the social processes by which *morisco* readers and scribes worked through issues of cultural and individual death, the texts dealing with Alexander, because of their explicit and persistent reckoning with empire, death, and knowledge, follow this pattern in very different, per-haps even more powerful ways.[10]

With regard to the *moriscos* of Portugal (referred to in Portuguese as *mouriscos*), it is necessary to alter a bit the terms of our discussion. In the first place, their numbers were always a fraction of those in Castile and Aragon, and they were for the most part—at least after the expulsions of 1497—made up of recent immigrants from the Maghreb that had been allowed to enter Portugal (in some cases, as official translators for the Crown) either through the granting of individual royal licenses or as slaves. These immigrants from Morocco and other parts of the Maghreb naturally possessed a much higher level of Arabic fluency than their counterparts in Castile and Aragon; how-ever, there is reason to suspect that the use of Arabic was starting to wane by the middle of the sixteenth century, as the Portuguese Inquisition labored to effect the religious, linguistic, and cultural assimilation of these small com-munities.[11] One of the results of this waning of Arabic fluency, coupled with a strong commitment to maintain the observance of Islam within Portugal, was the development of a system of Aljamiado writing in Portuguese that was never adopted—as far as is now known—on a wide scale.[12]

Turning our attention back to Castile and Aragon, it is important to point out that the textual and lectoral practices of Aragonese and Castilian Crypto-Muslims were relatively short-lived, coming to an abrupt and tragic end at the start of the seventeenth century. Facing increasing pressure from his advisers and church officials, King Felipe III ordered the expulsion of his *morisco* subjects in 1609. This order affected all but a very few *moriscos*, whether their conversion to Christianity (or that of their parents or grand-parents, as the case may have been) had been sincere or not. Pushed out of the Iberian Peninsula and forced to fend for themselves, many of these people, in-cluding children and the elderly, drowned in the Mediterranean as they made their way to various coastal cities in the Maghreb. A fair number of those who survived the journey settled in cities along the Atlantic coast of Morocco and in Tunis, where they seem to have likewise resisted cultural assimilation even as they were absorbed once again into Muslim society. Left behind in Aragon, under false floors and in the walls of houses (many of these would come spilling out as these houses were demolished in the nineteenth century), were the Aljamiado texts that had shaped their continued observance of Islam and helped them to theorize their own being-in-the-world while in Castile and Aragon. Among these texts was the *Rekontamiento del rey Ališandre*.

The Rekontamiento del rey Ališandre *in Its Manuscript Context*

The *Rekontamiento del rey Ališandre* is, as both Francisco Guillén Robles and A. R. Nykl have pointed out in their respective editions of the text, an Aljamiado translation of the popular Arabic narrative *Qiṣṣat Dhū al-Qarnayn* (Story of the Two-Horned One), a version of the Alexander story that for the most part blends aspects of the *Greek Alexander Romance* with the Qur'ān and other oral traditions.[13] It is extant in one manuscript copy currently located in Spain's National Library in Madrid (MS 5254, *olim* Gg-48). The text, copied out in Aragon during the second half of the sixteenth century, occupies 125 folios within a manuscript codex that contains a total of 144 folios (150 × 100 mm) of relatively rough but well-preserved paper.[14] The *Rekontamiento del rey Ališandre* is the only narrative text within this manuscript; however, there are other short texts, dealing with specific aspects of Muslim prayer and practice, in the opening and closing folios. The first two folios and the recto of the third are blank, but on folio 3v (see figure 5.1) we find a set of instructions regarding invocations to be uttered after performing one's ritual ablutions (*al-wuḍū'*):

Diráš tᶜreš vezeš: "Ašhadu an lā ilahu ilā Allahu wa ašhadu an Muhammadun rasūllullahu." Dešpuʷeš diráš tᶜreš vezeš: "Allahumma ṣali ʿalá Muhammadin il-karīmi wa ʿalá ālihi." Depuʷeš diráš tᶜreš vezeš: "Istaghfiru wa [sic] Allahi wa atūbu ileyhi." Kata no dešeš de dezirlo todo ešto dešpuʷeš ke abráš tomado al-wadu, ke en dezirlo por ello ay gᵃran guʷalardón.[15]

[You will say three times: "I affirm that there is no god but the One God, and I affirm that Muḥammad is His messenger." Afterward, you will say three times: "May God bless Muḥammad the Generous and his family." Afterward, you will say three times: "I ask forgiveness of God and I repent

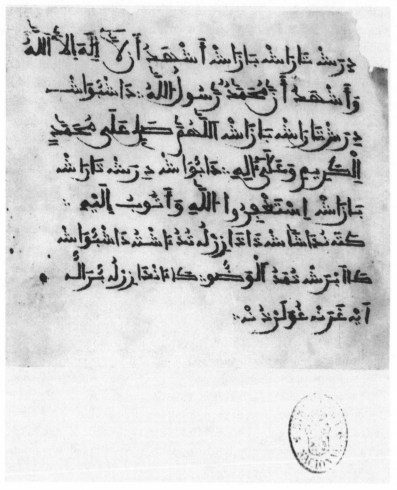

FIGURE 5.1   Madrid, BN MS 5254 (f. 3v.). Courtesy of the Biblioteca Nacional, Madrid.

to Him." Be sure not to neglect to say all of this after having performed the
ablution, as in saying it there is great benefit.]

This brief text is explicitly concerned with standardizing Muslim practice
(and ritual speech) within the Crypto-Muslim community that held this codex; however, it also demonstrates, especially at the beginning of the third
invocation, the tenuous understanding that the scribe had of Qur'ānic Ara-

bic. In any case, it is highly likely that the entire text was copied, with the scribal errors that often accompanied this process, from an earlier source.[16] The three folios (4r–7v) that follow the instructions on folio 3v are blank. On folio 8r, we find a text written, according to Francisco Guillén Robles, by Juan de Iriarte (1702–1771), who served as chief librarian of Spain's Royal Library during the eighteenth century: "Libro en castellano, con caracteres Arabes, intitulado *Libro del Racontamiento del Rey Alexandro*, en que se refieren sus batallas victorias y conquistas. Un tomo en 4° de muy buena letra, sin nombre de autor, ni fecha" (A book in Castilian, with Arabic characters, entitled, *Book of the Story of King Alexander*, in which are related his battles, victories, and conquests. A quarto volume written in a very fine hand, with no author's name or date).[17]

On the verso of the same folio, the *Rekontamiento del rey Ališandre* itself begins, in a hand different from that found on folio 3v, with: "Ešte eš el libro del rrekontami^yento del rrey Ališand^ere; bismillāhi al-raḥmāni al-raḥīmi wa ṣallá Allahu ʿalá sayidinā Muḥammadin wa ʿalá rālihi wa salam tasliman. Kitābu ḥadīthi Dhī al-Qarnayni" (This is the book of the story of King Alexander, in the name of God, the compassionate and merciful; may the blessings of God and peace be upon our chief, Muḥammad, and his family. The book is called *The Book of the Two-Horned One*).[18] There are several significant features to this introductory passage, but two in particular stand out. In the first place, the passage contains an invocation that parallels that found in the short text on folio 3v: "Allahumma ṣali ʿalá Muḥammadin il-karīmi wa ʿalá ālihi" (May God bless Muḥammad the Generous and his family). The beginning of the *Rekontamiento del rey Ališandre* presents a more standard form of this invocation: "Ṣallá Allahu ʿalá sayidinā Muḥammadin wa ʿalá ālihi wa salam tasliman" (May the blessings of God and peace be upon our chief, Muḥammad, and his family).[19] The point here is not that there should necessarily be word-for-word correspondence between these two texts, or that one text is in some sense a source for the other (these formulas were, and still are, fairly common within Muslim discourse); rather, the significance of this blessing of the Prophet and his family is to fold both the performing of ritual ablutions and the telling of the story of Alexander into an explicitly Islamic activity framework; that is, both are presented as components of communal, even ritual, practice. This much is reinforced by the first line of the text itself, which begins by providing an authoritative line of transmission (*isnād*) as in the *sunna* itself: "Bismillāhi al-raḥmāni al-raḥīmi.

Fuᵂe rrekontado por ʿAbd al-Rahmāni fijo Beni Ziyād-ibni fijo Anuʿmin, por ʿan Saʿīd-ibn fijo Alm[u]sayyabi por ʿan Saʿīd-ibn Abī Waqāṣin. Qala dišo" (In the name of God, the compassionate and merciful. It was recounted by ʿAbd al-Rahmān, son of Ibn Ziyād, son *fijo* of Anuʿmin, [who received it] *por* from Saʿīd, son *fijo* of Almusayyab, [who received it] *por* from Saʿīd, son of Abī Waqāṣin. He said *dišo*).²⁰ Within this chain of transmission, the Aljamiado text juxtaposes intrasentential translations of Arabic terms such as the noun *ibn* (son), the preposition ʿ*an* (from), and the verb *qala* (he said) with the Arabic terms themselves. The purpose of preserving the Arabic terms alongside their Aljamiado translations resides in the significance that the Arabic terms—like the invocation of God that initiates the text—have in the formation of an *isnād* and the resulting authority of the *matn* (main text) that follows it. Although it is true that the translation is less than precise (*por* (by) works grammatically with the opening clause "Fuᵂe rrekontado" (It was recounted), but it undermines to some extent the explicit sense of transmission that is conveyed by the original Arabic ʿ*an*, not to mention its role as an index of *sunna* discourse), it does nevertheless link this passage, and the narrative as a whole, to highly authoritative and even orthodox genres of Arabic literature and Muslim practice.

The explicit reference to authoritative Islamic discourse—at both the deictic and the semantico-referential level of signification—that we find in the opening of the *Rekontamiento del rey Ališandre* operates at the start of the main text, as well. The story begins with Muḥammad (after having performed his own ritual ablutions) responding to the questions of a group of Jews regarding Dhū al-Qarnayn. At the beginning of their exchange, the Jews test Muḥammad to see if he is able to intuit what it is that they wish to ask him:

Dijeronle: "Yā rasūla [*sic*] Allāh haslo a šaber a nošotroš por lo ke benimoš a demandarte por ello." Dijoleš: "Beníšme a demandar por a Dhū al-Qarnayni, i de lo ke fuᵂe de šuš nuᵂebaš, i de šu rrekontamiʸento, i de šu fecho, i de šu linaje, i de šu parenteško, i de šuš padreš, i de šuš aweloš, i de lo ke llego de šu fecho, i komo akošiguio lo ke okošiʸo, i de lo ke le diʸo Allāh de la potensiʸa i del forsamiʸento šobre laš billaš." Dijeronle: "Yā menšajero de Allāh, por ešo te benišoš [*sic*] a demandar." Dijoleš la ora el menšajero de Allāh, ṣalallahu ʿaleyhi wa salam: "Era Dhū al-Qarnayn, ke šu lombre era Aleskandar, de loš hijoš de los rreyeš de los rreyeš [*sic*] kⁱristianoš. I era Dhū̵-al̵-Qarnayni̵ šu padre šoberbiʸo de loš šoberbioš de loš kⁱrištianoš."²¹

[They said to them: "Oh Messenger of God, you must tell us what it is that we have come to ask you about." He said to them: "You've come to me to ask about Dhū al-Qarnayn, and to ask me to speak of him, his story, and his deeds, as well as his lineage, his family, his parents, and his grandparents. You also want me to speak of how he took what he took and of what God gave to him in terms of power and authority over the cities." They said to him: "Oh Messenger of God, that is what we came to ask you." The Messenger of God, may the blessings of God and peace be upon him, then said to them: "Dhū al-Qarnayn, whose name was Alexander, was the son of Christian kings. And D̶h̶ū̶ ̶a̶l̶-̶Q̶a̶r̶n̶a̶y̶n̶i̶ his father was the greatest of the great among the Christians."]

This passage, which contains a number of scribal errors (throughout the manuscript there are many marginal emendations to the main text), serves as a kind of *amplificatio* of *sura* 18, verse 83 of the Qur'ān, which begins: "They ask you about Dhū al-Qarnayn." The Qur'ān then launches into what the Prophet is to say about Dhū al-Qarnayn, while the Aljamiado text—as well as the Arabic text upon which it is based—dramatizes it in narrative through the use of, among other techniques, direct discourse. In essence, the Qur'ān implies this scene, while the narrative presents it as part of a possible world.[22] The crossed-out "Dhū al-Qarnayn" in the last line of the passage represents a scribal error provoked by the "i era Dhū al-Qarnayn" of the preceding line; the latter line begins with "i era" as well, but the subject is Dhū al-Qarnayn's father and not the prophet himself. This scribal error lends weight to Nykl's contention that Madrid, BN MS 5254, is a copy of an earlier Aljamiado translation of the Arabic original, and not a translation itself.

The other significant aspect of this text is that from its very beginning it links the Qur'ānic figure of Dhū al-Qarnayn with Alexander the Great: "Era Dhū al-Qarnayn, ke šu lombre era Aleskandar" (Dhū al-Qarnayn, whose name was Alexander). The significance of this reference is that it provides concrete evidence that Castilian and Aragonese *moriscos* understood Dhū al-Qarnayn to be Alexander, although in the Qur'ān it is by no means clear who Dhū al-Qarnayn might be. Even today, there are many Islamic scholars who contest the conventional link established between these two figures in Qur'ānic exegesis and popular Islamic narratives such as the *Rekontamiento del rey Ališandre*. Brannon M. Wheeler discusses these alternative readings while revealing his own belief that the Qur'ānic Dhū al-Qarnayn refers to Alexander the Great:

One possibility is that Dhū al-Qarnayn refers to the Lakhmīd ruler al-Mundhir al-Akbar III (r. 506–554), who supposedly killed the poet ʿAbid b. al-Abraṣ and put Abū Duʿād al-Iyādī in charge of his horses. This reference is not likely because there is no evidence that al-Mundhir III is reported to have done the things attributed to Dhū al-Qarnayn in Q 18:83–101. Another possibility is that Dhū al-Qarnayn is Cyrus the Great. This identification is based upon the reference to the ram with two horns, which are the kings of Media and Persia in Daniel 8:21. Given what is known of the conquests of Cyrus, it would be possible to identify him with the actions of Dhū al-Qarnayn in Q 18:83–101. There is no evidence, however, from the Arabic histories that Cyrus was thought to have conquered the world as is described in Q 18:83–101, nor is there any evidence in early exegesis that Dhū al-Qarnayn was identified with Cyrus.[23]

In another Aljamiado manuscript, part of the cache of books found at Almonacid de la Sierra (Aragon) in 1884, we find a more ambiguous reference to Dhū al-Qarnayn/Alexander. The manuscript is located in the Library of the Institute of Philology of CSIC (Centro Superior de Investigaciones Científicas) in Madrid (MS 26), and it contains cabbalistic formulas for making astrological predictions.[24] The concrete link that these predictions have to Dhū al-Qarnayn/Alexander is that the text frames him as the source of this knowledge: "Dixo Dhū al-Qarnayn: 'Kuʷando verna a tú algun demandante para demandarte alguna coša de laš demandaš akellaš ke še nonbᵃraran depueš dešto ši kerra Allah puʷeš konta šu nombᶜre i ʸel nombᶜre del diʸa akel ke tú ereš en el'" (Dhū al-Qarnayn said: "When some questioner comes to you and asks you a question regarding what, God willing, will be, simply count out his or her name and that of the present day").[25] Such connections between Dhū al-Qarnayn/Alexander and prophetic/scientific forms of knowledge (as both a devout Muslim and a former student of Aristotle) were very much a part of the Islamic tradition, and they surface in the *Rekontamiento del rey Ališandre*, as well. Also part of the Almonacid cache, it should be mentioned, is an Arabic copy of the *Qiṣṣat Dhū al-Qarnayn* (Madrid, Biblioteca del Instituto de Filología del CSIC MS 27), which forms the basis of Emilio García Gómez's 1929 study and explicitly links the Qurʾānic figure of Dhū al-Qarnayn to Alexander the Great.[26] Whether these texts refer explicitly to Alexander as Dhū al-Qarnayn (and Qurʾānic exegesis is not the principle concern of the present chapter), what remains clear is that the *morisco* scribes and readers who copied out and read (whether aloud in groups or silently) the *Rekontamiento del rey Ališandre* certainly equated the Macedonian king with the Qurʾānic figure from *sura* 18:83–102.

The text of the *Rekontamiento del rey Ališandre* ends on folio 133v (folio 125v according to the folio numbers added to the codex by a modern hand) with:

Akešto eš lo ke a noš llego de laš nuʷevaš da Dhū al-Qarnayni i lo ke conkišto en laš villaš i ʸafino de loš rreyeš i ʸafino de loš šiʸervoš i lo ke v[en]iʸa a él de laš wešteš i de laš kompannaš. Wa al-ḥamdu lillāhi rab al-ʿalamīn wa salawāt Allah al-tayyibāt wa salām ʿalá sayidinā Muḥammad khātim al-nabīyīn wa al-rasulīn wa ʿalá ālihi wa asḥabihi ajmaʿīna wa salama taslīman.[27]

[This is what came to us regarding Dhū al-Qarnayn, including the cities that he conquered and the end that he gave to kings and to slaves and what came to him from their armies and forces. And thanks be to God the Lord of the created world, and may the blessings of God and peace be upon our chief, Muḥammad, the seal of the prophets and the messengers, and upon his family and all his companions, and may he have complete peace.]

As Nykl points out in his edition of this text, there are numerous errors in the Arabic portion of this closing that speak to the decreased fluency that *morisco* scribes had in that language by the middle of the sixteenth century. Aside from these errors, we find once again the invocation—with minimal changes—that opened both the *Rekontamiento del rey Ališandre* and the set of instructions on folio 3v regarding invocations to be uttered after the performance of ritual ablutions (*al-wuḍūʾ*). This strongly suggests, as I have argued above, that reading this text, at least within one Aragonese *morisco* community, involved situating the *Rekontamiento del rey Ališandre* within established modes of Muslim practice in both storytelling and ritual settings.

After the close of the *Rekontamiento del rey Ališandre*, there is another short text in Aljamiado on folio 134v. This text, copied out in three hands that differ from those of the prayer invocation on folio 3v and the *Rekontamiento del rey Ališandre*, records two differing accounts of the days on which the Islamic month of Ramaḍān began in 1588. The first account reads: "Bismillāhi al-raḥmāni al-raḥīm. Memoriʸa šiʸa de kuʷando še vido la luna de Ramaḍān del año 1588. Aparesiʸo luneš a la tarde, ke še kontara el marteš el pʲrimero del meš de Ramaḍān i fuʷe a loš veyntišeyš de julio" (In the name of God the compassionate and merciful. May it be recorded when the moon of Ramaḍān appeared in the year 1588. It appeared on Monday afternoon, making that Tuesday the first day of the month of Ramaḍān and it was on the twenty-sixth of July).²⁸ This record is correct, because the first moon of Ramaḍān in the Gregorian year 1588 (996 AH) did in fact appear in the afternoon of Monday, July 25. Just below this account, written in a different hand, is what appears to a partial copy of the first: "Memoriʸa šiʸa de kuʷando še vido la luna de Ramaḍān del año 1588. Paresiʸo luneš a la tar[de]" (May it be recorded when the moon of Ramaḍān appeared in the year 1588. It appeared on Monday afternoon).²⁹ Just below this phrase, in a third hand, we find a different account of the first day of Ramaḍān in the Gregorian year of 1588: "Paresiʸo la luna de Ramaḍān tarde de luneš a nuʷeve diʸaš del meš de Janero" (The moon of Ramaḍān appeared on Monday afternoon, on the ninth day of the month of January).³⁰ As Nykl has pointed out, there is an obvious error in this account.³¹ It is possible, although the word nuʷeve (nine) is written out in this account, that the scribe meant to write out "five," because in the year 1573 the first day of Ramaḍān fell on Monday, January 5. The other, perhaps stronger possibility (although it is quite late, just three years before the final expulsion of the moriscos) is the year 1606, during which the first moon of Ramaḍān appeared in the evening of Monday, January 9. Whatever the case, this last phrase is copied out again in Latin script—in a late sixteenth-century hand—just below it: "a nueve dias del mes de Jenaro" (on the ninth day of the month of January).³² After this folio, there are further "scribbled, disconnected phrases" in Aljamiado and Arabic.³³ These include portions of Qurʾānic suras 108 and the whole of sura 111 (in Arabic) with numerous orthographic errors. According to Nykl, it is likely that scribes used these folios to test their pens.³⁴ The codex ends with a brief passage from the Libro de las luces (Book of the Lights) that lists the day of Muḥammad's birth: "Bismillāhi al-raḥmāni al-raḥīm. Nasiʸo al-nabī ʿaleyhi al-salam diʸa de al-iṯnayn a doze diʸaš de la luna de Rabīʿa al-awwal dešpueš de la venida de la conpaña del al-fīl kon sinkuʷenta diʸaš i fuʷe entᵉre al-fīl i ʸel fᵃraguʷamiʸento de la kaša de Makka kinze añoš" (In the name of God the compassionate and merciful. The Prophet, may peace be upon him, was born on Monday, the twelfth day of the month of Rabīʿa al-awwal, fifty days after the coming of the company of the elephant and fifteen years before the [re]construction of the House of Mecca [i.e., the Kaʿba]). The following folio (141r) contains a brief and somewhat jumbled phrase in Aljamiado regarding the unity and nobility of God: "Šab aderešeme Allah i ʸa tu ke še adebdese ke šepa ke Allah onrrado eš i noble šolo en šu reišmo" (Know that God holds fast to me and to you, and so we are commanded to know that God is praiseworthy and the sole noble in his kingdom).[35]

I have mentioned all of these texts, including the brief passages that occupy the first and last folios of Madrid, BN MS 5254, in part to provide a more complete sense of the manuscript codex that contains the *Rekontamiento del rey Ališandre*. Beyond this ultimately practical concern, however, I wish also to underscore the deeply pragmatic and devotional frame within which the *Rekontamiento del rey Ališandre* took on meaning and social force within the cultural practice of Castilian-Aragonese Crypto-Muslims during the second half of the sixteenth century. The juxtaposition, if not complete interpenetration, of various Islamic speech genres and genres of practice—the *sunna*, the formation of a chain of authoritative transmission (*isnād*), the prayers and invocations that accompany the performing of ritual ablutions (*al-wuḍū'*) and the mention of this same ritual practice within the story itself, the explicit *amplificatio* of the Qur'ānic verse 18:83 that opens the story, and the computations of the start of the lunar month of Ramaḍān scribbled in at the end of the codex—all situate Alexander not only within an explicitly Islamic tradition of popular literature, but also within discursive frameworks with strong and direct connections to various modes of devotional practice in the Crypto-Muslim communities of sixteenth-century Castile and Aragon. Such connections powerfully link Alexander to modes of being-in-the-world and action specific to the *morisco* communities of sixteenth-century Castile and Aragon.

What remains is to consider how the pragmatic and phenomenological features encoded in the short texts that surround and introduce the *Rekontamiento del rey Ališandre* intersect with the narrative itself (a narrative explicitly concerned with the interplay between the temporal world over which Alexander would rule and the eternal one of which, at the end of the story, Aristotle admonishes him to be mindful). At the heart of this consideration is an account of the persistent division that is made throughout the *Rekontamiento del rey Ališandre* between *al-dunyā* and *al-akhira*, or the spatiotemporal world and the afterlife, and the limits of human agency (reached in violent and dramatic fashion by Alexander) in the face of a death that comes from beyond, always too soon, to take us into it. To begin to address these matters in anything but a superficial way, however, it is necessary to return to the issue of how precisely the figure of Alexander came to be referred to as the "Two-Horned One" in the Islamic tradition and how the *Rekontamiento del rey Ališandre* draws from this legend to shape its account of epic achievement, devotional practice, and human mortality.

Siwa ʿAjamiyya

In November of 332 BCE, after a seven-month amphibious siege at Tyre followed shortly thereafter by a quick rout of Mazaces, the Persian satrap of Egypt, Alexander and his army arrived in Memphis. Here Alexander made it a point to pay very public homage to the Egyptian gods (something the Persians had consistently refused to do), and it was likely not long after this scene that he was recognized as pharaoh, a title that officially raised the Macedonian king to the status of a living deity for his new Egyptian subjects.[36] What psychological effect his new, quasi-divine status within Egypt may have had on Alexander is not known; however, it is evident that he did his best to cultivate this pharaonic image publicly, as evidenced by a bas-relief within the temple of Luxor that depicts him as a pharaoh paying homage to the ithyphallic Egyptian god Amun-Min.

Ironically enough, it is not Alexander's coronation/apotheosis as the new ruler of Egypt that has become a central feature of the legendary and historical narratives surrounding the Macedonian king, but rather a (relatively) short trip that he then made to Siwa, a large oasis in the Libyan desert. This journey to Siwa has had particular resonance within the Islamic tradition of legends, narratives, and even Qurʾanic verses involving Alexander, owing in large part to Alexander's subsequent affiliation with the god Amun, whose oracle was situated there. Alexander's connection to Amun was not merely devotional; he believed—and the priests of the oracle, perhaps overly eager to please their new pharaoh, confirmed this belief—that he was in fact Amun's son. This revelation meant little to the Egyptians, who already considered Alexander, as pharaoh, to be a living god, but it made a significant impact upon Alexander, who thereafter demanded of the much more skeptical Greeks and Macedonians that they recognize him as divine.

The story begins almost immediately after Alexander leaves Memphis for the Mediterranean coast of Egypt in early 331 BCE. At some point on that trip up the Nile River, Alexander latched onto the idea of traveling overland to the oasis of Siwa to consult the oracle of Amun. Arrian sets the scene:

> a longing [*póthos*] seized Alexander to pay a visit to Ammon in Libya, for one reason to consult the god, since the oracle of Ammon was said to be infallible, and to have been consulted by Perseus, when he was sent by Polydectes against the Gorgon, and by Heracles when he was on his way into Libya to find Antaeus, and into Egypt to find Busiris. Alexander sought to rival Perseus and Heracles [*Alexándrô dè philotimía ên pròs Perséa kaì 'Hrakléa*], as he was descended from them both; and in addition he himself traced his birth in part to Ammon, just as the legends traced that of Heracles and Perseus to Zeus. In any case he set out for Ammon with this idea, hoping to secure more exact knowledge of his affairs, or at least to say that he had secured it.[37]

Arrian is clear about Alexander's political motivations with regard to the oracle at Siwa, speaking first of the young king's *póthos*, or "Dionysiac urge to do something extraordinary."[38] This urge, as Arrian presents it, is connected to Alexander's ambitious desire (*philotimos*) to eclipse in every way the accomplishments of his ancestor Heracles and his perceived predecessor as Persian emperor, Perseus.

In strictly political terms, in fact, the journey to Siwa was a key piece of the complex strategy by which Alexander was fighting to keep Greek (particularly Athenian) public opinion on his side as he planned for deeper incursions into Asia. John Maxwell O'Brien supports this argument:

> In Alexander's mind, the undertaking made perfect sense. He was a religious man on the brink of the most important battle in his life [his final battle with Darius III at Gaugamela], and so a consultation with a prestigious oracle was perfectly consistent with his priorities. The trip might be perilous, but for him that would be an incentive rather than a deterrent. Aristotle had spoken with respect about a pious pilgrim who made the journey. The Greek world, whose opinion was always a concern of Alexander, ranked Siwah alongside Delphi and Dodona in the forefront of prophetic authorities. Given the infallible reputation of its oracular pronouncements, approval at Siwah could lend *imprimatur* to whatever Alexander believed or wished to undertake.[39]

Seen from a practical perspective, one in which Alexander was not only king of Macedonia but also the *hêgemôn* of the League of Corinth (a league invented by Alexander's father as a means of consolidating Macedonian power within Greece), the possible benefits of a journey to Siwa seem to have outweighed the foreseeable risks and costs.

Beyond the more or less solid political calculations and pious intentions involved in Alexander's decision to make the trip to Siwa, Arrian does suggest, albeit subtly, that there were other motivations at work as well: "kaì ti kaì autòs tês genéseôs tês heautou es Ammôna anéphere, katháper hoi muthoi tên Herakléous te kaì Perséôs es Día" (and in addition he himself traced his birth in part to Ammon, just as the legends traced that of Heracles and Perseus to Zeus).[40] Quintus Curtius, whose account of Alexander's life was second only to that of Paulus Orosius in terms of its popularity during the late Middle Ages, is much less subtle in speaking of the Macedonian king's immoderate desire to confirm at Siwa the theory of his divine parentage, although in Quintus Curtius's account the god in question is Jupiter rather than Amun—a reflection of the common Greek practice of conflating Amun with Zeus: "Sed ingens cupido animum stimulabat adeundi Iovem, quem generis sui auctorem haud contentus mortali fastigio aut credebat esse aut credi volebat" (Alexander was goaded by an overwhelming desire to visit the temple of Jupiter—dissatisfied with elevation on the mortal level, he either considered, or wanted others to believe, that Jupiter was his ancestor).[41] The fuzzy boundaries that existed, both in Alexander's mind and in many of his contemporaries', between the legendary and the historical are made explicit in both Arrian's and Quintus Curtius's accounts, as is Alexander's desire (the Greek word *póthos* once again serves nicely) to be recognized as the son of a god by the Greeks and Macedonians. This was no small challenge, as O'Brien points out: "The Egyptians had already accepted him as both the son of a god and a god in his own right, but among Macedonians and Greeks these issues had to be treated with sensitivity and tact. The authority of the oracle could be decisive with any such claim made in the future."[42] Seen, then, from a less practical (though by no means less important, at least for Alexander's imperial politics) point of view, the journey to Siwa could help Alexander to secure, within both the Greco-Macedonian and the Egyptian political context, his place among the immortals, something that even the most spectacular victory over the Persians could not do.

In all fairness to Alexander, he was encouraged from an early age to see himself as the son of a god. According to Justin's summary account of Pompeius Trogus's extensive *Historiae philippicae* (Philippine Histories), Alexander's mother, Olympias,

> confessa viro suo Philippo fuerat Alexandrum non ex eo se, sed ex serpente ingentis magnitudinis, concepisse. Denique Philippus ultimo prope vitae suae tempore filium suum non esse palam praedicauerat; qua ex causa Olympiada velut stupri conpertam repudio dimiserat.[43]

> [had confessed to her husband, Philip, that she had conceived Alexander not by him, but by a serpent of extraordinary size. Philip too, towards the end of his life, had publicly declared that Alexander was not his son; and he accordingly divorced Olympias, as having been guilty of adultery.]

Plutarch, who is more measured in his treatment of both Philip and Olympias, goes into more detail regarding the snake with which Olympias may or may not have had intercourse. He relates the story of how one day Philip came into his wife's room and found a large snake in bed with her as she slept. It is not clear, according to Plutarch (who cites twenty-four different source texts in the course of his brief summary of Alexander's life), whether Philip afterward feared Alexander's mother as a sorceress or suspected that she was having sexual relations with some god, but the result of this encounter was that he ceased to visit her bedroom altogether. Plutarch then explains away Olympias's perceived intimacy with the serpent in religious terms, citing her active participation in Orphic rites that frequently involved the presence of tame serpents and that "made a spectacle which men could not look upon without terror."[44]

On the specific issue of Olympias's role in pressing the notion that Alexander's father was a god, we may turn once again to Arrian, who explains that when the court historian Callisthenes, not incidentally the nephew of Alexander's former tutor Aristotle, was attempting to underscore the important role that he played in the king's greater designs, he (foolishly) made the claim that "Alexander's share in divinity did not depend on Olympias's intervention about his birth, but on the account he [himself] would write and publish in Alexander's interest."[45] Implicit in this statement, of course, is the idea that Alexander's claim to divine parentage was in fact nothing more than an invention—either pieced together by his mother or by the Olynthian

historian so busily sending narrative panegyrics back to Athens in install-
ments.[46] Sadly for Callisthenes, he was able to write very little if anything
after this exchange, given that Alexander subsequently had him charged with
treason in connection with the so-called Pages' Conspiracy and executed. As
Justin tells it, Callisthenes was first mutilated by having his nose, ears, and
lips cut off and then was held in a cage along with a dog until Lysimachus,
one of Alexander's bodyguards, poisoned him out of pity—a mercy killing
that has inspired the focused reflection of philosophers such as Seneca the
Younger and Montesquieu.[47]

It bears mentioning too that within Egypt a rumor spread that Alexander was not only the newly recognized pharaoh who had ended Persian rule
in Egypt, but also the illegitimate son of the last native Egyptian pharaoh,
Nectanebo II. This pharaoh was defeated by the Persian King Artaxerxes III
in 343 BCE and forced to flee Egypt, ending a period known in ancient Egyptian history as the Thirtieth Dynasty. Between the defeat of Nectanebo II
and Alexander's arrival in Egypt in 332 BCE, Egypt had been governed by a
Persian satrap, and it was perhaps natural for at least some Egyptians to see
Alexander—who readily paid homage to the Egyptian gods—as the em-
bodiment of a dynastic restoration rather than a Macedonian conqueror.
The weight of this tradition was of course augmented by the official propaganda of the Ptolemaic Dynasty, which ruled in Egypt from the time of Alexander's death to the defeat of Mark Antony and Cleopatra VII at Actium in
31 BCE: their authority derived directly from their link to Alexander through
Ptolemy I Soter (367–283 BCE), and they benefited enormously from the
belief that their rule was in essence the continuation, through Alexander's
purported direct descent from Nectanebo II, of the last line of native Egyptian kings. Alexander's theoretical Egyptian parentage is picked up in the
legendary tradition as well (a tradition with origins, not coincidentally, in
Ptolemaic Alexandria), in which Nectanebo is supposed to have arrived in
Pella and impregnated Olympias disguised as a large snake.

Whether or not the events at Siwa actually smoothed a path toward divinity for Alexander with respect to the Greeks and Macedonians remains an
open question. What is generally accepted, however, is that the journey was
in general a very difficult one. As Quintus Curtius describes it:

> The journey that had to be made could scarcely be managed even by a
> small band of soldiers lightly armed: land and sky lack moisture; the sands

lie flat and barren, and when they are seared by the blazing sun the ground swelters and burns the feet and the heat is intolerable. Apart from the high temperatures and dryness of the terrain one also has to contend with the tenacious quality of the sand which, because of its depth and the fact that it gives way to the tread, is difficult to negotiate on foot.[48]

Plutarch paints a similar picture of the difficulties associated with the journey but then moves almost seamlessly into a nearly miraculous account of Alexander's trip to Siwa, made in the spring of 331 BCE:

In this journey, the relief and assistance the gods afforded him in his distresses were more remarkable, and obtained greater belief than the oracles he received afterwards, which, however, were valued and credited the more on account of these occurrences. For first, plentiful rains that fell preserved them from any fear of perishing by drought, and, allaying the extreme dryness of the sand, which now became moist and firm to travel on, cleared and purified the air. Besides this, when they were out of their way, and were wandering up and down, because the marks which were wont to direct the guides were disordered and lost, they were set right again by some ravens, which flew before them when on their march, and waited for them when they lingered and fell behind; and the greatest miracle, as Callisthenes tells us, was that if any of the company went astray in the night, they never ceased croaking and making a noise till by that means they had brought them into the right way again. Having passed through the wilderness, they came to the place where the high priest, at the first salutation[,] bade Alexander welcome from his father Ammon.[49]

Plutarch's sources for this account of the journey to Siwa are Callisthenes (whom he mentions by name), Ptolemy, Aristoboulus, and Cleitarchus. Tellingly, he leaves out Ptolemy's fantastic account of the twin talking snakes that led Alexander and his men to the oracle at Siwa. Arrian makes mention of these snakes, but only to discount Ptolemy's version of the story before admitting that some sort of divine intervention had nonetheless likely occurred: "That some divine help was given him I can confidently assert, because probability suggests it too; but the exact truth of the story cannot be told; that is precluded by the way in which different writers about Alexander have given different accounts."[50]

As Arrian admits, the events at Siwa are shrouded in almost willful mystery. Whether the priests at the oracle confirmed that Amun was Alexander's father or not is a matter of much historical speculation. Plutarch even mentions the theory that the head priest at Siwa, whose proficiency in Greek was highly suspect, merely misspoke when addressing Alexander: "Others say that the priest, desirous as a piece of courtesy to address him in Greek, 'O Paidion' [Oh my child/son], by a slip in pronunciation ended with the *s* instead of the *n*, and said 'O Paidios' [Oh son of Zeus], which mistake Alexander was well enough pleased with, and it went for current that the oracle had called him so."[51] Arrian, for his part, states merely that Alexander "received the answer his heart desired" from the oracle and leaves it at that.[52]

Quintus Curtius, who like Justin/Trogus employed Cleitarchus as his main source, is a bit more unreserved in both his account of Alexander's visit to Siwa and his judgment of Alexander's subsequent claim to divine parentage. He first cites the priest's greeting of him as "son of Zeus," and then goes on to recount the questions that Alexander asks of the oracle and the answers that were supposedly given to him:

> Forgetting his mortal state, Alexander said that he accepted and acknowledged the title, and he proceeded to ask whether he was fated to rule over the entire world. The priest, who was as ready as anyone else to flatter him, answered that he was going to rule over all the earth. After this Alexander went on to inquire whether his father's murderers had all received their punishment. The priest's answer was that no harm could come to his father from anybody's wrongdoing, but that as far as Philip was concerned all had paid the penalty; and he added that he would remain undefeated until he went to join the gods. Alexander thereupon offered sacrifice, presented gifts both to the priests and to the god, and also allowed his friends to consult Jupiter on their own account. Their only question was whether the god authorized their according divine honours to their king, and this, too, so the priest replied, would be agreeable to Jupiter.[53]

The subtext of Curtius's account, merely alluded to in Arrian, is that Alexander was abetted by an Egyptian priest eager to flatter the new Hellenophone pharaoh and receive favors in return. As Spencer argues, Curtius was a staunch opponent of the Roman ruler cults of the Julio-Claudian period, and his account of Alexander often reveals this sentiment.[54] This is perhaps nowhere more apparent than at the end of Curtius's account of the journey to Siwa: "Someone making a sound and honest judgment of the oracle's reliability might well have found these responses disingenuous, but fortune generally makes those whom she has compelled to put their trust in her alone more thirsty for glory than capable of coping with it."[55] Justin goes on to conclude that the net effect of the visit to Siwa was that "hinc illi aucta insolentia mirusque animo increuit tumor exempta comitate quam et Graecorum litteris et Macedonum institutis didicerat" (Alexander's haughtiness was so much increased, and a strange arrogance arose in his mind, the agreeableness of demeanor, which he had contracted from the philosophy of the Greeks and the habits of the Macedonians, being entirely laid aside).[56]

Whatever occurred at Siwa, the events that followed afterward did much to shape legendary accounts of Alexander, especially within Islam. While Alexander undoubtedly pressed his Macedonian and Greek subjects to view him as the son of Amun (whom they equated with Zeus), he also moved within a parallel Egyptian tradition, taking on the physical attributes—primarily on coins—of this Egyptian god. Cartledge underscores the significance of this Egyptian tradition and its imagery for Alexander:

> At all events, it is absolutely clear that after the Siwah visit Alexander claimed a close relationship, possibly even physical filiation, with non-Greek Ammon, not with the syncretistic or hybrid Zeus-Ammon. . . . [A] silver coin issued in Alexander's own lifetime depicts him wearing the horns of Ammon. After his death, Ptolemy I [Soter] went one better and issued a coin showing him wearing not only Ammon's horns but also an elephant scalp-headdress in token of his great victory over Porus at the Hydaspes River in 326 [BCE]. Clinchingly, it was to Ammon at Siwah that Alexander sent in 324 [BCE] when he wanted to discover the most sensitive issue of the moment—how precisely should the recently deceased Hephaestion be posthumously venerated: as a god, or as a hero?[57]

The answer that came back from Siwa on this last question, posed from fifteen hundred miles away in Ecbatana (modern-day Hamadan, Iran), was that Hephaestion could not be worshipped as a god, but could be honored as a hero. Although this was presumably not the answer that Alexander wanted from the oracle, he nonetheless followed it to the letter.

The iconography of Amun would surround Alexander even after his own death: "The god Ammon became increasingly important to Alexander after Siwah . . . [and] after his death the men who knew him well would incorporate the horn of Ammon into the canonical iconography of Alexander."[58] To support his claims to divinity as the son of Amun (whom the

Greeks venerated as an avatar of Zeus), Alexander began to sanction official graphic representations of himself with the ram's horns of Amun curling through his hair. This image of Alexander fitted with the horns of a ram— horns that, incidentally, had also been part of the royal iconography of earlier pharaohs such as Amenhotep III (d. 1391 BCE)—can still be seen on various ancient coins. The best-known of these is likely the silver *tetradrachm* issued by King Lysimachus of Thrace (360–281 BCE) from the Pergamum mint shortly after Alexander's death, which displays Alexander in profile with large eyes, tousled hair, and both the royal diadem and a prominent pair of ram's horns on his head.[59]

Within the Hellenophone Ptolemaic Dynasty, the Alexandrian link to Amun was repeatedly invoked. This move made particular sense for the Ptolemies, in part because they ruled in Egypt and also because they derived power directly from the association of their first king, Ptolemy I Soter, with Alexander. Beryl Barr-Sharrar states succinctly that "members of the Ptolemeic [sic] dynasty—both male and female—borrowed the elephant's scalp from Alexander's image for portrayals in several media, as they did the ram's horns."[60] The most prominent female of the Ptolemaic line to employ the horns of Amun as part of a politicoreligious program was Arsinoe II (316–270 BCE), daughter of Ptolemy I Soter and eventually the wife of her brother, Ptolemy II (309–246 BCE). Her brother/husband actively sought to elevate her to the status of an Egyptian and Greek goddess through an association with Amun: "coins were minted bearing the portrait of the queen, on which she wears the ram's horns of Amun, among other features."[61] It is during this period that the first rescension of the Greek Alexander legend gained widespread popularity, prompting various emendations, accretions, and translations, among them the fifth-century CE Christian Syriac version that would find its way into the Qur'ān as the story of Dhū al-Qarnayn.[62] It is this Qur'ānic Alexander, already transformed in the Syriac version from a pagan Hellenic emperor into a bicornual instrument of the Abrahamic God, that eventually found his way into popular Ibero-Islamic texts such as the *Qiṣṣat Dhū al-Qarnayn* and its Aljamiado translation, the *Rekontamiento del rey Ališandre*.[63]

Through the two horns of Alexander we establish a direct link between the Macedonian king's efforts to establish his divine status and thus ensure his immortality and the broader Islamic concern with mortality and the afterlife. My point is that these horns, which according to some Qur'ānic scholars symbolize the spatial totality of the earth (the Arabic term *qrn* can be translated literally as "horn" or more figuratively as "nation"), can also be read along different, nonspatial vertices as the temporal expanse that extends from beginning to end, from birth to death. It is thus what lies beyond the span of these two horns (on either side), as the text of the *Rekontamiento del rey Ališandre* makes explicit, that becomes the principal concern of the narrative. At every turn in the text, the reader is reminded of the limits of human life and knowledge, of God's power, and of the final judgment that occurs just beyond the temporal-spatial expanse of this world and life (a concept summed up very neatly by the Arabic term *al-dunyā*). This intertwining of time and space—a kind of Islamic chronotope symbolized by Dhū al-Qarnayn's horns, or more accurately, the space between them—is made explicit at the very beginning of the narrative, when a group of Jews asks Muḥammad about the time that it took for Dhū al-Qarnayn to travel the entire expanse of the world, from East to West: "Dijeron: Yā menšajero de Allāh, i en ku^{w}ánto ti^{y}enpo rrodeó lal-dunyā ṭoda? Dišo: Den dose años" (They said: Messenger of God, in how much time did he travel around the entire world? He said: In twelve years).[64] In this way, the space of the world is measured out in terms of the time it took for Dhū al-Qarnayn to cross it—a complex mix of space, time, and agentive (if divinely inspired) action.

It should be pointed out that the *Rekontamiento del rey Ališandre* actually offers a multitude of theories regarding how Dhū al-Qarnayn received his name, all of which intersect in different ways with the temporal and ontological themes that I have just mentioned. Responding once again to the opening questions of his Jewish interviewers, Muḥammad states the following regarding the meaning and source of the name Dhū al-Qarnayn:

Dišřo Ka'bun: Hadīthanoš Abū Dharrin ke Allāh di^{y}o ada Dhū al-Qarnayni fecho ke no lo di^{y}o a nenguno de šuš formadoš i potensi^{y}a ke no pu^{w}ede šobrella nenguno de šuš formadoš, ke dise: "dimošle de toda koša šaber." Porke še lonb^{a}ra a Dhū al-Qarnayni? Dišřo: Rrekóntame Hišām, hijo de Ka'bin; dišřo ke teni^{y}a doš ku^{w}ernoš ke ligaba šobrelloš šuš ṭokaš. Dišřo enpero: lonb^{o}rólo Allāh a Dhū al-Qarnayn porkél ~~lleg~~ llegó a loš kaboš de la ti^{y}erra, a šol šali^{y}ente i ^{y}a šol poni^{y}ente, i bi^{y}o el šol de donde šali^{y}a, i lo bi^{y}o donde še poni^{y}a, i por akello lo lonb^{o}ró Allāh Dhū al-Qarnayni. Dišřo Muchāsir: lonb^{o}rólo Allāh Dhū al-Qarnayni porkél era barragán, i ^{y}era k-enkont^{a}raba la pele^{y}a, i š[e] aserṭaba él ku^{w}ando še ap^{c}retaba i ku^{w}ando paraban mi^{y}ent^{e}reš šuš konpañaš adelantábanše a morir, i laš o[t]raš vensi^{y}a kon lo ke keriᵞa, i feriᵞa šobre šuš quᵂernoš doš feridaš kon la špada šobre šu quᵂerno el derecho i šobre šu kuᵂerno el iskiᵞerdo.⁶⁵

[Kaʿbu said: Abū Dharri has told us that God gave to Dhū al-Qarnayn something that he gave to none of his other creatures and power such that none of his creatures could best him; that is: "We gave to him knowledge of all things." Why is he named Dhū al-Qarnayn [The Two-Horned One]? [Muḥammad] said: ʿHišām ibn Kaʿbi told me that he had two horns that he covered with his headpiece. [The Prophet] then said, however: God called him Dhū al-Qarnayn because he reached the ends of the earth, to the rising and setting sun, and he saw the point from where the sun rose and where it set, and for that reason God called him Dhū al-Qarnayn. Mujāsir said: God called him Dhū al-Qarnayn because he was courageous and never shied away from battle; he grew in strength when he was pressed, and when his troops reflected upon this they rushed forward to die, and he vanquished others at will. He gave himself two sword wounds on his horns, one on his right horn and one on the left.]

We find in this description of Alexander as Dhū al-Qarnayn a rich intersection of the major themes of the text as a whole. In the first place, according to what Muḥammad states, God gave Alexander "knowledge of all things." This knowledge is clearly presented as a divine gift, but it does not come by means of a one-time revelation, but rather through Alexander's lived experience— in large part shaped by his studies with Aristotle—and actions over time. Through this experience, Alexander *becomes* Dhū al-Qarnayn, a name that he receives from God upon having "reached the ends of the earth, to the rising and setting sun," and seeing "the point from where the sun rose and where it set." In this way, the text links knowledge both to the generosity of God and to lived experience, action, and perception ("he *saw* the point . . ."). Most importantly, it links Alexander to the spatiotemporal boundaries of human existence and the hereafter that stretches out beyond them. In the penultimate example from the above citation, taken from Mujāsir, Alexander supposedly gains the title of Dhū al-Qarnayn because of his courage in battle—a form of courage that produces the effect of helping his troops to overcome their own fear of death and rush forward to meet it, and whatever lies beyond.

The themes of knowledge, experience, and courage all come together in Alexander, and are framed by the horns (*kuᵂernoš*) that signify both the spatial expanse of Alexander's travels during his life and the temporal expanse of that life itself. Tellingly, the *Rekontamiento del rey Ališandre* ends with Aristotle admonishing Alexander to take into full consideration the end of his life and the judgment that will follow: "Ke loš diyaš še van i tu pᵃlaso š-aserka de tu i tu dešaras tu al-dunyā; apᵃreššate para al-akhira pᵒrovišiʸon de temor i ʸobra buʷena anteš ke te venga la muʷert i tu dello nigligente" (The days are passing, your end is nearing, and you will leave this world; take for yourself the provision of fear and good works for the afterlife before your death comes to you and finds you unmindful of it).[66] The Arabic term *al-dunyā* is central here, as it is in other Aljamiado texts dealing with moral comportment and the afterlife.[67] In basic terms, *al-dunyā* refers to the spatiotemporal world and the human lifespan; however, it does so always in relation to the concept of *al-akhira*, or the afterlife. Jane I. Smith and Yvonne Yazbeck Haddad, in their study of death and the afterlife in Sunni Islam, make this point explicitly:

> The terms *dunyā* and *akhira* themselves are related both to time and space: *dunyā* is the earth in the physical sense but at the same time refers to the period every individual spends on earth, related to its activities, as well as to the total time frame continuing until the coming of the hour of judgment. *Akhira* correspondingly refers both to the heavens, *samāwāt*, as the specific abodes of the angels and of the saved, and to the antithesis of *dunyā*, the hereafter or eternity. The very term used repeatedly in the Qur'ān for eternity is *dār al-akhira*, the "abode" of the hereafter, in itself illustrating the coincidence of the spatial and the temporal.[68]

In a deeper sense, then, the passage of the *Rekontamiento del rey Ališandre* in which Aristotle speaks to Alexander about the afterlife and God's judgment is principally concerned with a moral framework that is at once pragmatic, temporal, spatial, and eschatological. The question here is not about death per se, but also about the value of one's actions and fear of God (as a kind of footing) accumulated within the *dunyā* in the face of the judgment to come within the *akhira*. It is thus a reckoning with the fullness of *al-dunyā* and what lies beyond it (*al-akhira*) that most directly shapes the significance of Dhū al-Qarnayn's two horns and the *Rekontamiento del rey Ališandre* itself. Seen in this way, the prayer invocations that accompany ritual ablution and precede the text of the *Rekontamiento del rey Ališandre*, as well as the astronomical observations contained in the folios that follow it, intersect with the text's own concern with issues of life (as an activity framework) and the divine judgment to come.

The *Rekontamiento del rey Alisandre* begins, as I have stated above, with a narrative frame within which Muḥammad is asked a series of questions by a group of Jews. His answers to these men make up the rest of the story, which is mapped out by Nykl:

> Alexander is portrayed as an Islamic leader whose mission is to spread the true religion all over the inhabited world, by fire and sword, if necessary. With the exception of the Gog and Magog, the Snakes, and some peoples who resemble rather animals than human beings, his success is complete. He is not a prophet, but merely an admonisher, a model (*ḥujja*) for people to follow in order to escape the punishment of the Day of Judgment, f. 5v. The Jews become Muslims, 10. Alexander proclaims his mission in f. 11v. Urges the people of Yūnus to say the *kelima*, but finds them already converted to Islām, 16v. Summons the Gog and Magog to believe in Allāh, 19. Cave dwellers summoned to adopt Islām, 22v. Angel repeats to Alexander God's summons to make war on the unbelievers, 39v, 40, 40v. Alexander sends letters to the kings of the East and of the West summoning them to the true belief, 41. Writes to Darius in Quranic terms, 41v ff. Writes to his armies, calling himself "šanto fijo de Yūneš," and encourages them to put their trust in Allāh and in him, Allāh's viceregent on earth, 42v ff. Writes threatening letters to idolatrous kings, replete with praises of Allāh in Quranic terms, 44–47v. Darius pretends to be God's viceregent, and uses the standard Quranic expressions, 49. Alexander's answer refutes this in still more powerful terms, 53ff. Soldiers of Darius, dragged out of the frozen river, become Muslims, 59. Darius shows himself a thorough Muslim, his mother and daughter likewise, 66–66v. (Strangely enough, in 63v Alexander is rather liberal and leaves it to the Persians to believe in Islām or not. This is in harmony with the original [Greek legend] and was probably overlooked by the Arab compilers.) Destruction of idols and temples in India, 73v. Reassertion of the divine mission, 73v. The Turjamānīn episode is replete with Islamic tradition and superstitions, 74v–85v. Queen Semiramis summoned to become a convert of Islām, 86v. Reassertion of the divine mission, 97v, 99 ff, 107, 110. Submission of the Chinese ruler to the "rrey šanto," 118–120. Alexander builds a mosque, 124. Alexander admonished by Aristotle (also a Muslim) to think of the next world, 125.[69]

Nykl finishes this brief sketch of the text with a short statement, taken in part from Francisco Guillén Robles, regarding the "rather limited" literary merit of the *Rekontamiento del rey Ališandre*: "The literary merit of the text Sr. Robles says is 'bastante escaso.' This is on the whole true, with a few exceptions, where the author rises to the point of eloquence and shows excellent touches of consistent characterization of the principal hero."[70] In keeping with my broader concern with the ways in which the *Rekontamiento del rey Ališandre* intersects both with the theme of imperial expansion and with deeper, phenomenological issues of human existence and death, I am not necessarily interested in "literary merits" of the text. What most interests me is uncovering the ways in which this manuscript text theorizes death and the afterlife within a frame that is both traditionally Islamic and of a piece with the larger current of Alexander literature written and/or recopied within the Iberian Peninsula during the fifteenth and sixteenth centuries. To this end, it is worth looking briefly at the episode in *Rekontamiento del rey Ališandre* in which Alexander and his men travel through the land of total darkness and reach the fountain of life at its center.

Darkness and Light

Alexander's expedition through the land of darkness occurs just prior to the war with Darius, and it is on the basis of this journey that Alexander comes to understand that God has given him the right to rule over all the people of the earth: "Allāh, 'azza wa jalla, ya me a dado šu šenyorⁱʸo šobre todoš loš del mundo" (God, the mighty and noble, has given me power over all on earth).[71] It is also this journey to the beyond that more or less sets the terms of Alexander's power and life: it is here that he learns he will have power upon the earth but will not achieve immortality. His empire will correspond to and be limited by *al-dunyā* (symbolized by the two horns of his Arabic name), and his power—a gift from God—is wholly contingent upon his resolute focus upon *al-akhira*.

   This episode in the land of darkness occurs near the beginning of the *Rekontamiento del rey Ališandre*, just after Alexander converts the severely sunburned and largely nocturnal inhabitants of the city of Jābalqā to Islam. Within the *Rekontamiento del rey Ališandre*, the city of Jābalqā is the easternmost city of the known world, and the point from which the sun rises (in other versions of the story it is the westernmost, where the sun sets).[72] The text presents Alexander's interaction with this city:

Depu^wéš Dhū al-Qarnayni fu^weše a la sibdad de Jābalqā i bi^yo una sibdad ke teni^ya dose pu^wertaš i šobre kadda pu^werta nobenta mil porteroš
k-ent^araba kada di^ya si^yen mil per^sonaš para šuš meneštereš i šali^ya kada
di^ya šenbalante de akello por kada pu^werta i ent^ere pu^werta i pu^werta andadura de rete t^ereš millaš i vi^yo šuš khaleqadoš ke no teni^yan peloš ni barbaš
ni poštañaš en šuš ojoš ni sejaš ke ya leš ende abi^ya kemado el šol i elloš
ti^yenen ku^webaš de debajo de la ti^yerra ke nellaš abi^ya kašaš i šakaban laš
ollaš šobre la kara de la ti^yerra i loš paneš kosi^yan al kalor del šol i ku^wando
beni^ya el sol al ponimi^yento šali^yan de šuš ku^webaš i bendi^yan i konp^araban
i kaminaban i ^yelloš iban de noche i š-eškondi^yan de di^ya i llamóloš a-Dhū
al-Qarnayni a la k^ere^yensi^ya kon Allāh ta'alá i ^yatorgar k-él eš šeñor ke no ay
šeñor šino él i k^ere^yeron i ^yaberdadesi^yeron i rrešpondi^yeron i ^yobedesi^yeron
i eštaba awardando a-Dhū al-Qarnayni komo sali^ya el šol de šu rru^weda
šobrelloš.⁷³

[Afterward Dhū al-Qarnayn went to the city of Jābalqā and saw there a city
that had twelve doors and above each there were 90,000 guards; each day
100,000 people entered these doors to perform their necessary tasks and
each day a similar number left through them. The distance between these
doors was three miles. Dhū al-Qarnayni saw that the city's people had neither hair, beards, eyelashes, nor eyebrows, as the sun had burned these off.
These people have caves below the earth in which they had houses, and they
took out their pots on the surface of the earth and baked their bread with
the heat of the sun. When the sun began to set they came out of their caves
to sell and purchase goods and walk around; that is, they moved around at
night and hid during the day. Dhū al-Qarnayn called them to the worship
of God, and to attest that he is the Lord and that there is no Lord but he.
And they believed, affirmed this belief, and responded to and obeyed this
call. Dhū al-Qarnayn was then watching how the sun rose on its wheel
above them.]

The brief description of Jābalqā, followed by the almost perfunctory conversion of the city's residents and Alexander's contemplation of the rising sun,
seeks to describe the easternmost point of Alexander's earthly journey. It is
from this point that he ventures beyond the realm of human experience and
into the land of complete darkness, where his companion al-Khaḍir is called
to drink from the fountain of life, but Alexander is not.

What follows the perhaps overly economical description of the city of
Jābalqā and its conversion, after a line break, is a bilingual description of an
image most likely found in the Arabic manuscript that served as the source

for the Aljamiado translation from which the text in Madrid, BN MS 5254, was copied. This description reads: "*Ṣūratu* La fegura *Dhī al-Qarnayni* da Dhū al-Qarnayni *yanẓuru* ke wardaba *ilá al-šamsi* al šol *kayfa* komo *taṭluʻu* šaliʸa *min dawrihā* de šu ruʷeda *wa al-qawmu* i laš genteš *warāʻahu* saga dél *yanẓuruna* parando miʸentʻres *ilayhi* a él *kayfa* komo *yanẓuru* wardaba *ilaha* a él" (*Ṣūratu* The image *Dhī al-Qarnayni* of Dhū al-Qarnayn *yanẓuruna* he watches *ilá al-šamsi* the sun *kayfa* how *taṭluʻu* it rose *min dawrihā* from its wheel *wa al-qawmu* and the people *warāʻahu* behind him *yanẓuruna* contemplate *ilayhi* him *kayfa* how *yanẓuru* he watches *ilaha* it).[74] The described image corresponds to the end of the Aljamiado Jābalqā episode. Alexander has already converted the people of Jābalqā to Islam, and he is contemplating the rising sun, a scene that simultaneously presents his powers of conversion, the distance and time that he has traveled, and the power of God (there is no suggestion that the nearby sun has burned Dhū al-Qarnayn in any way). What this description of the original image also presents is a participation framework that speaks to models of conquest, heroism, and conversion in late medieval Islam: Alexander is looking directly at the rising sun, while the residents of Jābalqā look at him, likely in wonder of both his power and that of the God that he serves. In this way the economy of the text is offset by the depth of the image that complements it, even if in Madrid, BN MS 5254, the image does not actually appear but is merely presented ekphrastically.

Directly after Alexander finishes his imperial/religious business in Jābalqā, at the easternmost end of the world, he begins to desire to seek out a land of total darkness that he has read of in the book of an author from Alexandria:

Depuʷeš fuʷeše kišiʸendo buškar laškuridad Dhū al-Qarnayni i ʸašentoše kon šuš wešteš en la tiʸerra poblada de laš partidaš de akella sibdad de Jābalqā en la sageriʸa de šu tiʸerra i era Dhū al-Qarnayni ke abiʸa bišto en el libro del Eskenderiʸus ken la tiʸerra abiʸa una ešquridad i ʸen la mitad de laškuridad una fuʷente ke šu awa eš el awa de la bida i ʸubo konfiʸansa en beber della i beber de šu awa el i šuš wešteš kizaw ke durariʸan kon el mundo i durariʸa šu šeñoriʸo kon el duramiʸento del mundo dakiʸa el diʸa del afinamiʸento.[75]

[Afterward Dhū al-Qarnayn left, wishing to look for the darkness and he situated his troops in the outskirts of the city of Jābalqā, just behind their land. Dhū al-Qarnayn had seen in the book of the Alexandrian that in the land there was a darkness and in the middle of that darkness a fountain from which flowed the water of life. And he believed that if he and his troops drank the fountain's water that they would live as long as the earth itself and his power would endure until the end of the earth and the day of judgment.]

The book in question is quite probably the *Greek Alexander Romance*, thought to have been first pieced together in Alexandria during the third century BCE by an author/editor now commonly referred to as Pseudo-Callisthenes. This text, which was translated into Syriac sometime during the sixth century CE and then into Arabic around 800 CE, serves as the ultimate source for the *Rekontamiento del rey Ališandre*, although there are many differences between the Arabic (and Aljamiado) text and the extant Greek rescencions.[76]

In the second book of the *Greek Alexander Romance*, Alexander and a small portion of his troops travel to a land of complete darkness that is known as the Land of the Blessed. Guided by a wise old man among them, Alexander and his men come to a clear spring that grants immortality to those who drink from it:

We came to a place where there was a clear spring, whose water flashed like lightning, and some other streams besides. The air in this place was very fragrant and less dark than before. I was hungry and wanted some bread, so I called the cook Andreas by name and said, "Prepare some food for us." He took a dried fish and waded into the clear water of the spring to wash it. As soon as it was dipped in the water, it came to life and leapt out of the cook's hands. He was frightened, and did not tell me what had happened; instead he drank some of the water himself, and scooped some up in a silver vessel and kept it. The whole place was abounding in water, and we drank of its various streams. Alas for my misfortune, that it was not fated for me to drink of the spring of immortality, which gives life to what is dead, as my cook was fortunate enough to do.[77]

Alexander fails to drink from the fountain in the Aljamiado version of this episode as well. In fact, in the *Rekontamiento del rey Ališandre* he never even arrives at the fountain; left in the darkness, Alexander waits with his troops while his wise counselor, al-Khaḍir, receives a visit from an angel, who leads him to the fountain and allows him to drink from it.

The episode begins with the angel Zayāfil visiting Alexander to inform him that no one but God has knowledge of this land of darkness, and that it will take twenty years to reach its center, at which rests the fountain of eternal life. Alexander consults his advisers about what to do, and they inform him about how best to carry out the expedition. Beyond the earthly trick of deciding to ride on virgin mares (which apparently see best in darkness), Alexander and his men make use of a glowing rock that Adam had brought down from heaven (al-janna) to be passed down from one prophet to another. Alexander had received it directly from Aristotle, and he takes it out at the beginning of their journey and hands it to al-Khaḍir. Alexander then divides his army into three parts: he places an advance cavalry force of two thousand under the command of al-Khaḍir, he himself leads a larger expeditionary force of four thousand, and the rest stay behind with orders to wait up to twelve years for their king's return.

Al-Khaḍir places the glowing rock on the tip of his spear and holds it high to light the way through the darkness. As a result of the light given off by the rock and God's power, Alexander and his combined force are able to reach the center of the darkness in twenty days instead of twenty years. Once there, God sends an angel to al-Khaḍir to lead him alone to the fountain of life, where he drinks the water, performs his ritual ablutions (al-wuḍūʾ), and prays:

I fuʷeše Dhū al-Qarnayni, i kuʷando llego a laškuridad bajaroše de šuš kabalgaduraš i še apañaron i komensaron a dentʰrar en laškuridad i tomo al-Khaḍir la piʸedra i ligola en el fiʸerro de su lansa i tomó la lansa kon šu mano i ʸalsola porke viʸešen laš genteš la pidra i fuʷeron aši dakiʸa ke še kumpʲliʸo a elloš veyte diʸaš i fuʷeron en veyt diʸaš andadura de veyte años kon el poder de Allāh depuʷeš mando Allāh šobre al-Khaḍir un al-malak i ʸamošt°role donde eštaba la fuʷent akella kenella ešta ell awwa .: de la vida :. i diššole viʸen a la fuʷente i bebe de šu aguʷa i pararonše šuš konpañaš i fuʷeše el a la fuʷente i la piʸedra en šu mano ke še guiʸaba kon ella i bediʸa la fuʷent kon šu kʰlaredad dakiʸa ke llego a la fuʷent i bebiʸo della i fizo al-waḍḍū i fizo al-ṣallā i tornoše a šu gente i kaminaron dakiʸa ke saliʸeron de laškuridad por el poder de Allāh taʿālā en kuʷarenta diʸas.[78]

[And Dhū al-Qarnayni left, and when he arrived at the darkness they got down off their horses, covered themselves, and began to enter the darkness. Al-Khaḍir took the stone, fixed it to the point of his lance, took the lance in his hand, and held it high so that they could all see it. They went along this way for twenty days, completing in those twenty days, through the power of God, a journey of twenty years. Afterward, God sent an angel to al-Khaḍir to show him where the fountain that contained the water .: of life :. was. [The angel] said to him: "Come to the fountain and drink from its water." Everyone stopped marching, and he went to the fountain with the stone in his hand to guide him. He saw the fountain with all its clarity and he went to it and drank from it before performing his ablutions and praying. Then he went back to where the other were and they marched from there until they came out of the darkness, through the power of God, in forty days.]

Implicit in this passage, made somewhat confusing by the frequent use of subject pronouns (one is in fact tempted to think that the "he" (*él*) who drinks from the fountain is Alexander rather than al-Khaḍir), is the fact that Alexander will not be granted immortality.[79] More explicitly, we also see how the text once again underscores the practical aspects of Muslim prayer, especially the performance of ritual ablutions (*al-wuḍū'*) before prayer: after al-Khaḍir drinks from the fountain of life (with the phrase "of life" (*de la vida*) adorned in the text by a small cluster of dots) and before he prays, he performs his ablutions, thus linking for the reader of this manuscript a specific (and key) passage of the *Rekontamiento del rey Ališandre* with at least one of the paratexts that surround it. Al-Khaḍir's attainment of immortality thus is pragmatically linked to the daily practice not only of Muslims in some generic sense, but of a specific and concrete group of Crypto-Muslims in sixteenth-century Aragon. We find evidence of this link on the folio that precedes the arrival of al-Khaḍir at the fountain of life. On folio 35v, there is a long marginal correction made to the narrative in a hand different from that of the main text block: the phrase "daki^ya ke šalgaš dello inša'Allāh t'ālā dixo i tomo de al-Khaḍir la pi^yedra kon su mano" (until you leave it, God willing, he said, and al-Khaḍir took the stone from his hand), written in the outer margin, is meant to correct the following line: "i gui^yanoš por laškuridad; i ~~dijo kon šu mano~~ . . . i fu^weron kon el" (and guide us through the darkness; and ~~he said with his hand~~ . . . and they went with him). This correction, the addition by a second scribe of a portion of text that was left out of the first draft of the copy, is a minor one; however, it provides concrete proof not only that the *Rekontamiento del rey Ališandre* was read in its late sixteenth-century setting but that *morisco* readers also engaged this particular portion of the text. That is, the marginal textual emendation on folio 35v allows us to conclude that the section of the narrative that deals with al-Khaḍir at the fountain of life was read by at least one actual *morisco* reader. It also allows us to posit a concrete link—through both the act of reading and that of Muslim prayer—between al-Khaḍir's performance of *al-wuḍū'* and the more immediate concern over its performance in the prefatory material.

The pragmatic connection formed here between Muslim ritual and traditional narrative is striking enough, but underneath it also is a deeper theorization of the question of temporality, death, and the afterlife. As I have already pointed out, the space between the horns of Dhū al-Qarnayn is at once a physical expanse and a temporal demarcation: it represents *al-dunyā* and Alexander's dominion over it, through the power of God. What is beyond Alexander's power in the *Rekontamiento del rey Ališandre*, as it was beyond him in life—a fact that he tried to overcome at Siwa but which overtook him in Babylon—is precisely the world that extends beyond *al-dunyā*: the realm of everlasting life, or *al-akhira*. As Aristotle puts it at the very end of the *Rekontamiento del rey Ališandre*: "Loš diyaš še van i tu pᵃlaso š-aserka de tu i tu dešaras tu al-dunyā; apᵃreššate para al-akhira pᵒrovišiᵞon de temor i ᵞobra buᵂena anteš ke te venga la muᵂert i tu dello nigligente" (The days are passing, your end is nearing, and you will leave this world; take for yourself the provision of fear and good works for the afterlife before your death comes to you and finds you unmindful of it).[80] Here death is framed as the end of possibilities, as a moment that continually approaches Alexander, preparing to take him by force: "tu pᵃlaso š-aserka" (your end is nearing). This very particular image of Alexander borrows almost equally from Pseudo-Callisthenes and the historical episode at Siwa; however, these are now embedded within an Islamic ethicotemporal framework of *al-dunyā/al-akhira* and the Day of Judgment to come.

What is meant by immortality and mortality in this case? Coming from the *Greek Alexander Romance*, it is directly linked to Ptolemaic and later Latin Western legendary constructions of Alexander (e.g., Leo of Naples, the *Libro de Alexandre*, Walter of Châtillon, and Alexandre of Paris) and the classical tradition traced in chapter 2. It also passes, however, through an explicitly Muslim pragmatic field as elaborated by the *moriscos* within their difficult circumstances. Situated within the Iberian metropole, but very much on the wrong end of imperial power politics during the sixteenth century, the *morisco* scribes and readers who made use of the *Rekontamiento del rey Ališandre* did so ultimately to reckon with deeply felt and all too proximal anxieties regarding death and the afterlife, and the linguistic and spiritual practices that would help them prepare for both. In a very literal sense, it is possible to see the copying out of this book and its engagement by Aragonese *moriscos* as a means of giving shape to the performance of ritual ablution and so effectively prepare for the Day of Judgment—a time when *al-dunyā* would come to an end and, with it, Christian domination.

CHAPTER 6

CONCLUSIONS

IN A PHRASE THAT HAS BECOME SOMETHING OF A SOCIO-
linguistic and political maxim, the Castilian humanist Antonio de Nebrija
(1441–1522) opens the prologue to his *Gramática de la lengua castellana*
(Grammar of the Castilian Language) by making the historical claim that
"siempre la lengua fue companera del imperio" (language was always the
companion of empire).[1] Published in the aftermath of the fall of the Naṣri
kingdom of Granada and the expulsion of Castilian and Aragonese Jews in
1492, Nebrija's linking of empire to national language comes at a key moment in the history of Castile, even if we leave aside for the moment the
world-changing events that would take place (after the publication of the
Gramática de la lengua castellana) as a result of Christopher Columbus's
westward voyages.

As scholars such as Walter Mignolo and Lucia Binotti have argued, it
is anachronistic to read Nebrija's prologue to the *Gramática de la lengua
castellana* as a prediction of Castile's (and the Castilian language's) American future.[2] According to Mignolo, Nebrija's linguisticopolitical manifesto
to Queen Isabel I of Castile is first and foremost a response to the preface
with which Lorenzo Valla (1405–1457) had begun his *De elegantia latinae
linguae* (On the Eloquence of the Latin Language) and has as its focus both
Castile's relation to Rome and its potential role in the Mediterranean.[3] Valla
had begun work on his Latin grammar in 1435 while working in the Neapolitan court of Alfons V of Aragon, and he was almost certainly aware of the
influence that his new Latin grammar—which posits a break from inherited

forms of medieval and ecclesiastical Latin in favor of a return to modes of expression current during the Julio-Claudian period—would have in the political sphere, specifically with regard to the Italian ambitions of his patron. Nebrija, like many fifteenth-century humanists, was highly influenced by Valla's work, as Mignolo argues:

> Valla realized that rebuilding an empire was not a goal that could be reached by means of arms. Instead, he intended to achieve it by the expedient of letters. By contrasting the Latin used by his ancestors with the expansion of the Roman Empire, and by underlying the strength of the language as a unifying force over the geographical conquests, Valla foresaw the Roman recovery of its lost power and, as a consequence, predicted the central role that Italy was assigned to play in the future. Certainly, in 1492 it was difficult for Nebrija to anticipate much about the future colonization of the New World. It should have been clear to him, however, that Castile had an opportunity to take the place of the Roman Empire. If the preface to the *Gramática castellana* was indeed a rewriting of Valla's preface, the historical condition had changed: while Valla was attempting to save an already established empire in decadence, Nebrija was predicting the construction of a new one.[4]

By the end of the fifteenth century, it was abundantly clear that power in the Mediterranean would not rest with the Aragonese (see chapter 1 of the present volume on Joanot Martorell's *Tirant lo Blanc*), and it is logical to assume that Nebrija saw Castile as the most likely candidate to fill the vacuum left by Aragon's decline (a decline that the Castilians, not incidentally, had done much to speed along).

Foregrounding what he considers to be a kind of symbiotic relation between language and political dominion—"junta mente començaron, crecieron y florecieron, y después junta fue la caída de entrambos" (together they began, grew, and flourished, and later they also fell as one)—Nebrija speaks to the inherently political nature of language and, of equal importance, the linguistic foundations of power and empire.[5]

Placing aside for the moment the canonical status of Nebrija's conclusions regarding language and empire, and also his debt to Valla, the present volume examines what might be considered a corollary of Nebrija's and Valla's intersecting axiom of language, nation, and power. This corollary posits the central place of specific modes of text-mediated language use such as storytelling, poetry, and historiography in the processes by which the subjects of empire (in both senses of the term) reckon with deep anxieties regarding death and alterity. What I wish to argue for is not so much an alteration of Nebrija's statement as a call to focus on a specific aspect of it, namely that, beyond the general understanding of "language" as a companion of empire, we would do well to consider the extent to which specifically poetic, historiographical, and narrative forms of language use revolving around the figure of Alexander the Great accompanied and even helped to engender Iberian imperial projects that from even before the publication of the *Gramática de la lengua castellana* had been shaping social life and experience in Africa, Asia, and Europe.

We find an example of such processes, and Alexander's role in them, in Diego Ortúñez de Calahorra's *Espejo de príncipes y cavalleros* (Mirror of Princes and Nobles), first published in Zaragoza by Esteban de Nájera in 1555. Dedicating his text to Martín Cortés (1533–1589), the son of Hernán Cortés (1485–1547) and Juana Ramírez de Arellano de Zúñiga (not to be confused with his mestizo half-brother of the same name) and Second Marquis of the Valley of Oaxaca, Ortúñez de Calahorra writes of Alexander:

> Rezia cosa es que çufra uno la dureza de un señor tirano, y que no sepa çufrir la de su propio padre. Que aun quando no fuesse bueno, no han de redargüir los hijos las costumbres de los padres, mas çufrirlas. Que ninguna cosa más fea se lee Alexandre aver hecho, que aver no solamente denostado a su padre, mas aver avido embidia y pena de sus alabanças. Dizen bien los sabios que no ay sobre la tierra otro imperio más justo que el del padre, ni más onesta sujeción que la del hijo.[6]

> [It is a rough situation when one is able to tolerate the severity of his lord but not that of his own father. Even when he is not a good man, sons must not criticize the habits of their fathers, but rather tolerate them. One reads of no more repugnant thing done by Alexander than not only defaming his father but also feeling envy and pain when [Philip] was praised. The wise men say it well when they claim that there is no worldly empire more just than that of the father, nor subjection more honest than that of the son.]

The link that Ortúñez de Calahorra draws between the imperium of the family and home (*oikos*) and that of the broader political sphere (*polis*) has its origins in Augustine of Hippo, who, in his sprawling *De civitate Dei* (City of God), imagines "a kind of micro/macrocosmic relationship" between the household and the city that is to be reproduced on a worldwide scale as a chain of interconnected cities/households.[7] As Giorgio Agamben has recently pointed out, this relationship flies in the face of the stark division that Aristotle makes between *oikos* and *polis* at the very beginning of his *Politics*.[8] According to Agamben, "Aristotle takes the greatest care to distinguish the *oikonomos* (the head of an estate) and the *despotēs* (the head of a family), both of whom are concerned with the reproduction and the subsistence of life, from the politician, and he scorns those who think the difference between the two is one of quantity and not of kind."[9] In the context of the imperial and dynastic politics of sixteenth-century Castile, Cortés's status vis-à-vis his own conquistador father, and the complex genre to which the *Espejo de príncipes y cavalleros* corresponds (i.e., romances of chivalry), it is perhaps chilling that Ortúñez de Calahorra's explicit conflation of *pater* and *imperator* (the latter framed, by the sixteenth century, as a *despotēs*, but of a very different order) should be held up to Alexander's tortured and possibly patricidal relationship with his own father.[10] One might argue, in fact, that the entire passage stands as a symptom of the growing influence, within early modern Iberia, of the sort of biopolitics that Agamben, using consciously Foucauldian vocabulary, criticizes.[11] It is clear, at least, that the political model that Ortúñez de Calahorra both describes and constructs is one in which familial bonds and paternal powers are couched in the discourse of political dominion and vice versa.

There is, however, something that lurks beneath the surface of the narrative of neo-Roman moral supremacy Ortúñez de Calahorra constructs around the figure of Alexander the Great. Beyond making explicit reference to dispreferred modes of language use (e.g., criticism and defamation) in relation to the actions of the *pater/imperator*, Ortúñez de Calahorra in his condemnation of Alexander also subtly calls to his reader's attention the distinction between the temporal world and the world beyond. Like the distinction between *al-dunyā* and *al-akhira* developed in the *Rekontamiento del rey Ališandre*, neatly demarcated temporal/existential domains—and concern for them within a Christian cultural framework—are similarly made use of by Ortúñez de Calahorra to help him drive home his point and thus shape social practice. In all of this Alexander functions both as an imperial hero and a recalcitrant son: a conquering Caesar and a defiant Cain.

In the end, Ortúñez de Calahorra and other late medieval and early modern authors (as well as most modern ones) have all been more concerned with the ghost of Alexander than with what he may actually have been and done while he was alive. At once legendary, mythological, and historical, the ghost of Alexander is intricately related to the European, and more specifically Iberian, colonial adventures that took place in Muslim Africa and Asia during the fifteenth and sixteenth centuries. A disembodied presence, this phantom passed through the walls of customs houses, stole aboard caravels, rounded the Cape of Good Hope, sailed up the Persian Gulf, and marched into Gujarat. It crossed the Oued Makhzen and rode on to al-Qaṣr al-Kbīr, where it hovered briefly over the swollen bodies of horses and men before drifting back to Lisbon, Madrid, and Valencia. It haunted the mountains near Granada and chilled the exposed skin of royal soldiers and Muslim rebels alike. It washed up near Tlemcen, shipwrecked and full of seawater, but still invoking its right to conquest and conversion. Most significantly for the present book, this specter moved through the pens of those who had seen or imagined all of this activity, the spastic pecking of empire at the inside of its shell.

We end as we began, with Aschenbach at the streetcar stop on the Ungererstraße, staring at a stranger and being stared at in return. How do we respond to this returned stare, to this disruptive alterity that threatens to convert us into objects of judgment and dominion? Will we do better than Barros, Martorell, or Camões when faced with a presence that points to what will inevitably overcome our possibilities? How will we face the mortal fear that the Other inspires in us? Will we attempt to write it away with ghosts such as the one left behind by Alexander at Babylon (along with his bloated corpse)? Will we write at all?

I bring up (and here conclude with) the question of writing and literature because what Mann strongly points to in *Death in Venice*, beyond the scene that has more or less framed the present volume, is the fact that narrative, beyond all else, most potently serves as a domain for the consideration of other options, for possible worlds of side-shadowing and play. One of the most powerful lessons that we learn from Camões, Martorell, and the *Rekontamiento del rey Ališandre* (among others) is that the world can always be otherwise. The principal focus of the present book is, in the end, on the fact that even within the totalizing vision of empire, of hard-and-fast divisions between the subject and the object of colonial authority, narrative allows for the infinite to be given play, for a conversation to be taken up.

NOTES

Preface

1. Peter Green, *Alexander of Macedon, 356–323 B.C.: A Historical Biography* (Berkeley: University of California Press, 1991), xi.

Chapter 1

1. See, for example, H. J. Chaytor, *A History of Aragon and Catalonia* (London: Methuen, 1933), 229; Steven Runciman, *The Fall of Constantinople, 1453* (Cambridge: Cambridge University Press, 1990), 62 and 166; Montserrat Piera, "Rehistoricizing the 'Other' Reconquista," in *Tirant lo Blanc: New Approaches*, ed. Arthur Terry (London: Tamesis, 1999); Martí de Riquer, *Història de la literatura catalana*, 3 vols. (Barcelona: Ariel, 1964–66), vol. 2, 696; and Roberto González-Casanova, "Western Narratives of Eastern Adventures: The Cultural Poetics and Politics of Catalan Expansion, 1300–1500," *Catalan Review* 8, nos. 1–2 (1994).

2. For a general study of the image of North Africa in early modern Castile, see Miguel Angel Bunes Ibarra, *La imagen de los musulmanes y del Norte de Africa en la España de los siglos XVI y XVII: Los caracteres de una hostilidad* (Madrid: Consejo Superior de Investigaciones Científicas, 1989). For an examination of the Maghreb in Cervantes's work, see María Antonia Garcés, *Cervantes en Argel: Historia de un cautivo* (Madrid: Editorial Gredos, 2005).

3. Fernão Mendes Pinto, *Peregrinação*, ed. Fernando Ribeiro de Mello, 2 vols. (Lisbon: Edições Afrodite, 1971), vol.1, 10.

4. The Ottoman Turks, who also considered themselves heirs to Rome, likewise made good use of Greco-Roman accounts of Alexander the Great. Mehmed II (1432–1481), for example, was an avid reader of not only Homer but also of Arrian. Suleyman the Magnificent went so far as to declare himself "the second Alexander" in response to Carlos V's (1500–1558) claim to the mantle of Julius Caesar. For more on this, see Gülru Necipoglu, "Süleyman the Magnificent and the Representation of Power in the Context of Ottoman-Hapsburg-Papal Rivalry," *Art Bulletin* 71, no. 3 (1989); and Su Fang Ng, "Global Renaissance: Alexander the

Great and Early Modern Classicism from the British Isles to the Malay Archipelago," *Comparative Literature* 58 (2006).

5. C. R. Boxer, *The Portuguese Seaborne Empire, 1415–1825* (London: Hutchinson, 1969), 49.

6. Gomes Eanes de Zurara, *Crónica da tomada de Ceuta*, ed. Reis Brasil (Mems Martins Codex, Portugal: Publicações Europa-América, 1992).

7. Ibid., 79.

8. *Curial e Güelfa*, ed. Marina Gustà, 6th ed. (Barcelona: Edicions 62, 2004), 271–72.

9. The text of *Curial e Güelfa* in fact mentions Alexander the Great on two occasions, both in the third and final book. The first instance occurs in the narrator's invocation of the Muses at the beginning of the third book: "Veritat és que aquest noble e valerós cavaller, del qual s'escriu lo present llibre, no fonc gran capità, ne gran guerrer o conquistador, així com diríem Alexandre, Cèsar, Aníbal, Pirro o Cipió o altres molts, los quals per llur indústria, mesclada emperò ab cavalleria, conquistaren los uns quaix tot, los altres grans trosses o partides del món" (It is true that this noble and valorous knight, about which the present book is written, was no great captain, nor a great warrior or conqueror, as were Alexander, Caesar, Hanibal, Pirrus, or Scipio or many others, who by their initiative, combined with chivalry, managed to conquer in some cases almost the whole world and in others great parts of it) (ibid., 236). The other mention of Alexander comes in a long argument between Fortune and Juno. At one point, Fortune calls on a string of mythological, legendary, and historical figures to aid her in battling Juno; among these is Alexander's mother, as she is described in the *Greek Alexander Romance*: "¡E tu, reina de Macedònia, qui, segons se diu, tractant Nectanabo, gran filòsof e astròleg, haguist del déu Amon Alexandre, ton fill, lo qual déu era Jovis mudat en forma de moltó!" (And you, queen of Macedonia, who, according to what is said, through the help of a great philosopher and astrologer named Nectanabo, had a son, Alexander, by the god Amon, who was none other than Jupiter in the form of a ram!) (*Curial e Güelfa*, 254).

10. Luis del Mármol Carvajal, *Historia de la rebelión y castigo de los moriscos del Reino de Granada* (Barcelona: Linkgua, 2007), 67–68.

11. Thomas Mann, *Death in Venice*, trans. Michael Henry Heim (New York: HarperCollins, 2005), 3–5.

12. Immanuel Kant, *Critique of Judgement*, ed. Nicholas Walker, trans. James Creed Meredith (Oxford: Oxford University Press, 2007).

13. Mann, *Death in Venice*, 142.

14. Joanot Martorell, *Tirant lo Blanc*, ed. Manuel Sanromà and Martí de Riquer (Tarragona: Fundació Ciutat de Tarragona, 2008); http://www.tinet.org/bdt/tirant/capitols/cap299.html.

15. Martorell, *Tirant lo Blanc*; http://www.tinet.org/bdt/tirant/capitols/cap303.html.

16. Piera, "Rehistoricizing the 'Other' Reconquista," 57.

17. Rafael Beltrán, *Tirant lo Blanc, de Joanot Martorell* (Madrid: Síntesis, 2007), 92, attributes Tirant's death to his inability to adhere to the "ascetic prototype proposed since Ramon Llull." For Beltrán, Tirant's death can be attributed to his amorous desire for Car-

mesina, a "passionate fever." Martorell describes the illness that kills Tirant with a certain amount of precision, however: it is pleurisy (*mal de costat*), an inflammation of the lungs that will reduce Tirant once again, and now definitively, to the status of an object of perception. The lesson here is not, I think, one of the rightness of ascetic severity, but rather of the imminence of death—as a murderous, surprising force—that runs through the discourse of Iberian empire. And it is here that the intersections with the figure of Alexander (who may also have died of pleurisy) are most striking.

18. Josiah Blackmore, *Manifest Perdition: Shipwreck Narrative and the Disruption of Empire* (Minneapolis: University of Minnesota Press, 2002); Blackmore, "Imagining the Moor in Medieval Portugal," *Diacritics* 36, nos. 3–4 (2006); and Blackmore, *Moorings: Portuguese Expansion and the Writing of Africa* (Minneapolis: University of Minnesota Press, 2008).

19. For more on this topic, see Rafael Beltrán, "La muerte de Tirant: Elementos para una autopsia," in *Actes del Col.loqui internacional Tirant lo Blanc, Aix-en-Provence, 21–22 October 1994* (Barcelona: Centre Aixois de Recherches Hispaniques, Institut Interuniversitari de Filologia Valenciana, Publicacions de l'Abadia de Montserrat, 1997); Beltrán, *Tirant lo Blanc, de Joanot Martorell*; and Jeremy Lawrence, "Death in *Tirant lo Blanc*," in *Tirant lo Blanc: New Approaches*, ed. Arthur Terry (London: Tamesis, 1999).

20. Jorge Luis Borges, *Narraciones*, ed. Marcos Ricardo Barnatán (Madrid: Cátedra, 1980), 129: "En aquel Imperio, el Arte de la Cartografía logró tal Perfección que el mapa de una sola Provincia ocupaba toda una Ciudad, y el mapa del imperio, toda una Provincia. Con el tiempo, esos Mapas Desmesurados no satisfacieron y los Colegios de Cartógrafos levantaron un Mapa del Imperio, que tenía el tamaño del Imperio y coincidía puntualmente con él. Menos Adictas al Estudio de la Cartografía, las Generaciones Siguientes entendieron que ese dilatado Mapa era Inútil y no sin Impiedad lo entregaron a las Inclemencias del Sol y de los Inviernos. En los desiertos del Oeste perduran despedazadas Ruinas del Mapa, habitadas por Animales y Por Mendigos; en todo el País no hay otra reliquia de las Disciplinas Geográficas" (In that Empire, the Art of Cartography attained such Perfection that the map of a single Province occupied the entirety of a City, and the map of the Empire, the entirety of a Province. In time, those Unconscionable Maps no longer satisfied, and the Cartographers Guilds struck a Map of the Empire whose size was that of the Empire, and which coincided point for point with it. The following Generations, who were not so fond of the Study of Cartography as their Forebears had been, saw that that vast Map was Useless, and not without some Pitilessness was it, that they delivered it up to the Inclemencies of Sun and Winters. In the Deserts of the West, still today, there are Tattered Ruins of that Map, inhabited by Animals and Beggars; in all the Land there is no other Relic of the Disciplines of Geography).

21. Quintus Curtius Rufus, *De gestis Alexandri Magni, Regis Macedonum: Libri qui supersunt VIII* (Philadelphia: Lea & Blanchard, 1849), 312.

22. Quintus Curtius Rufus, *The History of Alexander*, trans. John Yardley (London: Penguin Books, 2004), 245–46.

23. Diodorus Siculus, *Bibliothèque historique, livre XVIII*, ed. Paul Goukowsky (Paris: Belles Lettres, 1978), 14.

06 NOTES TO PAGES 19–31

24. Marcus Junianus Justinus, *Trogi Pompei: Historiarum philippicarum epitoma*, ed. Justus Ieep (Leipzig: B. G. Teubner, 1872), 88.

25. For more on the reception of Pier Candido Decembrio's work in the Iberian Peninsula, see Antonio Pedro Bravo García, "Sobre las traducciones de Plutarco y de Quinto Curcio Rufo echas por Pier Candido Decembrio y su fortuna en España," *Cuadernos de filología clásica* 12 (1977): 143–87.

26. Madrid, Biblioteca Nacional MS 8549, f. 334v; and Madrid, Biblioteca Nacional MS 10140, ff. 268v–69r.

27. Diodorus Siculus, *Bibliothèque historique, livre XVII*, ed. Paul Goukowsky (Paris: Belles Lettres, 1976), 162.

28. Arrian, *Anabasis of Alexander*, trans. P. A. Brunt, 2 vols. (Cambridge, Mass.: Harvard University Press, 1983), vol. 2, 294–95.

29. Justinus, *Trogi Pompei*, 88–89.

30. Diana Spencer, *The Roman Alexander: Reading a Cultural Myth* (Exeter: University of Exeter Press, 2002).

31. Justinus, *Trogi Pompei*, 89.

32. Emmanuel Levinas, *Time and the Other*, trans. Richard A. Cohen (Pittsburgh, Pa.: Duquesne University Press, 1987), 71.

33. Ibid., 72.

34. Emmanuel Levinas, *Totality and Infinity: An Essay on Exteriority*, trans. Alphonso Lingis (Pittsburgh, Pa.: Duquesne University Press, 1969), 234–35.

35. Levinas, *Time and the Other*, 74.

36. Ibid., 70–71.

37. Ibid., 74.

38. Richard A. Cohen, Introduction to *Emmanuel Levinas: Time and the Other*, ed. Richard A. Cohen (Pittsburgh, Pa.: Duquesne University Press, 1987), 8–9.

39. Levinas, *Totality and Infinity*, 233.

40. Ibid., 233–34.

41. Ibid., 234.

42. Ibid.

43. Simon Critchley, introduction to *The Cambridge Companion to Levinas*, ed. Simon Critchley and Robert Bernasconi (Cambridge: Cambridge University Press, 2002), 13–14.

44. Ibid., 14; and Hilary Putnam, "Levinas and Judaism," in *The Cambridge Companion to Levinas*, ed. Simon Critchley and Robert Bernasconi (Cambridge: Cambridge University Press, 2002).

45. Emmanuel Levinas, "The Trace of the Other," in *Deconstruction in Context*, ed. Mark Taylor (Chicago: University of Chicago Press, 1986), 346.

46. Levinas, *Time and the Other*, 75.

47. Ibid., 77–78.

48. Levinas, *Totality and Infinity*, 235.

49. Paulus Orosius, *Orose: Histoires (contre les païens)*, ed. Marie-Pierre Arnaud-Lindet, 3 vols. (Paris: Les Belles Lettres, 1990), vol. 1, 147.

50. Lucius Annaeus Seneca, *Ad Lucilium Epistolae morales*, ed. Johann Gottfried Schweighaeuser, 2 vols. (Strassburg: Societatis Bipontinae, 1809), vol. 1, 54. For an analysis of this text, see Spencer, *The Roman Alexander*.

Chapter 2

1. Plutarch, *The Life of Alexander the Great*, trans. John Dryden (New York: Modern Library, 2004), 68.

2. Arrian, *Anabasis of Alexander*, vol. 2, 251.

3. See Herodotus, *The Histories*, trans. Robin Waterfield (Oxford: Oxford University Press, 1998), 419–20. According to Siculus, *Bibliothèque historique, livre XVII*:

> [Xerxes' engineers] then began to build bridges across the Hellespont from Abydos to that headland between Sestus and Madytus (the Phoenicians building one of ropes made from white flax and the Egyptians papyrus), taking Abydus as their starting-point and directing their efforts towards the headland on the opposite coast—a distance of seven stades. They had just finished bridging the straits when a violent storm erupted which completely smashed and destroyed everything.
>
> This news made Xerxes furious. He ordered his men to give the Hellespont three hundred lashes and to sink a pair of shackles into the sea. I once heard that he also dispatched men to brand the Hellespont as well. Be that as it may, he did tell the men he had thrashing the sea to revile it in terms you would never hear from a Greek. "Bitter water," they said, "this is your punishment for wronging your master when he did no wrong to you. King Xerxes will cross you, with or without your consent. People are right not to sacrifice to a muddy, brackish stream like you!" So the sea was punished at his orders, and he had the supervisors of the bridging of the Hellespont beheaded.

4. Diodorus Siculus, who is generally favorable to Alexander in his *Bibliotheka historika*, justifies the expedition against the Cossaeans as part of a planned military strategy. See Siculus, *Bibliothèque historique, livre XVII*, 154: "Alexander launched a campaign with light troops against the Cossaeans, who refused to obey him. This people, possessing extreme bravery, lived in the mountains of Media. Relying on the ruggedness of the country and their abilities in war, they had never accepted a foreign master. They had remained unconquered throughout the whole period of Persian dominance, and now they were so fully confident in themselves that they were not afraid of Macedonian valor. The king, however, captured the routes of access into their country before they were aware of it, and he destroyed a large part of Cossaea. Obtaining the advantage in every engagement, Alexander killed many of the barbarians and made prisoners of many times more. Utterly defeated and distressed at the number of their captives, the Cossaeans were constrained to accept servitude in exchange for the lives of their captives. Placing themselves and their belongings in Alexander's hands, they were able to obtain peace on condition that they should obey the king's orders. Having vanquished this people in a total of forty days and then having

founded some important cities in this mountainous country, Alexander let his army catch its breath."

5. On the question of Alexander's destruction of Persepolis (330 BCE), Arrian offers a somewhat ambivalent judgment: he is openly critical of the act itself, but he cites verbatim the official justification for the holy city's destruction, namely that it was a form of payback for Xerxes' earlier attack on the acropolis at Athens. See Arrian, *Anabasis of Alexander*, vol. 1, 287–89.

6. The title of Arrian's history of Alexander means, somewhat inelegantly in English translation, an "overland expedition to the sea" and directly evokes Xenophon's work of Persian history by the same name, written c. 390 BCE and used by Alexander as a field guide. On the issue of Alexander's emulation of Cyrus, John Maxwell O'Brien, *Alexander the Great: The Invisible Enemy* (London: Routledge, 1992), 51, argues, for example, that "Alexander knew his Xenophon, and seems to have been particularly influenced by the *Cyropaedia*, a fictionalized and laudatory account of the life of Cyrus the Great (d. 529), the founder of the Persian Empire." James Tatum, *Xenophon's Imperial Fiction: On the Education of Cyrus* (Princeton, N.J.: Princeton University Press, 1989), 238–39, makes a more dramatic claim: "The difficulty for Xenophon was that although he had invented the imperial fiction of the *Cyropaedia*, he was himself far from being a romantic. Inescapable proof of the wisdom of his revisionist thoughts about what he had created lay no more than a generation away, in the career of Cyrus's first imitator, Alexander. With Xenophon an important inspiration, he [Alexander] made an empire by imposing a romantic fiction on the world about him; in life and even more in death he was the inspiration for romance. You might say that Alexander the Great followed the *Cyropaedia* to the letter, its final chapter as well as its prologue." The importance of Xenophon's *Cyropaedia* extends well into the late medieval period as well: it figures among Greek texts such as Aristotle's *History of Animals*, which the Aragonese king Alfons V (1396–1458) had translated into Latin by his court in Naples (the translator of the *Cyropaedia* was the Florentine humanist Poggio Bracciolini).

7. Alfred Heuss, "Alexander der Grosse und die politische Ideologie der Altertums," *Antike und Abendland* 21 (1954): 102. The original German text reads: "Er gleicht einem Schlauch, der sich mit diesem und jenem Wein füllen lässt" (He resembles a wineskin [or bottle] that can be filled with any wine).

8. Spencer, *The Roman Alexander*, 38.

9. Ibid., 37.

10. For more on Roman notions of *imperium* and their impact on early modern Europe, see Anthony Pagden, *Lords of All the World: Ideologies of Empire in Spain, Britain and France, c. 1500–c. 1800* (New Haven, Conn.: Yale University Press, 1995), 11–28.

11. Douglas Frame, *The Myth of Return in Early Greek Epic* (New Haven, Conn.: Yale University Press, 1978).

12. Karen Bassi, "Nostos, Domos, and the Architecture of the Ancient Stage," *South Atlantic Quarterly* 98, no. 3 (1999): 417–18.

13. For more on the connection between *nostos* and *nóos*, see Frame, *The Myth of Return*. For a useful précis of Frame's arguments, see Gregory Nagy, *Greek Mythology and Poetics* (Ithaca, N.Y.: Cornell University Press, 1990), 217–20.

14. Nagy, *Greek Mythology and Poetics*, 219.

15. O'Brien, *Alexander the Great*.

16. The Learned Alfonso X, *General estoria: Primera parte*, ed. Pedro Sánchez-Prieto Borja, 2 vols. (Madrid: Fundación José Antonio de Castro, 2001), vol. 1, 85.

17. Blackmore, *Moorings*, 39.

18. Green, *Alexander of Macedon*, 469–70.

19. Plutarch, *The Life of Alexander the Great*, 70.

20. Arrian, *Anabasis of Alexander*, vol. 2, 289.

21. Plutarch offers a slightly different version of Dionysius's confession, contending that the Messenian claimed to have been ordered to sit silently on Alexander's throne by the syncretic Hellenistic-Egyptian god Serapis. See Plutarch, *The Life of Alexander the Great*, 69; and O'Brien, *Alexander the Great*, 222.

22. Plutarch, *The Life of Alexander the Great*, 71.

23. Ibid., 71–72; and Arrian, *Anabasis of Alexander*, vol. 2, 295–96.

24. Curtius Rufus, *De gestis Alexandri Magni*, 325–26.

25. Curtius Rufus, *The History of Alexander*, 256–57.

26. Green, *Alexander of Macedon*, 477.

27. Ibid.

28. These manuscripts are El Escorial, Biblioteca de San Lorenzo de El Escorial MS &. II. 8, ff. 8r–10r and 80v–83r; El Escorial, Biblioteca de San Lorenzo de El Escorial MS h. ii. 22, ff. 47r–50v; Lisbon, Biblioteca da Ajuda MS 52-XIII-24, ff. 1r–7v; Madrid, Biblioteca Nacional MS 3666, ff. 20r–22v; Madrid, Biblioteca Nacional MS 12672, ff. 157r–61v; Madrid, Biblioteca Nacional MS 9608, ff. 81r–83r; Madrid, Biblioteca Nacional MS 9522; and Madrid, Biblioteca Nacional MS 9513, ff. 140r–41v; and Salamanca, Biblioteca Universitaria MS 1890, ff. 43r–48v.

29. Lucian, *The Works of Lucian of Samosata*, ed. H. W. Fowler and F. G. Fowler (Oxford: Clarendon Press, 1905), 128.

30. Ibid.

31. Ibid., 129.

32. Ibid.

33. Ibid., 129–30.

34. *Libro de Alexandre*, ed. Jesús Cañas (Madrid: Cátedra, 1995), 573–74. In chapter 353 of *Tirant lo Blanc*, Plaerdemavida, in a long monologue directed at Tirant, likewise claims that Alexander (along with Hannibal) was poisoned.

35. Lucian, *The Works of Lucian of Samosata*, 131.

36. Ibid., 131–32.

37. Ibid., 132.

38. Ibid., 132–33.

39. Edward W. Said, *Orientalism* (New York: Vintage Books, 1978), 58.

40. Demosthenes, *The Third Philippic*, ed. Michael Lahanas, in Hellenica, http://www.mlahanas.de/Greeks/Texts/Demosthenes/TheThirdPhilippic.html.

41. For more on slavery in ancient Greece, see Yvon Garlan, *Slavery in Ancient Greece* (Ithaca, N.Y.: Cornell University Press, 1988); Michael Grant, *A Social History of Greece and Rome* (New York: Charles Scribner's Sons, 1992), 92–99; and William Linn Westermann, *The*

Slave Systems of Greek and Roman Antiquity (Philadelphia: American Philosophical Society, 1955).

42. Spencer, *The Roman Alexander*, 9–10.

43. Plato, "Menexenus," in *The Collected Dialogues of Plato*, ed. Edith Hamilton and Huntington Cairns (Princeton, N.J.: Princeton University Press, 1982), 195–96.

44. Aristotle, *The Basic Works of Aristotle*, trans. Richard Peter McKeon (New York: Random House, 1941), 1280.

45. Ibid., 1198.

46. Ibid., 1144.

47. Ibid.

48. Ibid., 1181.

49. Patricia Springborg, *Western Republicanism and the Oriental Prince* (Austin: University of Texas Press, 1992), 182–83.

50. Important texts composed in the Alexandria of the Ptolemies include the hymns of Callimachus (c. 305–c. 240 BCE), the pastoral poetry of Theocritus (c. 300–260 BCE), the epic *Argonautica* of Apollonius of Rhodes (c. 295–215 BCE), and the *Alexandra* of Lycophron of Chalcis (fl. 280 BCE).

51. Arrian, *Anabasis of Alexander*, vol. 1, 288–89.

52. Paul Cartledge, *Alexander the Great: The Hunt for a New Past* (Woodstock, N.Y.: Overlook Press, 2004), 280.

53. Siculus, *Bibliothèque historique, livre XVII*, 72.1–6.

54. Plutarch, *The Life of Alexander the Great*, 39.

55. Spencer, *The Roman Alexander*.

56. Lucius Annaeus Seneca, *Ad Lucilium epistulae morales*, ed. L. D. Reynolds (Oxford: Clarendon Press, 1965), 283–84.

57. In the *Diálogos* (Dialogues) of Amador Arrais, published in 1589 (and subsequently republished in Coimbra in 1604), Seneca's treatment of Alexander, linked to the issue of mortality, comes once again to the fore. In dialogue 2, chapter 18, entitled "Porque fez Deos o homem mortal, & o entregou a fraqueza do corpo, & da alma" (Why God Made Man Mortal and Handed Him Over to the Weakness of the Body and the Soul), Arrais writes: "De Alexandre Magno conta Seneca, que andando ao redor dos muros, no cerco de hûa Cidade foy ferido na coxa de hûa seta, & crescendolhe a dor da chaga foy constrangido a se recolher, & dizer aos seus: 'Todos jurão que eu sou filho de Jupiter, mas esta ferida clama que sou eu homem'" (Seneca speaks of Alexander the Great, recounting how while riding around the walls of a city under siege he was wounded in the thigh by an arrow, and as the pain of the wound increased he was compelled to gather himself and say to his men: "Everyone swears that I am the son of Jupiter, but this wound cries out that I am a man"). The text to which Arrais refers is Seneca's 59th Epistle.

58. Spencer, *The Roman Alexander*, 11; Spencer also argues that "in the *Aeneid*, Virgil confronts a legend buried in Roman self-consciousness, a legend of a mythical connection between early Rome and Greece, binding Greeks and Romans together through literary continuity and the development of a Roman foundation myth that made the first Romans the

direct heirs of the fallen Troy. From the increasingly Rome-dominated Mediterranean of the third century BCE, this myth demanded that Greeks should ally themselves with a growing power that celebrated its foundation by refugees from their one-time eastern enemies, the Trojans. The newly constructed eastern enemy, taking the place of Troy or even Persia in the discourse of a clash between East and West, was the Phoenician-founded Carthaginian Empire. In this way Carthage was inexorably forced into a nexus of ancient, mythological, cultural and literary myths that would demand an eastern enemy not just for the Achaeans, for the Greek states, or for Alexander, but also for Rome" (ibid., 10).

59. Ibid., 2–3.

60. Livy, *Livy: Book IX*, ed. W. B. Anderson (Cambridge: Cambridge University Press, 1912), 27. For more on Livy's antimonarchical stance and its relation to his view of Augustus, see Ruth Morello, "Livy's Alexander Digression (9.17–19): Counterfactuals and Apologetics," *Journal of Roman Studies* 92 (2002).

61. Justinus, *Trogi Pompei*, 79–80.

62. Curtius Rufus, *The History of Alexander*, 247–48. The Milanese humanist Pier Candido Decembrio (1399–1477) translated Quintus Curtius's text into Italian in 1438, and various fifteenth-century Ibero-Romance translations of his text can still be found in Peninsular archives. The extant manuscripts are (1) Barcelona, Biblioteca de Catalunya MS. 1560 ff. 1–188v (in Catalan); (2) Lisbon, Biblioteca da Ajuda MS 52-XIII-24 ff. 7v–165v (in Portuguese); (3) Madrid, Biblioteca Nacional MS 8549 (in Castilian); (4) Madrid, Biblioteca Nacional MS 9220 (in Castilian); (5) Madrid, Biblioteca Nacional MS 10140 (in Castilian); (6) Madrid: Real Biblioteca MS II/1290 (in Castilian); and (7) San Lorenzo de El Escorial: Escorial MS T.III.4, f. 306r–v (excerpts in Castilian). For more on Decembrio's translation of Quintus Curtius, see Julio Berzunza, "Preliminary Notes on the Three Italian Versions of Quintus Curtius Rufus' *Historiae Alexandri Magni*," *Italica* 18, no. 3 (1941). For an early print translation into Catalan of Decembrio's work, see Lluís de Fenollet, *La vida del Rey Alexandre scrita per aquell singularissim hystorial Plutarcho, fins en aquella part on lo Quinto Curcio Ruffo comença: "Alexandre entre tan"* (Barcelona: Pere Posa i Pere Bru, 1481).

63. Curtius Rufus, *The History of Alexander*, 248.

64. Jacques Derrida, "Plato's Pharmacy," in *Dissemination* (Chicago: University of Chicago Press, 2004).

65. Cartledge, *Alexander the Great*, 202–3.

66. Ibid., 203.

67. For more on the fecund intersection between political jurisdiction and power apparatuses in the medieval West, see Jesús Rodríguez-Velasco, *Ciudadanía, soberanía monárquica y caballería: Poética del orden de caballería* (Madrid: Akal, 2009).

68. Augustine also makes mention of Alexander in his *De civitate Dei* (City of God), specifically in 4, 4; 4, 7; 8, 5; 8, 27; 12, 10; 12, 25; 18, 42; and 18, 45. Particularly striking is the mention of Alexander that Augustine makes in 4, 4, in which a pirate offers a sharp riposte to the Macedonian king upon being captured: "Remove justice, and what are kingdoms but gangs of criminals on a large scale? What are criminal gangs but petty kingdoms? A gang is a group of men under the command of a leader, bound by a compact of association, in

which the plunder is divided according to an agreed convention. If this villainy wins so many recruits from the ranks of the demoralized that it acquires territory, establishes a base, captures cities and subdues peoples, it then openly arrogates to itself the title of kingdom, which is conferred on it in the eyes of the world, not by the renouncing of aggression but by the attainment of impunity. For it was a witty and truthful rejoinder which was given by a captured pirate to Alexander the Great. The king asked the fellow, 'What is your idea, in infesting the sea?' And the pirate answered, with uninhibited insolence, 'The same as yours in infesting the earth! But because I do it with a tiny craft, I'm called a pirate: because you have a mighty navy, you're called an emperor'" (Augustine, *City of God*, ed. G. R. Evans, trans. Henry Scowcroft Bettenson [London: Penguin Books, 2003], 139).

69. Although it is true that Augustine had begun work on his *De civitate Dei* before urging Orosius to compose his own response to the complaints of the pagans, Augustine's *magnum opus* was not completed until at least five years after the appearance of the *Historiarum adversus pagnos libri septem* in late 417 CE. On the origins of Orosius, Marie-Pierre Arnaud-Lindet, introduction to *Orose: Histoires (contre les païens)*, ed. Marie-Pierre Arnaud-Lindet (Paris: Les Belles Lettres, 1990), ix, writes: "When Orosius the priest arrived in Africa, he was coming from Galicia, where he had been part of the Church of Braga." Elsewhere (Arnaud-Lindet, introduction, xi–xii), she discusses the theory that he was a native of Bretagne who had been forced to emigrate to the Iberian Peninsula as well as the possibility that he was a native of Brigantia, or modern-day La Coruña. On these points, Adolf Lippold, introduction to *Orosio: Le storie contro i pagani*, ed. Adolf Lippold (Milan: Fondazione Lorenzo Valla 1976), xi, argues: "Given that, as Augustine states, [Orosius] joins him in Africa from the Atlantic coast of Spain; that [*sic*] Avito de Bracara (Braga, Northern Portugal) refers to him as *compresbyter meus* and that the Barbarian invasion of which he was a victim at first affected only the Northwest region of the Iberian Peninsula, it is rightly maintained today that Orosius's homeland was the area of Bracara, in the province of Galicia." Roy J. Deferrari, introduction to *Orosius: The Seven Books of History against the Pagans*, ed. Roy J. Deferrari (Washington, D.C.: Catholic University of America Press, 1964), xv, states simply that "Paulus Orosius was probably born at Bracara, now Braga, in Portugal, between 380 and 390." Orosius himself speaks of *Hispania Tarraconem nostram* in the seventh book of his *Historiae adversus paganos*, leading such scholars as María Carmen Jiménez Vicente, *La razón de estado en Alfonso X el Sabio: Paulo Orosio en la Primera Crónica General* (Valladolid: Secretariado de Publicaciones, Universidad, D.L., 1993) to suggest that he was a native of the Catalan city of Tarragona. The problem with this theory is that Hispania Tarraconensis was also a large Roman province (with Tarragona as its capital) that included within it the city of Bracara Augusta. Orosius writes, for example, of the city of Tarragona in book 7, chapter 22, 8: "Exstant adhuc per diversas provincias, in magnarum urbium ruinis, parvae et pauperes sedes, signa miseriarum et nominum indicia servantes, ex quibus nos quoque in Hispania Tarraconem nostram ad consolationem miseriae recentis ostendimus" (There still exist, throughout the different provinces, in the ruins of great cities, some small and poverty-stricken settlements that preserve below their names signs of their misfortunes, from which we may point out in Hispania our Tarragona as a consolation of recent misery; Paulus Orosius, *Orose: Histoires (contre les païens)*, ed. Marie-Pierre Arnaud-Lindet, 3 vols. (Paris: Les Belles Lettres, 1990),

vol. 1, 59). In the Latin text, Orosius refers to the peninsula as "Hispania" (its name under Roman rule), and while he speaks of "Tarraconem nostram" as though he came from that place and therefore it held some special value for him, Arnaud-Lindet rightly points out that the use of the "possessive *nostra* by which he qualifies the city . . . signifies only that Tarragona remained part of Rome" while most of the Iberian peninsula had been taken by barbarians: "Certains ont voulu faire de Tarragone la patrie d'Orose, en s'appuyant sur le possessif *nostra* dont il qualifie la ville (*Hist.* VII,22,8), mais l'usage du possessif signifie seulement que Tarragone est restée romaine dans une péninsule aux mains des barbares" (Arnaud-Lindet, introduction, xii n. 14).

70. Isidore cites Orosius directly in his brief mention of Alexander within the *Historia de regibus gothorum, vandalorum, et suevorum*: "Interpretatio autem nominis eorum in linguam nostram tecti, quo significatur fortitudo; et re vera, nulla enim gens in orbe fuit quae Romanum imperium adeo fatigaverit ut hi. Isti enim sunt quos etiam Alexander vitandos pronuntiavit, Pyrrhus pertimuit, Caesar exhorruit. (Ex Oros.) Per multa quippe retro saecula ducibus usi sunt, postea regibus, quorum oportet tempora per ordinem cursim exponere, et quo nomine actuque regnaverint, de historiis libata retexere" (The meaning of their name in our language is *tecti* [protected], which signifies fortitude; and in truth, there has never been a people in the world that has so strained Roman power. These are the people who even Alexander declared should be avoided, whom Pyrrhus dreaded, and Caesar feared. For many centuries they were led by chieftains, and then by kings, whose times we must briefly present in order along with their names and deeds, extracting these from existing chronicles).] Alfonso X also makes liberal use both of Orosius and Justin in the sections of his *General estoria* that deal with Alexander, as pointed out in Jiménez Vicente, *La razón de estado*.

71. For more on these manuscripts, see J. M. Bately and D. J. A. Ross, "A Checklist of Manuscripts of Orosius' *Historiarum adversum paganos libri septem*," *Scriptorium* 15 (1961); D. J. A. Ross, "Illustrated Manuscripts of Orosius," *Scriptorium* 9 (1955); and Ross, *Alexander Historiatus: A Guide to Medieval Illustrated Alexander Literature* (Frankfurt: Athenäum, 1988).

72. Orosius, *Orose: Histoires*, vol. 1, 147.

73. Ibid.

74. Ibid. The original text reads: "Quam ingressu Carthaginiesium in Italiam malorum grandinem secuturam continuarumque miserarium tenebras iuges historiarum fides locorumque infamia et abominatio dierum, quibus ea gesta sunt, protestantur. Tunc etiam nox usque ad plurimam diei partem tendi visa est et saxea de nubibus grando descendens veris terram lapidibus verberavit" (The faithfulness of the histories and places, and the horror of the days in which these things occurred, all testify that the entrance of the Carthaginians into Italy would be followed by a hailstorm of evils and a perpetual night of continued miseries. At that time, night ceaselessly blackened the day and a hailstorm of rocks descended down from the clouds and struck the earth).

75. Ibid., vol. 1, 147–48.

76. Ibid.

77. Ibid., vol. 1, 166. For more on Orosius's brief treatment of Alexander, see Fabrizio Fabbrini, *Paolo Orosio: Uno storico* (Rome: Edizione di Storia e Letteratura, 1979), 224–25.

78. George Cary, *The Medieval Alexander*, ed. David J. A. Ross (Cambridge: Cambridge University Press, 1956).

79. Ibid., x–xi.

80. Ibid., 194.

81. Ibid., 368. See also Emilio García Gómez, *Un texto árabe occidental de la leyenda de Alejandro, según el manuscrito ár. XXVII de la Biblioteca de la Junta para Ampliación de Estudios* (Madrid: Instituto de Valencia de don Juan, 1929); and A. R. Nykl, *A Compendium of Aljamiado Literature* (New York: Protat, 1929).

82. Cary, *The Medieval Alexander*, 61.

83. Ibid., 4.

84. María Rosa Lida de Malkiel, "La leyenda de Alejandro en la literatura medieval," *Romance Philology* 15 (1961–62).

85. Ibid.: 313.

86. D. S. Robertson, foreword to Cary, *The Medieval Alexander*, v.

87. María Rosa Lida de Malkiel, "Datos para la leyenda de Alejandro en la Edad Media castellana," *Romance Philology* 15 (1961–62); reprinted in Lida de Malkiel, *La tradición clásica en España* (Barcelona: Ariel, 1975), 165–97.

88. See, for example, Michael Agnew, "'Como un libro abierto': La construcción de un modelo exegético en el Libro de Alexandre," *La corónica* 29, no. 2 (2001); Ivy A. Corfis, "Libro de Alexandre: Fantastic Didacticism," *Hispanic Review* 62, no. 4 (1994); Ian Michael, "Interpretation of the Libro de Alexandre: The Author's Attitude towards His Hero's Death," *Bulletin of Hispanic Studies* 38 (1960); Michael, *The Treatment of Classical Material in the Libro de Alexandre* (Manchester: Manchester University Press, 1970); Dana A. Nelson, "El Libro de Alixandre y Gonzalo de Berceo: Un problema filológico," *La corónica* 28, no. 1 (1999); Francisco Rico, "La clerecía del mester," *Hispanic Review* 53 (1985); Isabel Uría Maqua, "El Libro de Alexandre y la Universidad de Palencia," in *Actas del I Congreso de Historia de Palencia* (Palencia: Diputación Provincial de Palencia, 1987); Raymond S. Willis, "Mester de clerecía: A Definition of the Libro de Alexandre," *Romance Philology* 10 (1956–57); Willis, "The Artistry and Enigmas of the Libro de Alexandre: A Review Article," *Hispanic Review* 42, no. 1 (1974); Willis, *The Debt of the Spanish Libro de Alexandre to the French Roman d'Alexandre* (Princeton, N.J.: Princeton University Press; Paris: Presses Universitaires de France, 1935); Willis, *El Libro de Alexandre: Texts of the Paris and the Madrid Manuscripts* (Princeton, N.J.: Princeton University Press; Paris: Presses Universitaires de France, 1934); and Willis, *The Relationship of the Spanish Libro de Alexandre to the Alexandreis of Gautier de Châtillon* (Princeton, N.J.: Princeton University Press; Paris: Presses Universitaires de France, 1934).

89. For analyses of the Aljamiado *Libro del recontamiento del rey Alixandre* (Book of the Story of King Alexander), Nykl, *A Compendium of Aljamiado Literature*, is still the best source; however, also indispensable are Francisco Guillén Robles, *Leyendas de José hijo de Jacob y de Alejandro Magno: Sacadas de dos manuscritos moriscos de la Biblioteca Nacional de Madrid* (Zaragoza: Imprenta del Hospicio Provincial, 1888), and the much more recent philological work in Z. David Zuwiyya, "Alexander's Journey through the Seven Climes of Antiquity and the Structure of the Aljamiado-Morisco Rrekontamiento del Rrey Alisandre," in *Entre oriente y occidente : Ciudades y viajeros en la Edad Media*, ed. María Do-

lores Rodríguez Gómez and Juan Pedro Monferrer Sala (Granada: Editorial Universidad de Granada, 2005); Zuwiyya, *Islamic Legends Concerning Alexander the Great: Taken from Two Medieval Arabic Manuscripts in Madrid* (Binghamton, N.Y.: Global Publications, 2001); Zuwiyya, "Royal Fame and Royal Honor in the Rrekontamiento del rrey Alisandre," *La corónica* 25, no. 1 (1996); and Zuwiyya, "A Study of Two Potential Sources for the Aljamiado-Morisco Legend of Alexander the Great: The Rrekontamiento del rrey Alisandre," *MIFLC Review* 9 (2000). For the broader Arabo-Islamic Alexander tradition in medieval Iberia, the most comprehensive study remains Emilio García Gómez's critical edition of Madrid, Junta ms. 27 (García Gómez, *Un texto árabe occidental de la leyenda de Alejandro*), although Zuwiyya's neo-Lachmannian edition of the Iberian *Qiṣṣat Dhū al-Qarnayn* (listed above) is also an important resource. J. A. Decourdemanche, "La légende d'Alexandre chez les Musulmans," *Revue de l'histoire des religions* 4, no. 1 (1882), and Tilman Nagel, *Alexander der Grosse in der frühislamischen Volksliteratur* (Walldorf-Hessen: Verlag für Orientkunde H. Vorndran, 1978), offer accounts of Alexander in Muslim folk literature that are also very informative, although they seek to cover a much broader body of literature. More general, though by no means comprehensive, treatments of Alexandrian literature in medieval Iberia can be found in, for example, Juan Beneyto, "Una versión en prosa castellana de la leyenda de Alejandro Magno," *Insula* 37 (1949); Jesús Cañas Murillo, "Un nuevo dato sobre la leyenda de Alejandro Magno en España: El manuscrito 3892 de la Biblioteca Nacional de Madrid," *Anuario de estudios filológicos* 7 (1984); Ian Michael, "Typological Problems in Medieval Alexander," in *Alexander the Great in the Middle Ages* (Groningen: Alfa Nijmegen, 1978); D. J. A. Ross, "Alexander Iconography in Spain: El Libro de Alexandre," *Scriptorium* 21 (1967); Fernando Rubio, "Un texto castellano occidental de la leyenda de Alejandro Magno," *La Ciudad de Dios* 178 (1966); Rubio, "Las leyendas sobre Alejandro Magno en la General Estoria de Alfonso el Sabio," *La Ciudad de Dios* 179 (1966); Dorothy Sherman Severin and Harvey L. Sharrer, "A Fifteenth-Century Spanish Fragment of a Lost Prose Alexander," *Medium Aevum* 48, no. 2 (1979); Harvey L. Sharrer, "Evidence of a Thirteenth-Century Libro del Infante Don Pedro de Portugal and Its Relationship to the Alexander Cycle," *Journal of Hispanic Philology* 1 (1977); and Nora Vela González, *El Libre de Alexandri: Versión catalana medieval*, Ph.D. diss. (Barcelona: Universitat Autónoma de Barcelona, 1973).

90. Richard Stoneman, *Alexander the Great: A Life in Legend* (New Haven, Conn.: Yale University Press, 2008).

91. Madrid, Biblioteca Nacional MS 10011, ff. 37v–38r.

92. This passage is reproduced, almost verbatim, in *Tirant lo Blanc* (chapter 181), although Alexander is left off the list.

Chapter 3

1. For more on the history of Catalano-Aragonese imperial expansion, see, for example, Stephen P. Bensch, *Barcelona and Its Rulers, 1096–1291* (Cambridge: Cambridge University Press, 2002), 277–346; Thomas N. Bisson, *Medieval Crown of Aragon: A Short History* (Oxford: Clarendon Press, 1986); Chaytor, *A History of Aragon and Catalonia*, 142–203 and 12–33; Francesco Giunta, *Aragonesi e Catalani nel Mediterraneo: La presenza Catalana nel Levante*

dalle origini a Giacomo II (Palermo: U. Manfredi, 1959); González-Casanova, "Western Narratives of Eastern Adventures"; Constantin Marinescu, *La politique orientale d'Alfonse V d'Aragon, roi de Naples (1416–1458)* (Barcelona: Institut d'Estudis Catalans, 1994); Piera, "Rehistoricizing the 'Other' Reconquista"; Antonio Rubió y Lluch and Maria Teresa Ferrer i Mallol, *Diplomatari de l'Orient català (1301–1409): Col·lecció de documents per a la història de l'expedició catalana a Orient i dels ducats d'Atenes i Neopàtria* (Barcelona: Institut d'Estudis Catalans, 2001); and Kenneth M. Setton, *Catalan Domination of Athens, 1311–1388* (London: Variorum, 1975).

2. On the history of Portuguese expansion into Morocco, see António Dias Farinha, *Os Portugueses em Marrocos* (Lisbon: Instituto Camões, 2002); Dias Farinha, "Os Xarifes de Marrocos (Notas sobre a expansão portuguesa no Norte de África)," in *Estudos de História de Portugal*, vol. 2, *Sécs. XVI–XX: Homenagem a A. H. de Oliveira Marques* (Lisbon: Estampa, 1983); Augusto Ferreira do Amaral, *Mazagão: A epopeia Portuguesa em Marrocos* (Lisbon: Tribuna da História, 2007); Luís Filipe Thomaz, "A evolução da política expansionista Portuguesa na primeira metade de quatrocentos," in *De Ceuta a Timor* (Lisbon: Difel, 1994); Andrew C. Hess, *The Forgotten Frontier: A History of the Sixteenth-Century Ibero-African Frontier* (Chicago: University of Chicago Press, 1978); and Maria Augusta Lima Cruz, "Os Portugueses em Marrocos nos séculos XV e XVI," in *História dos Descobrimentos e Expansão Portuguesa* (Lisbon: Universidade Aberta, 1999).

3. Blackmore, "Imagining the Moor," 28.

4. Ibid. See also Blackmore, *Moorings*, for a more detailed discussion of early modern Portuguese accounts of African Otherness.

5. Levinas, *Time and the Other*.

6. See, for example, Bunes Ibarra, *La imagen de los musulmanes*, 318–31; Richard L. Smith, *Ahmad al-Mansur: Islamic Visionary* (New York: Pearson Longman, 2006); and Dahiru Yahya, *Morocco in the Sixteenth Century: Problems and Patterns in African Foreign Policy* (Atlantic Highlands, N.J.: Humanities Press, 1981).

7. For more on the complex politics of the Sa'adis at the end of the sixteenth century, see Yahya, *Morocco in the Sixteenth Century*.

8. Ibid., 77.

9. For a recent account of Yaḥyá's career in Safi, see Maria Augusta Lima Cruz, "Mouro para os cristãos e cristão para os mouros: O caso Bentafufa," *Anais de história de Além-Mar* 3 (2002).

10. Vincent J. Cornell, "Socioeconomic Dimensions of Reconquista and Jihad in Morocco: Portuguese Dukkala and the Sadid Sus, 1450–1557," *International Journal of Middle East Studies*, 22, no. 4 (1990): 386; and David Lopes, *Textos em Aljamía Portuguesa: Documentos para a história do Domínio Português em Safim, extrahidos dos originaes da Torre do Tombo* (Lisbon: Imprensa Nacional, 1897), 118–37.

11. Joseph Goulven, *Safi au vieux temps des Portugais* (Lisbon: N.p., 1938), 91–92.

12. Lopes, *Textos em Aljamía Portuguesa*, 86–87.

13. Goulven, *Safi au vieux temps des Portugais*, 84.

14. Lopes, *Textos em Aljamía Portuguesa*, 62–65.

15. The scholar who has most steadily shined a light on the theological and imperial

spirit of Zurara's work is Josiah Blackmore. See Blackmore, "Imagining the Moor"; Blackmore, "Africa and the Epic Imagination of Camões," *Portuguese Literary and Cultural Studies* 9 (2003); and Blackmore, *Moorings*.

16. Zurara, *Crónica da tomada de Ceuta*, 144.

17. Ibid., 144–45.

18. For more on the redaction and transmission of the original Arabic text, see Mahmoud Manzalaoui, "The Pseudo-Aristotelian *Kitāb Sirr al-asrār*: Facts and Problems," *Oriens* 23 (1974): 147–257; and Steven J. Williams, *The Secret of Secrets: The Scholarly Career of a Pseudo-Aristotelian Text in the Latin Middle Ages* (Ann Arbor: University of Michigan Press, 2003). For a comprehensive assessment of the Castilian *Poridat de las poridades*, see Lloyd A. Kasten, *Poridat de las poridades* (Madrid: S. Aguirre, 1957).

19. Zurara, *Crónica da tomada de Ceuta*, 145.

20. Arrian, *Anabasis of Alexander*, vol. 1, 51. The episode is also mentioned in canto 5, stanza 93 of *Os Lusíadas*. See Luís Vaz de Camões, *Os Lusíadas* (Lisbon: António Gonçalves, 1572), f. 95r: "Não tinha em tanto os feitos gloriosos / De Aquiles, Alexandro, na peleja, / Quanto de quem o canta os numerosos / Versos: isso só louva, isso deseja. / Os troféus de / Melcíades, famosos, / Temístocles despertam só de enveja; / E diz que nada tanto o deleitava / Como a voz que seus feitos celebrava" (Alexander was not as impressed by Achilles's glorious feats in battle as he was by the man who sang so many verses about him: this only does he praise, this only does he desire).

21. Zurara, *Crónica da tomada de Ceuta*, 145. Livy narrates the story of Lucretia in book 1, chapters 57–60 of his *History of Rome*; the story of Verginia appears in book 3, chapter 44.

22. Levinas, *Time and the Other*, 74.

23. For a concise account of the chivalric underpinnings of the Portuguese expedition to Ceuta, as well as subsequent Portuguese actions in Morocco, see Peter Russell, *Prince Henry "The Navigator": A Life* (New Haven, Conn.: Yale University Press, 2000), 39–42.

24. Zurara, *Crónica da tomada de Ceuta*, 56.

25. Ibid., 146–47.

26. Ibid., 147.

27. Ibid.: "algumas pessoas que ela sabia eram de boa vida."

28. Ibid., 152.

29. Ibid., 153.

30. For more on the notion of natural bonds and chivalric investiture, see Rodríguez-Velasco, *Poética del orden de caballería*.

31. Zurara, *Crónica da tomada de Ceuta*, 162–63. The reference to Solomon is from Song of Songs 8:6.

32. Zurara, *Crónica da tomada de Ceuta*, 164.

33. Russell, *Prince Henry*, 46, speaks of the very brief period of mourning that João I established for Queen Philippa and its relation to the Ceuta expedition:

The queen's death coincided with what was thought by many to be yet another ill-omen—a long eclipse of the sun. The patent opposition to the whole enterprise among some of the king's own counselors once more came out into the open. They pointed out that the death of Queen Philippa created ceremonial and administrative problems that made it desirable to postpone the expedition's departure— already behind schedule—for at least a month. The delay would have the advantage, they stressed, that the danger of pestilence breaking out among the soldiers and sailors might have abated. Zurara claims that Prince Henry and his brothers rejected any idea of further postponement, doubtless insisting that their mother would not have wished her death to imperial the crusade. Their determination once again carried the day. The newly widowed king drastically curtailed the initial funeral ceremonies associated with a royal death, cutting the period of official mourning for Philippa to a barely decent minimum. On Friday, 26 July, eight days after her demise, the fleet set sail out of the Tagus estuary.

34. Zurara, *Crónica da tomada de Ceuta*, 164.

35. William Allison Laidlaw, *Latin Literature* (London: Methuen, 1951), 166.

36. Zurara, *Crónica da tomada de Ceuta*, 164.

37. Ibid., 164–65.

38. Levinas, *Time and the Other*, 74:

Death becomes the limit of the subject's virility, the virility made possible by the hypostasis at the heart of anonymous being, and manifest in the phenomenon of the present, in the light. It is not just that there exist ventures impossible for the subject, that its powers are in some way finite; death does not announce a reality against which nothing can be done, against which our powers are insufficient— realities exceeding our strength already arise in the world of light. What is important about the approach of death is that at a certain moment we are no longer *able to be able* [*nous ne "pouvons plus pouvoir"*]. It is exactly thus that the subject loses its very mastery as a subject.

39. Zurara, *Crónica da tomada de Ceuta*, 226.

40. Ibid.

41. The *Libro de Alexandre* (Book of Alexander), a thirteenth-century Castilian poetic work, introduces the siege of Gaza with an assassination attempt. As Alexander arrives at the city, a "bewitched man" (*omne endiabado*) disguised as a pilgrim pulls a sword out of his clothing and tries to kill Alexander. He is unsuccessful, and Alexander has the man's right hand chopped off as punishment. Alexander then unleashes his fury against Gaza, and although he is wounded in the shoulder by an arrow and in the thigh by a hurled stone, he manages to take the city in a short amount of time. See *Libro de Alexandre*, 339–40.

42. Quintus Curtius Rufus, *Life and Exploits of Alexander the Great*, ed. Christoph Cellarius (New York: D. Appleton, 1883), 257; Curtius Rufus, *The History of Alexander*, 248.

43. Siculus, *Bibliothèque historique, livre XVII*, 28. See also Justinus, *Trogi Pompei*, 70.

44. O'Brien, *Alexander the Great*, 253n. 91.

45. Zurara, *Crónica da tomada de Ceuta*, 225.

46. Curtius Rufus, *Life and Exploits of Alexander the Great*, 49.

47. Curtius Rufus, *The History of Alexander*, 64–65.

48. Arrian, *Anabasis of Alexander*, vol. 1, 214–15.

49. Zurara, *Crónica da tomada de Ceuta*, 226.

50. Camões, *Os Lusíadas*, f. 186v: "A minha já estimada e leda Musa / Fico que em todo o mundo de vós cante, / De sorte que Alexandro em vós se veja, / Sem à dita de Aquiles ter enveja" (I affirm that my now esteemed and happy muse / Will sing of you thoughout the entire world, / Such that Alexander will see himself in you, / And cease to envy the good fortune of Achilles). As is perhaps apparent, this reference has as much to do with the supreme confidence that Camões had in his own poetic prowess as it did with any perceived parallels between Sebastião and Alexander.

51. Nehemia Levitzion, "The Western Maghrib and Sudan," in *The Cambridge History of Africa*, ed. J. D. Fage and Roland Anthony Oliver (Cambridge: Cambridge University Press, 1975), vol. 3, 408–9. See also Muhammad al-Saghīr ibn Muhammad Ifrānī, *Nozhet-elhādi: Histoire de la dynastie Saadienne au Maroc (1511–1670)*, trans. Octave Victor Houdas, 2 vols. (Paris: Ernest Leroux, 1889), vol. 1, 109.

52. Yahya, *Morocco in the Sixteenth Century*, 69.

53. Bailey W. Diffie and George D. Winius, *Foundations of the Portuguese Empire, 1415–1580* (Minneapolis: University of Minnesota Press, 1977), 423 and 27. See also José Maria de Queiroz Velloso, *Dom Sebastião, 1554–1578* (Lisbon: Emprêsa Nacional de Publicidade, 1935), and Boxer, *The Portuguese Seaborne Empire*, 368–69.

54. For an analysis of the reception of Plutarch in Renaissance Portugal, see Nair de Nazaré Castro Soares, "Plutarco no Humanismo Renascentista em Portugal," in *Os fragmentos de Plutarco e a recepção da sua obra* (Coimbra: Instituto de Estudos Clássicos, 2003). Paulo Mendes Pinto, "Os sefarditas portugueses e a ciência do Renascimento" (Lisbon: Cátedra de Estudos Sefarditas "Alberto Benveniste," Universidade de Lisboa, 2008; http://www.fl .ul.pt/unidades/sefarditas/textos/sefarditas_renascimento.pdf), cites the fifteenth-century *Itinerário* of the Portuguese Franciscan Gaspar de São Bernardino, which includes references to Diodorus Siculus, Quintus Curtius, and Plutarch. For a detailed analysis of Plutarch's reception in fifteenth-century Italy, see Marianne Pade, *The Reception of Plutarch's Lives in Fifteenth-Century Italy*, 2 vols. (Copenhagen: Museum Tusculanum Press and University of Copenhagen, 2007).

55. The most focused account of Sebastião's sexual practices is Howard B. Johnson, *Dois estudos polémicos* (Tucson: Fenestra, 2004), which attributes Sebastião's genital pains to a case of chronic gonorrhea contracted through the sexual abuse the young king suffered at the hands of his confessor between 1560 and 1566, Luís Gonçalves da Câmara. Johnson's medical diagnosis is based on very circumstantial evidence (i.e., that Gonçalves da Câmara was blind in one eye, a symptom of untreated gonorrhea, and that he had served as a confessor in Tetuán, Morocco, where he had shared sleeping quarters with Christian prisoners); however, his account of the motives behind Sebastião's nighttime meetings with men across the Tagus and in the woods near Lisbon—Sebastião's private "wrestling match" with an escaped black slave in the forest near Sintra is especially suggestive—is compatible with the conclusions of other historians, including those working as early as the seventeenth century.

56. Joaquim Veríssimo Serrão, *Itinerários de el-Rei D. Sebastião*, 2 vols. (Lisbon: Academia Portuguesa da História, 1963), vol. 2, 223.

57. Andrew C. Hess, "The Battle of Lepanto and Its Place in Mediterranean History," *Past and Present* 57 (1972): 66.

58. Ibid.

59. Ibid., 66-67.

60. Serrão, *Itinerários de el-Rei D. Sebastião*, vol. 2, 222.

61. Hess, "The Battle of Lepanto," 67.

62. Serrão, *Itinerários de el-Rei D. Sebastião*, vol. 2, 223.

63. Among these was António de Saldanha, who spent several years in Marrakech as a captive of Aḥmad al-Manṣūr and composed a history of his reign from 1578 to 1603. See António de Saldanha, *Crónica de Almançor, Sultão de Marrocos (1578-1603)*, ed. António Dias Farinha (Lisbon: Instituto de Investigação Científica Tropical, 1997).

64. Luís de Camões, *Obras de Luiz de Camões: Precedidas de um ensaio biographico, no qual se relatam alguns factos não conhecidos da sua vida; augmentadas com algumas composições ineditas do poeta, pelo visconde de Juromenha*, ed. Visconde de Juromenha João Antonio de Lemos Pereira de Lacerda, 7 vols. (Lisbon: Imprensa Nacional, 1860-1924), vol. 1, 26.

65. Serrão, *Itinerários de el-Rei D. Sebastião*, vol. 2, 222.

66. Queiroz Velloso, *Dom Sebastião, 1554-1578*. As Boxer, *The Portuguese Seaborne Empire*, 368, describes him:

The young monarch had a fiery and exalted temperament, which was greatly excited when reading about Portuguese exploits overseas, and he was correspondingly upset when he read about the evacuation of the Moroccan coastal strongholds by order of his grandfather in 1549-50. While still a child he contemplated the conquest of Morocco, writing on the flyleaf of a missal which his Jesuit tutors gave him: 'Fathers, pray to God that He will make me very chaste, and very zealous to expand the Faith to all parts of the world.' His great desire was to be 'a captain of Christ,' and a crusading *conquistador* spirit permeates the instructions which he gave to the Viceroy and the Archbishop at Goa.

67. The very term Saʿadī, which has become the standard name used to refer to this dynasty, stems from attempts in the seventeenth century to contest the dynasty's genealogical link to the prophet Muḥammad by linking them to Muḥammad's wet-nurse and foster mother, Halima bint ʿAbd Allah. She was a member of the Banu Saʿad tribe from northern Arabia.

68. For a discussion of the Castilian use of the term *xarif*, see Bunes Ibarra, *La imagen de los musulmanes*, 318.

69. Levitzion, "The Western Maghrib and Sudan," vol. 3, 407.

70. Blackmore, "Imagining the Moor," 28, has described these politics, from the perspective of the Portuguese, very succinctly: "The Portuguese model (or better, practice) of

empire in Africa was not a simple exercise of dominance or subjugation but was regularly more negotiated, as practical and pragmatic as it was ideological."

71. Williams James, "Does Consciousness Exist?," *Journal of Philosophy, Psychology, and Scientific Methods* 1 (1904).

72. For more on Pierre Bourdieu's theory of *méconaissance*, see part 1 of Pierre Bourdieu and Jean-Claude Passeron, *Reproduction in Education, Society and Culture*, trans. Richard Nice (London: Sage, 1977).

73. Cohen, introduction to *Emmanuel Levinas: Time and the Other*, 9.

Chapter 4

1. João de Barros, *Da Ásia de João de Barros*, 24 vols. (Lisbon: Livraria Sam Carlos, 1973), vol. 1, 1.

2. Ibid.

3. Diogo do Couto offers a decidedly pragmatic frame for his use of Alexander in *O soldado prático*, invoking the Plutarchan (and medieval) commonplace regarding Alexander's generosity. See Diogo do Couto, *O soldado prático*, ed. Reis Brasil (Mem Martins: Publicacões Europa-América, 1988), 108: "E assi costumava a dizer o grande Alexandre que aquele era bom rei ou capitão, que aos amigos conservava com dadivas e merces, e aos imigos atraia a si com beneficios e boas obras" (Alexander the Great used to say that he was a great king or captain who sustained his friends with gifts and grants, and attracted his enemies with benefits and good works). Do Couto then refers to Alexander's father, Philip II of Macedon, using similar language. See Couto, *O soldado prático*, 109: "Trouxe estas particularidades pera mostrar a liberalidade e grandeza, com que se conquistou o mundo, e como aqueles capitaes venciam com mais merces que com armas. Com nenhuma outra cousa subiu Filipe, pai de Alexandre, a tanta grandeza senão com mão aberta; e muitas vezes dizia que não havia fortaleza tão forte que se não conquistasse, se a ela pudesse subir um asno carregado de ouro" (I bring up these things to show the generosity and largesse with which the world was conquered, and to show how those captains conquered more with grants than with arms. Through no other thing did Philip, the father of Alexander, rise to such greatness except through an open hand; and many times he said that there was no fort so strong that it could not be conquered if one were to approach it with a donkey loaded with gold).

4. Spencer, *The Roman Alexander*, 2.

5. See, for example, Hans Ulrich Gumbrecht, *Production of Presence: What Meaning Cannot Convey* (Stanford, Calif.: Stanford University Press, 2004), xv: "Presence effects . . . exclusively appeal to the senses. Therefore, the reactions that they provoke have nothing to do with *Einfühlung*, that is, with imagining what is going on in another's psyche."

6. Barros, *Da Ásia*, vol. 1, xiii–xiv.

7. Aristotle, *The Basic Works*, 561.

8. For more on this idea, see Ernst H. Kantorowicz, *The King's Two Bodies: A Study in Mediaeval Political Theology*, 7th ed. (Princeton, N.J.: Princeton University Press, 1997).

9. Barros, *Da Ásia*, vol. 1, xiv.

10. Ibid., xiv–xv.

11. For studies of Lullism in Renaissance Europe, see Jocelyn N. Hillgarth, *Ramon Lull and Lullism in Fourteenth-Century France* (Oxford: Clarendon Press, 1971); Jocelyn N. Hillgarth, Albert Soler i Llopart, Anna Alberni, and Joan Santanach i Suñol, *Ramon Llull i el naixement del lul·lisme* (Barcelona: Curial Edicions Catalanes i Publicacions de l'Abadia de Montserrat, 1998); Mark D. Johnston, "The Reception of the Lullian Art, 1450–1530," *Sixteenth Century Journal* 12, no. 1 (1981); and Joseph M. Victor, "The Revival of Lullism at Paris, 1499–1516," *Renaissance Quarterly* 28, no. 4 (1975). For a more comprehensive account of Llull's notion of *affatus*, see Mark D. Johnston, "Affatus: Natural Science as Moral Theology," *Estudios Lulianos* 30 (1990);Johnston, *The Evangelical Rhetoric of Ramon Llull: Lay Learning and Piety in the Christian West around 1300* (New York: Oxford University Press, 1996); and Ramon Llull, *Doctor Illuminatus: A Ramon Llull Reader*, ed. Anthony Bonner (Princeton, N.J.: Princeton University Press, 1993).

12. Johnston, *The Evangelical Rhetoric of Ramon Llull*, 66.

13. John Dagenais, "Speech as the Sixth Sense: Ramon Llull's *Affatus*," in *Actes del primer col·loqui d'estudis catalans a Nord-Amèrica/Actes del primer col·loqui d'estudis catalans à Nord-Amèrica*, ed. Spurgeon W. Baldwin, Alberto Porqueras Mayo, and Jaume Martí-Olivella (Montserrat: Publicacions de l'Abadia de Montserrat, 1978), 162.

14. Ibid., 168. The manuscript from which Dagenais cites Llull's text is Munich, Bayerische Staatsbibliothek Cod.hisp. 60, ff. 93ra–101rb. The Catalan text that he cites in this passage can be translated as: "[*affatus*] is nobler than *auditus*, because *auditus* is a passive sense in that it receives the voice, while *affatus* is an active sense, because it forms it."

15. João de Barros, *Grammatica da língua portuguesa* (Lisbon: Luís Rodrigues, 1540), 1.

16. For more on the influence of Erasmus on Barros, see Américo da Costa Ramalho, *Para a história do humanismo em Portugal* (Coimbra: Instituto Nacional de Investigação Científica, 1988), 201; José V. de Pina Martins, *Humanismo e Erasmismo na cultura portuguesa do século XVI: Estudo e textos* (Paris: Fundação Calouste Gulbenkian, 1973), 49–61; and José Sebastião da Silva Dias, *A política cultural da época de D. João III* (Coimbra: Instituto de Estudos Filosóficos, Universidade de Coimbra, 1969), 253–86.

17. Barros, *Da Ásia*, vol.1, xv.

18. Herodotus, *The Histories*, 3.

19. For an in-depth account of the ways in which written language intersected with processes of memorization in medieval Europe, see Mary J. Carruthers, *The Book of Memory: A Study of Memory in Medieval Culture* (Cambridge: Cambridge University Press, 1990).

20. Barros, *Da Ásia*, vol. 1, xv–xvi.

21. Ibid., vol. 1, xvi–xvii.

22. Ibid., vol. 1, xvii.

23. See Pero de Magalhães de Gandavo, *História da província Santa Cruz* (São Paulo: Editora Obelisco, 1964). The title of Camões's poem is "Ao muito ilustre Senhor D. Leonis Pereira sobre o livro que lhe oferece Pêro de Magalhães" (To the Very Illustrious Sir D. Leonis Pereira on the Book Offered to Him by Pêro de Magalhães). It can be said that Camões is acutely concerned with plumbing depths even darker than those explored by Barros. For an

example of this we need only look at the final stanza of *Os Lusíadas*, in which Camões directly addresses the young Portuguese king, Sebastião I (1554–1578), who would die, perhaps ironically, just six years after the publication of *Os Lusíadas* in a poorly planned military campaign in northern Morocco. See Camões, *Os Lusíadas*, f. 186v: "Ou fazendo que mais que a de Medusa, / A vista vossa tema o monte Atlante, / Ou rompendo nos campos de Ampelusa / Os muros de Marrocos e Trudante, / A minha ja estimada e leda Musa, / Fico, que em todo o mundo de vós cante, / De sorte que Alexandro em vós se veja, / Sem aa dita de Achiles ter enveja" (Whether you are striking more fear into Mount Atlas than the sight of Medusa could, or destroying in the fields of Cape Spartel the walls of Morocco and Taroudant, I affirm that my now esteemed and happy muse will sing of you throughout the entire world, such that Alexander will see himself in you, and cease to envy the good fortune of Achilles). The last verse of Camões's long epic poem invokes the episode related by Arrian of Alexander's visit to the tomb of Achilles in Troy. After placing a wreath on the tomb (Hephaestion is said to have placed one on the tomb of Patroclus), "Alexander, so the story goes, blessed Achilles for having Homer to proclaim his fame to posterity." Camões seems to be attempting to strike a deal here with Portugal's boy king: if Sebastião will carry out his plans to invade Morocco (something he had been planning to do since attaining majority in 1568), Camões will employ his considerable poetic talents to extol the king's accomplishments in such a way that Alexander the Great will see himself in Sebastião. More important, in light of Camões's attempt to gain royal patronage, these verses will compel Alexander (or rather, his shade) to cease to envy the poetic treatment given to Achilles by Homer and long instead for that given to Sebastião by Camões. That this plan would fail so spectacularly for the Portuguese is something that even the normally pessimistic Camões could not have predicted.

24. Camões also argues, in his "Oda VII," dedicated to King Manuel I of Portugal, that strong leaders have a central role in the cultivation of the sciences and the arts. See Luís de Camões, *Obras de Luiz de Camões*, ed. João António de Lemos Pereira de Lacerda, Segundo Visconde de Juromenha, 2 vols. (Lisbon: Imprensa Nacional, 1861), vol. 2, 275: "Mas altos corações dignos d'Imperio, / Que vencem a Fortuna, / Forão sempre coluna / Da sciencia gentil: Octaviano, / Scipião, Alexandre e Graciano. / Que vemos immortais; / E vós, que o nosso seculo dourais" (But high hearts worthy of Empire that vanquish Fortune were always the backbone of gentle learning: Octavian, Scipio, Alexander, and Gratian. We see them as immortal, and you as well, who makes our age golden).

25. Camões, *Os Lusíadas*, 95v.

26. Barros, *Da Ásia*, vol.1, xvii–xviii.

27. Ibid., vol. 1, xviii.

28. Ramalho, *Para a história do humanismo em Portugal*, 199, has argued that Barros actually knew very little Greek. See also Américo da Costa Ramalho, "Ropicapnefma: Um bibliónimo mal enxertado," *Humanitas* 27–28 (1975–76): 201–8.

29. For more on Barros's use of Plutarch, especially in the *Diálogo da viciosa vergonha*, see Jorge A. Osório, "Plutarco revisitado por João de Barros," *Ágora: Estudos clássicos em debate* 3 (2001), and Ramalho, *Para a história do humanismo em Portugal*, 198–203. For a modern edition of the *Diálogo da viciosa vergonha*, along with the *Gramática da língua por-*

tuguesa, see João de Barros, *Gramática da língua portuguesa: Cartinha, gramática, diálogo em louvor da nossa linguagem e Diálogo da viciosa vergonha*, ed. Maria Leonor Carvalhão Buescu (Lisbon: Publicações da Faculdade de Letras da Universidade de Lisboa, 1971).

30. Camões, *Os Lusíadas*, f. 1v.

31. Ibid., f. 129v–30r.

32. When I discovered in 2003 that Oliver Stone was in the process of producing a film version of Alexander based largely on Roman sources, I assumed that Stone's interest in the subject derived from the then-recent U.S. invasion of Iraq and Afghanistan, territories once held by Alexander. Before seeing the film, and aware of Stone's long commitment to engaging in political commentary in his films, I somewhat naively assumed that his film would read as a twenty-first-century American update of the Roman treatment of Alexander as a simultaneously "quaint" (as a Macedonian king) and "awesome" (as both a powerful emperor and orientalized degenerate) predecessor to Rome. The film, which stars the Irish actor Colin Farrell in the title role, does not, in my opinion, support such a historically weighty reading. In fairness to Stone, however, it might be that the film's very lightness is the more powerful statement on contemporary American political discourse, namely that we are more concerned with breaking away from history than from theorizing our connection to it. As Milan Kundera might frame it, our stubborn refusal to be haunted by Alexander in the context of our own Eastern conquests casts us as a nation more devoted to forgetting than to (Dionysian) laughter.

33. Camões, *Os Lusíadas*, f. 184v.

34. Before Vasco da Gama's successful voyage to India, Manuel I held the titles "King of Portugal, the Algarves, and of Africa, Lord of Guinea"; afterward, he added the titles "Lord of the Conquest, Navigation and Commerce with Ethiopia, Arabia, Persia, and India."

35. For Barros's and Góis's treatment of Monçaide, on which Camões based his own epic presentation of the Tunisian would-be Mourisco, see Damião de Góis, *Crónica do Felicíssimo Rei D. Manuel* (Coimbra: Impr. da Universidade, 1926), 82; and Barros, *Da Ásia*, vol. 1, 330.

36. Álvaro Velho, *Roteiro da primeira viagem de Vasco da Gama (1497–1499)*, ed. A. Fontoura da Costa (Lisbon: Agência Geral do Ultramar, 1960), 40.

37. Gaspar Correia, *The Three Voyages of Vasco da Gama, and His Viceroyalty*, ed. and trans. Henry E. L. Stanley (London: Hakluyt Society, 1869), 159; and Alvaro Velho, *A Journal of the First Voyage of Vasco da Gama*, ed. and trans. Ernest George Ravenstein (London: Hakluyt Society, 1898), 179.

38. Gil Vicente, *Auto da Índia: Farsa*, ed. Mário Fiúza (Porto: Porto Editora: 1986). For more on the notion of blackness in Renaissance Portugal, see Blackmore, *Moorings*.

39. Livy, *The History of Rome*, trans. George Baker, 6 vols. (London: Jones, 1830); Zurara, *Crónica da tomada de Ceuta*; and Zurara, *Crónica dos feitos notáveis que se passaram na conquista da Guiné por mandado do infante D. Henrique*, ed. Torquato de Sousa Soares, 2 vols. (Lisbon: Academia Portuguesa da História, 1978).

40. Vicente Suárez de Deza y Avila, *Parte primera de los donayres de Tersícore* (Madrid: Melchor Sánchez, 1663), 104v.

41. Barros, *Da Ásia*, 1–2.

42. Ibid., 2–3.

43. Ibid., 2.

44. Ibid., vol. 3, 108.

45. Abū 'Ja'far Muḥammad ibn Jarīr al-Tabarī, *The History of Al-Tabarī*, 40 vols. (Albany: State University of New York Press, 1988–2007).

46. Barros, *Da Ásia*, vol. 1, 3.

47. For different account of this idea, see Miguel Asín Palacios, *Dante y el Islam* (Madrid: Editorial Voluntad, 1927); Asín Palacios, *La escatologia musulmana en la Divina comedia* (Madrid: E. Maestre, 1919); Marie-Thérèse D'Alverny, *La connaissance de l'Islam dans l'Occident médiéval* (Aldershot: Variorum, 1994); Ugo Monneret de Villard, *Lo studio dell'Islam in Europa nel XII e nel XIII secolo* (Vatican City: Biblioteca Apostolica Vaticana, 1944); Philippe Sénac, *L'image de l'autre: L'Occident médiéval face à l'Islam* (Paris: Flammarion, 1983); and John Victor Tolan, *Saracens: Islam in the Medieval European Imagination* (New York: Columbia University Press, 2002).

48. On Dante's portrayal of Muhammad in the *Inferno*, see Asín Palacios, *Dante y el Islam*; Asín Palacios, *La escatologia musulmana*; Otfried Lieberknecht, *Allegorese und Philologie: Überlegungen zum mehrfachen Schriftsinn in Dantes Commedia* (Stuttgart: Franz Steiner Verlag, 1999); and Lieberknecht, "A Medieval View of Islam: Dante's Encounter with Mohammed in *Inferno* XXVIII" (Department of Italian Studies and the Townsend Center for the Humanities Working Group, University of California at Berkeley, 1997; http://www.lieberknecht.de/~diss/papers/p_moham.pdf).

49. Barros, *Da Ásia*, 9–10.

50. Giorgio Agamben, *Homo Sacer: Sovereign Power and Bare Life*, trans. Daniel Heller-Roazen (Stanford, Calif.: Stanford University Press, 1998).

51. Barros, *Da Ásia*, 10–11.

52. These are themes that Fernão Lopes de Castanheda (ca. 1500–1559) brings up in his own *História do descubrimento e conquista da Índia* (History of the Discovery and Conquest of India), first published in Coimbra in 1552. See Castanheda, *Historia do descobrimento e conqvista da India pelos Portvgveses*, 8 vols. (Lisbon: Typographia Rollandiana, 1833), vol. 1, ii–iii: "a que estas dos Portugueses e as dos Borbaros tem grande e conhecida avantage, porque as suas conquistas foram todas per terra, assi como a de Semiramis, de Ciro, de Xerxes, do grande Alexandre, de Julio Cesar, e doutros borbaros, gregos e latinos, e indo eles com suas gentes. E a da India foi feita por mar e por vossos capitães, e com navegação dum ano e d'oito meses e de seis ao menos: e não a vista de terra senão a fastados trezentas e seiscentas leguas partindo do fim do Occidente e navegando até ho do Oriente sem verem mais que agua e ceo, rodeando toda a sphera, cousa nunca cometida dos mortais, nem imaginada pera se fazer. Com imensos trabalhos de fome, de sede, de doenças e de perigos de morte, com a furia e impeto dos ventos e passados estes se vem na Índia em outras despantosas e crueis batalhas com a mais feroz gente e mais sabedor na guerra e abastada das munições parela, que outra nenhuma d'Ásia" (to which [the conquests of the Greeks and Romans] enjoy a great advantage over those of Portuguese and the Barbarians, because they were all undertaken by land, like those of Semiramis, Cyrus, Xerxes, Alexander the Great, Julius Caesar, and other Barbarians, Greeks, and Latins, and they involved a large number of their people. The Portuguese conquest of India, on the other hand, was carried out by sea and by

your captains, with a one-year eight-month, or at least one-year six-month, sea voyage: and not with land in sight, but 360 leagues away from the border of the West and sailing to that of the Orient without seeing anything but water and sky, sailing around the entire globe, a thing that had never been done by any mortal, nor had any imagined doing it. They suffered through immense hunger, thirst, sicknesses, and mortal danger, with the fury and force of the winds. Beyond all this they found themselves in India engaged in frightful and cruel battles with the most ferocious and well trained, and well supplied, fighting forces in all of Asia).

53. Ibid., vol. 3, i.

54. For more on this episode, see chapter 16 of Plutarch's *How a Man May Become Aware of His Progress in Virtue* (*Moralia*): "It is reported of Alexander, that one night seeing a messenger joyfully running towards him and stretching out his hand, as if he had something to deliver to him, he said to the apparition, Friend, what news do you bring me? Is Homer risen from the dead? That admirable monarch thought that nothing was wanting to his great exploits but such a herald as Homer."

55. *Libro de Alexandre*, 201.

56. Ibid.

57. Ibid.

58. Castanheda, *Historia*, vol. 3, i.

59. João de Barros, "Ropicapnefma," in *Corpus do Português (45 million words, 1300s–1900s)*, ed. Mark Davies and Michael Ferreira; http://www.corpusdoportugues.org: 2006–.

60. Justinus, *Trogi Pompei*, 73–74; Curtius Rufus, *The History of Alexander*, 27. The fourteenth-century *Libro de Alexandre* likewise repeats the Vulgate version of the story, taking out his sword and cutting through the knot. See *Libro de Alexandre*, 292.

61. For an introduction to Barros and his work, see C. Boxer, *João de Barros, Portuguese Humanist and Historian of Asia* (New Delhi: Concept, 1981).

62. Beyond what he relates about his travels, little is known of Teixeira, aside from the fact that he was a Portuguese *converso*, or Jewish convert to Christianity. As for his account of Hormuz, it is based on his own experiences as well as his reading of a lost chronicle of Hormuz written by Padisha Turan Shah (no longer extant), both of which he seems to have studied in the original Persian. His *Relaciones de Pedro Teixeira d'el origen descendecia y succession de los reyes de Persia, y de Harmuz, de un viage hecho por el mismo autor dende la India Oriental hasta Italia por tierra* (Accounts of Pedro Teixeira on the Origen, Descent, and Succession of the Kings of Persia and Hormuz, from a Voyage Made by the Author from East India to Italy by Land) was written in Spanish and published in Antwerp by Hieronymo Verdussen in 1610. For an English translation of the *Relaciones*, see Pedro Teixeira, *The Travels of Pedro Teixeira: with his "Kings of Harmuz" and Extracts from His "Kings of Persia,"* trans. W. F. Sinclair (London: Hakluyt Society, 1902). The earliest Portuguese translation of the *Chronicles of the Kings of Hormuz* that mentions Turan Shah as its author is found as an appendix to Frei Gaspar da Cruz's *Tratado das cousas da China* (Treatise on Matters of China), published in Evora in 1570. The appendix bears the title "Relação da Cronica dos Reyes Dormuz, e da fundaçam da cidade Dormuz, tirada de hũa Cronica que compos hũ Rey do mesmo Reyno, chamado Pachaturunxa, scripta em Arabigo [*sic*], e sumariamente traduzida em lingoajem Portugues por hum religioso da ordem de Sam Domingos, que na ilha dormuz

fundou hūa casa de sua ordem" (Account of the Chronicle of the Kings of Hormuz and of the Foundation of the City of Hormuz, Taken from a Chronicle Composed by a King of the Same Kingdom Named Padisha Turan Shah, Written in Arabic [*sic*] and Summarily Translated into the Portuguese Language by a Cleric in the Order of Saint Dominic, Who on the Island of Hormuz Founded a House of His Order). As Donald Ferguson points out in his introduction to the Hakluyt Society's English edition of Teixeira's *Relaciones*, "The 'Dominican monk' was, apparently, Gaspar da Cruz himself. Teixeira does not appear to have known of this translation: at any rate, he does not refer to it" (Teixeira, *The Travels of Pedro Teixeira*, xcvii). Duarte Barbosa's text was first published in Venice in 1554 as part of Gian Battista Ramusio's *Delle navigatione et viaggi* (Some Navigations and Voyages); however, most modern editions are based on the Portuguese manuscript discovered in Lisbon and published in 1813 by the Royal Academy of Science. For an English edition, see D. Barbosa, *The Book of Duarte Barbosa*, 2 vols., trans. M. Longworth Dames (London: Hakluyt Society, 1918–21). For a contemporary study of Hormuz and the Portuguese occupation, see L. Lockhart, "European Contacts with Persia, 1350–1736," *The Cambridge History of Iran in Seven Volumes* (Cambridge: Cambridge University Press, 1986), vol. 6, 373–411.

    63. Barros, *Da Ásia*, vol. 3, 92.

    64. Ibid., vol. 3, 124.

    65. Ibid., vol. 3, 127–28.

    66. Ibid., vol. 2, 318.

    67. Ibid., vol.1, xviii.

    68. Ibid., vol. 2, 318.

    69. Luís Pereira, in his epic account of the final campaign of the Portuguese King Sebastião I, published in 1588 and highly influenced by Camões, reworks the final verses of *Os Lusíadas*: "No coração do imigo espanto imprime, / Oo quem tivera aqui Meonia pluma, / Para fazer (no como aqui peleja) / Espanto a Achilles, e Alexandre inveja" (In the heart of the enemy he imprints fear, / Oh, that there might come one with a Meonian pen, / to instill (not as I struggle here) / fear in Achilles and envy in Alexander). Luís Pereira, *Elegiada* (Lisbon: Manuel de Lira, 1588), 395.

Chapter 5

    1. Louis Cardaillac, *Morisques et chrétiens: Un affrontement polémique (1492–1640)*. (Paris: Klincksieck, 1977); Antonio Domínguez Ortiz and Bernard Vincent, *Historia de los moriscos: Vida y tragedia de una minoría* (Madrid: Revista de Occidente, 1978); Isabel M. R. Mendes Drummond Braga, *Mouriscos e cristãos no Portugal quinhentista* (Lisbon: Hugin Editores, 1999); Mikel de Epalza, *Los moriscos antes y después de la expulsión* (Madrid: MAPFRE, 1992); Mercedes García Arenal, *Los moriscos* (Madrid: Nacional, 1975); L. P. Harvey, *Muslims in Spain: 1500 to 1614* (Chicago: University of Chicago Press, 2005); Henry Charles Lea, *The Moriscos of Spain: Their Conversion and Expulsion* (London: B. Quaritch, 1901); Pedro Longás Bartibás, *La vida religiosa de los moriscos* (Madrid: Ibérica, 1915); and Rogério de Oliveira Ribas, "Filhos de Mafoma: Mouriscos, Cripto-Islamismo e Inquisição no Portugal quinhentista" (Universidade de Lisboa, 2005).

2. Luis F. Bernabé Pons and María Jesús Rubiera Mata, "La lengua de mudéjares y moriscos: Estado de la cuestión," in *VII Simposio Internacional de Mudejarismo, Teruel, 19–21 de septiembre de 1996* (Teruel: Centro de Estudios Mudéjares, 1999); Dolors Bramon, "Les morisques et leur langue," *Cahiers d'études romanes* 16 (1990); Ottmar Hegyi, "Tradition and Linguistic Assimilation among the Spanish Moriscos During the Sixteenth Century," in *Conversion and Continuity: Indigenous Christian Communities in Islamic Lands*, ed. Michael Gervers and Ramzi Jibran Bikhazi (Toronto: Pontifical Institute of Medieval Studies, 1990); and Consuelo López-Morillas, "Language and Identity in Late Spanish Islam," *Hispanic Review* 63 (1995). Gerard A. Wiegers, *Islamic Literature in Spanish and Aljamiado: Yça of Segovia (fl. 1450), His Antecedents and Successors* (Leiden and New York: E. J. Brill, 1994), 67, argues that "already before 1455, some Mudejars [i.e., Muslims residing in Christian territory] of Aragon and Castile made use of Hispanic dialects to draw up documents, and also to copy out translations of works on *fiqh* . . . , devotional treatises, and polemical works. It can be seen that the earliest texts seem to date from the early 14th century. When Mudejars wrote in Romance they used both the Arabic and the Latin script. . . . Although the evidence does not allow us to say that Spanish is in use as a firmly established literary language, there can be no doubt that the Mudejars used the vernacular as a literary medium well before 1455." As López-Morillas, "Language and Identity," 198, succintly puts it: "The Aljamiado phenomenon, so characteristic of the Castilian and Aragonese Muslims, has its roots in the Mudéjar period."

3. For a detailed analysis of this author's work, see Wiegers, *Islamic Literature in Spanish and Aljamiado*.

4. See, for example, Mohamed Al-Aouani, "À la recherche des influences andalouses dans les campagnes tunisiennes: Essai de mise au point," in *Études sur les moriscos andalous en Tunisie*, ed. Mikel de Epalza and Ramón Petit (Madrid-Tunis: Dirección General de Relaciones Culturales, 1973); Beji Ben Mami, "Quelques aspects de la présence andalouse à la Médina de Tunis pendant le période Hafside," in *Actes du II Symposium International du C.I.E.M.: Religion, identité et sources documentaires sur les morisques andalous*, ed. Abdeljelil Temimi (Tunis: Institut Supérieur de Documentation, 1984); Luis F. Bernabé Pons, "La literatura en español de los moriscos en Túnez, mudéjares y moriscos, cambios sociales y culturales: Actas" (Teruel: Centro de Estudios Mudéjares, 2004); Abdelmouneim Bounou, "Los moriscos en Marruecos: Poder de una minoría," in *La política y los moriscos en la época de los Austria: Actas del encuentro* (Madrid: La Fundación del Sur-Ediciones Especiales, 1999); António Dias Farinha, "De mouriscos em Marrocos na epoca do Sultan Ahmad Al Mansur," in *La política y los moriscos en la época de los Austria: Actas del encuentro* (Madrid: La Fundación del Sur-Ediciones Especiales, 1999); Mikel de Epalza, "Moriscos y andalusíes en Túnez en el siglo XVII," *Al-Andalus* 34 (1969); Epalza, "Trabajos actuales sobre la comunidad de moriscos refugiados en Túnez: desde el siglo XVII a nuestros días," in *Actas del Coloquio internacional de literatura aljamiada y morisca (Oviedo, 1972)*, ed. Álvaro Galmés de Fuentes and Emilio García Gómez (Oviedo: Gredos, 1978); Epalza, "La vie intellectuelle en espagnol des morisques au Maghreb (XVIIe. siècle)," *Revue d'histoire maghrébine* 59–60 (1990); Guillermo Gozalbes Busto, "Presencia de los moriscos en Tetuán y Xauen (Marruecos sep-

tentrional)," in *Actes du II Symposium International du C.I.E.M.: Religion, dentité et sources documentaires sur les morisques andalous*, ed. Abdeljelil Temimi (Tunis: Institut Supérieur de Documentation, 1984); Luce López Baralt, "La angustia secreta del exilio: El testimonio de un morisco de Túnez," *Hispanic Review* 55, no. 1 (1987); Juan Penella Roma, "El sentimiento religioso de los moriscos españoles emigrados: Notas para una literatura morisca en Túnez," in *Actas del Coloquio internacional de literatura aljamiada y morisca*, ed. Alvaro Galmés de Fuentes and Emilio García Gómez (Madrid: Gredos, 1978); and Abdeljelil Temimi, "Las influencias de los moriscos andalusíes en la sociedad magrebina (el ejemplo de Túnez)," in *Actas del XIe congreso de estudios moriscos sobre: Huellas literarias e impactos de los moriscos en Túnez y en América Latina*, ed. Abdeljelil Temimi (Tunis: FTERSI, 2005).

5. Manuel Barrios Aguilera, *Granada morisca, la convivencia negada: Historia y textos* (Granada: Editorial COMARES, 2002), 82.

6. For information regarding the number of Iberian Muslims who converted to Christianity and remained in the Iberian Peninsula, see ; Julio Caro Baroja, *Los moriscos del reino de Granada: Ensayo de historia social* (Madrid: Instituto de Estudios Políticos, 1957); Domínguez Ortiz and Vincent, *Historia de los moriscos*; and Francisco Núñez Muley, *A Memorandum for the President of the Royal Audiencia and Chancery Court of the City and Kingdom of Granada*, ed. and trans. Vincent Barletta (Chicago: University of Chicago Press, 2007).

7. See Vincent Barletta, *Covert Gestures: Crypto-Islamic Literature as Cultural Practice in Early Modern Spain* (Minneapolis: University of Minnesota Press, 2005), and Jacqueline Fournel-Guerin, "Le livre et la civilisation écrite dans la communauté morisque aragonaise (1540–1620)," *Mélanges de la Casa de Velázquez* 15 (1979).

8. Luce López Baralt, "Crónica de la destrucción de un mundo: La literatura aljamiado-morisca," *Bulletin Hispanique* 82, nos. 1–2 (1980): 24.

9. López-Morillas, "Language and Identity," 195.

10. See Barletta, *Covert Gestures*; and Vincent Barletta, "Deixis, *Taqiyya*, and Textual Mediation in Crypto-Muslim Aragon," *Text and Talk* 28, no. 5 (2008).

11. For an account of the persecution of *moriscos* by the Portuguese Inquisition, see Ahmed Boucharb, *Os pseudo-mouriscos de Portugal no séc. XVI*, trans. Maria Filomena Lopes de Barros (Lisbon: Hugin Editores, 2004); Drummond Braga, *Mouriscos e cristãos no Portugal quinhentista*; María Filomena Lopes de Barros, "De mudéjares a mouriscos: O caso português," in *Actas del VIII Simposio Internacional de Mudejarismo: De mudéjares a moriscos; Una conversión forzada* (Teruel: Centro de Estudios Mudéjares, 2002); Ribas, "Filhos de Mafoma"; and François Soyer, *The Persecution of the Jews and Muslims of Portugal: King Manuel I and the End of Religious Tolerance (1496–7)* (Leiden: Brill, 2007).

12. For more on the production and use of Aljamiado texts in Portugal, see L. P. Harvey, "Aljamia Portuguesa Revisited," *Portuguese Studies* 2 (1986); Lopes, *Textos em Aljamía Portuguesa: Documentos para a História do Domínio Português em Safim, extrahidos dos originaes da Torre do Tombo* (Lisbon: Imprensa Nacional, 1897); Rogério de Oliveira Ribas, "'Cide Abdella': Um marabuto na corte de D. João III," in *D. João III e o império: Actas do Congresso Internacional comemorativo do seu nascimento*, ed. Roberto Carneiro and Artur Teodoro de

Matos (Lisbon: Centro de História Além-Mar/Centro de Estudos dos Povos e Culturas de Expressão Portuguesa, 2004); and Ribas, "Filhos de Mafoma."

13. Francisco Guillén Robles, *Leyendas de José hijo de Jacob y de Alejandro Magno: Sacadas de dos manuscritos moriscos de la Biblioteca Nacional de Madrid* (Zaragoza: Imprenta del Hospicio Provincial, 1888); and A. R. Nykl, *A Compendium of Aljamiado Literature* (New York: Protat, 1929). For a discussion of the origins of the Qiṣṣat Dhū al-Qarnayn, see Emilio García Gómez, *Un texto árabe occidental de la leyenda de Alejandro, según el manuscrito ár. XXVII de la Biblioteca de la Junta para Ampliación de Estudios* (Madrid: Instituto de Valencia de don Juan, 1929); and Z. David Zuwiyya, *Islamic Legends Concerning Alexander the Great: Taken from Two Medieval Arabic Manuscripts in Madrid* (Binghamton, N.Y.: Global, 2001), 1–47.

14. On the Aragonese provenance of the manscript, Guillén Robles, *Leyendas de José hijo de Jacob y de Alejandro Magno*, lvi, argues: "I have no doubt that this translation was made by Aragonese Moriscos, nor would any native of Aragon upon having read the first few pages."

15. Madrid, Biblioteca Nacional MS 5254, f. 3v.

16. Nykl, *A Compendium of Aljamiado Literature*, 38–39.

17. Madrid, Biblioteca Nacional MS 5254, f. 8r. On the reference to Iriarte, see Guillén Robles, *Leyendas de José hijo de Jacob y de Alejandro Magno*, lv; and Nykl, *A Compendium of Aljamiado Literature*, 34.

18. Madrid, Biblioteca Nacional MS 5254, f. 1v.

19. Ibid., f. 8v.

20. Ibid.

21. Ibid., f. 10r.

22. On the concept of narrative and "possible worlds," see Jerome S. Bruner, *Actual Minds, Possible Worlds* (Cambridge, Mass.: Harvard University Press, 1986).

23. Brannon M. Wheeler, *Moses in the Quran and Islamic Exegesis* (London: Routledge, 2002), 16.

24. The library was formerly known as the Biblioteca de la Junta para Ampliación de Estudios e Investigaciones Científicas; for this reason it is also commonly referred to as the Biblioteca de la Junta.

25. Madrid, Biblioteca del Instituto de Filología del CSIC/Junta, MS 26, f. 3v.

26. García Gómez, *Un texto árabe occidental.*

27. Madrid, Biblioteca Nacional MS 5254, 133v.

28. Ibid., f. 134v.

29. Ibid.

30. Ibid.

31. Nykl, *A Compendium of Aljamiado Literature*, 35n. 2.

32. Madrid, Biblioteca Nacional MS 5254, f. 134v.

33. Nykl, *A Compendium of Aljamiado Literature*, 35.

34. Ibid.

35. Madrid, Biblioteca Nacional MS 5254, f. 141r.

36. At the end of the Second Persian Period, Egyptian pharaohs were considered to be earthly avatars of Horus the Younger, the son of Isis and Osiris. As the legend goes, Osiris

was killed and chopped into pieces by his main adversary, Set. Isis, wishing to have a child by the slain Osiris, pieced together his scattered body parts. She was apparently unable to make much use of the murdered god's genitals (Set had thrown them into a river to be eaten by fish), so she fashioned some out of clay and attached them to Osiris's body. Mounting the lifeless body, Isis become pregnant, and Horus was soon born. Once he reached adulthood, Horus managed to avenge his father's murder by establishing dominion over Set and both Lower and Upper Egypt. For more on this story, see William Kelly Simpson, *The Literature of Ancient Egypt: An Anthology of Stories, Instructions, Stelae, Autobiographies, and Poetry*, 3rd ed. (New Haven, Conn.: Yale University Press, 2003), 91–103.

37. Arrian, *Anabasis of Alexander*, vol. 1, 229.

38. O'Brien, *Alexander the Great*, 88.

39. Ibid. See also Green, *Alexander of Macedon*, 272–73.

40. Arrian, *Anabasis of Alexander*, vol. 1, 229.

41. Curtius Rufus, *Life and Exploits of Alexander the Great*, 51–52; and Curtius Rufus, *The History of Alexander*, 67. On the late medieval popularity of Orosius's *Seven Books of History Against the Pagans* (*Historiarum adversus paganos libri septem*), see chapter 2 of the present volume.

42. O'Brien, *Alexander the Great*, 88.

43. Justinus, *Trogi Pompei*, 74. Trogus's principal source is Cleitarchus of Alexandria, whom Paul Cartledge, *Alexander the Great*, 278, describes: "Cleitarchus [a respected historian of Persia] was too young to accompany Alexander on his expedition, but this lack of first-hand experience was somewhat compensated for by his freedom from the pressures of writing more or less official history. Moreover, based as he was at Athens after 322 [BCE], Cleitarchus was able to consult at leisure all those Greeks (politicians, ambassadors, artists, technicians, ordinary soldiers) connected either with Alexander or with the Persian side. He could therefore enrich his reading of Callisthenes and other eyewitness authors with an abundant oral tradition lacking in Arrian's sources."

44. Plutarch, *The Life of Alexander the Great*, 4.

45. Arrian, *Anabasis of Alexander*, vol. 1, 371.

46. As I discussed in chapter 4, Camões would go on to echo Callisthenes's conceit in his own metapoetical address to Portuguese king Sebastião I (1554–1578 CE) within *Os Lusíadas*, although for him the source of this idea would be Alexander himself, contemplating the role of Homer in immortalizing Achilles.

47. Justinus, *Trogi Pompei*, 104–5; For Seneca's thoughts on Lysimachus and Alexander, see Spencer, *The Roman Alexander*, 100–112; for Montesquieu's reworking of the Lysimachus/Callisthenes/Alexander triangle, see Charles de Secondat Montesquieu, "Lysimachus," in *The Complete Works of M. de Montesquieu* (Dublin: W. Watson, W. Whitestone, J. Williams, et al., 1777), vol. 4, 191–95.

48. Curtius Rufus, *The History of Alexander*, 67.

49. Plutarch, *The Life of Alexander the Great*, 28.

50. Arrian, *Anabasis of Alexander*, vol. 1, 231.

51. Plutarch, *The Life of Alexander the Great*, 28.

52. Arrian, *Anabasis of Alexander*, vol. 1, 233.

53. Curtius Rufus, *The History of Alexander*, 68.

54. Spencer, *The Roman Alexander*, 79–82.

55. Curtius Rufus, *The History of Alexander*, 68.

56. Justinus, *Trogi Pompei*, 74.

57. Cartledge, *Alexander the Great*, 244.

58. O'Brien, *Alexander the Great*, 89.

59. Alan Fildes and Joann Fletcher, *Alexander the Great: Son of the Gods* (Los Angeles, Calif.: J. Paul Getty Museum, 2002), 58. In 1992, at the start of a naming-rights dispute between Greece and the newly formed Republic of Macedonia, the former issued an alloy remake of this coin valued at 100 drachmas; on its obverse, in Greek letters, it reads, "Alexander the Great, King of Macedon," and on its reverse it states, "Greek Republic" just above the sixteen-ray Vergina sun, a symbol of the royal Macedonian family to which Alexander had belonged.

60. Beryl Barr-Sharrar, review of Blanche Brown, *Royal Portraits in Sculpture and Coins: Pyrrhos and the Successors of Alexander the Great* (New York: Peter Lang, 1995) and Dominique Svenson, *Darstellungen hellenistischer Könige mit Götterattributen* (New York: Peter Lang, 1995), *American Journal of Archaeology* 103 (1999): 367.

61. Günther Hölbl, *A History of the Ptolemaic Empire*, trans. Tina Saavedra (London and New York: Routledge, 2001), 103.

62. For more on the relation between the Syriac version of the Alexander legend and the Qur'ān, see Ernest A. Wallis Budge, *The Alexander Book in Ethiopia: The Ethiopic Versions of Pseudo-Callisthenes, The Chronicle of Al-Makīn, the Narrative of Joseph ben Gorion, and a Christian Romance of Alexander* (London: Oxford University Press, 1933); Budge, *The Life and Exploits of Alexander the Great, Being a Series of Ethiopic Texts Edited from Manuscripts in the British Museum and the Bibliothèque Nationale, Paris, with an English Translation and Notes*, 2 vols. (London: C. J. Clay, 1896); García Gómez, *Un texto árabe occidental de la leyenda de Alejandro*, xxxi; Nykl, *A Compendium of Aljamiado Literature*, 40; and Zuwiyya, *Islamic Legends Concerning Alexander the Great*, 16.

63. As Zuwiyya demonstrates, the extant manuscripts of the *Qiṣṣat Dhū al-Qarnayn* found in Madrid were not the direct sources for the Aljamiado *Rekontamiento del rey Ališandre*.

64. Madrid, Biblioteca Nacional MS 5254, f. 14v.

65. Ibid., ff. 21v–22r.

66. Ibid., f. 133r–v.

67. See, for example, Vincent Barletta, "The Aljamiado 'Sacrifice of Ishmael': Genre, Power, and Narrative Performance," *Revista de estudios hispánicos* 40, no. 3 (2006); and Barletta, "Toward a Morisco Philosophy of Suffering and Action: The *Alhadith sobre el sacrificio de Ismail*," *Mediterranean Studies* 13 (2004).

68. Jane I. Smith and Yvonne Yazbeck Haddad, *The Islamic Understanding of Death and Resurrection* (Oxford: Oxford University Press, 2002), 6.

69. Nykl, *A Compendium of Aljamiado Literature*, 37–38.

70. Ibid., 38. See also Guillén Robles, *Leyendas de José hijo de Jacob y de Alejandro Magno*, lvi.

71. Madrid, Biblioteca Nacional MS 5254, f. 51v.

72. To compare the Aljamiado version to an earlier Andalusi version in Arabic (which did not, however, serve as a source for the Aljamiado text) see Zuwiyya, *Islamic Legends Concerning Alexander the Great*, 124–27. For a discussion of the various renderings of the Jābalqā episode, especially in relation to the Persian versions of the Alexander legend and the night journey of Muḥammad as related by al-Ṭabari, see Wheeler, *Moses in the Quran and Islamic Exegesis*, 95–98.

73. Madrid, Biblioteca Nacional MS 5254, f. 29v.

74. Ibid., 30r.

75. Ibid., 30v.

76. For a discussion of the Arabic tradition, see García Gómez, *Un texto árabe occidental de la leyenda de Alejandro*; Zuwiyya, *Islamic Legends Concerning Alexander the Great*, 1–45; and Zuwiyya, "A Study of Two Potential Sources for the Aljamiado-Morisco Legend of Alexander the Great: The *Rrekontamiento del rrey Alisandre*," *MIFLC Review* 9 (2000). For a summary of the Greek tradition, see Richard Stoneman, *Alexander the Great: A Life in Legend* (New Haven, Conn.: Yale University Press, 2008); and Stoneman, introduction to *The Greek Alexander Romance*, ed. Richard Stoneman (London: Penguin Books, 1991).

77. *The Greek Alexander Romance*, ed. Richard Stoneman (London: Penguin Books, 1991), 121.

78. Madrid, Biblioteca Nacional MS 5254, f. 31v.

79. In the Arabic versions of the narrative this is much clearer. See, for example, Zuwiyya, *Islamic Legends Concerning Alexander the Great*, 131–32.

80. Madrid, Biblioteca Nacional MS 5254, f. 132r–v.

Chapter 6

1. Antonio de Nebrija, *Gramática de la lengua española*, ed. Antonio Quilis (Madrid: Centro de Estudios Ramón Areces, 1989), 109.

2. See Walter Mignolo, *Local Histories/Global Designs: Coloniality, Subaltern Knowledges, and Border Thinking* (Princeton, N.J.: Princeton University Press, 2000), 258; and Lucia Binotti, "La lengua compañera del imperio: Observaciones sobre el desarrollo de un discurso de colonialismo lingüístico en el Renacimiento español," in *Las gramáticas misioneras de tradición hispánica (siglos XVI–XVII)*, ed. Otto Zwartjes (Amsterdam: Rodopi, 2000). See also Miguel Angel Esparza Torres, *Las ideas lingüísticas de Antonio de Nebrija* (Münster: Nodus, 1995).

3. Mignolo, *Local Histories/Global Designs*, 250–77.

4. Ibid., 258.

5. Nebrija, *Gramática de la lengua española*, 109.

6. Diego Ortúñez de Calahorra, *Espejo de príncipes y caballeros*, ed. Pedro de la Sierra and José Julio Martín Romero (Alcalá de Henares: CEC Centro de Estudios Cervantinos, 2003), vo. 5, 77–78.

7. Augustine, *City of God*, and John Milbank, *Theology and Social Theory: Beyond Secular Reason*, 2nd ed. (Malden, Mass.: Blackwell, 2006), 403.

8. See Aristotle, *The Basic Works*, 1127: "Some people think that the qualifications of a statesman, king, householder, and master are the same, and that they differ, not in kind, but only in the number of their subjects. . . . But all this is a mistake; for governments differ in kind, as will be evident to any one who considers the matter according to the method which has hitherto guided us."

9. Agamben, *Homo Sacer*, 2.

10. For more on the relation between chivalry and the social order, see Jesús Rodríguez-Velasco, *Poética del orden de caballería: La regulación de las instituciones caballerescas entre burguesía y nobleza* (Madrid: Akal, 2008).

11. Agamben, *Homo Sacer*; Giorgio Agamben, "What Is a Camp?," in *Means without End: Notes on Politics* (Minneapolis: University of Minneapolis Press, 2000), 37–45; Michel Foucault, *The History of Sexuality*, trans. Robert Hurley (New York: Vintage Books, 1990).

REFERENCES

Primary Sources

El Escorial, Biblioteca de San Lorenzo de El Escorial MS &. II. 8.
El Escorial, Biblioteca de San Lorenzo de El Escorial MS h. ii. 22.
Lisbon, Biblioteca da Ajuda MS 52-XIII-24.
Lisbon, Biblioteca Nacional MS IL 46.
Madrid, Biblioteca del Instituto de Filología del CSIC/Junta MS 26.
Madrid, Biblioteca Nacional MS 3666.
Madrid, Biblioteca Nacional MS 5254.
Madrid, Biblioteca Nacional MS 8549.
Madrid, Biblioteca Nacional MS 9513.
Madrid, Biblioteca Nacional MS 9522.
Madrid, Biblioteca Nacional MS 9608.
Madrid, Biblioteca Nacional MS 10011.
Madrid, Bibioteca Nacional MS 10140.
Madrid, Biblioteca Nacional MS 12672.
Madrid, Biblioteca Nacional MS Vitrina 5–10.
Paris, Bibliothèque Nationale MS Esp. 488.
Salamanca, Biblioteca Universitaria MS 1890.

Secondary Texts

Agamben, Giorgio. *Homo Sacer: Sovereign Power and Bare Life.* Translated by Daniel Heller-Roazen. Stanford, Calif.: Stanford University Press, 1998.

———. "What Is a Camp?" In *Means without End: Notes on Politics,* 37–45. Minneapolis: University of Minneapolis Press, 2000.

Agnew, Michael. "'Como un libro abierto': La construcción de un modelo exegético en el Libro de Alexandre." *La corónica* 29, no. 2 (2001): 159–83.

Al-Aouani, Mohamed. "À la recherche des influences andalouses dans les campagnes tunisiennes: essai de mise au point." In *Études sur les moriscos andalous en Tunisie*, edited by Mikel de Epalza and Ramón Petit, 374–77. Madrid-Tunis: Dirección General de Relaciones Culturales, 1973.

Alfonso X, The Learned. *General estoria: Primera parte.* Edited by Pedro Sánchez-Prieto Borja. 2 vols. Madrid: Fundación José Antonio de Castro, 2001.

Amaral, Augusto Ferreira do. *Mazagão: A epopeia Portuguesa em Marrocos.* Lisbon: Tribuna da História, 2007.

Aristotle. *The Basic Works of Aristotle.* Translated by Richard Peter McKeon. New York: Random House, 1941.

Arnaud-Lindet, Marie-Pierre. Introduction to *Orose: Histoires (contre les païens)*, edited by Marie-Pierre Arnaud-Lindet, vol. 1, vii–ciii. Paris: Les Belles Lettres, 1990.

Arrian. *Anabasis of Alexander.* Translated by P. A. Brunt. 2 vols. Cambridge, Mass.: Harvard University Press, 1983.

Asín Palacios, Miguel. *Dante y el Islam.* Madrid: Editorial Voluntad, 1927.

———. *La escatologia musulmana en la Divina comedia.* Madrid: E. Maestre, 1919.

Augustine. *City of God.* Edited by G. R. Evans. Translated by Henry Scowcroft Bettenson. London: Penguin Books, 2003.

Barbosa, D. *The Book of Duarte Barbosa.* 2 vols. Translated by M. Longworth Dames. London: Hakluyt Society, 1918–21.

Barletta, Vincent. "The Aljamiado 'Sacrifice of Ishmael': Genre, Power, and Narrative Performance." *Revista de estudios hispánicos* 40, no. 3 (2006): 513–36.

———. *Covert Gestures: Crypto-Islamic Literature as Cultural Practice in Early Modern Spain.* Minneapolis: University of Minnesota Press, 2005.

———. "Deixis, *Taqiyya,* and Textual Mediation in Crypto-Muslim Aragon." *Text and Talk* 28, no. 5 (2008): 561–79.

———. "Toward a Morisco Philosophy of Suffering and Action: The *Alhadith sobre el sacrificio de Ismail.*" *Mediterranean Studies* 13 (2004): 57–75.

Barr-Sharrar, Beryl. Review of Blanche Brown, *Royal Portraits in Sculpture and Coins: Pyrrhos and the Successors of Alexander the Great* (New York: Peter Lang, 1995) and Dominique Svenson, *Darstellungen hellenistischer Könige mit Götterattributen* (New York: Peter Lang, 1995). *American Journal of Archaeology* 103 (1999): 367–68.

Barrios Aguilera, Manuel. *Granada morisca, la convivencia negada: Historia y textos.* Granada: Editorial COMARES, 2002.

Barros, João de. *Da Ásia de João de Barros.* 24 vols. Lisbon: Livraria Sam Carlos, 1973.

———. *Grammatica da língua portuguesa.* Lisbon: Luís Rodrigues, 1540.

———. *Gramática da lingua portuguesa: Cartinha, gramática, diálogo em louvor da nossa linguagem e Diálogo da viciosa vergonha.* Edited by Maria Leonor Carvalhão Buescu. Lisbon: Publicações da Faculdade de Letras da Universidade de Lisboa, 1971.

———. "Ropicapnefma." In *Corpus do Português (45 million words, 1300s–1900s)*, edited by Mark Davies and Michael Ferreira. http://www.corpusdoportugues.org, 2006– (accessed October 30, 2008).

Barros, Maria Filomena Lopes de. "De mudéjares a mouriscos: O caso Portugués." In *Actas del VIII Simposio Internacional de Mudejarismo: De mudéjares a moriscos; una conversión forzada*, vol. 1, 567–74. Teruel: Centro de Estudios Mudéjares, 2002.

Bassi, Karen. "Nostos, Domos, and the Architecture of the Ancient Stage." *South Atlantic Quarterly* 98, no. 3 (1999): 415–49.

Bately, J. M., and D. J. A. Ross. "A Checklist of Manuscripts of Orosius' *Historiarum adversum paganos libri septem.*" *Scriptorium* 15 (1961): 329–34.

Beltrán, Rafael. "La muerte de Tirant: Elementos para una autopsia." In *Actes del Col.loqui internacional Tirant lo Blanc, Aix-en-Provence, 21–22 October 1994*, 75–93. Barcelona: Centre Aixois de Recherches Hispaniques, Institut Interuniversitari de Filologia Valenciana, Publicacions de l'Abadia de Montserrat, 1997.

———. *Tirant lo Blanc, de Joanot Martorell.* Madrid: Síntesis, 2007.

Ben Mami, Beji. "Quelques aspects de la présence andalouse à la Médina de Tunis pendant le période Hafside." In *Actes du II Symposium International du C.I.E.M.: Religion, identité et sources documentaires sur les morisques andalous*, edited by Abdeljelil Temimi, 291–92. Tunis: Institut Supérieur de Documentation, 1984.

Beneyto, Juan. "Una versión en prosa castellana de la leyenda de Alejandro Magno." *Insula* 37 (1949): 2.

Bensch, Stephen P. *Barcelona and Its Rulers, 1096–1291.* Cambridge: Cambridge University Press, 2002.

Bernabé Pons, Luis F. "La literatura en español de los moriscos en Túnez, mudéjares y moriscos, cambios sociales y culturales: Actas." Teruel: Centro de Estudios Mudéjares, 2004.

Bernabé Pons, Luis F., and María Jesús Rubiera Mata. "La lengua de mudéjares y moriscos: Estado de la cuestión." In *VII Simposio Internacional de Mudejarismo, Teruel, 19–21 de septiembre de 1996*, 599–631. Teruel: Centro de Estudios Mudéjares, 1999.

Berzunza, Julio. "Preliminary Notes on the Three Italian Versions of Quintus Curtius Rufus' *Historiae Alexandri Magni.*" *Italica* 18, no. 3 (1941): 133–37.

Binotti, Lucia. "La lengua compañera del imperio: Observaciones sobre el desarrollo de un discurso de colonialismo lingüístico en el Renacimiento español." In *Las gramáticas misioneras de tradición hispánica (siglos XVI–XVII)*, edited by Otto Zwartjes, 259–88. Amsterdam: Rodopi, 2000.

Bisson, Thomas N. *Medieval Crown of Aragon: A Short History.* Oxford: Clarendon Press, 1986.

Blackmore, Josiah. "Africa and the Epic Imagination of Camões." *Portuguese Literary and Cultural Studies* 9 (2003): 107–16.

———. "Imagining the Moor in Medieval Portugal." *Diacritics* 36, no. 3–4 (2006): 27–34.

———. *Manifest Perdition: Shipwreck Narrative and the Disruption of Empire.* Minneapolis: University of Minnesota Press, 2002.

———. *Moorings: Portuguese Expansion and the Writing of Africa.* Minneapolis: University of Minnesota Press, 2008.

Borges, Jorge Luis. *Narraciones.* Edited by Marcos Ricardo Barnatán. Madrid: Cátedra, 1980.

Boucharb, Ahmed. *Os pseudo-mouriscos de Portugal no séc. XVI.* Translated by Maria Filomena Lopes de Barros. Lisbon: Hugin Editores, 2004.

Bounou, Abdelmouneim. "Los moriscos en Marruecos: Poder de una minoría." In *La política y los moriscos en la época de los Austria: Actas del encuentro*. Madrid: La Fundación del Sur-Ediciones Especiales, 1999.

Bourdieu, Pierre, and Jean-Claude Passeron. *Reproduction in Education, Society and Culture*. Translated by Richard Nice. London: Sage, 1977.

Boxer, C. *João de Barros: Portuguese Humanist and Historian of Asia*. New Delhi: Concept, 1981.

Boxer, C. R. *The Portuguese Seaborne Empire, 1415–1825*. London: Hutchinson, 1969.

Bramon, Dolors. "Les morisques et leur langue." *Cahiers d'études romanes* 16 (1990): 1–25.

Bravo García, Antonio Pedro. "Sobre las traducciones de Plutarco y de Quinto Curcio Rufo echas por Pier Candido Decembrio y su fortuna en España." *Cuadernos de filología clásica* 12 (1977): 143–87.

Bruner, Jerome S. *Actual Minds, Possible Worlds*. Cambridge, Mass.: Harvard University Press, 1986.

Budge, Ernest A. Wallis. *The Alexander Book in Ethiopia: The Ethiopic Versions of Pseudo-Callisthenes, The Chronicle of Al-Makīn, the Narrative of Joseph ben Gorion, and a Christian Romance of Alexander*. London: Oxford University Press, 1933.

———. *The Life and Exploits of Alexander the Great, Being a Series of Ethiopic Texts Edited from Manuscripts in the British Museum and the Bibliothèque Nationale, Paris, with an English Translation and Notes*. 2 vols. London: C. J. Clay, 1896.

Bunes Ibarra, Miguel Angel. *La imagen de los musulmanes y del Norte de Africa en la España de los siglos XVI y XVII: Los caracteres de una hostilidad*. Madrid: Consejo Superior de Investigaciones Científicas, 1989.

Camões, Luís de. *Obras de Luiz de Camões*. Edited by João António de Lemos Pereira de Lacerda, Segundo Visconde de Juromenha. 2 vols. Lisbon: Imprensa Nacional, 1861.

———. *Obras de Luiz de Camões: Precedidas de um ensaio biographico, no qual se relatam alguns factos não conhecidos da sua vida; augmentadas com algumas composições ineditas do poeta, pelo visconde de Juromenha*. Edited by Visconde de Juromenha João Antonio de Lemos Pereira de Lacerda. 7 vols. Lisbon: Imprensa Nacional, 1860–1924.

Camões, Luís Vaz de. *Os Lusíadas*. Lisbon: António Gonçalves, 1572.

Cañas Murillo, Jesús. "Un nuevo dato sobre la leyenda de Alejandro Magno en España: El manuscrito 3892 de la Biblioteca Nacional de Madrid." *Anuario de estudios filológicos* 7 (1984): 57–60.

Cardaillac, Louis. *Morisques et chrétiens: Un affrontement polémique (1492–1640)*. Paris: Klincksieck, 1977.

Caro Baroja, Julio. *Los moriscos del reino de Granada: Ensayo de historia social*. Madrid: Instituto de Estudios Políticos, 1957.

Carruthers, Mary J. *The Book of Memory: A Study of Memory in Medieval Culture*. Cambridge: Cambridge University Press, 1990.

Cartledge, Paul. *Alexander the Great: The Hunt for a New Past*. Woodstock, N.Y.: Overlook Press, 2004.

Cary, George. *The Medieval Alexander*. Edited by David J. A. Ross. Cambridge: Cambridge University Press, 1956.

Castanheda, Fernão Lopes de. *Historia do descobrimento e conqvista da India pelos Portvgveses*. 8 vols. Lisbon: Typographia Rollandiana, 1833.

Castro Soares, Nair de Nazaré. "Plutarco no Humanismo Renascentista em Portugal." In *Os fragmentos de Plutarco e a recepção da sua obra*, 193–221. Coimbra: Instituto de Estudos Clássicos, 2003.

Chaytor, H. J. *A History of Aragon and Catalonia*. London: Methuen, 1933.

Cohen, Richard A. Introduction to *Emmanuel Levinas: Time and the Other*, edited by Richard A. Cohen, 1–27. Pittsburgh, Pa.: Duquesne University Press, 1987.

Corfis, Ivy A. "Libro de Alexandre: Fantastic Didacticism." *Hispanic Review* 62, no. 4 (1994): 477–86.

Cornell, Vincent J. "Socioeconomic Dimensions of Reconquista and Jihad in Morocco: Portuguese Dukkala and the Sadid Sus, 1450–1557." *International Journal of Middle East Studies*, 22, no. 4 (1990): 379–418.

Correia, Gaspar. *The Three Voyages of Vasco da Gama, and His Viceroyalty*. Edited and translated by Henry E. L. Stanley. London: Hakluyt Society, 1869.

Couto, Diogo do. *O soldado prático*. Edited by Reis Brasil. Mem Martins: Publicacões Europa–América, 1988.

Critchley, Simon. Introduction to *The Cambridge Companion to Levinas*, edited by Simon Critchley and Robert Bernasconi, 1–32. Cambridge: Cambridge University Press, 2002.

Cruz, Maria Augusta Lima. "Mouro para os cristãos e cristão para os mouros: O caso Bentafufa." *Anais de História de Além-Mar* 3 (2002): 39–63.

———. "Os Portugueses em Marrocos nos séculos XV e XVI." In *História dos Descobrimentos e Expansão Portuguesa*, 13–60. Lisbon: Universidade Aberta, 1999.

Curial e Güelfa. Edited by Marina Gustà. 6th ed. Barcelona: Edicions 62, 2004.

Curtius Rufus, Quintus. *De gestis Alexandri Magni, Regis Macedonum: Libri qui supersunt VIII*. Philadelphia: Lea & Blanchard, 1849.

———. *The History of Alexander*. Translated by John Yardley. London: Penguin Books, 2004.

———. *Life and Exploits of Alexander the Great*. Edited by Christoph Cellarius. New York: D. Appleton, 1883.

D'Alverny, Marie-Thérèse. *La connaissance de l'Islam dans l'Occident médiéval*. Aldershot: Variorum, 1994.

Dagenais, John. "Speech as the Sixth Sense: Ramon Llull's *Affatus*." In *Actes del primer col loqui d'estudis catalans a Nord-Amèrica/Actes del primer col-loqui d'estudis catalans à Nord-Amèrica*, edited by Spurgeon W. Baldwin Alberto Porqueras Mayo, and Jaume Martí-Olivella, 157–69. Montserrat: Publicacions de l'Abadia de Montserrat, 1978.

Decourdemanche, J.A. "La légende d'Alexandre chez les Musulmans." *Revue de l'histoire des religions* 4, no. 1 (1882): 98–113.

Deferrari, Roy J. Introduction to *Orosius: The Seven Books of History against the Pagans*, edited by Roy J. Deferrari, xxi, 422. Washington, D.C.: Catholic University of America Press, 1964.

Demosthenes. *The Third Philippic*. Edited by Michael Lahanas. In Hellenica, http://www

.mlahanas.de/Greeks/Texts/Demosthenes/TheThirdPhilippic.html (accessed January 5, 2009).

Derrida, Jacques. "Plato's Pharmacy." In *Dissemination*. Chicago: University of Chicago Press, 2004.

Dias Farinha, António. "De mouriscos em Marrocos na epoca do Sultan Ahmad Al Mansur." In *La política y los moriscos en la época de los Austria: Actas del encuentro*. Madrid: La Fundación del Sur-Ediciones Especiales, 1999.

———. *Os Portugueses em Marrocos*. Lisbon: Instituto Camões, 2002.

———. "Os Xarifes de Marrocos (Notas sobre a expansão portuguesa no Norte de África)." In *Estudos de História de Portugal*, vol. 2, *Sécs. XVI–XX: Homenagem a A. H. de Oliveira Marques*. Lisbon: Estampa, 1983.

Dias, José Sebastião da Silva. *A política cultural da época de D. João III*. Coimbra: Instituto de Estudos Filosóficos, Universidade de Coimbra, 1969.

Diffie, Bailey W., and George D. Winius. *Foundations of the Portuguese Empire, 1415–1580*. Minneapolis: University of Minnesota Press, 1977.

Domínguez Ortiz, Antonio, and Bernard Vincent. *Historia de los moriscos: Vida y tragedia de una minoría*. Madrid: Revista de Occidente, 1978.

Drummond Braga, Isabel M. R. Mendes. *Mouriscos e cristãos no Portugal quinhentista*. Lisbon: Hugin Editores, 1999.

Epalza, Mikel de. *Los moriscos antes y después de la expulsión*. Madrid: MAPFRE, 1992.

———. "Moriscos y andalusíes en Túnez en el siglo XVII." *Al-Andalus* 34 (1969): 247–327.

———. "Trabajos actuales sobre la comunidad de moriscos refugiados en Túnez: Desde el siglo XVII a nuestros días." In *Actas del Coloquio internacional de literatura aljamiada y morisca (Oviedo, 1972)*, edited by Álvaro Galmés de Fuentes and Emilio García Gómez, 427–44. Oviedo: Gredos, 1978.

———. "La vie intellectuelle en espagnol des morisques au Maghreb (XVIIe. siècle)." *Revue d'histoire maghrébine* 59–60 (1990): 73–78.

Esparza Torres, Miguel Angel. *Las ideas lingüísticas de Antonio de Nebrija*. Münster: Nodus, 1995.

Fabbrini, Fabrizio. *Paolo Orosio: Uno storico*. Rome: Edizione di Storia e Letteratura, 1979.

Farinha, António Dias. *Os Portugueses em Marrocos*. Lisbon: Instituto Camões, 2002.

———. "Os Xarifes de Marrocos (Notas sobre a expansão portuguesa no Norte de África)." In *Estudos de história de Portugal*, volume 2, *Sécs. XVI–XX: Homenagem a A. H. de Oliveira Marques*, 57–68. Lisbon: Estampa, 1983.

Fenollet, Lluís de. *La vida del Rey Alexandre scrita per aquell singularissim hystorial Plutarcho, fins en aquella part on lo Quinto Curcio Ruffo comença: "Alexandre entre tan."* Barcelona: Pere Posa i Pere Bru, 1481.

Fildes, Alan, and Joann Fletcher. *Alexander the Great: Son of the Gods*. Los Angeles: J. Paul Getty Museum, 2002.

Foucault, Michel. *The History of Sexuality*. Translated by Robert Hurley. New York: Vintage Books, 1990.

Fournel-Guerin, Jacqueline. "Le livre et la civilisation écrite dans la communauté morisque aragonaise (1540–1620)." *Mélanges de la Casa de Velázquez* 15 (1979): 241–59.

Frame, Douglas. *The Myth of Return in Early Greek Epic*. New Haven, Conn.: Yale University Press, 1978.

Gandavo, Pero de Magalhães de. *História da província Santa Cruz*. São Paulo: Editora Obelisco, 1964.

Garcés, María Antonia. *Cervantes en Argel: Historia de un cautivo*. Madrid: Editorial Gredos, 2005.

García Arenal, Mercedes. *Los moriscos*. Madrid: Nacional, 1975.

García Gómez, Emilio. *Un texto árabe occidental de la leyenda de Alejandro, según el manuscrito ár. XXVII de la Biblioteca de la Junta para Ampliación de Estudios*. Madrid: Instituto de Valencia de don Juan, 1929.

Garlan, Yvon. *Slavery in Ancient Greece*. Ithaca, N.Y.: Cornell University Press, 1988.

Giunta, Francesco. *Aragonesi e Catalani nel Mediterraneo: La presenza Catalana nel Levante dalle origini a Giacomo II*. Palermo: U. Manfredi, 1959.

Góis, Damião de. *Crónica do Felicíssimo Rei D. Manuel*. Coimbra: Impresa da Universidade, 1926.

González-Casanova, Roberto. "Western Narratives of Eastern Adventures: The Cultural Poetics and Politics of Catalan Expansion, 1300–1500." *Catalan Review* 8, nos. 1–2 (1994): 211–27.

Goulven, Joseph. *Safi au vieux temps des Portugais*. Lisbon: Gozalbes Busto, Guillermo. "Presencia de los moriscos en Tetuán y Xauen (Marruecos septentrional)." In *Actes du II Symposium International du C.I.E.M.: Religion, identité et sources documentaires sur les morisques andalous*, edited by Abdeljelil Temimi, vol. 1, 361–74. Tunis: Institut Supérieur de Documentation, 1984.

Grant, Michael. *A Social History of Greece and Rome*. New York: Charles Scribner's Sons, 1992.

The Greek Alexander Romance. Edited by Richard Stoneman. London: Penguin Books, 1991.

Green, Peter. *Alexander of Macedon, 356–323 B.C.: A Historical Biography*. Berkeley: University of California Press, 1991.

Guillén Robles, Francisco. *Leyendas de José hijo de Jacob y de Alejandro Magno: Sacadas de dos manuscritos moriscos de la Biblioteca Nacional de Madrid*. Zaragoza: Imprenta del Hospicio Provincial, 1888.

Gumbrecht, Hans Ulrich. *Production of Presence: What Meaning Cannot Convey*. Stanford, Calif.: Stanford University Press, 2004.

Harvey, L. P. "Aljamia Portuguesa Revisited." *Portuguese Studies* 2 (1986): 1–14.

———. *Muslims in Spain: 1500 to 1614*. Chicago: University of Chicago Press, 2005.

Hegyi, Ottmar. "Tradition and Linguistic Assimilation among the Spanish Moriscos During the Sixteenth Century." In *Conversion and Continuity: Indigenous Christian Communities in Islamic Lands*, edited by Michael Gervers and Ramzi Jibran Bikhazi, 381–88. Toronto: Pontifical Institute of Medieval Studies, 1990.

Herodotus. *The Histories*. Translated by Robin Waterfield. Oxford: Oxford University Press, 1998.

Hess, Andrew C. "The Battle of Lepanto and Its Place in Mediterranean History." *Past and Present* 57 (1972): 53–73.

——. *The Forgotten Frontier: A History of the Sixteenth-Century Ibero-African Frontier.* Chicago: University of Chicago Press, 1978.

Heuss, Alfred. "Alexander der Grosse und die politische Ideologie der Altertums." *Antike und Abendland* 21 (1954): 65–104.

Hillgarth, Jocelyn N. *Ramon Lull and Lullism in Fourteenth-Century France.* Oxford: Clarendon Press, 1971.

——, Albert Soler i Llopart, Anna Alberni, and Joan Santanach i Suñol. *Ramon Llull i el naixement del lul·lisme.* Barcelona: Curial Edicions Catalanes i Publicacions de l'Abadia de Montserrat, 1998.

Hölbl, Günther. *A History of the Ptolemaic Empire.* Translated by Tina Saavedra. London and New York: Routledge, 2001.

Ifrānī, Muhammad al-Saghīr ibn Muhammad. *Nozhet-elhādi: Histoire de la dynastie Saadienne au Maroc (1511–1670).* Translated by Octave Victor Houdas. 2 vols. Paris: Ernest Leroux, 1889.

James, Williams. "Does Consciousness Exist?" *Journal of Philosophy, Psychology, and Scientific Methods* 1 (1904): 477–91.

Jiménez Vicente, María Carmen. *La razón de estado en Alfonso X el Sabio: Paulo Orosio en la Primera Crónica General.* Valladolid: Secretariado de Publicaciones, Universidad, D.L., 1993.

Johnson, Howard B. *Dois estudos polémicos.* Tucson: Fenestra, 2004.

Johnston, Mark D. "Affatus: Natural Science as Moral Theology." *Estudios Lulianos* 30 (1990): 3–30; 139–59.

——. *The Evangelical Rhetoric of Ramon Llull: Lay Learning and Piety in the Christian West around 1300.* New York: Oxford University Press, 1996.

——. "The Reception of the Lullian Art, 1450–1530." *Sixteenth Century Journal* 12, no. 1 (1981): 31–48.

Justinus, Marcus Junianus. *Trogi Pompei: Historiarum philippicarum epitoma.* Edited by Justus Ieep. Leipzig: B. G. Teubner, 1872.

Kant, Immanuel. *Critique of Judgement.* Translated by James Creed Meredith. Edited by Nicholas Walker. Oxford: Oxford University Press, 2007.

Kantorowicz, Ernst H. *The King's Two Bodies: A Study in Mediaeval Political Theology.* 7th ed. Princeton, N.J.: Princeton University Press, 1997.

Kasten, Lloyd A. *Poridat de las poridades.* Madrid: S. Aguirre, 1957.

Laidlaw, William Allison. *Latin Literature.* London: Methuen, 1951.

Lawrence, Jeremy. "Death in *Tirant lo Blanc.*" In *Tirant lo Blanc: New Approaches,* edited by Arthur Terry, 91–107. London: Tamesis, 1999.

Lea, Henry Charles. *The Moriscos of Spain: Their Conversion and Expulsion.* London: B. Quaritch, 1901.

Levinas, Emmanuel. *Time and the Other.* Translated by Richard A. Cohen. Pittsburgh, Pa.: Duquesne University Press, 1987.

——. *Totality and Infinity: An Essay on Exteriority.* Translated by Alphonso Lingis. Pittsburgh, Pa.: Duquesne University Press, 1969.

———. "The Trace of the Other." In *Deconstruction in Context*, edited by Mark Taylor. Chicago: University of Chicago Press, 1986.

Levitzion, Nehemia. "The Western Maghrib and Sudan." In *The Cambridge History of Africa*, edited by J. D. Fage and Roland Anthony Oliver, 8 vols., vol. 3, 331–462. Cambridge: Cambridge University Press, 1975.

Libro de Alexandre. Edited by Jesús Cañas. Madrid: Cátedra, 1995.

Lida de Malkiel, María Rosa. "Datos para la leyenda de Alejandro en la Edad Media castellana." *Romance Philology* 15 (1961–62): 412–23.

———. "La leyenda de Alejandro en la literatura medieval." *Romance Philology* 15 (1961–62): 311–18.

———. *La tradición clásica en España.* Barcelona: Ariel, 1975.

Lieberknecht, Otfried. *Allegorese und Philologie: Überlegungen zum mehrfachen Schriftsinn in Dantes Commedia.* Stuttgart: Franz Steiner Verlag, 1999.

———. "A Medieval View of Islam: Dante's Encounter with Mohammed in *Inferno* XXVIII." Department of Italian Studies and the Townsend Center for the Humanities Working Group, University of California at Berkeley, 1997. http://www.lieberknecht.de/~diss/papers/p_moham.pdf (accessed September 26, 2008).

Lippold, Adolf. Introduction to *Orosio: Le storie contro i pagani*, edited by Adolf Lippold. Milan: Fondazione Lorenzo Valla 1976.

Livy. *Livy: Book IX.* Edited by W. B. Anderson. Cambridge: Cambridge University Press, 1912.

———. *The History of Rome.* Translated by George Baker. 6 vols. London: Jones, 1830.

Llull, Ramon. *Doctor Illuminatus: A Ramon Llull Reader.* Edited by Anthony Bonner. Princeton, N.J.: Princeton University Press, 1993.

Lockhart, L. "European Contacts with Persia, 1350–1736." In *The Cambridge History of Iran in Seven Volumes.* Cambridge: Cambridge University Press, 1986.

Longás Bartibás, Pedro. *La vida religiosa de los moriscos.* Madrid: Ibérica, 1915.

Lopes, David. *Textos em Aljamía Portuguesa: Documentos para a história do Domínio Português em Safim, extrahidos dos originaes da Torre do Tombo.* Lisbon: Imprensa Nacional, 1897.

López Baralt, Luce. "La angustia secreta del exilio: El testimonio de un morisco de Túnez." *Hispanic Review* 55, no. 1 (1987): 41–57.

———. "Crónica de la destrucción de un mundo: La literatura aljamiado-morisca." *Bulletin hispanique* 82, nos. 1–2 (1980): 16–58.

López-Morillas, Consuelo. "Language and Identity in Late Spanish Islam." *Hispanic Review* 63 (1995): 193–210.

———. *Textos aljamiados sobre la vida de Mahoma: El Profeta de los moriscos.* Madrid: CSIC, 1994.

Lucian. *Luciani Samosatensis Opera.* Edited by Wilhelm Dindorf. 4 vols. Lipsiae (Leipzig): Caroli Tachnutii, 1829.

———. *The Works of Lucian of Samosata.* Edited by H. W. Fowler and F. G. Fowler. Oxford: Clarendon Press, 1905.

Mann, Thomas. *Death in Venice*. Translated by Michael Henry Heim. New York: HarperCollins, 2005.

Manzalaoui, Mahmoud. "The Pseudo-Aristotelian *Kitāb Sirr al-asrār*: Facts and Problems." *Oriens* 23 (1974): 147–257.

Marinescu, Constantin. *La politique orientale d'Alfonse V d'Aragon, roi de Naples (1416–1458)*. Barcelona: Institut d'Estudis Catalans, 1994.

Mármol y Carvajal, Luis. *Historia de la rebelión y castigo de los moriscos del Reino de Granada*. Barcelona: Linkgua, 2007.

Martins, José V. de Pina. *Humanismo e Erasmismo na cultura portuguesa do século XVI: Estudo e textos*. Paris: Fundação Calouste Gulbenkian, 1973.

Martorell, Joanot. *Tirant lo Blanc*. Edited by Manuel Sanromà and Martí de Riquer. Tarragona: Fundació Ciutat de Tarragona, 2008. http://www.tinet.org/bdt/tirant/ (accessed December 18, 2008).

Mendes Pinto, Fernão. *Peregrinação*. Edited by Fernando Ribeiro de Mello. 2 vols. Lisbon: Edições Afrodite, 1971.

Michael, Ian. "Interpretation of the Libro de Alexandre: The Author's Attitude towards His Hero's Death." *Bulletin of Hispanic Studies* 38 (1960): 205–14.

———. *The Treatment of Classical Material in the Libro de Alexandre*. Manchester: Manchester University Press, 1970.

———. "Typological Problems in Medieval Alexander." In *Alexander the Great in the Middle Ages*, 131–47. Groningen: Alfa Nijmegen, 1978.

Mignolo, Walter. *Local Histories/Global Designs: Coloniality, Subaltern Knowledges, and Border Thinking*. Princeton, N.J.: Princeton University Press, 2000.

Milbank, John. *Theology and Social Theory: Beyond Secular Reason*. 2nd ed. Malden, Mass.: Blackwell, 2006.

Monneret de Villard, Ugo. *Lo studio dell'Islam in Europa nel XII e nel XIII secolo*. Vatican City: Biblioteca Apostolica Vaticana, 1944.

Montesquieu, Charles de Secondat. "Lysimachus." In *The Complete Works of M. de Montesquieu*, 4 vols., vol. 4, 191–95. Dublin: W. Watson, W. Whitestone, J. Williams, et al., 1777.

Morello, Ruth. "Livy's Alexander Digression (9.17–19): Counterfactuals and Apologetics." *The Journal of Roman Studies* 92 (2002): 62–85.

Nagel, Tilman. *Alexander der Grosse in der frühislamischen Volksliteratur*. Walldorf-Hessen: Verlag für Orientkunde H. Vorndran, 1978.

Nagy, Gregory. *Greek Mythology and Poetics*. Ithaca, N.Y.: Cornell University Press, 1990.

Nebrija, Antonio de. *Gramática de la lengua española*. Edited by Antonio Quilis. Madrid: Centro de Estudios Ramón Areces, 1989.

Necipoglu, Gülru. "Süleyman the Magnificent and the Representation of Power in the Context of Ottoman-Hapsburg-Papal Rivalry." *Art Bulletin* 71, no. 3 (1989): 401–27.

Nelson, Dana A. "El Libro de Alixandre y Gonzalo de Berceo: Un problema filológico." *La corónica* 28, no. 1 (1999): 93–136.

Ng, Su Fang. "Global Renaissance: Alexander the Great and Early Modern Classicism from the British Isles to the Malay Archipelago." *Comparative Literature* 58 (2006): 293–312.

Núñez Muley, Francisco. *A Memorandum for the President of the Royal Audiencia and Chancery Court of the City and Kingdom of Granada.* Edited and translated by Vincent Barletta. Chicago: University of Chicago Press, 2007.

Nykl, A. R. *A Compendium of Aljamiado literature.* New York: Protat, 1929.

O'Brien, John Maxwell. *Alexander the Great: The Invisible Enemy.* London: Routledge, 1992.

Orosius, Paulus. *Orose: Histoires (contre les païens).* Edited by Marie-Pierre Arnaud-Lindet. 3 vols. Paris: Les Belles Lettres, 1990.

Ortúñez de Calahorra, Diego. *Espejo de príncipes y caballeros.* Edited by Pedro de la Sierra and José Julio Martín Romero. Alcalá de Henares: CEC Centro de Estudios Cervantinos, 2003.

Osório, Jorge A. "Plutarco revisitado por João de Barros." *Ágora: Estudos clássicos em debate* 3 (2001): 139–55.

Pade, Marianne. *The Reception of Plutarch's Lives in Fifteenth-Century Italy.* 2 vols. Copenhagen: Museum Tusculanum Press and University of Copenhagen, 2007.

Pagden, Anthony. *Lords of All the World: Ideologies of Empire in Spain, Britain and France, c. 1500–c. 1800.* New Haven, Conn.: Yale University Press, 1995.

Penella Roma, Juan. "El sentimiento religioso de los moriscos españoles emigrados: Notas para una literatura morisca en Túnez." In *Actas del Coloquio internacional de literatura aljamiada y morisca,* edited by Alvaro Galmés de Fuentes and Emilio García Gómez, 447–74. Madrid: Gredos, 1978.

Pereira, Luís. *Elegiada.* Lisbon: Manuel de Lira, 1588.

Piera, Montserrat. "Rehistoricizing the 'Other' Reconquista." In *Tirant lo Blanc: New Approaches,* edited by Arthur Terry, 45–58. London: Tamesis, 1999.

Pinto, Paulo Mendes. *Os sefarditas portugueses e a ciência do Renascimento.* Lisbon: Cátedra de Estudos Sefarditas "Alberto Benveniste," Universidade de Lisboa, 2008. http://www.fl.ul.pt/unidades/sefarditas/textos/sefarditas_renascimento.pdf (accessed November 6, 2008).

Plato. "Menexenus." In *The Collected Dialogues of Plato,* edited by Edith Hamilton and Huntington Cairns, 186–99. Princeton, N. J.: Princeton University Press, 1982.

Plutarch. *The Life of Alexander the Great.* Translated by John Dryden. New York: Modern Library, 2004.

Putnam, Hilary. "Levinas and Judaism." In *The Cambridge Companion to Levinas,* edited by Simon Critchley and Robert Bernasconi, 33–64. Cambridge: Cambridge University Press, 2002.

Queiroz Velloso, José Maria de. *Dom Sebastião, 1554–1578.* Lisbon: Emprêsa Nacional de Publicidade, 1935.

Ramalho, Américo da Costa. *Para a história do humanismo em Portugal.* Coimbra: Instituto Nacional de Investigação Científica, 1988.

———. "Ropicapnefma: Um bibliónimo mal enxertado." *Humanitas* 27–28 (1975–76): 201–8.

Ribas, Rogério de Oliveira. "'Cide Abdella': Um marabuto na Corte de D. João III." In *D. João III e o império: Actas do Congresso Internacional comemorativo do seu nascimento,* edited by Roberto Carneiro and Artur Teodoro de Matos, 621–26. Lisbon: Centro de História Além-Mar/Centro de Estudos dos Povos e Culturas de Expressão Portuguesa, 2004.

————. "Filhos de Mafoma: Mouriscos, Cripto-Islamismo e Inquisição no Portugal quinhentista." Universidade de Lisboa, 2005.

Rico, Francisco. "La clerecía del mester." *Hispanic Review* 53 (1985): 1–12; 127–50.

Riquer, Martí de. *Història de la literatura catalana*. 3 vols. Barcelona: Ariel, 1964–66.

Robertson, D. S. Foreword to George Cary, *The Medieval Alexander*, edited by David J. A. Ross, v–vi. Cambridge: Cambridge University Press, 1956.

Rodríguez-Velasco, Jesús. *Ciudadanía, soberanía monárquica y caballería: Poética del orden de caballería*. Madrid: Akal, 2009.

Ross, D. J. A. *Alexander Historiatus: A Guide to Medieval Illustrated Alexander Literature*. Frankfurt: Athenäum, 1988.

————. "Alexander Iconography in Spain: el Libro de Alexandre." *Scriptorium* 21 (1967): 83–86.

————. "Illustrated Manuscripts of Orosius." *Scriptorium* 9 (1955): 35–56.

Rubio, Fernando. "Las leyendas sobre Alejandro Magno en la General Estoria de Alfonso el Sabio." *La Ciudad de Dios* 179 (1966): 431–62.

————. "Un texto castellano occidental de la leyenda de Alejandro Magno." *La Ciudad de Dios* 178 (1966): 431–62.

Rubió y Lluch, Antonio, and Maria Teresa Ferrer i Mallol. *Diplomatari de l'Orient català (1301–1409): Col·lecció de documents per a la història de l'expedició catalana a Orient i dels ducats d'Atenes i Neopàtria*. Barcelona: Institut d'Estudis Catalans, 2001.

Runciman, Steven. *The Fall of Constantinople, 1453*. Cambridge: Cambridge University Press, 1990.

Russell, Peter. *Prince Henry "The Navigator": A Life*. New Haven, Conn.: Yale University Press, 2000.

Said, Edward W. *Orientalism*. New York: Vintage Books, 1978.

Salamanca, Biblioteca Universitaria MS 1890.

Saldanha, António de. *Crónica de Almançor, Sultão de Marrocos (1578–1603)*. Edited by António Dias Farinha. Lisbon: Instituto de Investigação Científica Tropical, 1997.

Sénac, Philippe. *L'image de l'autre: L'Occident médiéval face à l'Islam*. Paris: Flammarion, 1983.

Seneca, Lucius Annaeus. *Ad Lucilium Epistolae morales*. Edited by Johann Gottfried Schweighaeuser. 2 vols. Strassburg: Societatis Bipontinae, 1809.

————. *Ad Lucilium epistulae morales*. Edited by L. D. Reynolds. Oxford: Clarendon Press, 1965.

Serrão, Joaquim Veríssimo. *Itinerários de el-Rei D. Sebastião*. 2 vols. Lisbon: Academia Portuguesa da História, 1963.

Setton, Kenneth M. *Catalan Domination of Athens, 1311–1388*. London: Variorum, 1975.

Severin, Dorothy Sherman, and Harvey L. Sharrer. "A Fifteenth-Century Spanish Fragment of a Lost Prose Alexander." *Medium Aevum* 48, no. 2 (1979): 205–12.

Sharrer, Harvey L. "Evidence of a Thirteenth-Century Libro del Infante Don Pedro de Portugal and Its Relationship to the Alexander Cycle." *Journal of Hispanic Philology* 1 (1977): 85–98.

Siculus, Diodorus. *Bibliothèque historique, livre XVII*. Edited by Paul Goukowsky. Paris: Belles Lettres, 1976.

————. *Bibliothèque historique, livre XVIII*. Edited by Paul Goukowsky. Paris: Belles Lettres, 1978.

Simpson, William Kelly. *The Literature of Ancient Egypt: An Anthology of Stories, Instructions, Stelae, Autobiographies, and Poetry*. 3rd ed. New Haven, Conn.: Yale University Press, 2003.

Smith, Jane I., and Yvonne Yazbeck Haddad. *The Islamic Understanding of Death and Resurrection*. Oxford: Oxford University Press, 2002.

Smith, Richard L. *Ahmad al-Mansur: Islamic Visionary*. New York: Pearson Longman, 2006.

Soyer, François. *The Persecution of the Jews and Muslims of Portugal: King Manuel I and the End of Religious Tolerance (1496–7)*. Leiden: Brill, 2007.

Spencer, Diana. *The Roman Alexander: Reading a Cultural Myth*. Exeter: University of Exeter Press, 2002.

Springborg, Patricia. *Western Republicanism and the Oriental Prince*. Austin: University of Texas Press, 1992.

Stoneman, Richard. *Alexander the Great: A Life in Legend*. New Haven, Conn.: Yale University Press, 2008.

————. Introduction to *The Greek Alexander Romance*, edited by Richard Stoneman, 1–32. London: Penguin Books, 1991.

Suárez de Deza y Avila, Vicente. *Parte primera de los donayres de Tersícore*. Madrid: Melchor Sánchez, 1663.

Tabarī, Abū Ja'far Muḥammad ibn Jarīr al-. *The History of Al-Tabarī*. 40 vols. Albany: State University of New York Press, 1988–2007.

Tatum, James. *Xenophon's Imperial Fiction: On the Education of Cyrus*. Princeton, N.J.: Princeton University Press, 1989.

Teixeira, Pedro. *The Travels of Pedro Teixeira: With his "Kings of Harmuz" and Extracts from His "Kings of Persia."* Translated by William F. Sinclair. London: Hakluyt Society, 1902.

Temimi, Abdeljelil. "Las influencias de los moriscos andalusíes en la sociedad magrebina (el ejemplo de Túnez)." In *Actas del XIe congreso de estudios moriscos sobre: Huellas literarias e impactos de los moriscos en Túnez y en América Latina*, edited by Abdeljelil Temimi, 215–28. Tunis: FTERSI, 2005.

Thomaz, Luís Filipe. "A evolução da política expansionista Portuguesa na primeira metade de quatrocentos." In *De Ceuta a Timor*, 43–147. Lisbon: Difel, 1994.

Tolan, John Victor. *Saracens: Islam in the Medieval European Imagination*. New York: Columbia University Press, 2002.

Uría Maqua, Isabel. "El Libro de Alexandre y la Universidad de Palencia." In *Actas del I Congreso de Historia de Palencia*, 431–42. Palencia: Diputación Provincial de Palencia, 1987.

Vela González, Nora. *El Libre de Alexandri: Versión catalana medieval*. Ph.D. diss. Barcelona: Universitat Autónoma de Barcelona, 1973.

Velho, Alvaro. *A Journal of the First Voyage of Vasco da Gama*. Edited and ranslated by Ernest George Ravenstein. London: Hakluyt Society, 1898.

Velho, Álvaro. *Roteiro da primeira viagem de Vasco da Gama (1497–1499)*. Edited by A. Fontoura da Costa. Lisbon: Agência Geral do Ultramar, 1960.

Vicente, Gil. *Auto da Índia: Farsa*. Edited by Mário Fiúza. Porto: Porto Editora, 1986.

Victor, Joseph M. "The Revival of Lullism at Paris, 1499–1516." *Renaissance Quarterly* 28, no. 4 (1975): 504–34.

Westermann, William Linn. *The Slave Systems of Greek and Roman Antiquity*. Philadelphia: American Philosophical Society, 1955.

Wheeler, Brannon M. *Moses in the Quran and Islamic Exegesis*. London: Routledge, 2002.

Wiegers, Gerard A. *Islamic Literature in Spanish and Aljamiado: Yça of Segovia (fl. 1450), His Antecedents and Successors*. Leiden and New York: E. J. Brill, 1994.

Williams, Steven J. *The Secret of Secrets: The Scholarly Career of a Pseudo-Aristotelian Text in the Latin Middle Ages*. Ann Arbor: University of Michigan Press, 2003.

Willis, Raymond S. "The Artistry and Enigmas of the Libro de Alexandre: A Review Article." *Hispanic Review* 42, no. 1 (1974): 33–42.

———. *The Debt of the Spanish Libro de Alexandre to the French Roman d'Alexandre*. Princeton, N. J.: Princeton University Press; Paris: Presses Universitaires de France, 1935.

———. *El Libro de Alexandre: Texts of the Paris and the Madrid Manuscripts*. Princeton, N.J.: Princeton University Press; Paris: Presses Universitaires de France, 1934.

———. "Mester de clerecía: A Definition of the Libro de Alexandre." *Romance Philology* 10 (1956–57): 212–24.

———. *The Relationship of the Spanish Libro de Alexandre to the Alexandreis of Gautier de Châtillon*. Princeton, N. J.: Princeton University Press; Paris: Presses Universitaires de France, 1934.

Yaḥyá, Dahiru. *Morocco in the Sixteenth Century: Problems and Patterns in African Foreign Policy*. Atlantic Highlands, N.J.: Humanities Press, 1981.

Zurara, Gomes Eanes de. *Crónica da tomada de Ceuta*. Edited by Reis Brasil. Mems Martins Codex, Portugal: Publicações Europa-América, 1992.

———. *Crónica dos feitos notáveis que se passaram na conquista da Guiné por mandado do infante D. Henrique*. Edited by Torquato de Sousa Soares. 2 vols. Lisbon: Academia Portuguesa da História, 1978.

Zuwiyya, Z. David. "Alexander's Journey through the Seven Climes of Antiquity and the Structure of the Aljamiado-Morisco Rrekontamiento del Rrey Alisandre." In *Entre oriente y occidente: Ciudades y viajeros en la Edad Media*, edited by María Dolores Rodríguez Gómez and Juan Pedro Monferrer Sala, 285–306. Granada: Editorial Universidad de Granada, 2005.

———. *Islamic Legends Concerning Alexander the Great: Taken from Two Medieval Arabic Manuscripts in Madrid*. Binghamton, N.Y.: Global Publications, 2001.

———. "Royal Fame and Royal Honor in the Rrekontamiento del rrey Alisandre." *La corónica* 25, no. 1 (1996): 128–45.

———. "A Study of Two Potential Sources for the Aljamiado-Morisco Legend of Alexander the Great: The *Rrekontamiento del rrey Alisandre*." *MIFLC Review* 9 (2000): 21–35.

INDEX